ORIENTAL TRANSLATION FUND.
NEW SERIES
VOLUME XII

A BUDDHIST MANUAL OF PSYCHOLOGICAL ETHICS

ORIENTAL TRANSLATION FUND.
NEW SERIES
VOLUME XII

A BUDDHIST MANUAL
OF
PSYCHOLOGICAL ETHICS

OF THE FOURTH CENTURY B.C.

BEING

A TRANSLATION, NOW MADE FOR THE FIRST TIME,
FROM THE ORIGINAL PALI
OF THE
FIRST BOOK IN THE ABHIDHAMMA PITAKA
ENTITLED

DHAMMA-SANGANI

(COMPENDIUM OF STATES OR PHENOMENA)

WITH INTRODUCTORY ESSAY AND NOTES
BY

CAROLINE A.F. RHYS DAVIDS, M.A.
FELLOW OF UNIVERSITY COLLEGE, LONDON.

GYAN

Published by

GYAN

Gyan Publishing House
5, Ansari Road
Daryaganj, New Delhi-110002
Phone: 011-47034999, 9811692060
E-mail: books@gyanbooks.com

Distribution Network
gyanbooks.com
India, USA, Canada, UK, Australia, France

ISBN : 978-81-212-2656-1 (HB)
First Published, 1900

2nd Impression 2021

Printed at: Gyan Press, Delhi.

A Buddhist Manual of Psychological Ethics
Author: Dhamma-Sangani

ORIENTAL TRANSLATION FUND.

NEW SERIES.

VOLUME XII.

A BUDDHIST MANUAL

OF

PSYCHOLOGICAL ETHICS

OF THE FOURTH CENTURY B.C.

BEING

A Translation, now made for the First Time, from the Original Pali,

OF THE

FIRST BOOK IN THE ABHIDHAMMA PIṬAKA

ENTITLED

DHAMMA-SANGANI

(COMPENDIUM OF STATES OR PHENOMENA).

With Introductory Essay and Notes

BY

CAROLINE A. F. RHYS DAVIDS, M.A.,

FELLOW OF UNIVERSITY COLLEGE, LONDON.

PRINTED AND PUBLISHED UNDER THE PATRONAGE OF THE ROYAL ASIATIC SOCIETY;

AND SOLD AT

22, ALBEMARLE STREET, LONDON.

1900.

TO

EDWARD T. STURDY,

BY

WHOSE GENEROUS ASSISTANCE

THE EDITION OF THE COMMENTARY

HAS BEEN RENDERED ACCESSIBLE TO SCHOLARS,

AND

A TRANSLATION OF THE TEXT TO READERS GENERALLY,

THIS VOLUME IS DEDICATED

WITH THE CORDIAL REGARD OF HIS FRIEND,

THE TRANSLATOR.

'Yaṃ kiñci dhammaṃ abhijaññā
ajjhattaṃ athavāpi bahiddhā.'

SUTTA NIPĀTA, 917.

'Api khvāham āvuso imasmiṃ yeva vyāmamatte kalevare saññimhi samanake lokaṃ paññāpemi . . .'

SAMYUTTA NIKĀYA, i. 62 ;=A., ii. 48.

'Kullūpamaṃ vo bhikkhave ājānantehi dhammā pi vo pahātabbā, pag-eva adhammā.'

MAJJHIMA NIKHĀYA, i. 135.

'Der Buddhismus ist die einzige, eigentlich positivistische Religion die uns die Geschichte zeigt.'

NIETZSCHE.

'We shall find that every important philosophical reformation, after a time of too highly strained metaphysical dogmatism or unsatisfying scepticism, has been begun by some man who saw *the necessity of looking deeper into the mental constitution.*'

. G. CROOM ROBERTSON.

CONTENTS.

CHAPTER IV.

CHAPTER V.

PART II.

BAD STATES OF CONSCIOUSNESS.

CHAPTER VI.

PART III.

INDETERMINATE STATES OF CONSCIOUSNESS.

CHAPTER I.

CHAPTER II.

BOOK II.

FORM (rūpakaṇḍaṃ).

CHAPTER I.

CHAPTER II.

CHAPTER III.

CHAPTER IV.

CHAPTER V.

CHAPTER VI.

CHAPTER VII.

CHAPTER VIII.

CHAPTER IX.

CHAPTER X.

CHAPTER XI.

BOOK III.

THE DIVISION ENTITLED 'ELIMINATION' (nikkhepa-kaṇḍaṃ).

PART I.

CHAPTER I.

CHAPTER II.

CHAPTER III.

CHAPTER IV.

CHAPTER V.

CHAPTER VI.

CHAPTER VII.

CHAPTER VIII.

CHAPTER IX.

CHAPTER X.

CHAPTER XI.

CHAPTER XII.

CHAPTER XIII.

CHAPTER XIV.

PART II.

APPENDIX I.

APPENDIX II.

ABBREVIATIONS.

1. BUDDHIST CANONICAL BOOKS

A.—Anguttara-Nikāya.
C.—Cullavagga.
D.—Dīgha-Nikāya.
Dhp.—Dhammapada.
Dh. K.—Dhātu-Kathā.
Dh. S.—Dhamma-Sangaṇi.
Jāt.—Jātaka.
K.—Siamese (Kambodian) edition of the text.
K. V.—Kathā Vatthu.
M.—Majjhima-Nikāya.
M. P. S.—Mahā-Parinibbāna Sutta (Childers).
P. P.—Puggala-Paññatti.
S.—Saṃyutta-Nikāya.
S. N.—Sutta-Nipāta.
Vin.—Vinaya.

2. OTHER BOOKS.

Abh. S.—Abhidhammattha-Sangaha.
Asl.—Atthasālinī.
Div.—Divyāvadāna.
J. P. T. S.—Journal of the Pali Text Society.
J. R. A. S.—Journal of the Royal Asiatic Society.
M. B. V.—Mahā Bodhi Vaṇsa.
Mah.—Mahā Vaṇsa.
Mil.—Milinda Pañho.
S. B. E.—Sacred Books of the East.
Sum.—Sumangala-Vilāsinī.
Vis. M.—Visuddhi Magga.

[By 'printed text,' or simply 'text,' is always meant the edition published in 1885 by the Pali Text Society, unless otherwise stated.]

INTRODUCTORY ESSAY.

I.

The Manual and the History of Psychology.

If the tombs of Egypt or the ruins of Greece itself were to give up, among their dead that are now and again being restored to us, a copy of some manual with which the young Socrates was put through the mill of current academic doctrine, the discovery would be hailed, especially by scholars of historical insight, as a contribution of peculiar interest. The contents would no doubt yield no new matter of philosophic tradition. But they would certainly teach something respecting such points as pre-Aristotelian logical methods, and the procedure followed in one or more schools for rendering students conversant with the concepts in psychology, ethics and metaphysic accepted or debated by the culture of the age.

Readers whose sympathies are not confined to the shores of the Mediterranean and Ægean seas will feel a stir of interest, similar in kind if fainter in degree, on becoming more closely acquainted with the Buddhist text-book entitled Dhamma-Sangaṇi. The English edition of the Pali text, prepared for the Pali Text Society by Professor Dr. Ed. Müller, and published fifteen years ago, has so far failed to elicit any critical discussion among Pali scholars. A cursory inspection may have revealed little but what seemed dry, prolix and sterile. Such was, at least, the verdict of a younger worker, now, alas! no more.[1] Closer study of the work will, I believe, prove less ungrateful, more especially if the conception of it as a student's manual be kept well in view. The method of the book is explicative, deductive; its object was, not to add to the Dhamma, but to unfold the orthodox import of terms in use among the body of the faithful, and, by organizing and systematizing the aggregate of doctrinal concepts, to render the learner's intellect both clear and efficient.

Even a superficial inspection of the Manual should yield great promise to anyone interested in the history of psychology. When upwards of six years ago my attention was first drawn to it, and the desirability of a translation pointed out by Professor Rhys Davids, I was at once attracted by the amount of psychological material embedded in its pages. Buddhist philosophy is ethical first and last. This is beyond dispute. But among ethical systems there is a world of difference in the degree of importance attached to the psychological prolegomena of ethics. In ethical problems we are on a basis of psychology, depending for our material largely upon the psychology of conation or will,[2] with its co-efficients of feeling and intelligence. And in the history of human ideas, in so far as it clusters about those problems, we find this dependence either made prominent or slurred over. Treated superficially, if suggestively and picturesquely, in Plato, the nature and functions of that faculty in man, whereby he is constituted an ethical and political 'animal,' are by Aristotle analyzed at length. But the Buddhists were, in a way, more advanced in the

---

[1] H. C. Warren, 'Buddhism in Translations,' xviii. *Cf.* Kern, 'Indian Buddhism,' p. 3.

[2] *Cf.* G. C. Robertson, 'Elements of General Philosophy,' pp. 191, 197; 'Philosophical Remains,' p. 3; A. Bain, 'Moral Science'—'The Psychological Data of Ethics.' 'Every ethical system involves a psychology of conduct, and depends for its development upon its idea of what conduct actually is' (C. Douglas, 'The Philosophy of J. S. Mill,' p. 251).

psychology of their ethics than Aristotle—in a way, that is, which would now be called scientific. Rejecting the assumption of a psyche and of its higher manifestations or noûs, they were content to resolve the consciousness of the Ethical Man, *as they found it*, into a complex continuum of subjective phenomena. They analyzed this continuum, as we might, exposing it, as it were, by transverse section. But their treatment was genetic. The distinguishable groups of dhammā—of states or mental psychoses—'arise' in every case in consciousness, in obedience to certain laws of causation, physical and moral[1]—that is, ultimately, as the outcome of antecedent states of consciousness. There is no exact equivalent in Pali, any more than there is in Aristotle, for the relatively modern term 'consciousness,' yet is the psychological standpoint of the Buddhist philosophy virtually as thoroughgoing in its perceptual basis as that of Berkeley. It was not solipsism any more than Berkeley's immaterialism was solipsistic. It postulated other percipients[2] as Berkeley did, together with, not a Divine cause or source of percepts, but the implicit Monism of early thought veiled by a deliberate Agnosticism. And just as Berkeley, approaching philosophical questions through psychology, 'was the first man to begin a perfectly scientific doctrine of sense-perception as a psychologist,'[3] so Buddhism, from a quite early stage of its development, set itself to analyze and classify mental processes with remarkable insight and sagacity. And on the results of that psychological analysis it sought to base the whole rationale of its practical doctrine and discipline. From studying the processes of attention, and the nature of sensation, the range and depth of feeling and the plasticity of the will in desire and in control, it organized its system of personal self-culture.

---

[1] Utu and kamma.
[2] *Cf. e.g.* below, p. 272 [1045].
[3] G. C. Robertson, *op. cit.*, p. 154.

Germany has already a history of psychology half completed on the old lines of the assumed monopoly of ancient thought by a small area of the inhabited world. England has not yet got so far. Is it too much to hope that, when such a work is put forth, the greater labour of a wider and juster initiative will have been undertaken, and the development of early psychological thought in the East have been assigned its due place in this branch of historical research?

II.

The Date of the Manual.

We can fortunately fix the date of the Dhamma-Sangaṇi within a limit that, for an Indian book, may be considered narrow. Its aim is to systematize or formulate certain doctrines, or at least to enumerate and define a number of scattered terms or categories of terms, occurring in the great books of dialogues and sundry discourse entitled the Nikāyas of the Sutta Piṭaka. The whole point of view, psychological and philosophical, adopted in them is, in our Manual, taken for granted. The technical terms used in them are used in it as if its hearers, subsequently its readers, would at once recognise them. No one acquainted with those books, and with the Dhamma-Sangaṇi, will hesitate in placing the latter, in point of time, after the Nikāyas.

On the other hand, the kind of questions raised in our Manual are on a different plane altogether from those raised in the third book in the Abhidhamma Piṭaka, viz., the Kathā Vatthu, which we know to have been composed by Tissa at Patna, in the middle of the third century B.C.[1] The Dhamma-Sangaṇi does not attempt to deal with any such advanced opinions and highly-elaborated points of doctrine as are put forward by those supposed opponents of the orthodox philosophy who are the interlocutors in the Kathā Vatthu. It remains altogether, or almost altogether, at the old standpoint of the Nikāyas as regards

---

[1] Atthasālinī, p. 3; Mahā Bodhi Vaṇsa, p. 110.

doctrine, differing only in method of treatment. The Kathā Vatthu raises new questions belonging to a later stage in the development of the faith.

The Dhamma-Sangaṇi is therefore younger than the Nikāyas, and older than the Kathā Vatthu. If we date it half-way between the two, that is, during the first third of the fourth century B.C. (contemporary, therefore, with the childhood of Aristotle, *b.* 384), we shall be on the safe side. But I am disposed to think that the interval between the completion of the Nikāyas and the compilation of the Dhamma-Sangaṇi is less than that between the latter work and the Kathā Vatthu; and that our manual should therefore be dated rather at the middle than at the end of the fourth century B.C., or even earlier. However that may be, it is important for the historian of psychology to remember that the ideas it systematizes are, of course, older. Practically all of them go back to the time of the Buddha himself. Some of them are older still.

The history of the text of our Manual belongs to that of the canonical texts taken collectively. There are, however, two interesting references to it, apart from the general narrative, in the Mahā Vaṇsa, which show, at least, that the Dhamma-Sangaṇi was by no means laid on the shelf among later Buddhists. King Kassapa V. of Ceylon (A.D. 929-939) had a copy of it engraved on gold plates studded with jewels, and took it in procession with great honour to a vihāra he had built, and there offered flowers to it.[1] Another King of Ceylon, Vijaya Bāhu I. (A.D. 1065-1120), shut himself up every morning for a time against his people in the beautiful Hall of Exhortation, and there made a translation of the Dhamma-Sangaṇi, no doubt from Pali into Sinhalese.[2]

I can testify to the seriousness of the task, and feel a keen sympathy with my royal predecessor, and envy withal for his proximity in time and place to the seat of orthodox tradition. Nothing, unfortunately, is now known, so far

---

[1] Mah., ch. l., vers. 50, 51, 56. [2] *Ibid.*, ch. lxx., ver. 17.

as I have been able to ascertain, of this work, in which the translator was very likely aided by the best scholarship of the day, and which might have saved me from many a doubt and difficulty.

III.

On the Commentaries and the Importance of the Atthasālinī.

It will be seen from Appendix I. that the last part of the text of our Manual is a supplement added to it by way of commentary, or rather of interpretation and digest. It is, perhaps, not surprising that so much of this kind of material has survived within the four corners of the Pitakas. We have the Old Commentary embedded in the Vinaya, and the Parivāra added as a sort of supplementary examination paper to it. Then there is the Niddesa, a whole book of commentary, on texts now included in the Sutta Nipāta, and there are passages clearly of a commentarial nature scattered through the Nikāyas. Lastly, there is the interesting fragment of commentary tacked on to the Dhamma-Sangaṇi itself (below, p. 357). As these older incorporated commentaries are varied both in form and in method, it is evident that commentary of different kinds had a very early beginning. And the probability is very great that the tradition is not so far wrong, when it tells us that commentaries on all the principal canonical books were handed down in schools of the Order *along with* the texts themselves.

This is not to maintain that all of the Commentaries were so handed down in all the schools, nor that each of them was exactly the same in each of the schools where it was taught. But wherever Commentaries were so handed down, tradition tells us that they were compiled, and subsequently written, in the dialect of the district where the school was situated. From two places, one in India and the other in Ceylon, we have works purporting to give in Pali the substance of such ancient traditional comment as had been handed down in the local vernacular. One of these is the Atthasālinī, Buddhaghosa's reconstruction, in Pali, of the Commentary on our present work, as handed down in Sinhalese at the school of the Great Monastery, the Mahā Vihāra at Anurādhapura in Ceylon.

The Mahā Vaṇsa, indeed, says (p. 251) that he wrote this work at Gayā, in North India, before he came to Anurādhapura. This, however, must be a mistake, if it refers to the work as we have it. For in that work he frequently quotes from and refers to another work which he certainly wrote after his arrival in Ceylon, namely, the Visuddhi Magga, and once or twice he refers to the Samanta Pāsādikā, which he also wrote in Ceylon.

The Sadhamma Sangaha[1] has two apparently inconsistent statements which suggest a solution. The first is that he wrote, at the Vihāra at Gayā, a work called the 'Uprising of Knowledge' (Ñāṇodaya), and a Commentary on the Dhamma-Sangaṇi, called the Atthasālinī, and began to write one on the Parittas. Then it was that he was urged to go, and actually did go, to Ceylon to obtain better materials for his work. The second is that, after he had arrived there and had written seven other works, he then wrote the Atthasālinī. When the same author makes two such statements as these, and in close conjunction, he may well mean to say that a work already written in the one place was revised or rewritten in the other.

Dhamma Kitti, the author of the Sadhamma Sangaha, adds the interesting fact that, in revising his Atthasālinī, Buddhaghosa relied, not on the Mahā Aṭṭhakathā in Sinhalese, but on another Commentary in that language called the Mahā Paccari.

We know, namely, that at the time when Buddhaghosa wrote—that is, in the early part of the fifth century A.D.—the Commentaries handed down in the schools had been, at various times and places, already put together into treatises and written books in the native dialects. And we know the names of several of those then existing. These are:

---

[1] Journal of the Pali Text Society, 1888, pp. 53, 56.

1. The Commentary of the dwellers in the 'North Minster'—the Uttara Vihāra—at Anurādhapura.[1]

2. The Mūla-, or Mahā-Aṭṭhakathā, or simply 'The Aṭṭhakathā,' of the dwellers in the 'Great Minster'—the Mahā Vihāra—also at Anurādhapura.[2]

3. The Andha-Aṭṭhakathā, handed down at Kāñcipura (Congevaram), in South India.

4. The Mahā Paccari, or Great Raft, said to be so called from its having been composed on a raft somewhere in Ceylon.[3]

5. The Kurunda Aṭṭhakathā, so called because it was composed at the Kurundavelu Vihāra in Ceylon.[4]

6. The Sankhepa Aṭṭhakathā or Short Commentary, which, as being mentioned together with the Andha Commentary,[5] may possibly be also South Indian.

Buddhaghosa himself says in the introductory verses to the Atthasālinī:[6]

'I will set forth, rejoicing in what I reveal, the explanation of the meaning of that Abhidhamma as it was chanted forth by Mahā Kassapa and the rest (at the first Council), and re-chanted later (at the second Council) by the Arahats, and by Mahinda brought to this wondrous isle and turned into the language of the dwellers therein. Rejecting now the tongue of the men of Tambapaṇṇi[7] and turning it into that pure tongue which harmonizes with the texts [I will set it forth] showing the opinion of the dwellers in the Great Minster, undefiled by and unmixed with the views of

---

[1] J. P. T. S., 1882, pp. 115, 116. English in Turnour's Mahā Vaṇsa, pp. xxxvii, xxxviii.

[2] Sum. 180, 182; Sadhamma Sangaha, 55; M. B. V. 134-136.

[3] Papañca Sūdanī on M. ii. 13; Sadhamma Sangaha, 55.

[4] Sadhamma Sangaha, 55.

[5] Vijesinha in the J. R. A. S., 1870 (vol. v., New Series), p. 298.

[6] Asl., p. 1, ver. 13 *et seq.*

[7] Taprobane = Ceylon.

the sects, and adducing also what ought to be adduced from the Nikāyas and the Commentaries.'[1]

It would be most interesting if the book as we have it had been written at Gayā in North India, or even if we could discriminate between the portion there written and the additions or alterations made in Ceylon. But this we can no longer hope to do. The numerous stories of Ceylon Theras occurring in the book are almost certainly due to the author's residence in Ceylon. And we cannot be certain that these and the reference to his own book, written in Ceylon, are the only additions. We cannot, therefore, take the opinions expressed in the book as evidence of Buddhist opinion as held in Gayā. That may, in great part, be so. But we cannot tell in which part.

In the course of his work Buddhaghosa quotes often from the Nikāyas without mentioning the source of his quotations; and also from the Vibhanga[2] and the Mahā Pakaraṇa[3] (that is, the Paṭṭhāna), giving their names. Besides these Pitaka texts, he quotes or refers to the following authorities:

1. His own Samanta Pāsādikā, *e.g.*, pp. 97, 98.
2. His own Visuddhi Magga, pp. 168, 183, 186, 187 (twice), 190, 198.[4]
3. The Mahā Aṭṭhakathā, pp. 80, 86, 107.
4. The Aṭṭhakathācariyā, pp. 85, 123, 217.
5. The Aṭṭhakathā, pp. 108, 113, 188, 267, 313.
6. The Aṭṭhakathā's, pp. 99, 188.
7. The Āgamaṭṭhakathā's, p. 86.[5]

---

[1] Āgamaṭṭhakathāsu, perhaps 'from the commentaries on the Nikāyas.' See note 5 below.

[2] For instance, pp. 165-170, 176, 178.

[3] For instance, pp. 7, 9, 87, 212, 409.

[4] The apparent references at pp. 195, 196 are not to the book.

[5] The reading in the printed text is āgamanaṭṭhakathāsu. But this is not intelligible. And as we have āgamaṭṭhakathāsu at p. 2, ver. 17, it is probable we must so read also here, where the meaning clearly is 'in the commentaries on the Nikāyas.'

8. Acariyānaṃ samānaṭṭhakathā, p. 90.
9. Porāṇā, pp. 84, 111, 291, 299, 313.
10. The Thera (that is Nāgasena), pp. 112, 121, 122.
11. Nāgasenatthera, p. 114.
12. Āyasmā Nāgasena, p. 119.
13. Ayasmā Nāgasenatthera, p. 142.
14. Thera Nāgasena, p. 120.
15. Dīgha-bhāṇakā, pp. 151, 399 (*cf.* p. 407).
16. Majjhima-bhāṇakā, p. 420.
17. Vitaṇḍa-vādī, pp. 3, 90, 92, 241.
18. Peṭaka, possibly Peṭakopadesa, p. 165.

I do not claim to have exhausted the passages in the Atthasālinī quoted from these authorities, or to be able to define precisely each work—what, for instance, is the distinction between 5 and 6, and whether 4 was not identical with either. Nor is it clear who were the Porāṇā or Ancients, though it seems likely, from the passages quoted, that they were Buddhist thinkers of an earlier age, but of a later date than that of our Manual, inasmuch as one of the citations shows that the 'Door-theory' of cognition was already developed (see below, p. lxviii., etc.). From the distinct references to 3 and to 7, it seems possible that the so-called 'Great Commentary' (3) dealt not so much with any particular book, or group of books, as with the doctrines of the Pitakas in general.

The foregoing notes may prove useful when the times are ready for a full inquiry into the history of the Buddhist Commentaries.[1] With respect to the extent to which the Atthasālinī itself has been quoted in the following pages, it may be judged that the scholastic teaching of eight centuries later is a very fallacious guide in the interpretation of original doctrines, and that we should but darken counsel

[1] I may add that a Ṭīkā, or sub-commentary on the Atthasālinī, written by a Siamese scholar, Ñāṇakitti, of unknown date, was edited in Sinhalese characters by Kodagoḍa Paññāsekhara of Kalutara, in Ceylon, and published there in 1890.

if we sought light on Aristotle from mediæval exegesis of the age of Duns Scotus.

Without admitting that the course of Buddhist and that of Western culture coincide sufficiently to warrant such a parallel, it may readily be granted that Buddhaghosa must not be accepted *en bloc*. The distance between the constructive genius of Gotama and his apostles as compared with the succeeding ages of epigoni needs no depreciatory criticism on the labours of the exegesists to make itself felt forcibly enough. Buddhaghosa's philology is doubtless crude, and he is apt to leave cruces unexplained, concerning which an Occidental is most in the dark.[1] Nevertheless, to me his work is not only highly suggestive, but also a mine of historic interest. To put it aside is to lose the historical perspective of the course of Buddhist philosophy. It is to regard the age of Gotama and of his early Church as constituting a wondrous 'freak' in the evolution of human ideas, instead of watching to see how the philosophical tradition implanted in that Church (itself based on earlier culture) had in the lapse of centuries been carefully handed down by the schools of Theras, the while the folklore that did duty for natural science had more or less fossilized, and the study of the conscious processes of the mind had been elaborated.

This is, however, a point of view that demands a fuller examination than can here be given it. I will now only maintain that it is even more suggestive to have at hand the best tradition of the Buddhist schools at the fulness of their maturity for the understanding of a work like the Dhamma-Sangaṇi than for the study of the Dialogues. Our manual is itself a book of reference to earlier books, and presents us with many terms and formulæ taken out of that setting of occasion and of discourse enshrined in which we meet them in the Nikāyas. The great scholar who comments on them had those Nikāyas, both as to letter and spirit, well pigeon-holed in memory, and cherished both

---

[1] *Cf.* Dr. Neumann in 'Die Reden Gotamo Buddhos,' p. xv *et seq.*

with the most reverent loyalty. That this is so, as well as the fact that we are bred on a culture so different in mould and methods (let alone the circumstances of its development) from that inherited by him, must lend his interpretations an importance and a suggestiveness far greater than that which the writings of any Christian commentator on the Greek philosophy can possess for us.

IV.

On the Method and Argument of the Manual.

The title given to my translation is not in any way a faithful rendering of the canonical name of the Manual. This is admitted on my title-page. There is nothing very intelligible for us in the expression 'Compendium of States,' or 'Compendium of Phenomena.' Whether the Buddhist might find it so or not, there is for him at all events a strong and ancient association of ideas attaching to the title Dhamma-Saṅgaṇi which for us is entirely non-existent. I have therefore let go the letter, in order to indicate what appears to me the real import of the work. Namely, that it is, in the first place, a manual or text-book, and not a treatise or disquisition, elaborated and rendered attractive and edifying after the manner of most of the Sutta Piṭaka. And then, that its subject is ethics, but that the inquiry is conducted from a psychological standpoint, and, indeed, is in great part an analysis of the psychological and psycho-physical data of ethics.

I do not mean to assert that the work was compiled solely for academic use. No such specialized function is assigned it in the Commentary. Buddhaghosa only maintains that, together with the rest of the Abhidhamma,[1] it was the *ipsissima verba* of the Buddha, not attempting to upset the mythical tradition that it was the special mode he adopted in teaching the doctrine to the 'hosts of devas come from all parts of the sixteen world-systems, he having

---

[1] But including the Mātikā only of the later Kathā Vatthu. *Cf.* 'Dialogues of the Buddha,' p. xi; Asl., p. 1.

placed his mother (re-incarnate as a devī) at their head because of the glory of her wisdom.'[1] Whether this myth had grown up to account for the formal, unpicturesque style of the Abhidhamma, on the ground that the devas were above the need of illustration and rhetoric of an earthly kind, I do not know. The Commentary frequently refers to the peculiar difference in style from that employed in the Suttanta as consisting in the Abhidhamma being nippariyāya-desanā—teaching which is not accompanied by explanation or disquisition.[2] And the definition it gives, at the outset, of the term Abhidhamma shows that this Pitaka, and *a fortiori* the Dhamma-Sangaṇi, was considered as a subject of study more advanced than the other Pitakas, and intended to serve as the complement and crown of the learner's earlier courses.[3] Acquaintance with the doctrine is, as I have said, taken for granted. The object is not so much to extend knowledge as to ensure mutual consistency in the *in*tension of ethical notions, and to systematize and formulate the theories and practical mechanism of intellectual and moral progress scattered in profusion throughout the Suttantas.[4]

It is interesting to note the methods adopted to carry out this object. The work was in the first instance inculcated by way of oral teaching respecting a quantity of matter which had been already learnt in the same way. And the memory, no longer borne along by the interest of

---

[1] Asl., p. 1.

[2] *E.g.*, Asl. 403. The meaning of this expression is illustrated by its use on p. 317 of the Cy.: na nippariyāyena dīghaṃ rūpāyatanaṃ; *i.e.*, 'that which is long (or short) is only *inferentially* a visual object.'

[3] Asl., p. 2. Translated by Mr. A. C. Taylor, J. R. A. S., 1894.

[4] Professor Edmond Hardy, in his Introduction to the fifth volume of the Anguttara Nikāya, expresses the belief that the Dhamma-Sangaṇi is 'entirely dependent upon the Anguttara.' For my part, I have found no reason to limit the manual's dependence on the Suttantas to any one book. Buddhaghosa does not specially connect the two works.

narrative or by the thread of an argument, had to be assisted by other devices. First of these is the catechetical method. Questions, according to Buddhist analysis, are put on five several grounds:[1]

- to throw light on what is not known;
- to compare what one knows with the knowledge of others;
- to clear up doubts;
- to get the premises in an argument granted;[2]
- to give a starting-point from which to set out the content of a statement.

The last is selected as the special motive of the catechizing here resorted to. It is literally the wish to discourse or expound (k a t h e t u k a m y a t ā), but the meaning is more clearly brought out by the familiar formula quoted, viz.: 'Four in number, brethren, are these Advances in Mindfulness. Now which are the Four?' Thus it was held that the questions in the Manual are analytic or explicative, having the object of unfolding and thereby of delimitating the implications of a mass of notions which a study of the Suttantas, if unaided, might leave insufficiently co-ordinated in the mind.

And the memory, helped by the interrogative stimulus, was yet further assisted by the symmetrical *form* of both question and answer, as well as by the generic uniformity in the *matter* of the questions. Throughout Book I., in the case of each inquiry which opens up a new subject, the answer is set out on a definite plan called u d d e s a—exposition—and is rounded off invariably by the a p p a n ā, or emphatic summing up: 'all these (whatever they may stand for on other occasions or in other systems) on this occasion = *x*.' The u d d e s a is succeeded by the n i d d e s a—de-position—*i.e.*, analytical question and answer on the details of the expository statement. This is indicated formally by the initial adverb t a t t h a—what *here* (in this

---

[1] Asl. 55, 56; *cf.* Sum. 68.

[2] A favourite method in the Dialogues. The Cy. quotes as an instance M. i. 232.

connexion) is *a . . b . . c?* Again, the work is in great part planned with careful regard to logical relation. The Buddhists had not elaborated the intellectual vehicle of genus and species, as the Greeks did, hence they had not the convenience of a logic of Definition. There is scarcely an answer in any of these Niddesas but may perhaps be judged to suffer in precision and lucidity from lack of it. They substitute for definition proper what J. S. Mill might have called predication of æquipollent terms—in other words, the method of the dictionary. In this way precision of meaning is not to be expected, since nearly all so-called synonyms do but mutually overlap in meaning without coinciding; and hence the only way to ensure no part of the connotation being left out is to lump together a number of approximate equivalents, and gather that the term in question is defined by such properties as the aggregate possesses in common. If this is the rationale of the Buddhist method, the inclusion, in the answer, of the very term which is to be defined becomes no longer the fallacy it is in Western logic. Indeed, where there is no pursuit of exact science, nor of sciences involving 'physical division,' but only a system of research into the intangible products and processes of mind and character, involving aspects and phases, *i.e.*, *logical* division, I am not sure that a good case might not be made out for Buddhist method. It is less rigid, and lends itself better, perhaps, to a field of thought where 'a difference in aspects *is* a difference in things.'[1]

However that may be, the absence of a development of the relation of Particular and Universal, of One and All, is met by a great attention to degree of Plurality. Number plays a great part in Buddhist classes and categories.[2] Whether this was inherited from a more ancient lore, such as Pythagoras is said to have drawn from, or whether this feature was artificially developed for mnemonic purposes, I do not know. Probably there is truth in both alternatives.

---

[1] Professor J. Ward, Ency. Brit., 9th ed., 'Psychology.'

[2] *Cf.* especially, not only Book II. of this work, but also the whole of the Anguttara.

But of all numbers none plays so great a part in aiding methodological coherency and logical consistency as that of duality. I refer of course especially to its application in the case of the correlatives, Positive and Negative.

Throughout most of Book II. the learner is greatly aided by being questioned on positive terms and their opposites, taken simply and also in combination with other similarly dichotomized pairs. The opposite is not always a contradictory. Room is then left in the 'universe of discourse' for a third class, which in its turn comes into question. Thus the whole of Book I. is a development of the triplet of questions with which Book III. begins (a-kusalaṃ being really the Contrary of kusalaṃ, though formally its Contradictory): What is *A?* What is *B?* What is (*ab*), *i.e.*, non-*A* and non-*B?* In Book III. there is no obvious ground of logic or method for the serial order or limits observed in the 'Clusters' or Groups, and the interpolated sets of 'Pairs' of miscellaneous questions. Nevertheless a uniform method of catechizing characterizes the former.

Finally, there is, in the way of mnemonic and intellectual aid, the simplifying and unifying effect attained by causing all the questions (exclusive of sub-inquiries) to refer to the one category of dhammā.

There is, it is true, a whole Book of questions referring to rūpaṃ, but this constitutes a very much elaborated sub-inquiry on 'form' as one sub-species of a species of dhammā—rūpino dhammā, as distinguished from all the rest, which are a-rūpino dhammā. This will appear more clearly if the argument of the work is very concisely stated.

Those who can consult the text will see that the Mātikā, or table of subjects of all the questions (which I have not held it useful to reproduce), refers exclusively to Book III. Book III. in fact contains the entire work considered as an inquiry (not necessarily exhaustive) into the concrete, or, as one might say, the applied ethics of Buddhism. In it many if not all fundamental concepts are taken as already defined and granted. Hence Books I. and II. are introductory and, as it were, of the nature of inquiry into data. Book II. is psycho-physical; Book I. is psychological. Together they constitute a very elaborate development, and again a sub-development, of the first triplet of questions in Book III., viz.: dhammā which are good, *i.e.*, make good karma, those which are bad, and those which make no karma (the indeterminates). Now, of these last some are simply and solely results[1] of good or bad dhammā, and some are not so, but are states of mind and expressions of mind entailing no moral result (on the agent).[2] Some again, while making no karma, are of neither of these two species, but are dhammā which might be called either unmoral (rūpaṃ),[3] or else *super*-moral (uncompounded element or Nirvana).[4] These are held to constitute a third and fourth species of the third class of dhammā called indeterminate. But the former of the two alone receives detailed and systematic treatment.

Hence the whole manual is shown to be, as it professes to be, a compendium, or, more literally, a co-enumeration of dhammā.

The method of treatment or procedure termed Abhidhamma (for Abhidhamma is treatment rather than matter) is, according to the Mātikā, held to end at the end of the chapter entitled Piṭṭhi-dukaṃ or Supplementary Set of Pairs. The last thirty-seven pairs of questions[5] and answers, on the other hand, are entitled Suttantika-dukaṃ. They are of a miscellaneous character, and are in many cases not logically opposed. Buddhaghosa has nothing to say by way of explaining their inclusion, nor the principle determining their choice or number. Nor is it easy to deduce any explanation from the nature or the treatment of them. The name Suttantika may mean that they are pairs of terms met with in the Dialogues, or

---

[1] Book I., Part III., ch. i.
[2] *Ibid.*, ch. ii.
[3] Book II.
[4] Appendix II.
[5] §§ 1296-1366.

in all the four Nikāyas. This is true and verifiable. But I for one cannot venture to predicate anything further respecting them.

V.

On the Chief Subject of Inquiry—Dhammā.

If I have called Buddhist ethics psychological, especially as the subject is treated in this work, it is much in the same way in which I should call Plato's psychology ethical. Neither the founders of Buddhism nor of Platonic Socratism had elaborated any organic system of psychology or of ethics respectively. Yet it is hardly overstating the case for either school of thought to say that whereas the latter psychologized from an ethical standpoint, the former built their ethical doctrine on a basis of psychological principles. For whatever the far-reaching term dhammo may in our manual have precisely signified to the early Buddhists, it invariably elicits, throughout Book I., a reply *in terms of subjective consciousness*. The discussion in the Commentary, which I have reproduced below, p. 2, note 3, on dhammārammaṇaṃ, leaves it practically beyond doubt that dhammo, when thus related to mano, is as a visual object to visual perception—is, namely, mental object in general. It thus is shown to be equivalent to Herbart's *Vorstellung*, to Locke's idea—'whatsoever is the immediate object of perception, thought or understanding'—and to Professor Ward's 'presentation.'[1]

The dhammā in question always prove to be, whatever their ethical value, factors of cittaṃ used evidently in its widest sense, *i.e.*, concrete mental process or state. Again, the analysis of rūpaṃ in Book II., as a species of 'indeterminate' dhammā, is almost wholly a study in the phenomena of sensation and of the human organism as sentient. Finally, in Book III. the questions on various dhammā are for the most part answered in terms of the four mental skandhas, of the cittāni dealt with in Book I., and of the springs of action as shown in their

[1] 'Ency. Brit.,' 9th ed., art. 'Psychology.'

effect on will. Thus the whole inquiry in its most generalized expression comes practically to this: Given man as a moral being, what do we find to be the content of his consciousness?

Now this term dhammo is, as readers are already aware, susceptible of more than one interpretation. Even when used for the body of ethical doctrine it was applied with varying extension, *i.e.*, either to the whole doctrine, or to the Suttantas as opposed to Vinaya and Abhidhamma, or to the doctrine of the Four Truths only. But whatever in this connexion is the denotation, the connotation is easy to fix. That this is not the case where the term has, so to speak, a secular or 'profane' meaning is seen in the various renderings and discussions of it.[1] The late H. C. Warren in particular has described the difficulties, first of determining what the word, in this or that connexion, was intended to convey, and then of discovering any word or words adequate to serve as equivalent to it. One step towards a solution may be made if we can get at a Buddhist survey of the meanings of dhammo from the Buddhists' own philosophical point of view. And this we are now enabled to do in consequence of the editing of the Atthasālinī. In it we read Buddhaghosa's analysis of the term, the various meanings it conveyed to Buddhists of the fifth century A.D., and his judgment, which would be held as authoritative, of the special significance it possessed in the questions of the Dhamma-saṅgaṇi. 'The word dhammo,' runs the passage (p. 38), 'is met with [as meaning] doctrine (pariyatti), condition or cause (hetu), virtue or good quality (guṇo), absence of essence or of living soul (nissatta-nijjīvatā),' etc. Illustrative texts are then given of each meaning, those referring to the last being the beginning of the answer in our Manual

[1] *Cf.*, *e.g.*, Oldenberg, 'Buddha,' etc., 3rd ed., p. 290; Warren, 'Buddhism in Translations,' pp. 116, 364; Kern, 'Indian Buddhism,' p. 51, n. 3; Neumann, 'Reden des Gotamo,' pp. 13, 23, 91; Gogerly, 'Ceylon Friend,' 1874, p. 21.

numbered [121]: 'Now at that time there are states'; and, further, the passage from the Satipaṭṭhānasutta[1]: 'Concerning dhammas he abides watchful over dhammas.' And it is with the fourth and last-named meaning of dhammo that the term is said to be used in the questions of the Manual. Again, a little later (p. 40), he gives a more positive expression to this particular meaning by saying that dhammo, so employed, signifies 'that which has the mark of bearing its nature' (or character or condition—sabhāvadhāraṇo). This to us somewhat obscure characterization may very likely, in view of the context, mean that dhammo as phenomenon is without substratum, is not a quality cohering in a substance. 'Phenomenon' is certainly our nearest equivalent to the negative definition of nissatta-nijjīvaṃ, and this is actually the rendering given to dhammo (when employed in this sense in the Sutta just quoted) by Dr. Neumann: 'Da wacht ein Mönch bei den Erscheinungen. . . .' If I have used states, or states of consciousness, instead of phenomena, it is merely because, in the modern tradition of British psychology, 'states of consciousness' is exactly equivalent to such phenomena as are mental, or at least conscious. And, further, because this use of 'states' has been taken up into that psychological tradition on the very same grounds as prompted this Buddhist interpretation of dhammā—the ground of non-committal, not to say negation, with respect to any psychical substance or entity.

That we have, in this country pre-eminently, gone to work after the manner of electrical science with respect to *its* subject-matter, and psychologized without a psyche, is of course due to the influence of Hume. In selecting a term so characteristic of the British tradition as 'states' of mind or consciousness, I am not concerned to justify its use in the face of a tendency to substitute terms more expressive of a dynamic conception of mental operations, or of otherwise altered standpoints. The Buddhists seem

[1] D. (suttanta 22); M. i. 61.

to have held, as our psychology has held, that for purposes of analysis it was justifiable to break up the mental continuum of the moral individuality into this or that congeries of states or mental phenomena. In and through these they sought to trace the working of moral causation. To look beneath or behind them for a 'thing in itself' they held to be a dangerous superstition. With Goethe they said: 'Suche nichts hinter den Phänomenen; sie selbst sind die Lehre!' And in view of this coincidence of implication and emphasis, 'states of mind' or 'of consciousness' seemed best to fit d h a m m ā when the reply was made in terms of mental phenomena.

In the book on Form, the standpoint is no doubt shifted to a relatively more objective consideration of the moral being and his contact with a world considered as external. But then the word d h a m m ā (and my rendering of it) is also superseded by r ū p a ṃ.

It is only when we come to the more synthetic matter of Book III. that d h a m m ā strains the scope of the term I have selected if 'states' be taken as strictly states of mind or of consciousness. It is true that the Buddhist view of things so far resembles the Berkeleian that all phenomena, or things or sequences or elements, or however else we may render d h a m m ā, may be regarded as in the last resort 'states of mind.' This in its turn may seem a straining of the significance which the term possessed for early Buddhists in a more general inquiry such as that of Book III. Yet consider the definitions of d h a m m ā, worthy of Berkeley himself, on p. 272 [1044-45].

The difficulty lay in the choice of another term, and none being satisfactory, I retained, for want of a better, the same rendering, which is, after all, indefinite enough to admit of its connoting other congeries of things or aspects beside consciousness.

The fundamental importance in Buddhist philosophy of this Phenomenalism or Non-substantialism as a protest against the prevailing Animism, which, beginning with projecting the self into objects, elaborated that projected self into noumenal substance, has by this time been more or less admitted. The testimony of the canonical books leaves no doubt on the matter, from Gotama's first sermon to his first converts,[1] and his first Dialogue in the 'Long Collection,' to the first book of the Kathā Vatthu.[2] There are other episodes in the books where the belief in a permanent spiritual essence is, together with a number of other speculations, waived aside as subjects calculated to waste time and energy. But in the portions referred to the doctrine of repudiation is more positive, and may be summed up in one of the refrains of the Majjhima Nikāya: Suññaṃ idaṃ attena vā attaniyena vā ti—Void is this of soul or of aught of the nature of soul![3] The force of the often repeated 'This is not mine, this is not I, this is not my Self,' is not intended to make directly for goodness but for truth and insight. 'And since neither self nor aught belonging to self, brethren, can really and truly be accepted, is not the heretical position which holds:—This is the world and this is the self, and I shall continue to be in the future, permanent, immutable, eternal, of a nature that knows no change, yea, I shall abide to eternity!—is not this simply and entirely a doctrine of fools?'[4]

And now that the later or scholastic doctrine, as shown in the writings of the greatest of the Buddhist scholastics, becomes accessible, it is seen how carefully and conscientiously this anti-substantialist position had been cherished and upheld. Half-way to the age of the Commentators, the Milinda-pañho places the question of soul-theory at the head of the problems discussed. Then turning to Buddhaghosa we find the emphatic negation of the Sumangala Vilāsinī (p. 194):—'Of aught within called self which looks forward or looks around, &c., there is none!' matched

---

[1] S. ii. 66-8; also in Mahā Vagga, i. 6, 38-47.

[2] *Cf.* Rhys Davids' 'American Lectures,' pp. 39, 40.

[3] Or 'self' (attena). M. i. 297; ii. 263 (*lege* suññaṃ); *cf.* S. iv. 54; and K. V. 67, 579. *Cf.* the 'Emptiness-concept,' below, p. 33.

[4] M. i. 138.

in the Atthasālinī, not only by the above-given definition of dhamma's, but also by the equally or even more emphatic affirmation respecting them, given in my *note* 1 to p. 33:—'There is no permanent entity or self which acquires the states . . . these are to be understood phenomenally (sabhāvaṭṭhena). There is no other essence or existence or personality or individual whatever.' Again, attention is drawn in the notes to his often-reiterated comment that when a disposition or emotion is referred to cittaṃ, *e.g.*, nandīrāgo cittassa,[1] the repudiation of an ego is thereby implied. Once more, the thoughts and acts which are tainted with 'Āsavas' or with corruptions are said to be só in virtue of their being centred in the soul or self,[2] and those which have attained that 'ideal Better,' and have no 'beyond' (an-uttarā) are interpreted as having transcended or rejected the soul or self.[3]

To appreciate the relative consistency with which the Buddhists tried to govern their philosophy, both in subject and in treatment, in accordance with this fundamental principle, we must open a book of Western psychology, more or less contemporary, such as the 'De Animâ,' and note the sharply contrasted position taken up at the outset.

'The object of our inquiry,' Aristotle says in his opening sentences, 'is to study and ascertain the nature and essence of the Psyche, as well as its accidents. . . . It may be well to distinguish . . . the genus to which the Psyche belongs, and determine what it is . . . whether it is a something and an essence, or quantity, or quality . . . whether it is among entities in potentiality, or whether rather it is a reality. . . . Now, the knowledge of anything in itself seems to be useful towards a right conception of the causes of the accidents in substances. . . . But the knowledge of the accidents contributes largely in its turn towards knowing what the thing essentially is. . . . Thus the

---

[1] P. 277, n. 2; also pp. 129, note 1; 298, note 3, &c.; and *cf.* p. 175, p. 1. See also on dhātu, p. lxxvii.

[2] P. 294, n. 7; 327, n. 1.

[3] P. 336, n. 2.

essence is the proper beginning for every demonstration. . . .'

The whole standpoint which the Buddhists brought into question, and decided to be untenable as a basis of sound doctrine, is here accepted and taken as granted. A phenomenon, or series of phenomena, is, on being held up for investigation, immediately and unhesitatingly looked upon under one of two aspects: *either* it must be a substance, essence, reality, *or* it belongs to one of those nine other 'Categories'—quantity, quality, etc.—which constitute the phenomenon an attribute or group of attributes cohering in a substance.

It is true that Aristotle was too progressive and original a thinker to stop here. In his theory of mind as εἶδος or 'form,' in itself mere potentiality, but becoming actuality as implicate in, and as energizing body, he endeavoured to transform the animism of current standpoints into a more rational conception. And in applying his theory he goes far virtually to resolve mind into phenomenal process (*De An.*, III., chaps. vii., viii.). But he did not, or would not, wrench himself radically out of the primitive soil and plant his thought on a fresh basis, as the Buddhist dared to do. Hence Greek thought abode, for all his rationalizing, saturated with substantialist methods, till it was found acceptable by and was brought up into an ecclesiastical philosophy which, from its Patristic stage, had inherited a tradition steeped in animistic standpoints.

Modern science, however, has been gradually training the popular mind to a phenomenalistic point of view, and joining hands in psychology with the anti-substantialist tradition of Hume. So that the way is being paved for a more general appreciation of the earnest effort made by Buddhism—an effort stupendous and astonishing if we consider its date and the forces against it—to sever the growth of philosophic and religious thought from its ancestral stem and rear it in a purely rational soil.

But the philosophic elaboration of soul-theory into Substantialism is complicated and strengthened by a deeply important factor, on which I have already touched. This factor is the exploitation by philosophy, not of a primitive *Weltanschauung*, but of a fundamental fact in intellectual procedure and intellectual economy. I refer to the process of assimilating an indefinite number of particular impressions, on the ground of a common resemblance, into a 'generic idea' or general notion, and of referring to each assimilated product by means of a common name. Every act of cognition, of coming-to-know anything, is reducible to this compound function of discerning the particular and of assimilating it into something relatively general. And this process, in its most abstract terms, is cognizing Unity in Diversity, the One through and beneath the Many.

Now no one, even slightly conversant with the history of philosophy, can have failed to note the connexion there has ever been set up between the concept of substratum and phenomena on the one hand, and that of the One and the Many on the other. They have become blended together, though they spring from distinct roots. And so essential, in every advance made by the intellect to extend knowledge and to reorganize its acquisitions, is the co-ordinating and economizing efficacy of this faculty of generalizing, that its alliance with any other deep-rooted traditional product of mind must prove a mighty stay. A fact in the growth of religious and of philosophic thought which so springs out of the very working and growth of thought in general as this tendency to unify, must seem to rest on unshakeable foundations.

And when this implicit logic of intellectual procedure, this subsuming the particular under the general, has been rendered explicit in a formal system of definition and predication and syllogism, such as was worked out by the Greeks, the breach of alliance becomes much harder. For the progress in positive knowledge, as organized by the logical methods, is brought into harmony with progress in religious and philosophic thought.

This advance in the West is still in force, except in so far as psychological advance, and scientific progress generally, tell on the traditional logic and philosophy. Psychological analysis, for instance, shows that we may confuse the effective registration of our knowledge with the actual disposition of the originals. That is to say, this perceiving and judging, by way of generalizing and unifying, is the only way by which we are able to master the infinite diversities and approximate uniformities of phenomena. Through such procedure great results are attained. Conceptions are widened and deepened. Laws are discovered and then taken up under more general laws. Knowledge groups all phenomena under a few aspects of all but supreme generality. Unification of knowledge is everywhere considered as the ideal aim of intellect.

But, after all, this is only the ideal *method* and *economy* of intellect. The stenographer's ideal is to compress recorded matter into the fewest symbols by which he can reproduce faithfully. The ideal of the phonograph is to reproduce without the intermediacy of an economical process. Limitations of time and faculty constrain us to become mental stenographers. Whatever be our view as to the reality of an external world outside our perception of it, psychology teaches us to distinguish our fetches of abstraction and generalization for what they are *psychologically*—*i.e.*, for effective mental shorthand—whatever they may represent besides. The logical form of Universal in term and in proposition is as much a token of our weakness in realizing the Particular as of our strength in constructing what is at best an abstract and hypothetical whole. The philosophical concept of the One is pregnant with powerful associations. To what extent is it simply as a mathematical symbol in a hypothetical cosmos of carefully selected data, whence the infinite concrete is eliminated lest it 'should flow in over us'[1] and overwhelm us?

Now, the Buddhistic phenomenalism had also both the one and the other member of this great alliance of

---

[1] *Infra*, p. 351: 'Yaṃ . . . pāpakā akusalā dhammā anvāssaveyyuṃ.'

Noumenon and Unity to contend with. But the alliance had, so far at least as we know or can infer, not yet been welded together by a logical organon, or by any development in inductive science. Gotama and his apostles were conversant with the best culture of their age, yet when they shape their discourse according to anything we should call logic, they fall into it rather than wield it after the conscious fashion of Plato or Aristotle. Nor is there, in the books, any clear method practised of definition according to genus and species, or of mutual exclusion among concepts. Thus freer in harness, the Buddhist revolutionary philosophy may be said to have attempted a relatively less impracticable task. The development of a science and art of logic in India, as we know it, was later in time; and though Buddhist thinkers helped in that development, it coincided precisely with the decline of Buddhistic non-substantialism, with the renascence of Pantheistic thought.

VI.

On the Inquiry into Rūpaṃ (Form), and the Buddhist Theory of Sense.

Taking dhammā, then, to mean *phenomena considered as knowledge*—in other words, as actually or potentially states of consciousness—we may next look more closely into that which the catechism brings out respecting rūpaṃ (Book II., and § 583) considered as a *species* of dhammā. By this procedure we shall best place ourselves at the threshold, so to speak, of the Buddhist position, both as to its psychology and its view of things in general, and be thus better led up to the ethical import of the questions in the first part.

The entire universe of dhammā is classed with respect to rūpaṃ in questions 1091, 1092 (Book III.). They are there shown to be either rūpino, having form, or a-rūpino, not having form. The positive category comprises 'the four great phenomena (four elements) and all their derivatives.' The negative term refers to what we should call modes or phases of consciousness, or subjective experience—that is, to 'the skandhas of feeling, perception, syntheses and intellect'—as well as to 'uncompounded element.' (The skandhas are also 'elements' —that is, irreducible but phenomenal factors (see p. 129, n. 1)—but *they* are compounds.[1]) Rūpaṃ would thus appear at first sight to be a name for the external world or for the Extended universe, as contrasted with the unextended, mental, psychical or subjective universe. Personally I do not find, so far, that the Eastern and Western concepts can be so easily made to coincide. It will be better before, and indeed without as yet, arriving at any such conclusive judgment, to inquire into the application made of the term in the Manual generally.

We find rūpaṃ used in three, at least, of the various meanings assigned to it in the lexicons. It occurs first, and very frequently, as the general name for the objects of the sense of sight. It may then stand as simply rūpaṃ (§ 617, 'this which is visual form,' as opposed to § 621, etc., 'this which is "sound," "odour,"' etc.). More usually it is spoken of as rūpārammaṇaṃ, object of sight (p. 1), or as rūpāyatanaṃ, sphere (province, *Gebiet*) of sights or of visual form (pp. 172, 183 *et seq.*). It includes both sensations of colour and lustre and the complex sensations of form. Used in this connexion, its specialization is, of course, only due to the psychological fact that sight is the spokesman and interpreter of all the senses, so that 'I see' often stands for 'I perceive or discern through two or more modes of sensation.'

On this point it is worth while pointing out an interesting flash of psychological discrimination in the Commentary. It will be noticed, in the various kinds of rūpāyatanaṃ enumerated in § 617 (p. 183, n. 9), that, after pure visual sensations have been instanced, different magnitudes and forms are added, such as 'long, short,' etc. On these

---

[1] *Cf.*, *e.g.*, Dhp. A., p. 413: . . . 'all the compounds, with their divisions of skandhas, elements and spheres.'

Buddhaghosa remarks: 'Here, inasmuch as we are able to tell "long," "short," etc., by touch, while we cannot so discern "blue," etc., therefore "long," "short" and the rest are *not* visual forms except inferentially (literally, not visual forms without explanation). *A*, *B*, placed in such a relation to *C*, *D*, is only by customary usage spoken of as something seen' (Asl. 316).[1] This may not bring us up to Berkeley, but it is a farther step in that direction than Aristotle's mere hint—'There is a movement which is perceptible both by Touch and Sight'—when he is alluding to magnitudes, etc., being 'common sensibles,' *i.e.*, perceptible by more than one sense.[2]

To resume: Rūpaṃ, in its wider sense (as 'all form'), may be due to the popular generalization and representative function of the sense of sight, expressed in Tennyson's line:

'For knowledge is of things we see . . .'

And thus, even as a philosophical concept, it may, loosely speaking, have stood for 'things seen,' as contrasted with the unseen world of dhammā arūpino. But this is by no means an adequate rendering of the term in its more careful and technical use in the second Book of our Manual. For, as may there be seen, much of the content of 'form' is explicitly declared to be invisible.[3]

Rūpaṃ occurs next, and, with almost equal frequency, together with its opposite, arūpaṃ, to signify those two other worlds, realms or planes[4] of temporal existence,

---

[1] The symbols are my own adaptation, not a literal rendering. In the account of the 'external senses' or Indriyas given in the (later) Sānkhya text-books, Professor Garbe points out that the objects of sight are limited to colour (rūpa), exclusive of form (Garbe, 'Die Sānkhya Philosophie,' p. 258).

[2] 'De Animâ,' II. vi.

[3] *Cf.* §§ 597 *et seq.*, 657, 658, 751, 752, etc.

[4] To the employment of 'universe' for avacaraṃ exception may be taken, since the latter term means only a *part* of the Oriental cosmos. I admit it calls for apology.

which Buddhism accepted along with other current mythology, and which, taken together with the lowest, or sensuous plane of existence, exhaust the possible modes of re-birth. These avacaras, or loci of form and non-form, are described in terms of vague localization (§§ 1280-85), but it is not easy to realize how far existence of either sort was conceived with anything like precision. Including the 'upper' grades of the world of sensuous existence, they were more popularly known as heaven or sagga (svarga), *i.e.*, the Bright. Their inhabitants were devas, distinguished into hosts variously named. Like the heaven of the West or the Near East, they were located 'above.' Unlike that heaven, life in them was temporal, not eternal.

But the Dhamma-saṅgaṇi throws no new light on the kind of states they were supposed to be. Nor does Buddhaghosa here figure as an Eastern Dante, essaying to body out more fully, either dogmatically or as in a dream, such ineffable oracles as were hinted at by a Paul 'caught up to the third heaven . . . whether in the body or out of the body I cannot tell—God knoweth,' or the ecstatic visions of a John in lonely exile. The Atthasālinī is not free from divagations on matters of equally secondary importance to the earnest Buddhist.[1] Yet it has nothing

---

If I have used it throughout Book I., it was because there the term avacaraṃ seemed more suggestive of the logician's term 'universe of discourse,' or 'of thought,' than of any physically conceived actuality. It seemed to fit De Morgan's definition of 'the universe of a proposition'—'a collection of all objects which are contemplated as objects about which assertion or denial may take place,' the universe of form, for instance, either as a vague, vast concept 'in' time and effort, or as a state of mind, a rapt abstraction—in either case a 'universe of thought' for the time being.

[1] *Cf.*, *e.g.*, on a similar subject, Sum. 110. He tells us, it is true (see below, p. 196, n. 4), that the food of the gods who inhabited the highest sphere of the *sensuous* world was of the maximum degree of refinement, leading

to tell of a mode of being endowed with rūpa, yet without the kāmā, or sensuous impulses held to be bound up with rūpa, when the term is used in its wider sense.[1] Nor does it enlighten us on the more impalpable denizens of a plane of being where rūpa itself is not, and for which no terms seem held appropriate save such as express high fetches of abstract thought.[2] We must go back, after all, to the Nikāyas for such brief hints as we can find. We do hear, at least, in the Dīgha Nikāya, of beings in one of the middle circles of the Form heavens termed Radiant (Ābhassara), as 'made of mind, feeding on joy, radiating light, traversing the firmament, continuing in beauty.'[3] Were it not that we miss here the unending melody sounding through each circle of the Western poet's Paradise,[4] we might well apply this description to Dante's 'anime liete,' who, like incandescent spheres:

> 'Fiammando forte, a guisa di comete,
> E come cerchi in tempra d' oriuoli
> Si giran.' . . .

Liker to those brilliant visions the heavens of Form seem to have been than to the 'quiet air' and 'the meadow of fresh verdure' on that slope of Limbo where

> 'Genti v' eran con occhi tardi e gravi,'

who

---

perhaps to the inference that in the two superior planes it was not required.

[1] See pp. 168-170: 'All form is that which is . . . related, or which belongs to the universe of sense, *not* to that of form, or to that of the formless.'

[2] See the four Āruppas, pp. 71-75.

[3] D. i. 17. Again we read (D. i. 195), that of the three possible 'personalities' of current tradition, one was made of mind, having form, and a complete organism, and one was without form and made of consciousness, or perception (arūpī saññāmayo).

[4] There is no lack of music in some of the lower Indian heavens. *Cf.*, *e.g.*, M. i. 252, on Sakka the god enjoying the music in his sensuous paradise. And see Vimāna Vatthu, *passim*.

'Parlavan rado, con voci soavi.'

Yet the rare, sweet utterances of these devas of Europe, discoursing with 'the Master of those who know,' may better have accorded with the Buddhist conception of 'beings made of mind' than the choric dances of the spheres above.

Among these shadowy beings, however, we are far from the fully bodied out idea of the 'all form' and the 'skandha of form' of the second and third Books of the Manual. It may be that the worlds of rūpa and arūpa were so called in popular tradition because in the former, visible, and in the latter, invisible, beings resided. But whereas attributes concerning either are 'sadly to seek,' there is no lack of information concerning the attributes of form in the 'sensuous universe' or kāmāvacaraṃ. If the list given of these in the first chapter of Book II. be consulted, it will be seen that I have not followed the reading of the P. T. S. edition when it states that all form is kāmāvacaram eva, rūpāvacaram eva, that is, is both related to the universe of sense and also to that of form. The Siamese edition reads kāmāvacaram eva, na rūpāvacaram eva. It may seem at first sight illogical to say that form is not related to the universe of form. But the better logic is really on the side of the Siamese. On page 334 of my translation,[1] it is seen that the avacaras were mutually exclusive as to their contents. To belong to the universe of form involved exclusion from that of sense. But in the inquiry into 'all form' we are clearly occupied with facts about this present world and about women and men as we know them—in a word, with the world of sense. Hence the 'all form' of Book II. is clearly *not* the form of the rūpāvacaraṃ. It is not used with the same implications.

Further than this, further than the vague avacara-geography gathered already from other sources, the Manual does not bring us, nor the Commentary either.

---

[1] §§ 1281-1284 of the P. T. S.'s edition.

We come then to rūpaṃ in the sensuous plane of being, or at least to such portion of that plane as is concerned with human beings: to sabbaṃ rūpaṃ and to its distribution in each human economy, termed rūpakkhandho. Whether taken generally, or under the more specialized aspect, there seems to be unanimity of teaching concerning the various manifestations of it.[1] Under it are comprised four ultimate primary, or underivable constituents and twenty-three secondary, dependent or derived modes. Thus:

Rūpaṃ

No upādā	Upādā
= (*a*) The Tangible (*i.e.*, earthy or solid, lambent or fiery, gaseous or aerial elements, or great phenomena),	= (*a*) The Five Senses,
(*b*) The Fluid (or moist) Element.	(*b*) The Four Objects of Sense (excluding Tangibles),
	(*c*) The Three Organic Faculties.
	(*d*) The Two Modes of Intimation,
	(*e*) The Element of Space,
	(*f*) Three Qualities of Form,
	(*g*) Three Phases in the Evolution of Form,
	(*h*) Impermanence of Form,
	(*i*) Bodily nutriment.

To enter with any fulness of discussion into this classification, so rich in interesting suggestions, would occupy itself a volume. In an introduction of mere notes I will offer only a few general considerations.

We are probably first impressed by the *psychological* aspect taken of a subject that might seem to lend itself to purely objective consideration. The main constituents of

---

[1] *Cf.*, *e.g.*, S. iii. 59, with Dh. S., § 584, and Vis. Mag.

the material world, classified in the East as we know them to have been classified, contemporaneously, in the West, are set down in terms of subjective or conscious experience. The āpo-dhātu is not called explicitly the Intangible; virtually, however, it and the other three 'Great Phenomena,' or literally 'Great things that have Become,'[1] are regarded from the point of view of how they affect us by way of sense. We might add, how they affect us most fundamentally by way of sense. In the selection of Touch among the senses the Indian tradition joins hands with Demokritus. But of this no more at present.

Again, in the second table, or secondary forms, the same standpoint is predominant. We have the action and re-action of sense-object and sense, the distinctive expressions of sex and of personality generally, and the phenomena of organic life, as 'sensed' or inferred, comprehended under the most general terms. Two modes of form alone are treated objectively: space and food. And of these, too, the aspect taken has close reference to the conscious personality. Ākāso is really okāso, room, or opportunity, for life and movement. Food, though described as to its varieties in objective terms, is referred to rather in the abstract sense of nutrition and nutriment than as nutritive *matter*. (*Cf.* p. 203, n. 3.)

---

[1] Better in Greek τὰ γιγνόμενα, or in German *die vier grossen Gewordenen*. How the Buddhist logic exactly reconciled the anomaly of āpodhātu as underived and yet as inaccessible to that sense which comes into contact with the underived is not, in the Manual, clearly made out. In *hot* water, as the Cy. says, there is heat, gas, and *solid*, and hence we feel it. Yet by the definition there must be in fluid a something underived from these three elements.

The Buddhist Sensationalism was opposed to the view taken in the Upanishad, where the senses are derived from prajñā (rendered by Prof. Deussen 'consciousness'), and again from the World Soul. In the Garbha Up., however, sight is spoken of as *fire*. The Buddhist view was subsequently again opposed by the Sāṅkhya philosophy, but not by the Nyāya.

Or we may be more especially struck by the curious selection and classification exercised in regard to the items of the catalogue of form.

Now, the compilers of this or of any of the canonical books were not interested in rūpaṃ on psychological grounds as such. Their object was not what we should term scientific. They were not inquiring into forms, either as objective existences, or as mental constructions, with any curiosity respecting the macrocosm, its parts, or its order. They were not concerned with problems of primordial ὕλη, of first causes, or of organic evolution, in the spirit which has been operative in Western thought from Thales (claimed by Europe) to Darwin. For them, as for the leaders of that other rival movement in our own culture, the tradition of Socrates and Plato, man was, first and last, the subject supremely worth thinking about. And man was worth thinking about as a moral being. The physical universe was the background and accessory, the support and the 'fuel' (upādānaṃ), of the evolution of the moral life. It was necessary to man as ethical (at least during his sojourn on the physical plane), but it was only in so far as it affected his ethical life that he could profitably study it. The Buddhist, like the Socratic view, was that of primitive man—'What is the *good* of it?'—transformed and sublimated by the evolution of the moral ideal. The early questioning: Is such and such good for life-preservation, for race-preservation, for fun? or is it bad? or is it indeterminate? becomes, in evolved ethics: Does it make for my perfection, for others' perfection, for noblest enjoyment? does it make for the contrary? does it make for neither?

And the advance in moral evolution which was attempted by Buddhist philosophy, coming as it did in an age of metaphysical dogmatism and withal of scepticism, brought with it the felt need of looking deeper into those data of mental procedure on which dogmatic speculation and ethical convictions were alike founded.[1]

---

[1] G. Croom Robertson, 'Philosophical Remains,' p. 3.

Viewed in this light, the category of rūpaṃ or of rūpakkhandho becomes fairly intelligible, both as to the selection and classification of subject matter and as to the standpoint from which it is regarded. As a learner of ethical doctrine, pursuing either the lower or the higher ideal, the Buddhist was concerned with the external world just as far as it directly and inevitably affected his moral welfare and that of other moral beings, that is to say, of all conscious animate beings. To this extent did he receive instruction concerning it.

In the first place, the great ultimate phenomena of his physical world were one and the same as the basis of his own physical being. That had form; so had this. That was built up of the four elements; so was this. That came into being, persisted, then dissolved; this was his destiny, too, as a temporary collocation or body, 'subject to erasion, abrasion, dissolution and disintegration.'[1] And all that side of life which we call mind or consciousness, similarly conceived as collocations or aggregates, was bound up therein and on that did it depend.

Here, then, was a vital kinship, a common basis of physical being which it behoved the student of man to recognise and take into account, so as to hold an intelligent and consistent attitude towards it. The bhikkhu sekho[2] 'who has not attained, who is aspiring after the unsurpassable goal,' has to know, *inter alia*, earth, water, flame, air, each for what it is, both as external and as part of himself[3] —must know 'unity' (ekattaṃ) for what it is; must indulge in no conceits of fancy (mā maññi) about it or them, and must so regard them that of him it may one day be said by the masters: Pariññātaṃ tassa!— 'He knows it thoroughly.'

To this point we shall return. That the elements are considered under the aspect of their tangibility involves

---

[1] D. i. 76, *e.g.*

[2] The brother in orders undergoing training. M. i. 4.

[3] M. i., pp. 185, *et seq.;* pp. 421, *et seq.*

for the Buddhist the further inquiry into the sensitive agency by which they affect him as tangibles, and so into the problem of sensation and sense-perception in general. On this subject the Dhamma-sangaṇi yields a positive and valuable contribution to our knowledge of the history of psychology in India in the fourth century B.C. It may contain no matter additional to that which is reproduced in Hardy's 'Manual of Buddhism' (pp. 399-404, 419-423). But Hardy drew *directly* from relatively modern sources, and though it is interesting to see how far and how faithfully the original tradition has been kept intact in these exegetical works, we turn gladly to the stronger attractions of the *first academic formulation* of a theory of sense which ancient India has hitherto preserved for us. There is no such analysis of sensation—full, sober, positive, so far as it goes—put forward in any Indian book of an equally early date. The pre-Buddhistic Upanishads (and those, too, of later date) yield only poetic adumbrations, sporadic aphorisms on the work of the senses. The Nyāya doctrine of pratyaksha or perception, the Jaina Sutras, the elaboration of the Vedânta and Sānkhya doctrines are, of course, of far later date. It may not, therefore, be uncalled for if I digress at some length on the Buddhist position in this matter, and look for parallel theories in the West rather than in India itself.

The theory of action and reaction between the five special[1] senses and their several objects is given in pages 172-190 and 197-200 of my translation. It may be summarized as follows:

A. The Senses.

First, a general statement relating each sense in turn (*a*) to Nature (the four elements), (*b*) to the individual

[1] They are called 'special' in modern psychology to distinguish them from organic, general or systemic sense, which works without specially adapted peripheral organs.

organism, and affirming its invisibility and its power of impact.

Secondly, an analysis of the sensory process, in each case, into

(*a*) A personal agency or apparatus capable of reacting to an impact not itself;

(*b*) An impingeing 'form,' or form producing an impact of one specific kind;

(*c*) Impact between (*a*) and (*b*);

(*d*) Resultant modification of the mental continuum, viz.: in the first place, contact (of a specific sort); then, hedonistic result, or intellectual result, or, presumably, both. The modification is twice stated in each case, emphasis being laid on the mutual impact, first as causing the modification, then as constituting the object of attention in the modified consciousness of the person affected.

B. The Sense-objects.

First, a general statement, relating each kind of sense-object in turn to Nature, describing some of the typical varieties, and affirming its invisibility, except in the case of visual objects,[1] and its power of producing impact.[2]

Secondly, an analysis of the sensory process in each case as under A, but, as it were, from the side of the sense-object, thus:

(*a*) A mode of form or sense-object, capable of producing impact on a special apparatus of the individual organism;

---

[1] This insistence on the invisibility of all the senses, as well as on that of all sense-objects except sights or visual forms, is to me only explicable on the ground that rūpaṃ recurring in each question and each answer, and signifying, whatever else it meant, in popular idiom, things *seen*, it was necessary, in philosophic usage, to indicate that the term, though referring to sense, did *not*, with one exception, connote things seen. Thus, even solid and fiery objects were, *quâ* tangibles, not visible. They were not visible to the kāyo, or skin-sensibility. They spelt visible only to the eye.

[2] See p. 183, n. 1.

(*b*) The impact of that apparatus;

(*c*) The reaction or complementary impact of the sense-object;

(*d*) Resultant modification of the mental continuum, viz.: in the first place, contact (of a specific sort); then hedonistic result, or intellectual result, or, presumably, both. The modification is twice stated, in each case emphasis being laid on the mutual impact, first as causing the modification, then as constituting the object of attention in the modified consciousness thus affected.

If we, for purposes of comparison, consult Greek views on sense-perception before Aristotle—say, down to B.C. 350—we shall find nothing to equal this for sobriety, consistency and thoroughness. The surviving fragments of Empedoklean writings on the subject read beside it like airy fancies; nor do the intact utterances of Plato bring us anything more scientific. Very possibly in Demokritus we might have found its match, had we more of him than a few quotations. And there is reason to surmise as much, or even more, in the case of Alkmæon.

Let me not, however, be understood to be reading into the Buddhist theory more than is actually there. In its sober, analytical prose, it is no less archaic, naïve, and inadequate as explanation than any pre-Aristotelian theory of the Greeks. The comment of Dr. Siebeck on Empedokles applies equally to it:[1] 'It sufficed him to have indicated the possibility of the external world penetrating the sense-organs, as though this were tantamount to an explanation of sensation. The whole working out of his theory is an attempt to translate in terms of a detailed and consecutive physiological process the primitive, naïve view of cognition.' Theory of this calibre was, in Greece, divided between *impact* (Alkmæon, Empedokles, with respect to *sight*, Demokritus, Plato, who, to impact, adds a *commingling* of sense and object) and *access* (efflux and pore theory of Empedokles) as the essential part of the process. The Buddhist

[1] 'Geschichte der Psychologie,' i. 107.

explanation confines itself to *impact*.[1] But neither East nor West, with the possible exception of Alkmæon, had yet gripped the notion of a conducting medium. In Aristotle all is changed. 'Eidôla' which collide, and 'aporrhoæ' which penetrate, have been thrown aside for an examination into 'metaxu.' And we find the point of view similarly shifted in Buddhaghosa's time, though how long before him this advance had been made we do not know. Nor was there, in the earlier thought of East or West, any clear dualistic distinction drawn between mind and matter, between physical (and physiological) motion or stimulus on the one hand, and consequent or concomitant mental modification on the other, in an act of sense-perception. The Greek explanations are what would now be called materialistic. The Buddhist description may be interpreted either way. It is true that in the Milinda-pañho, written some three or four centuries later than our Manual, the action and reaction of sense and sense-object are compared in realistic metaphor to the clash of two cymbals and the butting of two goats.[2] But, being metaphorical, this account brings us really no further. The West, while it retained the phraseology characterizing the earlier theory of sense, ceased to imply any direct physical impact or contact when speaking of being 'struck' by sights, sounds, or ideas. How far, and how early, was this also the case in the East?

The very fact that the Buddhist theory, with all its analytical and symmetrical fulness of exposition, yields so very abstract and schematic a result leaves the way open to surmise that, even in the time of our Manual, the process of sense impression was not materialistically conceived.[3]

---

[1] *Access* comes later into prominence with the development of the 'Door-theory.' See following section.

[2] 'Milindapañho,' p. 60. S.B.E., vol. xxxv., pp. 92, 93. *Cf.* below, p. 5, n. 2.

[3] Note 2, p. 175, below, suggests the eye, in the case of sight. If so, in what shape did the object get there?

We are not told, for instance, *where* the mutual impact takes place, nor *with what* a distant object impinges. And if dhammā are conceived, as in the Manual, as actual or potential states of consciousness, and rūpaṃ is conceived as a species of dhammā, it follows that both the rūpaṃ, which is 'external' and comes into contact with the rūpaṃ which is 'of the self,' and also this latter rūpaṃ are regarded in the light of the two *mental* factors necessary to constitute an act of sensory consciousness, actual or potential.

Such may have been the psychological aspect adumbrated, groped after—not to go further—in the Dhamma-saṅgaṇi itself. That the traditional interpretation of this impact-theory grew psychological with the progress of culture in the schools of Buddhism seems to be indicated by such a comment in the Atthasālinī as: '*strikes* (impinges) *on form* is a term for the eye (*i.e.*, the visual sense) being receptive of the object of consciousness.'[1] This seems to be a clear attempt to resolve the old metaphor, or, it may be, the old physical concept, into terms of subjective experience. Again, when alluding to the simile of the cymbals and the rams, we are told by Buddhaghosa to interpret 'eye' by 'visual cognition,' and to take the 'concussion' in the sense of *function*.[2] Once more, he tells us that when feeling arises through contact, the real causal antecedent is mental, though apparently external.[3]

Without pursuing this problem further, we cannot leave the subject of sense and sensation without a word of comment and comparison on the prominence given in the Buddhist theory to the notion of 'contact' and the sense of touch. As with us, both terms are from the same stem. But phasso (contact), on the one hand, is generalized to include all *receptive* experience, sensory as well as idea-

---

[1] Asl. 309. Cakkhuṃ ārammanaṃ sampaṭicchayamānam eva rūpamhi paṭihaññati nāma.

[2] *Ibid.* 108: 'kiccaṭṭhen' eva.

[3] See below, p. 5, n. 2.

tional,[1] and to represent the essential antecedent and condition of all feeling (or sensation = v e d a n ā). On the other hand, p h u s a t i, p h o ṭ ṭ h a b b a ṃ (to touch, the tangible) are specialized to express the activity of one of the senses. Now, the functioning of the tactile sense (termed body-sensibility or simply body, k ā y o, pp. 181, 182) is described in precisely the same terms as each of the other four senses. Nevertheless, it is plain, from the significant application of the term tangible, or object of touch, alluded to already—let alone the use of 'contact' in a wider sense—that the Buddhists regarded Touch as giving us knowledge of things 'without' in a more fundamental way than the other senses could. By the table of the contents of r ū p a ṃ given above, we have seen that it is only through Touch that a knowledge of the *underived elements* of the world of sense could be obtained, the fluid or moist element alone excepted. This interesting point in the psychology of early Buddhism may possibly be formulated somewhere in the Abhidhamma Piṭaka. I should feel more hopeful in this respect had the compilers been, in the first instance, not ethical thinkers, but impelled by the scientific curiosity of a Demokritus. The latter, as is well known, regarded all sensation as either bare touch or developments of touch—a view borne out to a great extent by modern biological research. This was, perhaps a corollary of his atomistic philosophy. Yet that Demokritus was no mere deductive system-spinner, but an inductive observer, is shown in the surviving quotation of his dictum, that we should proceed, in our inferences, 'from phenomena to that which is not manifest.' Now, as the Buddhist view of r ū p a ṃ calls three of the four elements 'underived' and 'the tangible,' while it calls the senses and all other sense-objects 'derived from that tangible' and from fluid, one might almost claim that their position with respect to Touch was in effect parallel to that of Demokritus. The Commentary does not assist us to any

[1] See below, p. 4, n. 2.

clear conclusion on this matter. But, in addition to the remark quoted above, in which visual magnitudes are pronounced to be really tactile sensations, it has one interesting illustration of our proverb, 'Seeing is believing, but Touch is the real thing.' It likens the four senses, excluding touch, to four balls of cotton-wool, intervening between hammer and four anvils (*i.e.*, Upādārūpaṃ, or derived form, without and within) and deadening the impact. But in Touch, hammer smites through wool, getting at the bare anvil.[1]

Further considerations on the Buddhist theory of sense, taking us beyond bare sensation to the working up of such material into concrete acts of perception, I propose to consider briefly in the following section. The remaining heads of the rūpa-skandha are very concisely treated in the niddesa answers (pp. 190-197), and, save in the significance of their selection, call for no special treatment.

It is not quite clear why senses and sense-objects should be followed by three indriyas—by three only and just these three. The senses themselves are often termed indriyas, and not only in Buddhism. In the indriyas of sex, however, and the phenomena of nutrition, the rūpa-skandha, in both the self and other selves, is certainly catalogued under two aspects as general and as impressive as that of sense. In fact, the whole organism as modifiable by the 'sabbaṃ rūpaṃ' without, may be said to be summed up under these three aspects. They fit fairly well into our division of the receptive side of the organism, considered, psychophysically, as *general* and *special* sensibility. From his ethical standpoint the learner did well to take the life in which he shared into account under its impressive aspects of sense, sex and nutrition. And this not only in so far as he was receptive. The very term indriyaṃ, which is best paralleled by the Greek δύναμις, or faculty—*i.e.*, 'powers in us, and in all other

---

[1] Asl. 263; below, p. 127, n. 1.

things, by which we do as we do'[1]—and which is interpreted to this effect by Buddhaghosa,[2] points to the active, self-expressive side of existence. Both as recipient, then, and as agent, the learner of the Dharma had to acquire and maintain a certain attitude with respect to these aspects of the rūpa-skandha.

The same considerations apply to the next two kinds of rūpaṃ, with which we may bracket the next after them. The two modes of 'intimation' or self-expression exhaust the active side of life as such, constituting, as one might say, a world of sub-derivative or tertiary form, and calling quite especially for modification by theory and practice (dassanena ca bhāvanāya ca). And the element of space, strange as it looks, at first sight, to find it listed just here, was of account for the Buddhist only as a necessary datum or postulate for his sentient and active life. The vacua of the body, as well as its *plena*, had to be reckoned in with the rūpa-skandha; likewise the space without by which bodies were delimitated, and which, yielding room for movement, afforded us the three dimensions.[3]

The grounds for excluding space from the four elements and for calling it derived remain in obscurity. In the Mahā Rāhulovāda-Sutta (cited below) it is ranked immediately after, and apparently as co-ordinate with, the other four. And it was so ranked, oftener than not, by Indian thought generally. Yet in another Sutta of the same Nikāya—the Mahā Hatthipadopama-Sutta—Sāriputta

---

[1] Republic, v. 477. [2] Asl., p. 119 and *passim*.

[3] See below, p. 194, n. 1; also M. i. 423. In the former passage space is described as if external to the organism; in the latter Gotama admonishes his son respecting the internal ākāso.

On the interesting point put forward by Professor von Schroeder of a connexion between ākāça and the Pythagorean ὄλκας, see Professor Garbe in the *Vienna Oriental Journal*, xiii., Nro. 4 (1899). The former scholar refers to the ranking of space as a fifth element, as a *schwankend uberlieferte Bezeichnung*. It was so for Buddhism.

describes four elements, leaving out ākāso. Eliminated for some reason from the Underived, when the Dhammasangaṇi was compiled, it was logically necessary to include it under Derived Rūpaṃ. That it was so included because it was held to be a mental construction, or a 'pure form of intuition,' is scarcely tenable.

And yet the next seven items of derived form are apparently to be accepted rather as concepts or aspects of form than as objective properties or 'primary qualities' of it. Be that as it may, all the seven are so many common facts about rūpaṃ, both as 'sabbaṃ' and as skandha. The Three Qualities[1] indicated the ideal efficiency for moral ends to which the rūpa-skandha, or any form serving such an end, should be brought. The Three Phases in the organic evolution of form and the great fact of Impermanence applied everywhere and always to all form. And as such all had to be borne in mind, all had to co-operate in shaping theory and practice.

Concerning, lastly, the āhāro, or support, of the rūpa-skandha, the hygiene and ethics of diet are held worthy of rational discussion in the Sutta Piṭaka.[2]

We have now gone with more or less details into the divisions of rūpaṃ in the 'sensuous universe,' with a view of seeing how far it coincided with any general philosophical concept in use among ourselves. For me it does not fit well with any, and the vague term 'form,' implicated as it is, like rūpaṃ, with 'things we see,' is perhaps the most serviceable. Its inclusion of faculties and abstract notions as integral factors prevent its coinciding with 'matter,' or 'the Extended,' or 'the External World.' If we turn to the list of attributes given in Chapter I. of Book II., rūpam appears as preeminently the *unmoral* (as to both cause and effect) and the *non-mental*. It was 'favourable' to *im*moral states, as the chief constituent of a world that had to be mastered

---

[1] Lightness, plasticity, wieldiness, pp. 194, 195.
[2] *Cf.*, *e.g.*, M. i., Suttas 54, 55, 65, 66, 70.

and transcended by moral culture, but the immoral states exploiting it were of the other four skandhas. It included the phenomena of sense, but rather on their physical pre-mental side than as full-fledged facts of consciousness. And it was sharply distinguished, as a constituent 'collocation' or 'aggregate' (skandha, rāsi), in the total aggregate of the individual organism from the three collocations called cetasikā (feelings, perceptions, syntheses), and from that called citta (intellect, thought, cognition). The attabhāvo, or personality, *minus* all mental and moral characteristics, is rūpam.

As such it is one with all rūpam not of its own composition. It is 'in touch' with the general impersonal rūpam, as well as with the mental and moral constituents of other personalities by way of *their* rūpam. That this intercommunication was held to be possible on the basis, and in virtue of, this common structure was probably as implicit in the Buddhist doctrine as it was explicit in many of the early Greek philosophers. It is not impossible that some open allusions to 'like being known by like' may be discovered in the Pitakas as a consciously held and deliberately stated principle or ground of the impressibility of the sentient organism. No such statement occurs in our Manual. But the phrase, recurring in the case of each of the special senses, 'derived from the four Great Phenomena,' may not have been inserted without this implication. Without further evidence, however, I should not be inclined to attach philosophical significance in this direction to it. But on the one hand we have an interesting hint in the Commentary that such a principle *was* held by early Buddhists. 'Where there is difference of kind (or creature), we read,[1] there is no sensory stimulus. According to the Ancients, "Sensory stimulus is of similar kinds, not of different kinds."'

---

[1] Asl. 313. Bhūta visese hi sati pasādo va na uppajjati. 'Samānānaṃ bhūtanaṃ hi pasādo, na visamānānan ti' Porāṇā.

And again: 'The solid, both within and without, becomes the condition of the sense of touch in the laying hold of the object of perception—in discerning the tangible.'[1] It is true that Buddhaghosa is discoursing, not on this question, but on what would now be called the specific energy, or specialized functioning, of nerve. Nevertheless, it seems inferable from the quotations that the principle was established. And we know also how widely accepted (and also contested)[2] this same principle—Ἡ γνῶσις τοῦ ὁμοίου τῷ ὁμοίῳ—was in Greece, from Empedokles to Plato and to Plotinus,[3] thinkers, all of them, who were affected, through Pythagorism or elsewise, by the East. The vivid description by Buddhaghosa (*cf.* below, pp. 173-174) of the presence in the seat of vision of the four elements is very suggestive of Plato's account of sight in the 'Timæus,' where the principle is admitted.

Whether as a principle, or merely as an empirical fact, the oneness of man's rūpaskandha with the sabbaṃ rūpaṃ without was thoroughly admitted, and carefully taught as orthodox doctrine. And with regard to this kinship, I repeat, a certain philosophical attitude, both theoretical and practical, was inculcated as generally binding. That attitude is, in one of the Majjhima discourses,[4] led up to and defined as follows: All good states (d h a m m ā) whatever are included in the Four Noble Truths concerning Ill.[5] Now the First Noble Truth unfolds the nature of Ill: that it lies in using the five skandhas for Grasping.[6] And the

---

[1] *Ibid.*, 315. Ajjhattika-bāhirā paṭhavī etassa kāyapasādassa ārammaṇagahane . . . phoṭṭhabbajānane paccayo hoti.

[2] *Cf.* Aristotle's discussion, *De An.*, i. 2, 5.

[3] *Cf.* the passage, Enn. i. 6, 9, reproduced by Göthe: οὐ γὰρ ἂν πώποτε εἶδεν ὀφθαλμὸς ἥλιον ἡλιοειδὴς μὴ γεγενημένος.

[4] M. i. 184, *et seq.* [5] See below, p. 276.

[6] *Ibid.*, p. 323. I have retained the meaning of 'Grasping' as dictated by Buddhaghosa for the group of the Four Kinds of Grasping. Dr. Neumann renders u p ā d ā n a k-

first of the five is that of rūpaṃ. Now rūpaṃ comprises the four Great Phenomena and all their derivatives. And the first of the four is Earth (the solid element). Then the solid *within*, or 'belonging to the self,' is catalogued, with the injunction that *it is to be regarded as it really is with right wisdom* (yathābhūtaṃ sammāpaññāya daṭṭhabbaṃ). And this means that—while recognizing his kinship with the element to the full—the good student should not identify himself with it so as to see in it a permanent unchanging substance *as which* he should persist amid transient phenomena. He was to reflect, 'This is not mine, it is not *I*, it is not the soul of me!' 'It is void of a Self.'[1] And so for the other three elements. In their mightiest manifestations—in the earthquake as in the flood, in conflagration as in tempest—they are but temporal, phenomenal; subject to change and decay. Much more is this true of them when collocated in the human organism. So far from losing himself in his meditation in the All, in Nature, in 'cosmic emotion' of any kind, he had to realize that the rūpaṃ in which he participated was but one of the five factors of that life which, in so far as it engulfed and mastered him and bore him drifting along, was the great Ill, the source of pain and delusion. From each of those five factors he had to detach himself in thought, and attain that position of mastery and emancipation whereby alone the true, the Ideal Self could emerge—temporary as a phenomenal

---

khandho by element of the impulse to live (Lebenstrieb; an expression doubtlessly prompted by Schopenhauer's philosophy). It would be very desirable to learn from the Papañca-Sūdanī (Buddhaghosa's 'Commentary on the Majjhima Nikāya), whether the Commentator interprets the term to the same effect in both passages. Dhammadinnā, the woman-apostle, explains upādānaṃ, used with a similar context, as meaning 'passionate desire in the five skandhas-of-grasping.' (M. i. 300.)

[1] See above, p. xxxvi, where the context leaves no doubt as to what the reflection is meant to emphasize.

collocation, eternal by its ethical aspiration. And the practical result of cultivating 'this earth-like culture' and the rest, as Gotama called it in teaching his son, was that 'the mind was no longer entranced by the consideration of things as affecting him pleasantly or disagreeably,'[1] but 'the disinterestedness which is based on that which is good was established.'[2] 'And he thereat is glad'—and rightly so—'for thus far he has wrought a great work!'

These seem to me some of the more essential features in the Buddhist Dharma concerning Rūpaṃ.

VII.

On the Buddhist Philosophy of Mind and Theory of Intellection.

It would have been the greatest possible gain to our knowledge of the extent to which Buddhism had developed any clear psychological data for its ethics, had it occurred to the compilers of the Dhamma-Sangaṇi to introduce an analysis of the other four skandhas parallel to that of the skandha of form. It is true that the whole work, except the book on rūpaṃ, is an inquiry into arūpino dhammā, conceived for the most part as mental phenomena, but there is no separate treatment of them divided up as such. Some glimpses we obtain incidentally, most of which have been pointed out in the footnotes to the translation. And it may prove useful to summarize briefly such contribution as may lie therein to the psychology of Buddhism.

And, first, it is very difficult to say to what extent, if at all, such psychological matter as we find is distinctively and originally Buddhist, or how much was merely adopted from contemporary culture and incorporated with the Dharma. Into this problem I do not here propose to inquire farther. If there be any originality, any new departure in the psychology scattered about the Nikāyas, it is more likely to be in aspect and treatment than in new

---

[1] M. i. 423, 424. [2] M. i. 186.

matter. Buddhism preached a doctrine of regenerate personality, to be sought after and developed by and out of the personal resources of the individual through a system of intellectual self-culture. Thrown back upon himself, he developed introspection, the study of consciousness. But, again, his doctrine imposed on him the study of psychical states without the psyche. Nature without and nature within met, acted and reacted, and the result told on the organism in a natural, orderly, necessary way.[1] But there was no one adjusting the machinery.[2] The Buddhist might have approved of Leibniz's amendment of Locke's 'Nihil est in intellectu quod non prius fuerit in sensu' in the addltional phrase 'nisi ipse intellectus.' But he would not thereby have exalted v i ñ ñ ā ṇ a ṃ, c i t t a ṃ, or m a n o to any hypostatic permanence as prior or as immanent. He would only admit the priority of intellect to particular sensations as a natural order, obtaining among the phenomenal factors of any given act of cognition.

Psychological earnestness, then, and psychological inquiry into mental phenomena, coexisting apart from, and in opposition to, the usual assumption of a psychical entity: such are the only distinctively Buddhist features which may, in the absence of more positive evidence than we yet possess, be claimed in such analysis of mind as appears in Buddhist ethics.

Of the results of this earnest spirit of inquiry into mental phenomena, in so far as they may be detached from ethical doctrine, and assigned their due place in the history of human ideas, it will be impossible, for several years, to prepare any adequate treatment. Much of the Abhidhamma Piṭaka, and even some of the Sutta Piṭaka, still remains unedited.

Of the former collection nothing has been translated with the exception of the attempt in this volume. And, since Buddhist psychology has an evolution to show covering nearly a thousand years, we have to await fresh materials

---

[1] *Cf.* Mil. 57-61. [2] Sum. 194.

from the yet unedited works of Buddhaghosa, the Buddhist Sanskrit texts, and such works as the Netti-pakaraṇa, Professor Hardy's edition of which is now in the press. Meanwhile there is an increasing store of accessible material which might be sifted by the historical investigator.

There are, for instance, in the Dhamma-Sangaṇi several passages suggesting that Buddhist scholars, in contemplating the consciousness or personality as affected by phenomena considered as external, were keenly alive to the distinction between the happening of the expected and the happening of the unexpected, between instinctive reaction of the mind and the organism generally, on occasion of sense, and the deliberate confronting of external phenomena with a carefully adjusted intelligence. Modern psychology has largely occupied itself with this distinction, and with the problems of consciousness and subconsciousness, of volition and of memory, involved in it. The subject of attention, involuntary and voluntary, figures prominently in the psychological literature of the last two decades. But it is not till the centuries of post-Aristotelian and of neo-Platonic thought that we see the distinction emerging in Western psychology contemporaneously with the development of the notion of consciousness.[1]

In the history of Buddhist thought, too, the distinction does not appear to have become explicitly and consciously made till the age of, or previous to, the writing of the great Commentaries (fifth century). A corresponding explicitness in the notion of consciousness and self-consciousness, or at least in the use of some equivalent terms, has yet to be traced.[2] Buddhism is so emphatically a philosophy, both in theory and practice, of the conscious will, with all that this involves of attention and concentration, that we hardly

---

[1] *Cf.* Siebeck, *op. cit.*, ii., pp. 200, 353, 388.

[2] In the Mahā Nidāna Sutta Gotama discourses on *sibi conscire* by way of n ā m a - r ū p a. See in Grimblot's 'Sept Suttas,' p. 255.

look to find terms discriminating such notions from among other mental characteristics. We are reminded instead of Matthew Arnold's well-known remark that as, at Soli, no one spoke *of* solecisms, so in England we had to import the term Philistine.

But, whereas it is the Atthasālinī, written from the standpoint of a later elaboration of thought, that makes explicit what it holds to be the intention of the classic manual, the latter work lends itself without straining to such interpretation. I pass over Buddhaghosa's comments on the limitations and the movements of attention reproduced below, pp. 198, n. 2, 200, n. 1, as derived very possibly from thought nearer to his own times. Again, with respect to the residual unspecified factors in good and bad thoughts—the 'or-whatever-other-states'[1]— among which the Commentator names, as a constant, manasikāra, or attention—this specifying may be considered as later elaboration. But when the Commentary refers the curious alternative emphasis in the description of the sensory act[2] to just this distinction between a percipient who is prepared or unprepared for the stimulus, it seems possible that he is indeed giving us the original interpretation.

---

[1] See below p. 5, n. 1; also Asl., pp. 168, 250, etc. The definition given of manasikāra in the 'ye-vā-panaka' passage of the Commentary (p. 133) is difficult to grasp fully, partly because, here and there, the reading seems doubtful in accuracy, partly because of the terms of the later Buddhist psychology employed, which it would first be necessary to discuss. But I gather that manasikāra may be set going in the first, middle, or last stage of an act of cognition—*i.e.*, on the ārammaṇaṃ or initial presentation, the vīthi (or āvajjanaṃ), and the javanaṃ; that in this connexion it is concerned with the first of the three; that it involves memory, association of the presentation with [mental] 'associates,' and confronting the presentation. And that it is a constructive and directing activity of mind, being compared to a charioteer.

[2] Below, p. 176, nn. 1, 2.

Again, the remarkable distinction drawn, in the case of every type of good or of bad thoughts, 'relating to the sensuous universe,' *i.e.*, to the average moral consciousness, between thoughts which are prompted by a conscious motive,[1] and such as are not, seems to me to indicate a groping after the distinction between instinctive or spontaneous intellection, on the one hand, and deliberate, purposive, or motivated thought on the other.

Taken in isolation, there is insufficient material here to establish this alternative state of mind as a dominant feature in Buddhist psychology. Taken in conjunction with the general mental attitude and intellectual culture involved in Buddhist ethical doctrine and continually inculcated in the canonical books, and emphasized as it is by later writings, the position gains in significance. The doctrine of karma, inherited and adopted from earlier and contemporary thought, never made the Buddhist fatalistic. He recognised the tremendous *vis a tergo* expressed in our doggerel:

'For 'tis their *nature* to.'

But he had unlimited faith in the saving power of *nurture*. He faced the grim realities of life with candour, and tolerated no mask. This honesty, to which we usually add a mistaken view of the course of thought and action he prescribed in consequence of the honesty, gains him the name of Pessimist. But the hope that was in him of what might be done to better nature through nurture, even in this present life, by human effort and goodwill, reveals him as a strong Optimist with an unshaken ideal of the joy springing from things made perfect. He even tried to 'pitchfork nature' in one or two respects, though opposed to asceticism generally—simply to make the Joy

---

[1] *Cf.* below, p. 34, n. 1. The thoughts which are not called sasankhārena are by the Cy. ruled as being a-sankhārena, though not explicitly said to be so (Asl. 71).

more easily attainable by those who dared to 'come out.' And this regenerating nurture resolves itself, theoretically, into a power of discrimination; practically, into an exercise of selection. The individual learner, pervious by way of his 'fivefold door' to an inflooding tide of impressions penetrating to the sixth door of the co-ordinating 'mind,' was to regulate the natural alertness of reception and perception by the special kind of attention termed yoniso manasikāra, or thorough attention, and by the clear-eyed insight referred to already as yathābhūtaṃ sammappaññāya daṭṭhabbaṃ, or the higher wisdom of regarding 'things as in themselves they really are'—to adopt Matthew Arnold's term. The stream of phenomena, whether of social life, of nature, or of his own social and organic growth, was not so much to be ignored by him as to be marked, measured and classed according to the criteria of one who has chosen 'to follow his own uttermost,'[1] and has recognised the power of that stream to imperil his enterprise, and its lack of power to give an equivalent satisfaction.[2] The often-recurring subject of sati-sampajaññaṃ, or that 'mindful and aware' attitude, which evokes satire in robust, if superficial, criticism, is the expansion and ethical application of this psychological state of prepared and pre-adjusted sense or voluntary attention.[3] The student was not to be taken by surprise—'evil states of covetousness and repining flowing in over him dwelling unprepared'—until he had

'. . . The nobler mastery learned
Where inward vision over impulse reigns.'[4]

---

[1] Seṭṭhaṃ upanamaṃ udeti . . . attano uttariṃ bhajetha (A. i. 126).

[2] *Cf.* M. i. 85-90 on kāmānaṃ assādañ ca ādīnavañ ca nissaraṇaṃ ca . . . yathābhūtaṃ pajānitvā.

[3] See below on guarding the door of the senses, pp. 350-353. Also note on D. i. 70 in 'Dialogues of the Buddha,' p. 81.

[4] George Eliot, 'Brother and Sister.'

Then indeed he might dwell at ease, strong in his emancipation.

Step by step with his progress in the cultivation of attention, he was also practising himself in that faculty of selection which it were perhaps more accurate not to distinguish from attention. Alertness is never long, and, indeed, never strictly, attending to anything and everything at once. We are reminded of Condillac's definition of attention as only an 'exclusive sensation.' From the multitude of excitations flowing in upon us, one is, more or less frequently, selected,[1] the rest being, for a time, either wholly excluded or perceived subconsciously. And this selective instinct, varying in strength, appears, not only in connexion with sense-impressions, but also in our more persisting tendencies and interests, as well as in a general disposition to concentration or to distraction.

Buddhism, in its earnest and hopeful system of self-culture, set itself strenuously against a distrait habit of mind, calling it tatra-tatrābhinandinī[2]—'the there-and-there-dalliance,' as it were of the butterfly. And it adopted and adapted that discipline in concentration (samādhi), both physical and psychical, both perceptual and conceptual, for which India is unsurpassed. But it appreciated the special practice of rapt absorbed concentrated thought called Dhyāna or Jhāna, not as an end in itself, but as a symbol and vehicle of that habit of selection and single-minded effort which governed 'life according to the Higher Ideal.' It did not hold with the robust creed, which gropes, it may be, after a yet stronger ideal:

> 'Greift nur hinein ins volle Menschenleben,
> Und wo Ihr's packt, da ist es interessant?'

'Full life' of the actual sort, viewed from the Buddhist standpoint, was too much compact of Vanity Fair, shambles

---

[1] *Cf.* Höffding's criticism of Condillac in 'Outlines of Psychology' (London, 1891), p. 120.

[2] M. i. 299.

and cemetery, to be worth the plunge. It had, on the other hand, great faith in experimenting on nature by a judicious pruning of everything it judged might wreck or hinder the evolution of a life of finer, higher *quality*. If we, admitting this intention, look on the frequent injunctions respecting what 'was to be put away' (pahātabbaṃ)[1] from the life of each disciple, whether by insight or by culture, whether by gentle or by forcible restraint,[2] not as so much mere self-mortification and crippling of energy, but as expressions of selective culture for the better 'forcing' of somewhat tender growths, we may, if we still would criticise, appraise more sympathetically.

If I have dwelt at some length on a side of Buddhist psychological ethics which is not thrown into obvious relief in our Manual, it was because I wished to connect that side with the specially characteristic feature in Buddhist psychology where it approximates to the trend of our own modern tradition. There, on the one hand, we have a philosophy manifestly looking deeper into the mental constitution than any other in the East, and giving especial heed to just those mental activities—attention and feeling, conation and choice—which seem most to imply a subject, or subjective unity *who* attends, feels, wills and chooses. And yet this same philosophy is emphatically one that attempts to 'extrude the Ego.' If, on the other hand, we leap over upwards of 2,000 years and consider one of the most notable contributions to our national psychology, we find that its two most salient features are a revival of the admission of an Ego or Subject of mental states, which had been practically extruded, and a theory of the ultimate nature of mental procedure set out entirely in terms of attention and feeling.[3]

---

[1] See, *e.g.*, below, p. 256 *et seq.*

[2] *Cf.* the Sabbāsava Sutta and *passim*, M. i., especially the Vitakkasanthāna Sutta.

[3] I refer to Professor Ward's 'Psychology,' Ency. Brit., 9th ed.

And yet the divergence between the two conclusions, widely removed though they are by time and space, is not so sharp as at first appears. The modern thinker, while he finds it more honest not to suppress the fact that all psychologists, not excepting Hume, do, implicitly or explicitly, assume the conception of 'a mind' or conscious subject, is careful to 'extrude' metaphysical dogma. That everything mental is referred to a Self or Subject is, for him, a psychological conception which may be kept as free from the metaphysical conception of a soul, mind-atom, or mind-stuff as is that of the individual organism in biology. In much the same way the Buddhists were content to adopt the term attabhāvo (self-hood or personality —for which Buddhaghosa half apologizes[1])—ajjhattikaṃ (belonging to the self, subjective[2]) and the like, as well as to speak of cittaṃ, mano and viññāṇaṃ where we might say 'mind.' It is true that by the two former terms they meant the totality of the five skandhas, that is to say, both mind and body, but this is not the case with the three last named. And if there was one thing which moved the Master to quit his wonted serenity and wield the lash of scorn and upbraiding, and his followers to use emphatic repudiation, it was just the reading into this convenient generalization of mind or personality that 'metaphysical conception of a soul, mind-atom, or mind-stuff,' which is put aside by the modern psychologist.

And I believe that the jealous way in which the Buddhists guarded their doctrine in this matter arose, not from the wish to assimilate mind to matter, or the whole personality to a machine, but from the too great danger that lay in the unchecked use of attā,[3] ahankāra, attabhāvo, *even as* a mere psychological datum, in that it afforded a foothold to the prevailing animism. They

---

[1] See below, p. 175, n. 1. [2] *Ibid.*, p. 207, n. 1.

[3] Svayaṃ (this one) is nearly always substituted for attā as a nominative, the latter term usually appearing in oblique cases.

were as Protestants in regard to the crucifix. They remembered with Ste. Beuve: 'La sauvagerie est toujours là à deux pas, et, dès qu'on lâche pied, elle recommence.'

What, then, was their view of mind, as merely phenomenal, in relation to the rūpa-skandha or non-mental part of the human individual? We have considered their doctrine of external phenomena impingeing on and modifying the internal or personal rūpaṃ by way of sense. Have we any clue to their theory of the propagation of the modifications, alleged in their statement[1] to take place in relation to those factors of personality which were arūpino, and not derived from material elements—the elements (dhātu's), namely, or skandhas of feeling, perception, syntheses and intellect? How did they regard that process of co-ordination by which, taking sensuous experience as the more obvious *starting-point* in mental experience, sensations are classed and made to cohere into groups or percepts, and are revived as memories, and are further co-ordinated into concepts or abstract ideas? And finally, and at back of all this, *who* feels, or attends, or wills?

Now the Dhamma-Saṅgaṇi does not place questions of this kind in the mouth of the catechist. In so far as it is psychological (not psycho-physical or ethical), it is so strictly *phenomenological*, that its treatment is restricted to the analysis of certain broadly defined states of mind, felt or inferred to have arisen in consequence of certain other mental states as conditions. There is no reference anywhere to a 'subjective factor' or agent *who has* the cittaṃ or thought, with all its associated factors of attention, feeling, conception and volition. Even in the case of Jhāna, where it is dealing with more active modes of regulated attention, involving a maximum of constructive thought with a minimum of receptive sense, the agent, *as conscious subject*, is kept in the background. The inflexion of the verb[2] alone implies a given personal agent, and the

---

[1] See answers in §§ 600, 604, etc.

[2] Bhāveti, viharati (cultivates, abides); p. 43 *et seq.*

Commentary even feels it incumbent to point him out. It is this psychologizing without a psyche that impressed me from the first, and seemed to bring the work, for all its remoteness in other respects, nearer to our own Experiential school of and since Locke, than anything we find in Greek traditions.

It is true that each of the four formless skandhas is defined or described, and this is done in connexion with the very first question of the book. But the answers are given, not in terms of respective function or of mutual relation, but of either synonyms, or of modes or constituent parts. For instance, feeling (v e d a n ā) is resolved into three modes,[1] perception (s a ñ ñ ā) is taken as practically self-evident and not really described at all,[2] the syntheses (s a n k h ā r ā) are resolved into modes or factors, intellect (v i ñ ñ ā ṇ a ṃ) is described by synonyms.

Again, whereas the skandhas are enumerated in the order in which, I believe, they are unvaryingly met with, there is nothing, in text or Commentary, from which we can infer that this order corresponds to any theory of genetic procedure in an act of cognition. In other words, we are not shown that feeling calls up perception, or that the sankhāras are a necessary link in the evolution of perception into conception or reasoning.[3] If we can infer

---

[1] See pp. 3-9, 27-29.

[2] It is on the other hand described with some fulness in the Cy. See my note *s.v.*

[3] *Cf.* the argument by Dr. Neumann, 'Buddhistische Anthologie,' xxiii, xxiv. If I have rendered s a n k h ā r ā by 'syntheses,' it is not because I see any coincidence between the Buddhist notion and the Kantian *Synthesis der Wahrnehmungen*. Still less am I persuaded that *Unterscheidungen* is a virtually equivalent term. Like the 'confections' of Professor Rhys Davids and the '*Gestaltungen*' of Professor Oldenberg, I use syntheses simply as, more or less, an etymological equivalent, and wait for more light. I may here add that I have used intellection and cognition interchangeably as comprehending the whole process of knowing, or coming to know.

anything in the nature of causal succession at all, it is such that the order of the skandhas as enumerated is upset. Thus, taking the first answer (and that is typical for the whole of Book I. when new ground is broken into): a certain sense-impression evokes, through 'contact,' a complex state of mind or psychosis called a thought or cittaṃ. *Born of this contact and the 'appropriate'* cittaṃ, now (*i.e.*, in answer 3) called, in terms of its synonym, representative intellection (manoviññāṇa-dhātu), feeling, we are told, is engendered. Perception is called up likewise and, apparently, simultaneously. So is 'thinking' (cetanā)—of the sankhāra-skandha. And 'associated with' the cittaṃ come all the rest of the constituent dhammas, both sankhāras, as well as specific *modes*[1] or different *aspects*[2] of the feeling and the thought already specified. In a word, we get contact evoking the *fifth* skandha, and, as the common co-ordinate resultant, the genesis or excitement of the other three. This is entirely in keeping with the many passages in the Nikāyas, where the concussion of sense and object are said to result in viññāṇaṃ = cittaṃ = the fifth skandha. 'Eye,' for instance, and 'form,' in mutual 'contact,' result in 'visual cognition.'

In the causal chain of that ancient formula, the Paticca-samuppāda,[3] on the other hand, we find quite another order of genesis, sankhāras inducing cognition or thought, and contact alone inducing feeling. This mysterious old rune must not further complicate our problem. I merely allude to it as not in the least supporting the view that the order of statement, in the skandhas, implies order of happening. What we may more surely gather from the canon is that, as our own psychological thought has now conceived it,[4] the, let us say, given

---

[1] *E.g.*, ease.

[2] *E.g.*, the 'faculties' of mind (ideation) and of pleasure.

[3] Given below on p. 348 [1336].

[4] Professor Ward, *op. cit.*

individual '*attends* to or cognizes (vijānāti) changes in the sensory continuum, and is, in consequence, either pleased or pained' (or has neutral feeling). And, further, in any and every degree of conscious or subconscious mood or disposition, he may be shown to be experiencing a number of 'associated states,' as enumerated. All this is in our Manual called a cittuppādā—a genesis of thought.

Of thought or of thinking. There seems to be a breadth and looseness of implication about cittaṃ fairly parallel to the popular vagueness of the English term. It is true that the Commentary does not sanction the interpretation of contact and all the rest (I refer to the type given in the first answer) as so many attributes of the thought which 'has arisen.' The sun rising, it says, is not different from its fiery glory, etc., arising. But the cittaṃ arising is a mere expression to fix the occasion for the induction of the whole concrete psychosis, and connotes no more and no less than it does as a particular constituent of that complex.[1]

This is a useful hint. On the other hand, when we consider the synonymous terms for cittaṃ, given in answer 6, and compare the various characteristics of these terms scattered through the Commentary, we find a considerable wealth of content and an inclusion of process and product similar to that of our 'thought.' For example, 'cittaṃ means mental object or presentation (ārammaṇaṃ); that is to say, he thinks; that is to say, he attends to a thought.'[2] Hence my translation might well

---

[1] Asl. 113. I gather, however, that the adjective cetasikaṃ had a wider and a narrower denotation. In the former it meant 'not bodily,' as on p. 6. In the latter it served to distinguish three of the incorporeal skandhas from the fourth, *i.e.*, cittaṃ, as on pp. 265, 318—citta-cetasikā dhammā. Or are we to take the Commentator's use of kāyikaṃ here to refer to those three skandhas, as is often the case (p. 43, n. 3)? Hardly, since this makes the two meanings of cetasikam self-contradictory.

[2] *Ibid.* 63.

have run: When a good thought . . . has arisen . . . *as* the object of this or that sense, etc. Again, cittaṃ is defined as a process of connecting (sandhānaṃ) the last (things) as they keep arising in consciousness with that which preceded them.[1] Further, it is a co-ordinating, relating, or synthesizing (sandahanaṃ);[2] and, again, it has the property of initiative action (pure cārikaṃ). For, when the sense-impression gets to the 'door' of the senses, cittaṃ confronts it before the rest of the mental congeries.[3] The sensations are, by cittaṃ, wrought up into that concrete stream of consciousness which they evoke.

Here we have cittaṃ covering both thinking and thought or idea. When we turn to its synonym or quasi-synonym mano we find, so far as I can discover, that only activity, or else spring, source or *nidus* of activity, is the aspect taken. The faculty of ideation (manindriyaṃ), for instance,[4] while expressly declared to be an equivalent (vevacanaṃ) of cittam, and, like it, to be that which attends or cognizes (vijānāti), is also called a *measuring* the mental object—declared above to *be* cittaṃ.[5] In a later passage (*ibid.*, 129), it is assigned the function of accepting, receiving, analogous, perhaps, to our technical expression 'assimilating' (sampaṭicchanaṃ). In thus appraising or approving, it has all sensory objects for its field, as well as its more especial province of dhammas.[6] These, when thus distinguished, I take to mean ideas, including images and general notions. And it is probably

---

[1] Asl., pp. 112, 113.

[2] *Cf.* the characteristic—samvidahanaṃ—of cetanā in my note, p. 8.

[3] The figure of the city-guardian, given in Mil. 62, is quoted by the Cy.

[4] See below, p. 18, and Asl. 123.

[5] It is at the same time said to result in (establishing) fact or conformity (tathābhāvo), and to succeed sense-perception as such.

[6] See p. 2, n. 3.

only in order to distinguish between mind in this abstract functioning and mind as cognition in its most comprehensive sense that we see the two terms held apart in the sentence: 'C i t t a ṃ cognizes the dhammas which are the objects of m a n o, just as it cognizes the visual forms, etc., which are the objects of the senses.'[1]

When c i t t a ṃ is thus occupied with the abstract functioning of m a n o[2]—when, that is, we are reflecting on past experience, in memory or ratiocination—then the more specific term is, I gather, *not* c i t t a ṃ, but m a n o v i ñ-ñ ā ṇ a m (corresponding to c a k k h u v i ñ ñ a ṇ a ṃ, etc.). This, in the Commentarial psychology, certainly stands for a further stage, a higher 'power' of intellection, for 'representative cognition,' its specific activity being distinguished as judging or deciding (s a n t ī r a ṇ a ṃ), and as fixing or determining (v o ṭ ṭ h a p p a n a ṃ).

The affix d h ā t u, whether appended to m a n o or to m a n o v i ñ ñ ā ṇ a m, probably stands for a slight distinction in *aspect* of the intellectual process. It may be intended to indicate either of these two stages as an irreducible element, a psychological ultimate, an activity regarded as its own spring or source or basis. Adopted from without by Buddhism, it seems to have been jealously guarded from noumenal implications by the orthodox. Buddhaghosa, indeed, seems to substitute the warning against its abuse for the reason why it had come to be used. According to him, the various lists of dhammas (*e.g.*, in the first answer), when considered under the aspect of phenomena, of 'emptiness,' of non-essence, may be grouped as together forming two classes of d h ā t u.[3] Moreover, each special sense can be so considered (c a k k h u - d h ā t u, etc.; see pp. 214, 215),

---

[1] Asl., p. 112.

[2] *Cf.* the expression suddha-manodvāro in my note, p. 3. And on what follows, *cf.* pp. 129, 132, nn.

[3] Viz., manoviññāṇa-dhātu and dhamma-dhātu see Asl. 153, and below, p. 26, n. 2. The term 'element' is similarly used in our own psychology.

and so may each kind of sense-object. For, with respect to sense, or the apprehension of form, they are so many phenomenal ultimates—the two terms, so to speak, in each sensory relation.

How far dhātu corresponds to vatthu—how far the one is a psychological, the other a physical conception[1] of source or base—is not easily determined. But it is interesting to note that the Commentator only alludes to a basis of thought (cittassa vatthu), that is, to the heart (hadaya-vatthu), when the catechizing is in terms of mano-dhātu.[2] His only comment on 'heart,' when it is included in the description of cittaṃ (answer [6]), is to say that, whereas it stands for cittaṃ, it simply represents the inwardness (*intimité*) of thought.[3] But in the subsequent comment he has a remark of great interest, namely, that the 'heart-basis' is the place whither all the 'door-objects' come, and where they are assimilated, or received into unity. In this matter the Buddhist philosophy carries on the old Upanishad lore about the heart, just as Aristotle elaborated the dictum of Empedokles, that perception and reasoning were carried on in 'the blood round the heart.'

---

[1] *Cf.* below, pp. 214, 215, with 209-211.

[2] Asl. 264; below, p. 129, fn.

[3] Asl. 140: 'Heart=thought (Hadayan ti cittaṃ). In the passage—"I will either tear out your mind or break your heart"—the heart in the breast is spoken of. In the passage (M. i. 32)—"Methinks he planes with a heart that knows heart" (like an expert)!—the mind is meant. In the passage—"The vakkam is the heart"—the basis of heart is meant. But *here* cittam is spoken of as heart in the sense of inwardness (abbhantaram).' It is interesting to note that, in enumerating the rūpaskandha in the Visuddhi Magga, Buddhaghosa's sole departure from conformity with the Dhamma-Saṅgaṇi is the *inclusion of* hadaya-vatthu *after* '*vitality*.'

The other term, 'that which is clear' (paṇḍaram), is an ethical metaphor. The mind is said to be naturally pure, but defiled by incoming corruptions. (*Cf.* A. i., p. 10.)

It is possible that this ancient and widely-received tradition of the heart (rather than the brain, for instance) as the seat of the soul or the mind is latent in the question put by Mahākoṭṭhito, a member of the Order, to Sāriputta, the leading apostle:[1] 'Inasmuch as these five indriyas (senses) are, in province and in gratification, mutually independent, what process of reference is there,[2] and who is it that is gratified by them in common?' So apparently thinks Dr. Neumann, who renders Sāriputta's answer—'The mind (mano)'—by *Herz*. This association must, however, not be pressed. For in another version of this dialogue more recently edited, Gotama himself being the person consulted, his interlocutor goes on to ask: What is the paṭisaraṇam of mano—of recollection (sati)—of emancipation—of Nirvana?[3] So that the meaning of the first question may simply be that as emancipation *looks to*, or *makes for* Nirvana, and recollection or mindfulness for emancipation, and ideation or thinking refers or looks

---

[1] M. i. 295.

[2] Kim paṭisaraṇaṃ. The word is a crux, and may bear more than one meaning. *Cf.* Vinaya Texts (S. B. E. xvii.), ii., p. 364, n.; 'Dialogues of the Buddha,' i., p. 122, n. Dr. Neumann renders it by *Hort*, following Childers.

It is worthy of note that, in connexion with the heresy of identifying the self with the physical organism generally (below, p. 259), the Cy. makes no allusion to heart, or other part of the rūpam, in connexion with views (2) or (4). These apparently resembled Augustine's belief: the soul is wholly present both in the entire body and in each part of it. With regard to view (3), is it possible that Plotinus heard it at Alexandria, or on his Eastern trip? For he, too, held that the body was 'in the soul,' permeated by it as air is by fire (Enn. iv.). Buddhaghosa's illustrative metaphor is 'as a flower being "in" its own perfume.' I regret that space fails me to reproduce his analysis of these twenty soul-hypotheses.

[3] S. v., p. 218. In the replies mano is referred to sati, sati to vimutti, and this to Nirvana.

to memory,[1] so sensation depends on thinking, on mental construction (to become effective as knowledge).

It is, indeed, far more likely that Buddhist teaching made little of and passed lightly over this question of a physical basis of thought or mind. It was too closely involved with the animistic point of view—how closely we may see, for instance, in the Bṛihadāraṇyaka Upanishad. When King Milinda puts a similar question respecting the subject of sensations,[2] he does so from so obviously animistic a standpoint that the sage, instead of discussing mano, or heart, with him, argues against any one central subjective factor whatever, and resolves the process of cognition into a number of 'connate' activities. The method itself of ranking mental activity as though it were a sixth kind of sense seems to point in the same direction, and reminds us of Hume's contention, that when he tried to 'catch himself' he always 'tumbled on some particular perception.' Indeed it was, in words attributed to Gotama himself, the lesser blunder in the average man to call 'this four-elementish body' his soul than to identify the self with 'what is called cittaṃ, that is, mano, that is, viññāṇam.' For whereas the body was a collocation that might hold together for many years, 'mind, by day and by night is ever arising as one thing, ceasing as another!'[3]

Impermanence of conscious phenomena was one of the two grounds of the Buddhist attack. So far it was on all fours with Hume. The other ground was the presence of law, or necessary sequence in mental procedure. The Soul was conceived as an entity, not only *above change*, an absolute constant, but also as an *entirely free agent*. Both

---

[1] *Cf.* the interesting inquiry into the various modes of *association in remembering*, given in Mil., pp. 78, 79, and 77, 78.

[2] Mil. 54. He calls it vedagū (knower), and, when cross-examined, abbhantare jīvo (the living principle within).

[3] S. ii., pp. 94-96.

grounds, be it noted, are laid down on psychological evidence—on the testimony of consciousness. And both grounds were put forward by Gotama in his very first sermon.[1] The standard formula for the latter only is reproduced in our Manual.[2] And it is interesting to see the same argument clothed in fresh dress in the dialogue with Milinda referred to above. The point made is this: that if any one of the skandhas could be identified with a self or soul, it would, as not subject to the conditions of phenomena, act through any other faculty it chose. It would be a principle, not only of the nature of what *we* should call will, but also of genuine free will.[3] Soul and Free Will, for the Buddhist, stand or fall together. But, he said, what we actually find is no such free agency. We only find certain organs (doors), with definite functions, natural sequence, the line of least resistance and association.[4] Hence we conclude there is no transcendent 'knower' about us.

Here I must leave the Buddhist philosophy of mind and theory of intellection. We are only at the threshold of its problems, and it is hence not strange if we find them as baffling as, let us say, our own confused usage of many psychological terms—feeling, will, mind—about which we ourselves greatly differ, would prove to an inquiring Buddhist. If I have not attempted to go into the crux of the sankhāra-skandha, it is because neither the Manual nor its Commentary brings us any nearer to a satisfactory hypothesis. For future discussion, however, the frequent enumerations of that skandha's content, varying with every changing mood, should prove pertinent. In every direction there is very much to be done. And each addition to the texts edited brings new light. Nor can philosophic interest fail in the long-run to accumulate about a system

---

[1] Vin. i. 14; = M. i. 138, 300; S. iii. 66; *cf.* iv. 34.

[2] P. 257 *et seq.*

[3] *Cf.* the writer's article on the Vedalla Suttas, J. R. A. S., April, 1894.

[4] Mil., *loc. cit.*

of thought which at that early time of day took up a task requiring such vigour and audacity—the task, namely, of opposing the prevailing metaphysic, not because problems of mind did not appeal to the founders of that system, but because further analysis of mind seemed to reveal a realm of law-governed phenomenal sequence for which the ready hypothesis of an unconditioned permanent Self *super grammaticam* was too cheap a solution.

VIII.

On the Buddhist Notions of 'Good, Bad, and Indeterminate.'

By way of dhammā, rūpaṃ and cittaṃ, by way of Buddhist phenomenology and psychology, we come at last to the ethical purport of the questions in the Manual. Given a human being known to us by way of these phenomenal states, what is implied when we say that some of them are good, some bad, others neither?

The Dhamma-Sangaṇi does not, to our loss be it said, define any one of these concepts. All it does is to show us the content of a number of 'thoughts' known as one or the other of these three species of dhammā. In a subsequent passage (pp. 345-348) it uses the substantival form of 'good' (kusalatā; another form is kosallam) in the sense of skill or proficiency as applied to various kinds of insight, theoretical or practical.

Now if we turn to the later expression of old tradition in the Commentaries, we find, on the one hand, an analysis of the meaning of 'good'; on the other, the rejection of precisely that sense of skill, and of that alone out of four possible meanings, with respect to 'good' *as used in Book I.* Kusalaṃ, we read,[1] may mean (*a*) wholesome, (*b*) virtuous, (*c*) skilful, (*d*) felicific, or productive of happy result. The illustrations make these clear statements clearer. *E.g.* of (*a*), from the Dasaratha Jātaka: 'Is it good for you, sir, is it wholesome?'[2] Of (*b*) 'What, sir, is good

---

[1] Asl. 38.

[2] The two adjectives are kusalaṃ, anāmayaṃ.

behaviour in act? Sire, it is conduct that is blameless (a n a v a j j o).' Of (*c*) 'You are good at knowing all about the make of a chariot.'[1] Again: 'The four girl-pupils are good at singing and dancing.' Of (*d*) 'Good states, brethren, are acquired through good karma having been wrought and stored up.'

Of these four, (*c*) is alone ruled out as not applicable to the eight types of good thoughts constituting d h a m m ā k u s a l ā. In so far, then, as we suffer the Buddhist culture of the fifth century to interpret the canon for us, 'good,' in the earlier ethics, meant that which insures soundness, physical and moral, as well as that which is felicific.

The further question immediately suggests itself, whether Buddhism held that these two attributes were at bottom identical. Are certain 'states' intrinsically good, *i.e.*, virtuous and right, independently of their results? Or is 'good,' in the long-run at least, felicitous result, and only on that account so called? Are Buddhists, in a word, Intuitionists, or are they Utilitarians? Or is not a decidedly eclectic standpoint revealed in the comprehensive interpretation given of k u s a l a ṃ?

These are, however, somewhat modern—I am tempted to say, somewhat British—distinctions to seek in an ancient theory of morals. They do not appear to have troubled Buddhism, early or late. The Buddhist might possibly have replied that he could not conceive of any thought, word, or deed as being intrinsically good and yet bad in its results, and that the distinction drawn by the Commentator was simply one of aspects.

If pressed, however, we can almost imagine the Buddhist well content with the relative or dependent good of Utilitarianism, so closely is his ethics bound up with cause and effect. Good, for him, is good with respect to karma—that is, to pleasurable effect or *eudæmonia*.

With respect to the supremely good effect, to arahatship

---

[1] *Cf.* M. ii. 94.

or Nirvana, he might, it is true, have admitted a difference, namely, that this state was absolutely good, and not good because of its results. It *was* the supreme Result or Fruit, and there was 'no beyond.' But then he did not rank Nirvana exactly in the category of good, and precisely for this reason, that in it moral causation culminated and ceased. He spoke of it as Indeterminate, as without result—as a Freedom, rather than as a Good.

He would not then have fallen in with Aristotle's definition of Good in terms of *aim*, viz., as 'that at which everything aims.' Good was rather *the means by and with which we aim.* But that at which we aim is, in all lower quests, Sukhaṃ, in the one high quest, Vimutti (emancipation), or Nirvana.

Nor must the substitution of these two last terms for that well-being, that well-ness, 'τὸ εὐ ζῆν,' which is the etymological equivalent of sukhaṃ,[1] be taken as indicating the limit of the consistent Hedonism or Eudæmonism of the Buddhist. For he did not scruple to speak of these two also (Emancipation and Nirvana) in terms of pleasurable feeling. Gotama attaining his supreme enlightenment beneath the Bo-tree is said to have 'experienced Emancipation-bliss' (vimutti-sukha-paṭisaṃvedi).[2] And to King Milinda the Sage emphatically declares Nirvana to be 'absolute (or entire) happiness' (ekanta-sukhaṃ).[3] And we know, too, that Buddhism defined all right conduct and the sufficient motive for it in terms of escape from ill (dukkhaṃ, the antithesis of sukhaṃ) or suffering. Here then again their psychological proclivity is manifested. They analyzed feeling, or subjective experience, into three modes: sukhaṃ, dukkhaṃ, adukkhaṃ-asukham. And in Good and Bad they saw, not ends or positions of attainment, but the vehicles or agencies, or, to speak less in abstractions, the characteristic mark of those kinds of

---

[1] *Cf.* p. 12, n. 3. [2] Vin. i. 2, 3, quoted Jāt. i. 77.
[3] Mil. 313.

conduct, by which well-being or ill-being might respectively be entailed.

The Buddhist, then, was a Hedonist, and hence, whether he himself would have admitted it or not, his morality was dependent, or, in the phrase of British ethics, utilitarian, and not intuitionist. Hedonist, let us say, rather than eudæmonistic, because of the more subjective (psychological) import of the former term. And he found the word s u k h a ṃ good enough to cover the whole ground of desirability, from satisfaction in connexion with sense—compare Buddhaghosa's traveller refreshed obtaining both joy and ease[1]—up to the ineffable 'Content' of Nirvana.[2] He did not find in it the inadequacy that some moral philosophers have found in our 'Pleasure.' His ethical system was so emphatically a study of *consequences*—of karma and v i p ā k a (effect of karma)—of seeing in every phenomenon a *reaping* of some previous sowing—that the notion of good became for him inevitably bound up with result. As my late master used to say (*ex cathedrâ*): If you bring forward consequences—how acts by way of result affect self and others—you *must* come to feeling. Thence pleasure becomes prominent. And did not folk suffer loose, lower associations to affect their judgment, there would be no objection to Hedonism. For pleasures are of all ranks, up to that of a good conscience.'

A reflection may here suggest itself to readers in this country who have, at the feet of Spencer, Bain, and Leslie Stephen, learnt to see, behind Nature's device of Pleasurable Feeling, the conservation of the species—'quantity of life, measured in breadth as well as in length'—as the more fundamental determinant of that which, in the long-run, becomes the end of conduct. Namely, that there seems a strange contradiction in a philosophic position which is content to find, in the avoidance of pain and the quest of pleasurable feeling, its fundamental spring of

---

[1] Below, p. 12, n. 3.

[2] S a n t u ṭ ṭ h i. See p. 358, n. 2.

moral action while, at the same time, it says of life—apart from which it admits no feeling to be possible—that the attainment of its *last phase* is the one supremely happy event.[1] Pleasurable feeling, from the evolutionist's standpoint, means, and is in order to, the increase, 'intensive and extensive,' of life. Yet to the Hedonistic Buddhist, the dissolution of the conditions of renewed existence is a happy event, *i.e.*, an event that causes pleasurable feeling in the thoughtful spectator.

I believe that the modern ethics of evolution would have profoundly interested the early Buddhists, who after their sort and their age were themselves evolutionists. And I believe, too, that they would have arisen from a discussion with our thinkers on this subject as stanch Buddhists and as stanch Hedonists as they had sat down. I admit that with respect to the desirableness of life taken quantitatively, and in two dimensions, they were frankly pessimistic. As I have already suggested,[2] and have put forward elsewhere,[3] to prize mere *quantity* of living stood by Gotama condemned as ignoble, as stupid, as a mortal bondage, as one of the four Asavas or Intoxicants.[4] The weary, heart-rending tragedies immanent in the life of the world he recognised and accepted as honestly and fully as the deepest pessimist. The complexities, the distractions, the burdens, the dogging sorrow, the haunting fear of its approaching tread, inevitable for life lived in participation of all that the human organism naturally calls for, and human society puts forward as desirable—all this he judged too heavy to be borne, not, indeed, by lay followers, but by those who should devote themselves to the higher life. To these he looked to exemplify and propagate and transmit

---

[1] *Cf.*, *e.g.*, M. P. S. 62; Mahā Sudassana-sutta, S. B. E. xi. 240, 289.

[2] See above, pp. lxix, lxx.

[3] In an article 'On the Will in Buddhism,' J. R. A. S., January, 1898.

[4] *Cf.* below, p. 290 *et seq.*

his doctrine. Theirs it was to lift the world to higher standpoints and nobler issues. Life in its fulness they at least could not afford to cultivate.

But if we take life of a certain *quality* where selective economy, making for a certain object, cuts off some lines of growth but forces others on—then Buddhism, so far from 'negating the will to live' that kind of life, pronounced it fair and lovely beyond all non-being, beyond all after-being. If final death, as it believed, followed inevitably on the fullest fruition of it, it was not this that made such life desirable. Final dissolution was accepted as welcome, not for its own sake, but as a corollary, so to speak, of the solved problem of emancipation. It merely signified that unhealthy moral conditions had wholly passed away.

Keeping in view, then, the notion of Good in thought, word and deed, as a means entailing various kinds of felicific result, we may see in Book I. of our Manual, first, the kind of conscious experience arising apart from systematic effort to obtain any such specific result, but which was bound, none the less, to lead to hedonistic consequences, pleasant or unpleasant (pp. 1-42). Next, we see a certain felicific result deliberately aimed at through self-cultivation in modes of consciousness called Good (pp. 43-97). And, incidentally, we learn something of the procedure adopted in that systematic culture.

The Commentary leaves us no room to doubt whether or not the phase rupūpapattiyā maggam bhāveti ('that he may attain to the heavens of Form he cultivates the way thereto') refers to a flight of imaginative power merely. 'Form = the rūpa-bhavo,' or mode of existence so called. 'Attainment = nibbatti, jāti, sañjāti'—all being terms for birth and re-birth.[1] So for the attaining to the Formless heavens. Through the mighty engine of 'good states,' induced and sustained, directed and developed

---

[1] Asl. 162. See below, pp. 43 *et seq.*, 71 *et seq.*

by intelligence and self-control, it was held that the student might modify his own destiny beyond this life, and insure, or at least promote, his chances of a happy future. The special culture or exercise required in either case was that called Jhāna, or rapt contemplation, the psychology of which, when adequately investigated, will one day evoke considerable interest. There was first intense attention by way of 'an exclusive sensation,'[1] to be entered upon only when all other activity was relaxed to the utmost, short of checking in any way the higher mental functions. After a time the sensation practically ceases. The wearied sense gives out. Change, indispensable to consciousness, has been eliminated; and we have realized, at all events since Hobbes wrote, how *idem semper sentire et non sentire ad idem recidunt*. Then comes the play of the 'after-image,' and then the emergence of the mental image, of purely ideational or representative construction. This will be, not of the sense-object first considered, but some attenuated abstraction of one of its qualities. And this serves as a background and a barrier against all further invasion of sense-impressions for the time being. To him thus purged and prepared there comes, through subconscious persistence, a *reinstatement* of some concept, associated with feeling and conation (*i.e.*, with desire or aspiration), which he had selected for preliminary meditation. And this conception he now proceeds by a sort of psychical involution to raise to a higher power, realizing it more fully, deepening its import, expanding its application.

Such seems to have been the Kasiṇa method according to the description in the Visuddhi Magga, chap. iv.,[2] but there were several methods, some of which, the method, *e.g.*, of respiration, are not given in our Manual. Of the thoughts for meditation, only a few occur in the Dhamma-

---

[1] See above, p. lxix.

[2] Translated in Warren's 'Buddhism in Translations,' p. 293 *et seq.* *Cf.* below, Book I., Part I., chap. ii. *Cf.* also Rhys Davids' 'Yogâvacara's Manual,' Introduction.

Sangaṇi, such as the 'Sublime Abodes' of thought—love, pity, etc. But in the former work we find numerous lists for exercise in the contemplative life, with or without the rapt musing called Jhāna.[1]

In the exercises calculated to bring out re-birth in the world of Form, it was chiefly necessary to ponder on things of this life in such a way as to get rid of all appetite and impulse in connexion with them, and to cultivate an attitude of the purest disinterestedness towards all worldly attractions. If the Formless sphere were the object of aspiration, it was then necessary, by the severest fetches of abstraction, to eliminate not only all sense-impression, but also all sensory images whatever, and to endeavour to realize conditions and relations other than those obtaining in actual experience.[2] Thus, in either method a foretaste of the mode of re-becoming aspired after was attempted.

But besides and beyond the sort of moral consciousness characterizing these exercises which were calculated to promote a virtuous and happy existence in any one of the three worlds, there were the special conditions of intellect and emotion termed lok'uttaram cittam.[3] Those exercises were open to the lay pupil and the bhikkhu alike. There was nothing especially 'holy,' nothing esoteric, about the practice of Jhāna. The diligent upāsaka or upāsikā, pursuing a temporary course of such religious and philosophic discipline as the rising schools of

---

[1] J. P. T. S., 1891-1893. Synopsis of the Vis. Mag., Parts II. and III.

[2] In translating the formula of the Third Āruppa or meditation on Nothingness, I might have drawn attention to Kant's development of the concept of None or Nothing, in the *Kritik der reinen Vernunft* (end of Div. i. of Transc. Logic). Some great adepts were credited with the power of actually partaking in other existences while yet in this, notably Mahā Moggallāna (*e.g.*, M. i.).

Gotama tells of another in the Kevaddha Sutta (D. i. 215), but tells it as a myth.

[3] P. 82 *et seq.* *Cf.* n. 2 on p. 81.

Buddhism afforded, might be expected to avail himself or herself of it more or less. But those 'good' dhammas alluded to were those which characterized the Four Paths, or Four Stages of the way, to the full 'emancipation' of Nirvana. If I have rendered lokuttaraṃ cittaṃ by 'thought engaged upon the higher ideal' instead of selecting a term more literally accurate, it is because there is, in a way, less of the 'supramundane' or 'transcendent,' as we usually understand these expressions, about this cittam than about the aspiring moods described above. For this sort of consciousness was that of the man or woman who regarded not heaven nor re-birth, but one thing only, as 'needful': the full and perfect efflorescence of mind and character to be brought about, if it might be, here and now.

The Dhamma-Sangaṇi never quits its severely dry and formal style to descant on the characteristics and methods of that progress to the Ideal, every step in which is elsewhere said to be loftier and sweeter than the last, with a wealth of eulogy besides that might be quoted. Edifying discourse it left to the Suttanta Books. But no rhetoric could more effectively describe the separateness and uncompromising other-ness of that higher quest than the one word A-pariyāpannaṃ—Unincluded—by which reference is made to it in Book III.

Yet for all this world of difference in the *quo vadis* of aspiration, there is a great deal of common ground covered by the moral consciousness in each case, as the respective expositions show. That of the Arahat *in spe* differs only in two sets of additional features conferring greater richness of content, and in the loftier quality of other features not in themselves additional.

This quality is due to the mental awakening or enlightenment of sambodhi. And the added factors are three constituents of the Noble Eightfold Path of conduct (which are, more obviously, modes of overt activity than of consciousness) and the progressive stages in the attainment of the sublime knowledge or insight termed a ñ ñ ā.[1] Our Western languages are scarcely rich enough to ring the changes on the words signifying 'to know' as those of India did on j ñ ā and v i d, d ṛ ś and p a ś. Our religious ideals have tended to be emotional in excess of our intellectual enthusiasm. 'Absence of dulness' has not ranked with us as a cardinal virtue or fundamental cause of good. Hence it is difficult to reproduce the Pali so as to give impressiveness to a term like a ñ ñ ā as compared with the mere ñ ā ṇ a ṃ,[2] usually implying less advanced insight, with which the 'first type of good thought' is said to be associated.

But I must pass on. As a compilation dealing with positive culture, undertaken for a positive end, it is only consistent that the Manual should deal briefly with the subject of bad states of consciousness. It is true that a k u s a l a ṃ, as a means leading to unhappy result, was not conceived as negatively as its logical form might lead us to suppose. Bad karma was a 'piling up,' no less than its opposite. Nevertheless, to a great extent, the difference between bad types of thought and good is described in terms of the contradictories, of the factors in the one kind and in the other. Nor are the negatives always on the side of evil. The three cardinal sources of misery are positive in form. And the five 'Path-factors' go to constitute what might have been called the Base Eightfold Path.

We come, finally, to the third ethical category of a - v y ā k a t a ṃ, the Inexplicit or Indeterminate. The subject is difficult if interesting, bringing us as it does within closer range of the Buddhist view of moral causation. The hall-mark of Indeterminate thought is said to be 'absence of result'[3]—that is, of pleasant or painful result. And there are said to be four species of such

[1] Viz, : Anaññāt'aññassāmītindriyaṃ, aññindriyaṃ, aññātāvindriyaṃ. Pp. 86, 96, 97, 150. *Cf.* Dh. K. 53.

[2] *Contra, cf.* M. i., 184.

[3] Asl. 39.

thought: (1) Vipāko, or thought which *is* a result; (2) Kiriyā, or consciousness leading to no result; (3) form, as outside moral causation; (4) uncompounded element (or, in later records, Nirvana), as above or beyond the further efficacy of moral causation.

Of these four, the third has been dealt with already; the fourth I cannot discuss here and now.[1] It is conceivable that the earlier Buddhists considered their *summun bonum* a subject too ineffably sublime and mysterious for logical and analytical discussion. Two instances, at least, occur to me in the Nikāyas,[2] where the talk was cut short, in the one case by Gotama himself, in the other by the woman-apostle Dhammadinnā, when the interlocutor brought up Nirvana for discussion of this sort. This is possibly the reason why, in a work like our Manual, the concept is presented—in all but the commentarial appendixes—under the quasi-metaphysical term 'uncompounded element.' It is classed here as a species of Indeterminate, because, although it was the outcome of the utmost carrying power of good karma, it could, as a state of mind and character, itself work no good effect *for that individual* mind and character. *These* represented pure effect. The Arahat could afford to live wholly on withdrawn capital and to use it up. His conduct, speech and thought are, of course, necessarily 'good,' but good with no 'heaping-up' potency.

Of the other two Indeterminates, it is not easy to say whether they represent *aspects* only of states considered with respect to moral efficacy, or whether they represent *divisions* in a more rigid and artificial view of moral causation than we should, at the present day, be prepared to maintain. To explain: every thought, word and deed (morally considered) is for us at once the effect of certain antecedents, and the cause, or part of the cause, of subsequent manifestations of character. It is a link, both held and holding. But in vipāko we have dhammas

---

[1] See Appendix II. [2] S. v. 218; M. i. 304.

considered, with respect to cause, *merely* as effects; in kiriyā[1] we have dhammas considered, with respect to effect, as having *none*. And the fact that both are divided off from Good and Bad—that is to say, from conduct or consciousness considered as *causally effective*—and are called Indeterminate, seems to point, not to aspects only, but to that artificial view alluded to. Yet in this matter I confess to the greater wisdom of imitating the angels, rather than rushing in with the fools. Life presented itself to the Buddhist much as the Surrey heath appeared to the watchful eyes of a Darwin—as a teeming soil, a khettaṃ,[2] where swarmed the seeds of previous karmas waiting for 'room,' for opportunity to come to effect. And in considering the seed as potential effect, they were not, to that extent, concerned with *that* seed as capable of producing, not only its own flower and fruit, but other seed in its turn.

However that may have been, one thing is clear, and for us suggestive. Moral experience as result pure and simple was not in itself uninteresting to the Buddhists. In dealing with good and bad dhammas, they show us a field of the struggle for moral life, the sowing of potential well-being or of ill. But in the Avyākatas we are either outside the struggle and concerned with the unmoral Rūpaṃ, or we walk among the sheaves of harvest. From the Western standpoint the struggle covers the whole field of temporal life. Good and bad 'war in the members' even of its Arahats. The ideal of the Buddhist, held as realizable under temporal conditions, was to walk

---

[1] I am indebted to the Rev. Suriyagoḍa Sumangala, of Ratmalanē, Ceylon, for information very kindly given concerning the term kiriyā or kriyā. He defines it as 'action ineffective as to result,' and kiriyā-cittaṃ as 'mind in relation to action ineffective as to result.' He adds a full analysis of the various modes of kiriyā taught by Buddhists at the present day.

[2] 'Origin of Species,' p. 56. A. i. 223, 224. *Cf.* Asl. 360.

among his sheaves 'beyond the Good and the Bad.'[1] The Good consisted in giving hostages to the future. His ideal was to be releasing them, and, in a span of final, but glorious existence, to be tasting of the finest fruit of living —the peace of insight, the joy of emancipation. This was life supremely worth living, for

> 'leben heisst
> In Freiheit leben und mit freiem Geist!'[2]

The Good, to take his own metaphor, was as a raft bearing him across the stream of danger. After that he was to leave it and go on. 'And ye, brethren, learn by the parable of the raft that ye must put away good conditions, let alone bad.'[3]

It is not easy for us, who have learnt from Plato to call our Absolute the Good and our Ideal a *summun bonum*, to sympathize really with this moral standpoint. Critics see in it an aspiration towards moral stultification and self-complacent egoism.

Yes, there is little fear but that in the long-run fuller knowledge will bring deeper insight into what in Buddhism is really worthy of admiration for all time. If it is now accused of weakening the concept of individuality by rejecting soul, and, at the same time, of fostering egoistic morality, it is just possible that criticism is here at fault. On the ruins of the animistic view, Buddhism had to reconstruct a new personality, wholly phenomenal, impermanent, law-determined, yet none the less able, and alone able, by indomitable faith and will, to work out a personal salvation, a personal perfection. Bearing this in mind and surveying the history of its altruistic missionary labours, we cannot rashly cast egoistic morality at it to much effect. Nor has it much to fear from charges of stultification, quietism, pessimism and the like. We are misled to a

---

[1] Nietzsche on Buddhism in 'Der Antichrist.'
[2] A. Pfungst, 'An Giordano Bruno.'
[3] See the third quotation, p. vii.

certain extent herein by the very thoroughness of its methods of getting at the moral life by way of psychical training. We see, as in our Manual, and other canonical records, elaborate systems for analyzing and cultivating the intellectual faculties, the will and feeling, and we take these as substitutes for overt moral activity, as ends when they are but means. And if the Dhamma-Saṅgaṇi seems to some calculated to foster introspective thought to a morbid extent, it must not be forgotten that it is not Buddhist philosophy alone which teaches that, for all the natural tendency to spend and be spent in efforts to cope, by thought and achievement, with the world without, 'it is in this little fathom-long mortal frame with its thinkings and its notions that the world'[1] itself and the whole problem of its misery and of the victory over it lies hid.

If I have succeeded to any extent in connecting the contents of this Manual with the rest of the Buddhist Pitakas, it is because I had at my disposal the mass of material accumulated in my husband's MS. Pali dictionary. Besides this, the selection of material for Sections II. and III. of my Introduction is his work. Besides this I owe him a debt of gratitude indefinitely great for advice and criticism generally.

---

[1] See second quotation, p. vii.

[BOOK I.

THE GENESIS OF THOUGHTS
(Cittuppāda-kaṇḍaṃ).

PART I.—GOOD STATES OF CONSCIOUSNESS.

CHAPTER I.

The Eight Main Types of Thought relating to the Sensuous Universe (Kāmāvacara-aṭṭha-mahācittāni).][1]

I.

[1] Which are the states that are good?[2]

When a good thought concerning the sensuous universe[3] has arisen, which is accompanied by happiness and associated with knowledge,[4] and has as its object a

---

1 The brackets enclosing this and all other headings indicate that the latter have been transposed from the position they occupy in the text. There each heading stands at the end of its section.

2 See Introduction. 3 *Ibid.*

4 Ñāṇa-sampayuttaṃ. According to the Cy., a good thought deserves to be thus distinguished on three grounds: from the karma it produces, from the maturity of the faculties it involves, and from the remoteness of mental and moral infirmity which it implies (Asl. 76). Sampayuttaṃ—lit., con-yoked—is, in the Kathāvatthu, quoted by the Cy. (p. 42), described as including the following relations (between one 'state' and another): concomitant (sahagatā), connate (sahajātā), contiguous

sight,[1] a sound, a smell, a taste, a touch,[2] a [mental] state,[3] or what not,[4] then there is

(i) contact (§ 2),
(ii) feeling (§ 3),

(saṃsaṭṭhā), having a common origin (ekuppādā), a common cessation (ekanirodhā), a common basis or embodiment (ekavatthukā), a common object of attention (ekārammaṇā). In the present work the term is subsequently rendered by 'connected,' *e.g.*, in § 1007, etc. The preceding adjectival phrase, somanassa-sahagatam, which I have rendered 'accompanied by happiness,' is virtually declared by the Cy. to be here equivalent to somanassa-sampayuttaṃ, inasmuch as it is to be interpreted in its fullest intension. Of its five distinguishable shades of meaning, the one here selected is that of 'conjoined' (saṃsaṭṭhaṃ). And of the four distinguishable connotations of 'conjoined,' the one here selected is that of 'connate.' Hence 'accompanied by' means here 'connate.' And further, inasmuch as the concomitance is not between two corporeal phenomena, or between a corporeal and an incorporeal phenomenon, it is of that persistent and thoroughgoing kind—persisting beyond the common origin—which is described under the word 'associated.'

Thus far the intricate Buddhaghosa. But I have yet to discover any attempt to analyze the laws governing the process of association between mental states, such as we first find in Aristotle.

On 'happiness,' see §§ 10, 18.

[1] Rūpārammaṇam, saddārammaṇaṃ, etc., *i.e.*, either as a present sensation or as a representative image relating to the past or future; in the language of Hume, as an impression or as an idea; in the more comprehensive German term, as *Vorstellung* (Asl. 71). See Introduction.

[2] Literally, an object that is tangible—the standard Pali term.

[3] Dhammārammaṇaṃ—the 'object,' that is, of representative imagination or ideation (mano, cittam, Asl., 71), just as a thing seen is the object of sight. Buddhaghosa rejects the opinion that a dhammārammaṇaṃ is something outside the range of the senses, and cites M. i. 295, where Sāriputta declares that, whereas

(iii) perception (§ 4),
(iv) thinking (§ 5),
(v) thought (§ 6),
(vi) conception (§ 7),
(vii) discursive thought (§ 8),
(viii) joy (§ 9),
(ix) ease (§ 10),
(x) self-collectedness (§ 11),
(xi) the faculty of faith (§ 12),
(xii) the faculty of energy (§ 13),
(xiii) the faculty of mindfulness (§ 14),
(xiv) the faculty of concentration (§ 15),
(xv) the faculty of wisdom (§ 16),

---

each sense has its specific field, the mano has all these five fields as its scope. At the moment when an object enters 'the door of the eye' or other sense, it enters also the door of the ideating faculty causing the consciousness, or one's being, to vibrate (bhavangacalanassa paccayo hoti), just as the alighting bird, at the same moment, strikes the bough and casts a shadow (*ibid.* 72).—As we might say, presentative cognition is invariably accompanied by representative cognition.—Then, in the course of the mental undulations arising through this disturbance by way of sense impact, one of these eight psychoses termed Mahācittāni may emerge. 'But in pure representative cognition (suddha-manodvāre) there is no process of sensory stimulation,' as when we recall past sense-experience.—The process of representation is illustrated in detail, and completes an interesting essay in ancient psychology. In the case of seeing, hearing, and smell, past pleasant sensations are described as being simply revived during a subsequent state of repose. In the case of taste and touch, it is present disagreeable sensations which suggest certain contrasted experience in the past. But the commentator is not here interested in 'association by contrast' as such.

[4] Lit., 'or whatever [object the thought] is about.' The gist of the somewhat obscure comment is that, while no new class of objects is here to be understood over and above those of present or past sensations, there is no serial or numerical order in which these become material for thought.

(xvi) the faculty of ideation (§ 17),
(xvii) the faculty of happiness (§ 18),
(xviii) the faculty of vitality (§ 19);
(xix) right views (§ 20),
(xx) right intention (§ 21),
(xxi) right endeavour (§ 22),
(xxii) right mindfulness (§ 23),
(xxiii) right concentration (§ 24);
(xxiv) the power of faith (§ 25),
(xxv) the power of energy (§ 26),
(xxvi) the power of mindfulness (§ 27),
(xxvii) the power of concentration (§ 28),
(xxviii) the power of wisdom (§ 29),
(xxix) the power of conscientiousness (§ 30),
(xxx) the power of the fear of blame (§ 31);
(xxxi) absence of lust (§ 32),
(xxxii) absence of hate (§ 33),
(xxxiii) absence of dulness (§ 34);
(xxxiv) absence of covetousness (§ 35),
(xxxv) absence of malice (§ 36),
(xxxvi) right views[1] (§ 37);
(xxxvii) conscientiousness (§ 38),
(xxxviii) fear of blame (§ 39);
(xxxix, xl) serenity in sense and thought (§§ 40, 41),
(xli, xlii) lightness in sense and thought (§§ 42, 43),
(xliii, xliv) plasticity in sense and thought (§§ 44, 45),
(xlv, xlvi) facility in sense and thought (§§ 46, 47),
(xlvii, xlviii) fitness in sense and thought (§§ 48, 49),
(xlix, l) directness in sense and thought (§§ 50, 51);
(li) mindfulness (§ 52),
(lii) intelligence (§ 53)
(liii) quiet (§ 54)

---

[1] According to Buddhaghosa the 'states' numbered xxxiv-vi are considered as equivalents of those numbered xxxi-iii respectively, but as taken under another aspect. In the prior enumeration the threefold 'root of good' is set out; in the latter, reference to the 'path of karma' is understood (Asl. 129).

(liv) insight (§ 55),
(lv) grasp (§ 56),
(lvi) balance (§ 57).

Now these—or whatever other incorporeal, causally induced states[1] there are on that occasion—these are states that are good.

[2] What on that occasion is contact (phasso)?[2]

---

[1] Nine other states, according to the Cy., are here implied as factors in this psychosis, viz., desire (or conation, or volition, chando), resolve (adhimokkho), attention (manasikāro), equanimity (tatramajjhattatā), pity (karuṇā), sympathy (muditā), abstinence from evil conduct in act, speech, and mode of livelihood. And the opening words of this and similar supplementary clauses in the text are coined into a technical term—ye-vā-panakā, 'the or-whatever' [states],—to signify such groups.

The Cy. then 'defines' the nine: desire, qualified as orthodox desire (dhammachando), to distinguish it from ethically undesirable desire (*cf.* § 1097, etc.), is the wish to act, the stretching forth the hand of the mind (*cf.* ὄρεξις) to grasp the object in idea. Resolve is steadfastness, decision, the being unshaken as a pillar. Attention is movement, direction of the mind, confronting the object. Equanimity—lit., the mean (medium) state—is the being borne along evenly, without defect or excess, without partiality. Pity and sympathy are described in § 258 *et seq.* The last three give those three factors of the Eightfold Path unrepresented in the analysis of the thought (Asl. 132, 133).

It is not without interest to note that in this supplementary category all the purely psychological states are wholly, or at least mainly, volitional or emotional.

[2] Touch or contact must be understood in a very general sense, as the outcome of three conditions: an impingeing sentient organ, an impingeing agency conceived as external to the sentient organ, and impact or collision. The similes in Mil. 60 of the rams and the cymbals are quoted in the Cy. The eye and its object are the usual illustration, but the representative imagination (mano or cittaṃ) and its object are included as proceeding by way of contact, only without impact (sanghaṭṭanaṃ). The real causal connexion in every case—so I understand the, to me, obscurely

The contact which on that occasion is touching, the being brought into contact, the state of having been brought into touch with—this is the contact that there then is.

[3] What on that occasion is feeling (vedanā)?[1]

The mental pleasure, the mental ease, which, on that occasion, is born of contact with the appropriate element of representative intellection;[2] the pleasurable, easeful sensa-

---

worded comment to say (Asl. 109)—is mental, even though we speak of an external agency, just as when lac melts with heat we speak of hot coals as the cause, though the heat is in the lac's own tissue.

'Contact' is given priority of place, as standing for the inception of the thought, and as being the *sine quâ non* of all the allied states, conditioning them much as the roof-tree of a storied house supports all the other combinations of material (*ibid.* 107).

[1] Vedanā is a term of very general import, meaning sentience or reaction, bodily or mental, on contact or impression. Sensation is scarcely so loyal a rendering as feeling, for though vedanā is often qualified as 'born of the contact' in sense-activity, it is always defined generally as consisting of the three species—pleasure (happiness), pain (ill), and neutral feeling—a hedonistic aspect to which the term 'feeling' is alone adequate. Moreover, it covers representative feeling.

This general psychical aspect of vedanā, as distinct from sensations localized bodily—*e.g.*, toothache—is probably emphasized by the term 'mental' (cetasikam) in the answer. The Cy. points out that by this expression (=cittanissitattaṃ) 'bodily pleasure is eliminated' (Asl. 139). It also illustrates the general scope of vedanā by the simile of a cook who, after preparing a number of dishes for his lord, tastes each critically to test them, the lord partaking of whichever he pleases. The cook represents all the associated states in the thought-complex, each functioning in one specific way. Vedanā, the master, 'enjoys the essence (taste) of the object' as a whole.

[2] Tajjā-manoviññāṇadhātu. Tajjā is paraphrased by anucchavikā, sarūpā. *Cf.* A. i. 207; S. iv. 215; M. i. 190, 191; Mil. 53. On the remainder of the com-

tion which is born of contact with thought;[1] the pleasurable, easeful feeling which is born of contact with thought—this is the feeling that there then is.

[4] What on that occasion is perception (s a ñ ñ ā) ?[2]

The perception, the perceiving, the state of having perceived which on that occasion is born of contact with the

---

pound term, see § 6. And on the hedonistic expressions in the answer, see § 10.

[1] Ceto-samphassajaṃ . . . vedayitaṃ. The latter term (experience) is, more literally, that which is felt, *das Empfundene.* Ceto, cittaṃ are used interchangeably in the Cy. on these terms (see § 6). The 'contact' is that between idea or object and thought, or the ideating agency, conceived as analogous to the impact between sense-organ and sense-object. In consequence of this contact or presentation, emotional affection arises in consciousness.

[2] The apparently capricious way in which the intension of the term s a ñ ñ ā is varied in the Pitakas makes it difficult to assign any one adequate English rendering. In the Mahāvedalla Sutta (M. i. 293) and elsewhere (*cf.* Mil. 61) it is explained as the relatively simple form of intellection or cognition which consists in the discernment, recognition, assimilation of sensations—*e.g.*, of colours, as 'blue,' etc.—the process termed in modern English psychology sense-perception, except that it is not quite clear that, in Buddhist psychology, as in English, the perception is made only *on occasion of sense-stimulation.* The answer, indeed, in our § 4 alludes to representative activity only. In the Mahāparinibbāna Sutta, however (*cf.* A. v. 105), s a ñ ñ ā stands for the intellectual realization of a number of highly complex concepts, such as impermanence, non-substantiality, etc. In the Poṭṭhapāda Sutta (D. i. 180-187), again, the s a ñ ñ ā discussed is clearly what we should call consciousness, whether as opposed to the unconsciousness of trance, or as the raw material of ñ ā ṇ a m, or as conceivably distinct from the soul or Ego. Lastly, in a more popular sense the term is used (notably in the Jātakas and in commentators' similes) for sign, mark, or token.

Here, if we follow the Cy. (Asl. 110), s a ñ ñ ā means simply that sense-perception which discerns, recognises and gives class-reference to (u p a ṭ ṭ h i t a - v i s a y a), the impressions of sense. Its procedure is likened to the carpenter's recognition of certain woods by the mark he had made on each;

appropriate element of representative intellection—this is the perception that there then is.

[5] What on that occasion is thinking (cetanā)?[1]

The thinking, the cogitating, the reflection, which is born of contact with the appropriate element of representative intellection—this is the thinking that there then is.

[6] What on that occasion is thought (cittaṃ)?

---

to the treasurer's specifying certain articles of jewelry by the ticket on each; to the wild animal's discernment in the scarecrow of the work of man. The essence of saññā is said to be recognition by way of a mark. In this notion of mark and marking lies such continuity of thought as may be claimed for the various uses of the term. The bare fact of consciousness means ability to discriminate—that is, to mark. To mark is to perceive. And the ideas or concepts of 'impermanence,' 'impurity,' and the like, were so many acts of marking, though of a highly 're-representative' character. Saññā, no less than cittaṃ (see Introduction), and 'thought,' stands for both faculty and any act or product of that faculty. And it is even objectified so far as to signify further the result of any such act—that is, in its connotation of mark or sign.

It is, I believe, when connoting the more specific sense of faculty, or of skandha, that it may safely be rendered by 'perception' or 'marking,' and may be taken to mean the relatively 'superficial,' 'transient' (Asl. 110, 111) play of cognition when concerned with objects of sense. In ch. xiv. of the Visuddhi Magga—in a passage the late Henry C. Warren was good enough to transcribe for me—saññā is in this way, and this way only, distinguished from viññāṇam and paññā. The latter terms stand for cognition at (as we might say) a relatively higher and a still higher power, in virtue of the greater depth and complexity of the concepts they were exercised about (see §§ 6, 16).

[1] There is no more difficult problem in interpreting the Dhamma Sangaṇi than to get at the grounds on which its compilers, and subsequently its commentator, saw fit to set out mutually independent descriptions of terms etymologically so identical as cetanā and cittaṃ. The only parallel that suggests itself to me is the distinction drawn, during a long period in British philosophy, between 'reasoning' and 'reason'—that is, between deductive inference and the noûs, or noëtic function. Both pairs of terms are quite

The thought which on that occasion is ideation, mind, heart, that which is clear, ideation as the sphere of mind, the faculty of mind, intellection, the skandha of intellection, the appropriate element of representative intellection —this is the thought that there then is.

---

popular in form. Compare, *e.g.*, in the Nidāna-kathā (Jāt. i. 74), Buddha's reply to Māra: 'I have here no conscious (or intelligent) witness. . . . Let this . . . earth, unconscious though it be, be witness. . . . Sacetano koci sakkhī, etc. . . . ayam acetanāpi . . . paṭhavī sakkhīti.' Again, in A. i., p. 224, the import seems simple and quite untechnical: 'Their thoughts (cetanā) and hopes (lit., thinking and hoping) are fixed on lower things.' Hence I have kept to terms popular in form. This does not justify the use of terms so undifferentiated as 'thinking' and 'thought'; yet I have returned to them, after essaying half a dozen substitutes, for various reasons. They show the close connection between the Buddhist pair of terms, instead of obscuring it; they are equally popular and vague in form and extension; the import of cetanā has much in common with a psychological account of thinking; no term *misfits* cittaṃ *less* than 'thought,' unless it be 'heart,' on which see Introduction. It is unfortunate that Buddhaghosa does not give a comparative analysis of the two, as he does in the case of vitakka-vicāra and pīti-sukhaṃ. Under cetanā he expatiates in forcible similes, describing it as a process of activity and toil, and as a co-ordinating, ordering function. He likens it to an energetic farmer, bustling about his fifty-five labourers (the fifty-five co-constituents in the thought-complex) to get in the harvest; to a senior apprentice at the carpenter's, working himself and supervising the tasks of the others; to the leader of a warrior band, fighting and inciting. To these notions the definition of Nāgasena (Mil. 61) only adds that of preparing (abhisankharaṇaṃ), the other qualifying term being merely a denominative form (as if we should say 'thinkifying').

In so far, then, as 'thinking' connotes representative, co-ordinative intellection, it coincides with cetanā. In its narrower, technical sense of intellection by way of general notions, it does not (see Introduction). Any way, to call it 'thinking' is sufficiently indefinite, and does not preclude the rendering of it elsewhere by such terms as 'reflecting,' 'cogitating,' 'considering,' etc. But the problem has still

[7] What on that occasion is conception (vitakko)?[1]

The ratiocination, the conception, which on that occasion is the disposition,[2] the fixation, the focussing,[3] the applica-

---

to be solved of how it is related to such terms as saññā, cittaṃ, and viññāṇaṃ. With regard to skandha, it is classed, not with cittaṃ, but under the sankhāra-skandha, § 62.

Cittaṃ, together with the terms in which it is described, is discussed in my Introduction.

[1] Vitakko and vicāro is another pair of terms which it is hard to fit with any one pair of English words. It is very possible that academic teaching came to attach a more pregnant and specialized import to them than was conveyed in popular and purely ethical usage. *Cf.* M. i., Suttas xix. and xx., where vitakkā would be adequately rendered by ideas, notions, or thoughts. In Asl. 114, 115, on the other hand (*cf.* Mil. 62, 63), the relation of the two to cittaṃ and to each other is set out with much metaphor, if with too little psychological grasp. Vitakko is distinctively mental procedure at the inception of a train of thought, the deliberate movement of voluntary attention. As a king ascends to his palace leaning on the arm of favourite or relative, so thought ascends to its object depending upon the conceptive act (vitakko; Asl. 114). Other metaphorical attributes are its impingeing upon, circum-impingeing upon (paryāhanaṃ), the object, and, again, bringing it near. Hence in selecting 'conception' in preference to 'reasoning,' by which vitakko has often been translated, I wished to bring out this grasping, constructive, reaching-out act of the mind, this incipient fetch of the imagination, elaborated in the Buddhist scholastic analysis of the term; but I had no wish to read our own logical or psychological import of conception as intellection by way of general notions, or the like, into the Eastern tradition. Yet just as conception may be so used as to include 'reasoning' or 'ratiocination,' so vitakko is, in the reply, described by takko, the term used for ratiocinative procedure, argument, or logic (*cf.* D. i. 12, 21). 'What,' asks the Cy., 'does one reason about (takkesi)? About a pot, a cart, the distance of anything. Well, vitakko is a stronger reasoning.'

[2] On 'disposition,' 'right intention,' see § 21.

[3] Appanā vyappanā, the latter an intensive form of the former (Asl. 142, 143). In the 'Yogāvacara's Manual' (p. xi and *passim*) appanā denotes the dawn of the desired

tion of the mind,[1] right intention—this is the conception that there then is.

[8] What on that occasion is discursive thought (vicāro)?[2]

The process, the sustained procedure (vicāro), the progress and access [of the mind] which on that occasion is the [continuous] adjusting and focussing of thought[3]—this is the discursive thought that there then is.

[9] What on that occasion is joy (pīti)?[4]

---

concept during the practice of regulated meditation. Buddhaghosa defines it thus:—ekaggaṃ cittaṃ ārammaṇe appenti.

[1] Cetaso abhiniropanā = ārammaṇe cittam . . . patiṭṭhapeti (*ibid.*)

[2] Vicāro, as compared with vitakko, was used to express the movement and maintenance of the voluntary thought-continuum, as distinguished from the initiative grappling with the subject of reflection. Examining in detail, as compared with grasping the whole, is also read into it by commentators (Asl. 114). It is a pounding up (anumajjanaṃ), as well as a linking together. Metaphors are multiplied, to show its relation to vitakko. It is as the reverberation of the beaten drum or bell is to the beating; as the planing movement of the bird's wings after the initial upsoaring; as the buzzing of the bee when it has alighted on the lotus; as the scouring of the dirty bowl when clutched; as the manipulating hand of the potter, vitakko being represented by the hand which holds the clay to the wheel, and so on. 'Investigation' would well represent the sustained activity; 'analysis,' the cogitation in details; 'discursive thought' gives some of the import of both, without introducing modern and Western implications.

[3] Like the adjusting of bow and arrow. 'Focussing' is anupekkhamāno.

[4] Pīti, as distinguished from sukhaṃ, is explicitly excluded from the skandha of feeling, considered as the irreducible hedonic constituent, and referred to the composite psychoses of the sankhāra skandha. It connotes emotion, as distinct from bare feeling; that is to say, pīti is a complex psychical phenomenon, implying a 'central psycho-physical origin' and a widely diffused 'somatic resonance' (*cf.* Sully, 'The Human Mind,' ii. 56).

The joy which on that occasion is gladness, rejoicing at, rejoicing over, mirth and merriment, felicity,[1] exultation, transport of mind[2]—this is the joy that there then is.

[10] What on that occasion is ease (s u k h a ṃ) ?[3]

It arises out of a present idea, and suffuses the whole being. By Buddhaghosa's day it was divided into five species: the thrill of joy, just causing 'the flesh to creep'; the flash of joy, like lightning; the flood of joy, like the breakers on a sea-shore; ecstasy or transport, in which the subject could float in the air; and overwhelming suffusing joy (Asl. 115, 116). Instances are related of the fourth species (u b b e g a - p ī t i), the inspiring idea being 'B u d d h ā r a m m a ṇ a ṃ' (see also Visuddhi Magga, ch. iv.; 'Yogāvacara's Manual,' vii.). The same word (u b b e g o) is used to describe the anguish or trembling over guilt discovered. See below, § 31 n.

[1] V i t t i, meaning literally, as the Cy. points out, prosperity, wealth, and used here by analogy as a state conditioned by a source of pleasure. 'Happiness arises to him who is joyful through his joy, as it arises to the wealthy through his rice-possessions.' (Asl. 143.)

[2] A t t a m a n a t ā c i t t a s s a. Buddhaghosa, who did not know the true etymology of this term, is ready as ever with a guess: a t t a n o m a n a t ā, or mentality of one's self, not of another, subjective experience. If I am pained or pleased, that is peculiarly my affair (*ibid.*). Psychologically it is interesting to note that he is prepared to find this intimate, subjective reference in a state of intense feeling. 'Feeling is subjective experience *par excellence* . . . our feelings . . . are all our own.' (Sully, 'The Human Mind,' ii. 2; G. C. Robertson, 'Elements of Psychology,' 185-188.)

[3] To contrast p ī t i with s u k h a ṃ, Buddhaghosa draws a charming picture of the traveller who, fordone with journeying through a desert, hears with joy of a pool in a grove, and with joy comes upon it, and who, on drinking, bathing, and resting in the shade is filled with ease. S u k h a m, it is true, is not bare quiescence; it is positive, pleasurable feeling, and may have active concomitants; its 'essence' is expansion or increase (u p a b r ū h a ṇ a ṃ). But just as d u k k h a ṃ means, not so much pain as ill-being or misery, so does s u k h a ṃ mean well-being or sane and sound cœnæsthesis. And as 'joy' is the satisfaction of

The mental pleasure, the mental ease which on that occasion is the pleasant, easeful experience born of contact with thought, the pleasant, easeful feeling born of contact with thought—this is the ease that there then is.

[11] What on that occasion is self-collectedness (cittass' ekaggatā)?[1]

The stability, solidity, absorbed steadfastness of thought[2] which on that occasion is the absence of distraction,

---

gaining (potentially or actually) what we desire, so is 'ease' the enjoyment of the flavour (French, *savourer*) of what we have gained (Asl. 117). See further § 60. 'Mental ease' (cetasikaṃ sukhaṃ) is perhaps more correctly somanassam, rendered (§ 1, etc.) by 'happiness,' sukhaṃ being sometimes distinguished as bodily (kāyikam) only. See S. v. 209.

[1] 'Citt' ekaggatā, the one-peaked condition of mind, is a name for concentration (samādhi),' says the Cy. (p. 118). And accordingly, whereas under § 15 it gives no further description of samādhi, it here applies to citt' ekaggatā the metaphors used in Mil. 38 to illustrate samādhi, viz., the centre part of a tent-shaped hut, and a chieftain leading his army. It then adds that 'this samādhi, which is called self-collectedness, has, as its characteristic mark, the absence of wandering, of distraction; as its essence, the binding together of the states of mind that arise with it, as water binds the lather of soap; and as its concomitants, calmness, or wisdom—for it is said, "he who is at peace he understands, he sees things as they really are"—and ease. The steadfastness of thought is likened to the steadiness of a lamp-flame in a windless place.' See 'Yogāvacara's Manual,' p. xxvi.

[2] These three cognate terms are in the text cittassa ṭhiti sanṭhiti avaṭṭhiti. According to the Cy. (p. 143), the standing unshaken in or on the object (ārammaṇe) connoted by ṭhiti is modified by the prefix saṃ to imply kneading together (sampiṇḍetvā) the associated states in the object, and by the prefix ava to imply the being immersed in the object. The last metaphor is in Buddhist doctrine held applicable to four good and three bad states—faith, mindfulness, concentration (= self-collectedness) and wisdom; craving, speculation and ignorance, but most of all to self-collectedness.

balance,[1] imperturbed mental procedure, quiet,[2] the faculty and the power of concentration, right concentration—this is the self-collectedness that there then is.

[12] What on that occasion is the faculty of faith (saddhindriyaṃ)?[3]

The faith which on that occasion is a trusting in, the professing confidence in,[4] the sense of assurance, faith,[5]

---

[1] Avisahāro, avikkhepo (*v.* § 57). Distraction and loss of equilibrium are attributed to the presence of 'excitement and perplexity' (§§ 425, 429 ; Asl. 144).

[2] Samatho. Distinguished as of three species : mental calm (so used here) ; legal pacification, or settlement ; calm in all the sanskāras, by which, according to the Cy. (144), is meant the peace of Nirvana.

[3] On 'faculty,' see Introduction.

Faith is characterized and illustrated in the same terms and approximately the same similes as are used in Mil., pp. 34-60. That is to say, it is shown to be a state of mind where the absence of perplexity sets free aspiration and energy. It is described as trust in the Buddha and his system. There is, however, no dwelling just here on any terminus *ad quem*, as St. Paul did in speaking of 'the prize for the mark of the high calling,' etc., towards which he pressed in ardent faith. There is, rather, an insistence on that self-confidence born of conviction of the soundness of one's methods and efforts which is, as it were, an aspect of faith as a *vis a tergo*. In the simile of the stream, the Cy. differs from Trenckner's version of the Milinda to the extent of making the folk afraid to cross because of alligators and other monsters, till the hero takes his sword and plunges in. See the note on 'faith' in the translation of Mil. i. 56.

[4] *I.e.*, in the Buddha, the Doctrine and the Order. Buddhaghosa is only interested in making the etymology bear on ethics, and compares the 'downward plunge' of confidence (o-kappanā) in the attitude of faith to the 'sinking' in 'mindfulness,' the 'grounded stand' in 'concentration,' and the 'sounding' penetration of 'wisdom' Asl. 144, 145).

[5] The Cy. puts forward an alternative explanation of the repetition in the description of this and following compounds of the first term of the compound, viz., 'faith.'

faith as a faculty and as a power—this is the faith that there then is.

[13] What on that occasion is the faculty of energy (viriyindriyaṃ)?[1]

The mental inception[2] of energy which there is on that occasion, the striving and the onward effort, the exertion

---

According to the former, it is the method of Abhidamma to set out in isolation the adjectival part of a compound on which the substantival part depends: faith-faculty = faith (faculty of). According to the latter, the identity between the two abstractions, faith and faith-faculty, is brought out. The case of woman and attribute of femininity, it remarks, is different. (This may be a groping after the distinction between concrete and abstract.)

[1] Viriyaṃ is by Buddhaghosa connected with (*a*) vīra, the dynamic effectiveness which is the essence of the genus 'hero' (vīro), (*b*) īriya, vibrating movement. He characterizes it by the two notions, 'supporting' and 'grasping at,' or 'stretching forward' (paggaho), and, again, by 'exerting' (ussāhanaṃ). *Cf.* Mil. 36; Sum. Vil. 63. And he cites the same similes as appear in the Milinda. He seems to have wished, as modern psychologists have done, to account for the two modes of conscious effort: Resistance and Free Energy. But he also emphasizes the fact that the energy in question is mental, not bodily (pp. 120 *et seq.*, 145).

[2] Ārambho (*cf.* ārammanaṃ), overt action as distinguished from inaction, hence action at its inception, is distinguished by the Cy. as having six different implications, according as there is reference to karma, to a fault committed, to slaying or injury, or to action as such (kiriyā), or energy as such.

I do not pretend that the four following pairs of words fit those in the text exactly. They are mere approximations. 'Endeavour' is vāyāmo, the term representing 'energy' in the Noble Eightfold Path. 'Unfaltering' effort (asithila-parakkamatā) is the attitude of one who has made the characteristic Buddhist vow: Verily may skin and nerve and bone dry up and wither, or ever I stay my energy, so long as I have not attained whatsoever by human vigour, energy, and effort is attainable! (M. i. 480). The desire sustained—lit., not cast down—is that felt on an occasion for making good karma.

and endeavour, the zeal and ardour, the vigour and fortitude, the state of unfaltering effort, the state of sustained desire, the state of unflinching endurance, the solid grip of the burden, energy, energy as faculty and as power, right endeavour—this is the energy that there then is.

[14] What on that occasion is the faculty of mindfulness (satindriyaṃ)?[1]

The mindfulness which on that occasion is recollecting, calling back to mind; the mindfulness[2] which is remembering, bearing in mind, the opposite of superficiality[3] and of obliviousness; mindfulness as faculty, mindfulness as power, right mindfulness—this is the faculty of mindfulness that there then is.

---

[1] Buddhaghosa's comment on sati, in which he closely follows and enlarges on the account in Mil. 37, 38, shows that the traditional conception of that aspect of consciousness had much in common with the Western modern theory of conscience or moral sense. Sati appears under the metaphor of an inward mentor, discriminating between good and bad and prompting choice. Hardy went so far as to render it by 'conscience,' but this slurs over the interesting divergencies between Eastern and Western thought. The former is quite unmystical on the subject of sati. It takes the psychological process of representative functioning (without bringing out the distinction between bare memory and judgment), and presents the same under an ethical aspect. See also under hiri, § 30; and the notion as described in 'Questions of Milinda,' 38, n. 2.

[2] The *three*fold mention of sati in the reply (*cf.* § 12) agrees with K., but not with Puggala Paññatti (p. 25). It is not noticed by the Cy.

[3] Apilāpanatā. The Atthasālinī solves the problem presented by this term (see Milinda (S.B.E.), vol. i., p. 58, n. 2) by deriving it from pilavati, to float, and interprets:—'not floating on the surface like pumpkins and pots on the water,' sati entering into and plunging down into the object of thought. *Cf.* § 11, n. 2; § 12, n. 2, in which connection the term is again used. The positive form occurs *infra*, § 1349. P. P. has (a)vilāpanatā (21, 25). (Asl. 147; *cf.* 405.) I should have rendered the word by 'profundity,'

[15] What on that occasion is the faculty of concentration (samādhindriyaṃ)?[1]

Answer as for 'self-collectedness,' § 11.

[16] What on that occasion is the faculty of wisdom (paññindriyaṃ)?[2]

---

had I not preferred to bring out the negative form of the original.

[1] Buddhaghosa's etymology—'ārammaṇe cittaṃ sammā adhīyati, ṭhapetī ti'—is no doubt incorrect, sam-ā-dhā being the sounder analysis; nevertheless, he brings out that voluntary and deliberate adjustment of the attention with a view to sustained mental effort which is connoted by samādhi (Asl. 122).

[2] To fit the term paññā with its approximate European equivalent is one of the cruces of Buddhist philosophy. I have tried in turn reason, intellect, insight, science, understanding, and knowledge. All of these have been, and are, used in the literature of philosophy with varying shades of connotation, according as the sense to be conveyed is popular and vague, psychological and precise, or transcendental and—*passez-moi le mot*—having precise vagueness. And each of them might, with one implication or another, represent paññā. The main difficulty in choice lay in determining whether, to the Buddhist, paññā stood for mental function, or for the aggregate product of certain mental functioning, or for both. When all the allusions to paññā in the Sutta Pitaka have been collated, a final translation may become possible. Here it must suffice to quote two. In M. i. 292, he who has paññā (paññavā) is declared in virtue thereof to understand (pajānāti) the nature of the phenomenon of pain or ill (the Four Noble Truths). In D. i. 124 Gotama asks: What is this paññā? and himself sets out its content as consisting in certain intellectual attainments, viz., the Jhānas, insight into the nature of impermanence, the mental image of one's self, the power of Iddhi, the cosmic Ear, insight into other minds, into one's own past lives, the cosmic Eye, and the elimination of all vitiating tendencies. Buddhaghosa also (Vis. M., ch. xiv.) distinguishes paññā from saññā and viññāṇa. He describes it as adequate to discern not only what these can, viz., sense-objects and the Three Marks (impermanence, pain, and non-substantiality) respectively, but *also* the

The wisdom which there is on that occasion is understanding, search, research, searching the Truth,[1] discernment, discrimination, differentiation, erudition, proficiency, subtlety, criticism, reflection, analysis, breadth,[2] sagacity,[3] leading,[4] insight, intelligence, incitement;[5] wisdom as faculty, wisdom as power, wisdom as a sword,[6] wisdom as a height,[7] wisdom as light,[8] wisdom as glory,[9] wisdom as splendour,[10] wisdom as a precious stone; the absence of dulness, searching the Truth,[11] right views—this is the wisdom that there then is.

[17] What on that occasion is the faculty of ideation (representative imagination, manindriyaṃ)?

Answer as for 'thought' (cittaṃ), § 6.

Path. For him, then, it might be called intellect 'at a higher power.' And in Gotama's reply, all those attainments are described in terms of *intellectual process*. Nevertheless, it is clear that the term did not stand for *bare mental process of a certain degree of complexity*, but that it also implied mental process as cultivated in accordance with a *certain system of concepts objectively valid* for all Buddhist adepts. Hence, I think it best to reject such terms as reason, intellect, and understanding, and to choose wisdom, or science, or knowledge, or philosophy. Only they must be understood in this connexion as implying the body of learning as assimilated and applied by the intellect of a given individual. See further under ñāṇaṃ (Introduction) and vijjā (§ 1296).

1 *I.e.*, the doctrines of the 'Four Truths' (Asl. 147). *Cf.* Mil. 83.

2 Wisdom compared to the breadth and amplitude of the earth (Asl. 147, 148).

3 Medhā. The Cy. explains the specific wisdom of this term to lie in 'slaying' vice, or else in 'grasping and bearing' (148).

4 Pariṇāyikā.

5 Literally, a goad.

6 'For the slaying of vices' (Asl. 148; *cf.* Jāt. iv. 174).

7 'In the sense of something lofty' (*ibid.*; *cf.* Dhp. v. 28 = Mil. 387).

8 Ang. ii. 139.

9 *Ibid.*

10 *Ibid.*

11 Repeated by way of antithesis to 'dulness' (Asl. 148).

[18] What on that occasion is the faculty of pleasure (somanassindriyaṃ)?

Answer as for 'ease' (sukhaṃ), § 10.

[19] What on that occasion is the faculty of vitality (jīvitindriyaṃ)?

The persistence of these incorporeal states, their subsistence, going on, their being kept going on, their progress, continuance, preservation, life, life as faculty[1]—this is the faculty of vitality that there then is.[2]

[20] What on that occasion are right views (sammā-ditthi)?[3]

Answer as for the 'faculty of wisdom,' § 16.

[21] What on that occasion is right intention (sammā-sankappo)?[4]

Answer as for 'conception,' § 7.

[22] What on that occasion is right endeavour (sammā-vāyāmo)?

Answer as for the 'faculty of energy,' § 13.

[23] What on that occasion is right-mindfulness (sammāsati)?

Answer as for the 'faculty of mindfulness,' § 14.

[24] What on that occasion is right concentration (sammāsamādhi)?

Answer as for 'self-collectedness,' § 11.

---

[1] In the text, hoti before idaṃ is probably an error.

[2] This answer is exceptional in the omission of tasmiṃ samaye (' on that occasion ') at the beginning of the sentence. *Cf.* §§ 82, 295, 441. The reason of its omission is probably that in the presence of life, by which the complex of dhammas is sustained as lotuses by water, or as an infant by its nurse (Asl. 124), there is nothing contingent on the *ethical* quality (good, bad, or indeterminate) of the given complex.

[3] For a discussion of the term diṭṭhi, see § 1003. On these five factors of the Path see Introduction.

[4] Sankappo is by the Cy. especially identified with the expression cetaso abhiniropanā, application of the mind, the disposition or adjustment of attention, that on which the heart is set, hence aspiration, intention, purpose, design.

[25] What on that occasion is the power of faith (saddhābalaṃ)?

Answer as for the 'faculty of faith,' § 12.

[26] What on that occasion is the power of energy (viriyabalaṃ)?

Answer as for the 'faculty of energy,' § 13.

[27] What on that occasion is the power of mindfulness (satibalaṃ)?

Answer as for the 'faculty of mindfulness,' § 14.

[28] What on that occasion is the power of concentration (samādhibalaṃ)?

Answer as for 'self-collectedness,' § 11.

[29] What on that occasion is the power of wisdom (paññābalaṃ)?

Answer as for the 'faculty of wisdom,' § 16.

[30] What on that occasion is the power of conscientiousness (hiribalaṃ)?[1]

---

[1] Hiri and ottappaṃ, as analyzed by Buddhaghosa, present points of considerable ethical interest. Taken together they give us the emotional and conative aspect of the modern notion of conscience, just as sati represents it on its intellectual side. The former term 'is equivalent to shame (lajjā),' the latter to 'anguish (ubbego) over evil-doing.' Hiri has its source within; ottappaṃ springs from without. Hiri is autonomous (attādhipati); ottappaṃ, heteronomous, influenced by society (lokādhipati). The former is established on shame; the latter on dread. The former is marked by consistency; the latter by discernment of the danger and fearsomeness of error. The subjective source of hiri is fourfold, viz., the idea of what is due to one's birth, age, worth and education. Thus, one having hiri will think, 'Only mean folk (fishers, etc.), children, poor wretches, the blind and ignorant, would do such an act,' and he refrains. The external source of ottappaṃ is the idea that 'the body of the faithful will blame you,' and hence one refrains. If a man have hiri, he is, as said the Buddha, his own best master. To one who is sensitive by way of ottappaṃ, the masters of the faith are the best guides (Asl. 126).

In a supplementary paragraph (p. 127) the 'marks' (consistency, etc.) are thus explained: In hiri one reflects

The feeling of conscientious scruple[1] which there is on that occasion when scruples ought to be felt, conscientious scruple at attaining to bad and evil states—this is the power of conscientiousness that there then is.

[31] What on that occasion is the power of the fear of blame (ottappabalaṃ)?

The sense of guilt,[2] which there is on that occasion, where a sense of guilt ought to be felt, a sense of guilt at attaining to bad and evil states—this is the fear of blame that there then is.

[32] What on that occasion is the absence of lust (alobho)?

The absence of lust, of lusting, of lustfulness, which there is on that occasion, the absence of infatuation, the feeling and being infatuated, the absence of covetousness, that absence of lust which is the root of good[3]—this is the absence of lust that there then is.

[33] What on that occasion is the absence of hate (adoso)?

---

on the worth of one's birth, one's teacher, one's estate, and one's fellow-students. In ottappaṃ one feels dread at self-reproach, the blame of others, chastisement, and retribution in another life.

[1] Hiriyati, paraphrased by jigucchati (Asl. 149; D. i. 174; M. i. 78).

[2] Ottappati, paraphrased by ubbego (Asl. 124).

[3] *I.e.*, the fundamental condition, the cause of goodness. On 'covetousness' and 'infatuation,' see §§ 35, 1059. Alobho and its two co-ordinate virtues, the threefold 'root' of goodness, lose all their force in English negatives, but to a Buddhist convey doubtless as much impressiveness, as much of positive import, as the negative 'immortality' does to the Christian. Alobho, *e.g.*, involves active altruism; adoso, active sympathy; amoho, a life of culture (see § 34, n.). I do not know any positive terms meet to represent them.

The 'mark' of the first is absence of greed, or of adhesion, as a drop of water runs off a lotus leaf. Its essence is independence, like that of the emancipated bhikshu (Asl. 127).

The absence of hate, of hating,[1] of hatred, which there is on that occasion, the absence of malice, of spleen,[2] the absence of hate which is the root of good—this is the absence of hate that there then is.

[34] What on that occasion is the absence of dulness (a m o h o)?

Answer as for the 'faculty of wisdom,' § 16.[3]

[35] What on that occasion is the absence of covetousness (a n a b h i j j h ā)?

Answer as for the 'absence of lust,' § 32.[4]

[36] What on that occasion is the absence of malice (a v y ā p ā d o)?[5]

Answer as for the 'absence of hate,' § 33.

[37] What on that occasion are right views (s a m m ā d i t t h i)?[6]

Answer as for the 'faculty of wisdom,' § 16.

---

[1] K. reads a d ū s a n ā, a d ū s i t a t t a ṃ. The 'mark' of a d o s o is said to be absence of churlishness and crossness (see § 1060); its essence the suppression of annoyance and fever; its immediate result is loveliness—like the full moon (Asl. 127).

[2] 'The opposite of the pain felt when one is angry' (Asl. 150).

[3] Buddhaghosa expatiates at some length on the excellencies of the fundamental trinity of Buddhist virtue. To take a few only: a l o b h o (1) involves health, a d o s o (2) youth (hate ages quickly), a m o h o (3) long life (through prudence). (1) tends to material good through generosity (*cf.* 'he that soweth plenteously,' etc.); (2) to the acquisition of friends, won and held by love; (3) to self-development. (1) leads to life in the devaloka, (2) to life in the Brahmaloka, (3) to Arahatship. (1) gives insight into impermanence, and, conversely, (2) and (3) into the other two marks ('pain' and 'non-substantiality,' respectively).

[4] A b h i j j h ā and l o b h o are synonymous. See §§ 1059 and 1136, where a b h i j j h ā stands for l o b h o.

[5] Described (Asl. 129) as the being void of any wish to destroy welfare of others, bodily or mental, their advantages in this or other worlds, or their good reputation.

[6] *Cf.* § 1 (xxxvi), footnote.

[38] What on that occasion is conscientiousness (h i r i)?

Answer as for the 'power of conscientiousness,' § 30.

[39] What on that occasion is the fear of blame (o t t a p p a ṃ)?

Answer as for the 'power of the fear of blame,' § 31.

[40] What on that occasion is repose of sense (k a y ā - p a s s a d d h i)?[1]

The serenity,[2] the composure which there is on that occasion, the calming, the tranquillizing, the tranquillity of the skandhas of feeling, perception and syntheses—this is the serenity of sense that there then is.

[41] What on that occasion is serenity of thought (c i t t a p a s s a d d h i)?

The serenity, the composure which there is on that occasion, the calming, the tranquillizing, the tranquillity of the skandha of intellect—this is the serenity of thought that there then is.

[42] What on that occasion is buoyancy[3] of sense (k ā y a l a h u t ā)?

The buoyancy which there is on that occasion, the alertness in varying,[4] the absence of sluggishness[5] and inertia, in the skandhas of feeling, perception and syntheses—this is the buoyancy of sense that there then is.

[43] What on that occasion is buoyancy of thought (c i t t a l ā h u t ā)?

---

[1] On the meaning of k ā y o see Introduction.

[2] P a s s a d d h i is described as a state free from pain—where pain is allayed and suppressed; where tremor or unquiet is replaced by 'coolness'—the opposite to the states called k i l e s a s, especially excitement (§ 1229). *Cf.* D. i. 73; M. i. 37.

[3] Literally, lightness, described as the opposite of heaviness, sluggishness and the rigidity of stolidity and stupor (§ 1185).

[4] 'The capacity of changing quickly' (Asl. 150). *Cf.* Childers' Dictionary, *s.v.* p a r i v a t t i.

[5] Read a d a n d h a n a t ā. K. reads a d a n d h a t ā, but a d a n d h a n a t ā in § 43 and § 639.

The buoyancy, etc. (*as in* § 42), in the skandha of intellect—this is the buoyancy of thought that there then is.

[44] What on that occasion is plasticity of sense (kāyamudutā)?[1]

The plasticity which there is on that occasion, the suavity, smoothness, absence of rigidity, in the skandhas of feeling, perception and syntheses—this is the plasticity of sense that there then is.

[45] What on that occasion is plasticity of thought (cittamudutā)?

The plasticity which, etc. (*as in* § 44), in the skandha of intellect—this is the plasticity of thought that there then is.

[46] What on that occasion is wieldiness[2] of sense (kāyakammaññatā)?

The wieldiness which there is on that occasion, the tractableness, the pliancy, of the skandhas of feeling, perception and syntheses—this is the wieldiness of sense that then is.

[47] What on that occasion is wieldiness of thought (cittakammaññatā)?

The wieldiness, etc. (*as in* § 46), of the skandha of intellect—this is the wieldiness of thought that there then is.

[48] What on that occasion is fitness[3] of sense (kāyapāguññatā)?

The fitness which there is on that occasion, the competence, the efficient state of the skandhas of feeling, perception and syntheses—this is the fitness of sense that there then is.

---

[1] The suppression of stiffness and resistance, or oppugnancy; the attitude antithetical to that belonging to the kilesas of opinionativeness and conceit.

[2] Kammaññatā, literally workableness, or serviceableness—for good action (Asl. 151), by which one 'succeeds in constructing objects of thought' (*ibid.* 130).

[3] The antithesis to illness and diffidence (*ibid.* 131).

[49] What on that occasion is fitness of thought (cittapāguññatā)?

The fitness, etc. (*as in* § 48), of the skandha of intellect—this is the fitness of thought that there then is.

[50] What on that occasion is rectitude[1] of sense (kāyujjukatā)?

The straightness which there is on that occasion, the rectitude, without deflection, twist or crookedness, of the skandhas of feeling, perception and syntheses—this is the directness of sense that there then is.

[51] What on that occasion is rectitude of thought (cittujjukatā)?

The straightness, etc. (*as in* § 50), of the skandha of intellect—this is the rectitude of thought that there then is.

[52] What on that occasion is mindfulness (sati)?

Answer as for the 'faculty of mindfulness,' § 14.

[53] What on that occasion is intelligence (sampajaññaṃ)?[2]

Answer as for 'wisdom,' § 16.

[54] What on that occasion is quiet (samatho)?

Answer as for 'self-collectedness,' § 11.

[55] What on that occasion is insight (vipassanā)?

Answer as for 'wisdom,' § 16.

[56] What on that occasion is grasp (paggāho)?

Answer as for the 'faculty of energy,' § 13.

[57] What on that occasion is balance (avikkhepo)?[3]

---

[1] Defined as the antithesis of crookedness, deception (māyā) and craftiness (Asl. 131).

[2] Or comprehension; to know anything according to its usefulness, its expediency, its scope, and to know it clearly. Named as approximately equivalent to 'wisdom,' the Cy. assigns to it as well the characteristics of mindfulness (*ibid.*). *Cf.* the frequent twin qualification of sati-sampajāno—*e.g.*, M. i. 274.

[3] 'The opposite of excitement or fluster' (Asl. *ibid.*). Literally, 'the absence of wavering' (or vacillation or unsteadiness).

Answer as for 'self-collectedness,' § 11.

These, or whatever other[1] incorporeal, causally induced states there are on that occasion—these are states that are good.

Here ends the delimitation of terms (Pada-bhājaniyaṃ).

End of the First Portion for Recitation.

[Summary of the constituents of the First Type of Thought (saṅgahavāraṃ or koṭṭhasavāraṃ).][2]

[58] Now, on that occasion
the skandhas are four,
the spheres (āyatanāni) are two,
the elements (dhātuyo) are two,
the nutriments (āhārā) are three,
the faculties (indriyāni) are eight,
the Jhāna is fivefold,
the Path is fivefold,
the powers (balāni) are seven,
the causes (hetū) are three;

---

[1] See above, p. 5.

[2] The constituent dhammas of the first of the eight schemata of 'good thoughts' (cittangāni) are now rehearsed with reference to class and number. The motive probably was to aid the student either to a conspectus of the psychosis in question, or mnemonically. Thus, if the constituent factors of the thought be regarded under the aspect of classified aggregates (rāsaṭṭhena, or khandhaṭṭhena), they all fall under four heads. All that do not belong to the skandhas of feeling, perception, or intellect, come under the sanskāra-skandha. Regarded under the aspect of collocation or conjuncture (āyatanaṃ), they all fall under two heads, corresponding to the fourth, and to the first, second, and third, of those four skandhas respectively. Regarded under the aspect of phenomena, of *non-noümena* (sabhāvaṭṭhena, suññataṭṭhena, nissattaṭṭhena), they all fall under two heads, corresponding to the two preceding. We then come to partial aspects.

contact,
feeling,
perception,
thinking,
thought,
} are each single [factors];

the skandhas of
feeling,
perception,
syntheses,
intellect,
} are each single [factors];

the sphere of ideation (manāyatanaṃ),
the faculty of ideation,
the element of representative intellection (manoviññāṇadhātu),
the sphere of a (representative) state,
the element of a (representative) state,
} are each single [factors].

These, or whatever other incorporeal, causally induced states there are on that occasion—these are states that are good.

[59] What on that occasion are the four skandhas?

The skandhas of feeling, perception, syntheses and intellection.

[60] (i.) What on that occasion is the skandha of feeling?

The mental pleasure, the mental ease, which there is on that occasion,[1] the pleasurable, easeful sensation which is born of contact with thought, the pleasant, easeful

---

[1] The omission in both this and the next answer of the phrase, used in §§ 3 and 4—'born of contact with the appropriate element of representative intellection'—is not noticed in the Cy. K. draws attention to it in a footnote, not at this passage, but at §§ 108-110. The omission is probably accidental.

feeling born of contact with thought—this is the skandha of feeling that there then is (§§ 3, 10, 18).

[61] (ii.) What on that occasion is the skandha of perception?

The perception, the perceiving, the state of having perceived, which there is on that occasion—this is the skandha of perception that there then is (§ 4).

[62] (iii.) What on that occasion is the skandha of syntheses?[1]

(i) Contact,
(ii) thinking,
(iii) conception,
(iv) discursive thought,
(v) joy,
(vi) self-collectedness,
(vii) the faculty of faith,
(viii) the faculty of energy,
(ix) the faculty of mindfulness,
(x) the faculty of concentration,
(xi) the faculty of wisdom,
(xii) the faculty of vitality,
(xiii) right views,
(xiv) right intention,
(xv) right endeavour,
(xvi) right mindfulness,
(xvii) right concentration,
(xviii) the power of faith,
(xix) the power of energy,
(xx) the power of mindfulness,
(xxi) the power of concentration,
(xxii) the power of wisdom,
(xxiii) the power of conscientiousness,
(xxiv) the power of the fear of blame,
(xxv) absence of lust,
(xxvi) absence of hate,
(xxvii) absence of dulness,

---

[1] See Introduction.

(xxviii) absence of covetousness,
(xxix) absence of malice,
(xxx) right views,
(xxxi) conscientiousness,
(xxxii) the fear of blame,
(xxxiii) serenity of sense,
(xxxiv) serenity of thought,
(xxxv) buoyancy of sense,
(xxxvi) buoyancy of thought,
(xxxvii) plasticity of sense,
(xxxviii) plasticity of thought,
(xxxix) wieldiness of sense,
(xl) wieldiness of thought,
(xli) fitness of sense,
(xlii) fitness of thought,
(xliii) rectitude of sense,
(xliv) rectitude of thought,
(xlv) mindfulness,
(xlvi) intelligence,
(xlvii) quiet,
(xlviii) insight,
(xlix) grasp,
(l) balance.

These, or whatever other incorporeal, causally induced states there are on that occasion, exclusive of the skandhas of feeling, perception and intellection—these are the skandha of syntheses.

[63] (iv.) What on that occasion is the skandha of intellect?

The thought which on that occasion is ideation, mind, the heart, that which is clear, ideation as the sphere of mind, as the faculty of mind, the skandha of intellect, the appropriate element of representative intellection—this is the skandha of intellect that there then is (§ 6).

These on that occasion are the four skandhas.

[64] What on that occasion are the two spheres?

The sphere of ideation, the sphere of (mental) states.

[65] What on that occasion is the sphere of ideation (m a n ā y a t a n a ṃ)?

Answer as for 'thought,' § 6, *and for the* 'skandha of intellection,' § 63.

[66] What on that occasion is the sphere of (mental) states (d h a m m ā y a t a n a ṃ)?

The skandhas of feeling, perception, syntheses—this is on that occasion the sphere of (mental) states.

These are on that occasion the two spheres.

[67] What on that occasion are the two elements?

The element of representative intellection, the element of (mental) states.

[68] What on that occasion is the element of representative intellection (m a n o v i ñ ñ ā ṇ a d h ā t u)?

Answer as for 'thought,' § 6; *cf.* §§ 63, 65.

[69] What on that occasion is the element of (mental) states (d h a m m a d h ā t u)?

The skandhas of feeling, of perception, of syntheses—these are on that occasion the element of (mental) states.

These are on that occasion the two elements.

[70] What on that occasion are the three nutriments?[1]

The nutriment of contact, the nutriment of representative cogitation, the nutriment of intellection.

[71] What on that occasion is the nutriment of contact (p h a s s ā h ā r o)?

---

[1] These three incorporeal nutriments or foods, together with the fourth or corporeal food, are given in the Sutta Pitaka: M. i. 261; S. ii. 11. In the A. they are not classified under the Catukka Nipāta; but in the Dasaka Nipāta (A. v. 136) ten species of ā h ā r o are named, which have no reference to the four. *E.g.*, 'appropriate action is the ā h ā r o of health.' Buddhaghosa, dwelling on the etymology, calls them not so much conditions as supplementary casual 'adducts' (ā - h ā r). Given, *e.g.*, a living individual, adduce contact, and you get feeling; adduce cogitation, and you get the three 'becomings' (in the universe of sense, etc.); adduce intellect, and you get conception and name-and-form (Asl. 153).

Answer as for 'contact,' § 2.

[72] What on that occasion is the nutriment of representative cogitation (manosañcetanāhāro)?

The thinking, the cogitating, the reflection which there is on that occasion—this is the representative cogitation that there then is.

[73] What on that occasion is the nutriment of intellection (viññāṇāhāro)?

Answer as for the 'skandha of intellection,' § 63.

These on that occasion are the three nutriments.

[74] What on that occasion are the eight faculties?

The faculties of faith, energy, mindfulness, concentration, wisdom, ideation, happiness, vitality.

[75-82] What on that occasion is the faculty of faith . . . vitality?

Answers as in §§ 12-19 *respectively.*

These on that occasion are the eight faculties.

[83] What on that occasion is the fivefold Jhāna (pañcangikaṃ jhānaṃ)?

Conception, discursive thought, joy, ease, self-collectedness.

[84-88] What on that occasion is conception . . . self-collectedness?

Answers as in §§ 7-11 *respectively.*

This on that occasion is the fivefold Jhāna.

[89] What on that occasion is the fivefold Path (pañcangiko maggo)?

Right views, right intention, right endeavour, right mindfulness, right concentration.

[90-94] What on that occasion are right views . . . is . . . right concentration?

Answers as in §§ 20-24 *respectively.*

This on that occasion is the fivefold Path.

[95] What on that occasion are the seven powers?

The power of faith, energy, mindfulness, concentration, wisdom, conscientiousness, the fear of blame.

[96-102] What on that occasion is the power of faith . . . the fear of blame?

Answers as in §§ 25-31 respectively.

These on that occasion are the seven powers.

[103] What on that occasion are the three causes (tayo hetū)?

The absence of lust, of hate, and of dulness.

[104-106] What on that occasion is the absence of lust . . . dulness?

Answers as in §§ 32-34 respectively.

These are on that occasion the three causes.

[107] What on that occasion is contact . . .
[108] feeling . . .
[109] perception . . .
[110] thinking . . .
[111] thought . . .
[112] the skandha of feeling . . .
[113] the skandha of perception . . .
[114] the skandha of syntheses . . .
[115] the skandha of intellection . . .
[116] the sphere of ideation . . .
[117] the faculty of ideation . . .
[118] the element of ideational intellection . . .
[119] the sphere of (mental) states . . .
[120] the element of (mental) states,
regarded as a single factor?

Answers as in §§ 2-6, 60-63, 65, 65, 65, 66, 66, respectively.

These, or whatever other incorporeal, causally induced states there are on that occasion—these are states that are good.

[Here ends] the Summary [of the constituents of the First Main Type of Good Thoughts].

[The 'Emptiness' Section (suññatavāro)].[1]

[121] Now, at that time there are
states (distinguishable constituents of the 'thought'),
skandhas,
spheres,
elements,
nutriments,
faculties,
Jhāna,
the Path,
powers,
causes,
contact,
feeling,
perception,
thinking,
thought,
the skandha of feeling,
the skandha of perception,
the skandha of syntheses,
the skandha of intellect,
the sphere of ideation,
the faculty of ideation,
the element of representative intellection,
the sphere of [mental] states,
the element of [mental] states.

These, or whatever other incorporeal, causally induced states there are on that occasion—these are states that are good.

---

[1] On the significance of the term 'emptiness,' see Introduction; *cf.* § 344. The significance of this section in the student's course of study seems to have consisted simply in this: That the interest being withdrawn from the nature and numbers of the particular constituents in each of the species of mental activity to which the thought-complex is reducible, emphasis is laid on the principle that this same thought-complex is an aggregate or combination of such phenomenal factors, *and nothing more*. 'There are states of consciousness' (dhammā honti); that is (Asl. 155), 'there is no permanent entity or self which acquires the states.' 'The states are to be understood phenomenally. There is no other being or existence or person or individual whatever.'

[122] What on that occasion are states?

The skandhas of feeling, of perception, of syntheses, of intellection.

[123] What on that occasion are skandhas?

Answer as in § 59.

[124-145] *Similar questions are then put respecting* 'spheres,' 'elements,' *and so on through the list of constituent species. The answers are identical with those given to similar questions in the previous* 'Summary,' *viz., in* §§ 64, 67, 70, 74, 83, 89, 95, 103, *and* 107-120.

[Here ends] the 'Emptiness' Section.

[Here ends] the First Main Type of Good Thoughts.

II.

[146] Which are the states that are good?

When a good thought concerning the sensuous universe has arisen by the prompting of a conscious motive,[1] a

---

[1] Sasankhārena. Buddhaghosa's explanation of the term is terse and explicit. Sa = co-, sankhāro = compound, is here used in the sense of concomitant with spring, motive, means, or cause (ussāho, payogo, upāyo, paccayo-gahaṇaṃ). For instance, a bhikshu dwelling in the neighbourhood of a vihāra is inclined, when duty calls him to sweep the terrace round the sthūpa, wait on the elders, or listen to the Dhamma, to find the way too far, and shirk attendance. Second thoughts, as to the impropriety of not going, induce him to go. These are prompted either by his own conscience (attano vā payogena), or by the exhortation of another who, showing the disadvantage in shirking, and the profit in attending, says, 'Come, do it!' And the 'good thought,' *i.e.*, of course, the resolve to go, is said 'to have arisen by way of a concomitant motive, by way of the taking hold of a cause.' Asl. 156.

This explanation is not discrepant with that of sasankhāriko, given to Childers by Vijesinha Mudliar. He

thought which is accompanied by pleasure, associated with knowledge, and having, as its object, a sight, a sound, a smell, a taste, a touch, a [mental] state, or what not, then there is contact, feeling, etc.[1] [*here follows the list of 'states' dealt with in §§ 1-145 and constituting the First Thought*]—these, or whatever other incorporeal, causally induced states there are on that occasion—these are states that are good. . . .

[Here ends] the Second Thought.[2]

III.

[147] Which are the states that are good?

When a good thought concerning the sensuous universe has arisen accompanied by pleasure, disconnected with knowledge, and having as its object, a sight, a sound, a

---

was not, I take it, so bad a Buddhist as to mean that an asankhārikaṃ cittaṃ was a thought in and for itself spontaneous, *i.e.*, uncaused. He would mean only that the subject of the thought experienced it without being conscious of its mental antecedent *as such*, without paccaya-gahaṇaṃ. In a cittaṃ sasankhārena, on the other hand, the thought presents itself in consciousness together with its mental conditions. In the Abhidhammattha-Sangaha the terms used in a similar connexion are asankhārikaṃ and sasankhārikaṃ. J. P. T. S., 1884, p. 1 *et seq*. Cf. Warren, 'Buddhism in Translations,' 490.

[1] In the text (§ 146), at the omitted repetitions indicated by '. . . pe . . .' reference is made to § 147. More correctly reference should be made to § 1. The second type-thought is in all respects (including Summary and 'Emptiness' Section) identical with the first (Asl. 156), with the sole exception of the additional implication 'by the prompting of a conscious motive.' With the same exception the fourth, sixth, and eighth type-thoughts are identical with the third, fifth, and seventh respectively. Hence the reference in § 159 of the text should have been to § 157.

[2] K. reads Dutiyaṃ Cittaṃ, and so on for the eight.

smell, a taste, a touch, a [mental] state, or what not, then there is

contact, conception,
feeling, discursive thought,
perception, joy,
thinking, ease,
thought, self-collectedness;
the faculty of
faith, concentration,
energy, ideation,
mindfulness, happiness,
vitality;
right intention,[1] right mindfulness,
right endeavour, right concentration;
the power of
faith, concentration,
energy, conscientiousness,
mindfulness, the fear of blame;
absence of lust,
absence of hate,
absence of covetousness,
absence of malice;
conscientiousness,
fear of blame;
serenity, wieldiness,
buoyancy, fitness,
plasticity, rectitude,
both of sense and thought;
mindfulness, grasp,
quiet, balance.

---

[1] Sammādiṭṭhi should have been here omitted in the text, just as it is rightly omitted at the place of its second mention between avyāpādo and hiri. Its absence from the third type of thought is involved in the qualifying phrase 'disconnected with knowledge,' just as 'wisdom,' 'insight,' etc., are. *Cf.* K. In 147*a* the Path is said to be *fourfold* only.

These, or whatever other incorporeal, causally induced states there are on that occasion—these are states that are good.

[Summary, *cf.* § 58 *et seq.*]

[147*a*] Now, on that occasion
the skandhas are four,
the spheres are two,
the elements are two,
the nutriments are three,
the faculties are seven,[1]
the Jhāna is fivefold,
the Path is fourfold,
the powers are six,[2]
the causes are two,[3]
contact, etc.

[*Continue as in* § 58.]

* * * * * *

[148] What on that occasion is the skandha of syntheses?
The content of the sanskāra-skandha is the same as in the First Type of Thought, § 62,[4] *with the following omissions:*
'The faculty of wisdom,'
'right views,'
'the power of wisdom,'
'the absence of dulness,'
'intelligence,'
'insight.'

---

1 That of 'wisdom' being omitted.
2 See preceding note.
3 'Absence of dulness' being omitted.
4 In the text the reader is referred to § 62 without reservation, and is thereby landed in inconsistencies. K. enumerates the content of the skandha in full, omitting all those factors which are incompatible with a thought divorced from knowledge. I have thought it sufficient to name only these excluded factors.

These are omitted as incompatible with the quality 'disconnected with knowledge.'

*   *   *   *   *   *

These, or whatever other incorporeal, etc.

*   *   *   *   *   *

[Here ends] the Third Type of Thought.[1]

IV.

[149] Which are the states that are good?

When a good thought concerning the sensuous universe has arisen by the prompting of a conscious motive, a thought which is accompanied by happiness, disconnected with knowledge, and having as its object a sight, a sound, a smell, a taste, a touch, a [mental] state, or what not, then there is contact, etc. [*continue as in* § 147]—these, or whatever other incorporeal, causally induced states there are on that occasion—these are states that are good. . . .[2]

*   *   *   *   *   *

[Here ends] the Fourth Thought.

---

[1] Placed erroneously in the text after § 147.

[2] So K. The text, by omitting not only the repetitions, but also the essentially distinctive factor sasankhārena, renders the insertion of the 'Fourth Thought' quite unintelligible.

Buddhaghosa gives a different illustration of this type of thought in harmony with its resemblance to and difference from the former cittaṃ sasankhārena, viz.: in its involving a pleasurable state of mind, but not any great understanding or discernment. Such is the thought of little boys, who, when their parents duck their heads to make them worship at a cetiya, willingly comply, though doing so without intelligent conviction. Asl. 156.

V.

[150] Which are the states that are good?

When a good thought concerning the sensuous universe has arisen, accompanied by disinterestedness,[1] associated with knowledge, and having as its object a sight, a sound, a smell, a taste, a touch, a [mental] state, or what not, then there is contact, etc. [*continue as in* § 1, *but for* 'joy' *and* 'happiness' *substitute* 'equanimity' (upekkhā), *and for* 'the faculty of happiness' *substitute* 'the faculty of disinterestedness'].[2]

[151] What on that occasion is contact?

Answer as in § 2.

[152] What on that occasion is feeling?

The mental [condition] neither pleasant nor unpleasant, which, on that occasion, is born of contact with the appropriate element of representative intellection; the sensation, born of contact with thought, which is neither easeful nor painful; the feeling, born of contact with thought, which is neither easeful nor painful—this is the feeling that there then is.

* * * * * *

[*Continue as in* §§ 4-8.]

[153] What on that occasion is disinterestedness?[3]

Answer as in preceding reply, omitting the phrase 'born

---

[1] Upekkhā. 'This is impartiality (lit., middleness) in connexion with the object of thought, and implies a discriminative knowledge' (Asl. 157). *Cf.* its significance in the cultivation of Jhāna, § 165. In the Jhāna that may arise in connexion with the first type of thought, which is concomitant with 'joy' and 'ease,' it is replaced by 'self-collectedness.' See § 83.

[2] Here, again, the excision, in the text, of practically the whole answer, and the reference to § 156, where the sixth thought is differentiated from this, the fifth thought, by the quality sasankhārena, quite obscures the classification adopted in the original.

[3] Substituted for 'joy' and 'ease,' §§ 9, 10.

of contact with the appropriate element of representative intellection.'

* * * * * *

[*Continue as in* §§ 11-17.]

[154] What on that occasion is the faculty of disinterestedness?

Answer as in preceding reply. Continue as in §§ 19-57.

[Summary.]

[154*a*] Now, on that occasion
the skandhas are four,
the spheres are two,
the elements are two,
the nutriments are three,
the faculties are eight,
the Jhāna is fourfold,[1]
the Path is fivefold,
the powers are seven,
the causes are three,
contact,
etc., etc. [*cf.* § 58],
the sphere of mental states is a single factor,
the element of mental states is a single factor.

These, or whatever other incorporeal, causally induced states there are on that occasion—these are states that are good. . . .

[*Continue as in* §§ 59-61.]

[155] What on that occasion is the skandha of syntheses?

---

[1] Consisting presumably in 'conception,' 'discursive thought,' 'disinterestedness' (superseding 'joy' and 'ease'), and 'self-collectedness.' *Cf.* § 83. The last-named attitude of mind does not usually figure in the Pitakas as the culminating (or other) stage of Jhāna (*cf.* § 160 *et seq.*). In the Abhidhammattha-Sangaha, however, it does occur as such, and side by side also with 'disinterestedness.' J. P. T. S., 1884, p. 3.

Answer as in § 62, *omitting* 'joy.'[1]

*   *   *   *   *   *

[*Continue as in the Summary and* 'Emptiness' *Section of the First Type of Thought.*]

[Here ends] the Fifth Type of Thought.]

VI.

[156] Which are the states that are good?

When a good thought concerning the sensuous universe has arisen, accompanied by disinterestedness, associated with knowledge, prompted by a conscious motive, and having, as its object, a sight, a sound, a smell, a taste, a touch, a [mental] state, or what not, then there is contact, etc.

*   *   *   *   *   *

[*Continue as in the Fifth Type of Thought.*]

*   *   *   *   *   *

[Here ends] the Sixth Type of Thought.

VII.

[157] Which are the states that are good?

When a good thought concerning the sensuous universe has arisen, accompanied by disinterestedness, disconnected with knowledge, and having, as its object, a sight, a sound, a smell, a taste, a touch, a [mental] state, or what not, then there is contact, etc. . . .

*   *   *   *   *   *

[*Continue as in the Third Type of Thought, substituting* 'disinterestedness' *for* 'joy' *and* 'ease,' *the* 'faculty of disinterestedness' *for that of* 'happiness,' *and* 'fourfold' *for* 'fivefold Jhāna.'[2]]

*   *   *   *   *   *

---

[1] K. gives the skandha in full, omitting 'joy,' joy and upekkhā being mutually exclusive.

[2] Ñāṇindriyaṃ in the text should be manindriyaṃ.

[Summary.]

[157*a*] Now, on that occasion
the skandhas are four,
etc., etc.

[*Continue as in the Third Type of Thought, substituting* 'fourfold' *for* 'fivefold Jhāna.']

* * * * * *

[158] What on that occasion is the skandha of syntheses?

The content of this skandha is the same as in the Third Type of Thought (*see* § 148), *with the further omission of* 'joy.'

* * * * * *

[*Continue as in the First Type of Thought.*]

* * * * * *

[Here ends] the Seventh Type of Thought.

VIII.

[159] Which are the states that are good?

When a good thought concerning the sensuous universe has arisen, accompanied by disinterestedness, disconnected with knowledge, prompted by a conscious motive, and having, as its object, a sight, a sound, a smell, a taste, a touch, a [mental] state, or what not, then there is contact, etc.

* * * * * *

[*Continue as in the Seventh Type of Thought.*]

* * * * * *

[Here ends] the Eighth Type of Thought.

[End of Chapter I. on] the Eight Main Types of Thought concerning the Sensuous Universe.

(Here ends the Second Portion for Recitation.)

Chapter II.

[Good in relation to the Universe of Form (rūpāvacara-kusalaṃ).

Methods for inducing Jhāna.

I.

The Eight Artifices (aṭṭhakasiṇaṃ).

1. The Earth Artifice (paṭhavīkasiṇaṃ).

(*a*) *The Fourfold System of Jhāna* (catukkanayo).]

[160] Which are the states that are good?

When, that he may attain to the heavens of Form,[1] he[2] cultivates the way thereto, aloof from sensuous appetites, aloof from evil ideas,[3] and so, by earth-gazing, enters[4] into

---

[1] See Introduction.

[2] The subject of these states of consciousness.

[3] Vivicc' eva kāmehi, vivicca akusalehi dhammehi. Lit., 'having separated one's self, having become without, having departed from' (Asl. 164). That is to say —again according to the Cy. (*ibid.*)—from the objects of sensual desires, and from the desires themselves, respectively (vatthukāmā, kilesakāmā. Childers' Dictionary, *s.v.* kāmo). The former phrase (vivicc' eva kāmehi) includes the whole psychological realm of sense-presentation (kāyo, or the three skandhas of feeling, perception and sanskāras); the latter, dhammehi, referring to the realm of ideation (cittaṃ) only.

The Cy. repudiates the idea that the emphatic enclitic eva, occurring only in the former of the two phrases, renders the latter less important, and quotes, in support, the opening words of the Cūla-sīhanāda Discourse (M. i. 63).

[4] Paṭhavikasinaṃ. The first of the Karmasṭhāna

and abides in[1] the First Jhāna (the first rapt meditation), wherein conception works and thought discursive,[2] which is born of solitude,[3] and full of joy[4] and ease—then the contact, the feeling . . . the grasp, the balance, which arise in him, or whatever other[5] incorporeal, causally induced states that there are on that occasion—these are states that are good.

*   *   *   *   *   *

---

methods, or quasi-hypnotic devices for attaining to temporary rapt oblivion of the outer world. The percept of the circle of mould induces the vivid image (nimittaṃ), and thereupon Jhāna supervenes.

[1] *I.e.*, sustains the mood indefinitely. The Cy. quotes the Vibhanga as paraphrasing the term by the same expressions, 'going on,' etc., as are used to describe above (§ 19) the 'faculty of vitality.'

[2] Savitakkaṃ savicāraṃ. Leaving the negative essential conditions of Jhāna, we pass to the positive features (Asl. 166). The meditation progresses by means of these two in particular, as a tree does by its flowers and fruit. According to the Vibhanga, they reveal the determined resolves of the individual student (puggalādhiṭṭhānā). (*Ibid.*)

[3] According to the Cy., the solitude is rather moral than physical, and means 'born in the seclusion which the student creates by thrusting from his heart the five hindrances (*ibid.*; *infra*, § 1152). According as it is said in the Peṭaka (? Peṭakopadesa), concentration opposes sensual desire; joy opposes malice; conception, or the onset of intellect, opposes stolidity and torpor; ease opposes excitement and worry; discursive thought opposes perplexity or doubt (Asl. 165). See D. i. 73, where the hindrances are explicitly mentioned in connection with Jhāna; also the notes in Rhys Davids' 'Dialogues of the Buddha,' I., p. 84.

[4] *I.e.*, joy of the fifth species, pharaṇa-pīti (Asl. 166), § 9; also compare the passage just referred to, D. i. 73. See above, so imam eva kāyaṃ . . . abhisandeti . . . parip-pharati.

[5] These are said to be the four first—desire, etc.—of the nine named above, p. 5, n. 1 (Asl. 168).

Continue as in the First Type of Thought relating to the sensuous universe, including the Summary and 'Emptiness' *divisions.*[1]

[161] Which are the states that are good?

When, that he may attain to the heavens of Form, he cultivates the way thereto, suppressing the working of conception and of thought discursive, and so, by earth-gazing, enters into and abides in the Second Jhāna (the second rapt meditation), which is self-evolved,[2] born of concentration, full of joy and ease, in that, set free from the working of conception and of thought discursive, the mind

---

[1] So the Cy. (*ibid.*). In the text, therefore, the reader should have been referred, not to (147), but to (1). K. indicates the elision simply by a . . . pe . . . at the point corresponding to the comma before 'or whatever . . .' in my translation, followed by 'ime dhammā kusalā.'

I am inclined, however, to think that the detailed catechism as to the nature of the various dhammas, such as occurs at §§ 2-57, is not to be understood as included in the passage elided, either here or in the remaining Jhānas. K. does not repeat the . . . pe . . . cited above at the corresponding point in the three remaining Jhānas, where the Summary is not elided, but given. Nor does it give the . . . pe . . . which stands in the text, in §§ 163, 165, before Tasmiṃ kho pana samaye. Similarly it omits the . . . pe . . . given in the text at the corresponding points in the formulæ for the 'five-fold Jhāna,' § 168 *et seq.*

[2] Ajjhattaṃ, *i.e.*, according to the Cy. (169), attano jātaṃ, attasantāne nibbattaṃ; according to the Vibhanga, paccattaṃ. It is not quite clear to me what is the special force of the term in just this Jhāna, unless it be that the 'earth-gazing' is not now continued—the individual becoming more rapt from external determinants of consciousness, more susceptible to purely subjective conditions.

grows calm and sure,[1] dwelling on high[2]—then the contact, the feeling, the perception, the thinking, the thought, the joy, the ease, the self-collectedness, the faculties of faith, energy, mindfulness, concentration, wisdom, ideation, happiness, and vitality, the right views,[3] right endeavour, . . .[4] the grasp, the balance that arises—these, or whatever other incorporeal, causally induced states that there are on that occasion—these are states that are good.

---

[1] Sampasādanaṃ, tranquillizing, paraphrased in the Cy. (*ibid.*) by saddhā, assurance or faith (above, § 12). It is a term for Jhāna itself, blent as it is with the whole contemplative discipline, 'just as cloth steeped in purple is "purple"'—to adapt the commentator's simile to our idiom. The following word cetaso, 'of the mind,' may be taken either with this term, or with that next after it, ekodibhāvaṃ (*ibid.*).

[2] In the text read ekodibhāvaṃ. Buddhaghosa's comments on this expression contain the original of the Thera Subhūti's quotation given in Childers. The substance of them is that the ceto (intellect, mind, heart), no longer overwhelmed or encumbered by vitakko and vicāro, rises up slowly pre-eminent (eko=seṭṭho or asahāyo) in its meditative concentration, or samādhi, this term being synonymous with ekodibhāvaṃ (Samādhiss' etaṃ adhivacanaṃ). The discursive intellection of the First Jhāna, troubling the ceto, as waves rendering water turgid, has in the Second Jhāna sunk to rest. And this uplifting is said (the commentator emphasizes) of ceto, and not of an individual entity, nor of a living soul (na sattassa na jīvassa). See Morris's note, J. P. T. S., 1885, p. 32.

[3] Sammāsankappo is here, its usual order of place, omitted. It involves vitakko; see § 7.

[4] The reference in the text to § 157 cannot be right. The subject has not yet banished pleasurable emotion, and attained to the calm of disinterestedness; nor is his state of mind 'disconnected with knowledge.' The type of thought, as to its remaining components, is still the first, *i.e.*, that of § 1.

[Summary.]

[161*a*] Now, on that occasion
the skandhas are four,
the spheres are two,
the elements are two,
the nutriments are three,
the faculties are eight,
the Jhāna is threefold,[1]
the Path is fourfold,[2]
the powers are seven,
the causes are three,
contact counts as a single factor,
etc., etc.

[*Continue as in* § 58 *et seq.*]

*　　*　　*　　*　　*　　*

[162] What on that occasion is the skandha of syntheses?

Contact,	joy,
thinking,	self-collectedness;
the faculties of	
faith,	concentration,
energy,	wisdom,
mindfulness,	vitality;

right views,
right endeavour,
etc., etc.

[*Continue as in* § 62 *et seq.*[3]]

---

[1] *Cf.* § 83. 'Conception' and 'discursive thought' are now suppressed.

[2] *Cf.* § 89. 'Right intention,' as involving 'conception,' is now suppressed. The mind is no longer occupied with overt activities concerned with this life. See p. 46, n. 3.

[3] Including, presumably,, the 'Emptiness' Section, as in the case of the First Jhāna.

[163] Which are the states that are good?

When, that he may attain to the heavens of Form, he cultivates the way thereto, and further, through the waning of all passion for joy,[1] holds himself unbiassed,[2] the while, mindful and self-possessed,[3] he experiences in his sense-consciousness[4] that ease whereof the Noble Ones[5] declare: 'He that is unbiassed and watchful dwelleth at ease'—and so, by earth-gazing, enters into and abides in the Third Jhāna—then the contact, the feeling, the perception, the thinking, the thought, the ease, the self-collectedness, the faculties of faith, energy, mindfulness,[6] concentration, wisdom, ideation, happiness and vitality, the right views, right endeavour,[7] etc. . . . the grasp, the balance that arises[8]—these, or whatever other incorporeal, causally induced states that there are on that occasion—these are states that are good.

---

[1] Pītiyā ca virāgā, 'meaning either distaste for joy or the transcending of it.' The ca indicates the progressive continuity from the preceding to the present Jhāna (Asl. 171).

[2] Upekkhako, or disinterested. He looks on from the standpoint of one who has arrived, says the Cy. (172). As we might say:

'E terra magnum alterius spectare laborem.'

Buddhaghosa expatiates here on the ten kinds of upekkhā enumerated in Hardy, 'Man. Buddhism,' 505.

[3] Sampajāno. Intelligently aware of his own procedure.

[4] Kāyo, see Introduction; *supra*, p. 43, n. 3.

[5] See *infra*, § 1003, n. 6.

[6] Omitted in the text, but not so in K. The context requires its insertion.

[7] Sammāsati, inserted in the text, but not in the right order, is of course required by the context, but is, here and in K., assumed in the 'etc.'

[8] § 157, to which the reader is referred in the text, is obviously wrong. § 1 would be nearer the mark.

[Summary.]

[163*a*] Now, on that occasion
the skandhas are four,
the spheres are two,
the elements are two,
the nutriments are three,
the faculties are eight,
the Jhāna is twofold,[1]
the Path is fourfold,[2]
the powers are seven,
the causes are three,
contact counts as a single factor,
etc., etc.

[*Continue as in* § 58.]

* * * * * *

[164] What on that occasion is the skandha of syntheses?

Contact,
thinking,
self-collectedness;
the faculties of
faith, concentration,
energy, wisdom,
mindfulness, vitality;
right views, right endeavour,
etc., etc.

[*Continue as in* § 62.]

* * * * * *

[1] 'Ease' remains and 'self-collectedness.'
[2] *Cf.* § 161[a] n. 2.

[165] Which are the states that are good?

When, that he may attain to the heavens of Form, he cultivates the way thereto, and, by the putting away of ease and by the putting away of ill, by the passing away of the happiness and of the misery[1] he was wont to feel, he thus, by earth-gazing, enters into and abides in the Fourth Jhāna (the fourth rapt meditation) of that utter purity of mindfulness which comes of disinterestedness,[2] where no ease is felt nor any ill—then the contact, the feeling, the perception, the thinking, the thought, the disinterestedness, the self-collectedness, the faculties of faith, energy, mindfulness, concentration, wisdom, ideation, disinterested-

---

[1] 'Ease' and 'ill,' according to the Cy., are kāyikaṃ, or relating to the three skandhas of feeling, etc.—relating to sense-consciousness. 'Happiness' and 'misery' (somanassaṃ, domanassaṃ) relate to the intellect, or ideational consciousness. 'Happiness' is the last of these to be transcended; the others have been expelled in the course of the previous stages of Jhāna (Asl. 175, 176). But all four are here enumerated, as if all were only in this Fourth Jhāna transcended, in order to show more clearly, by the method of exhaustive elimination, what is the subtle and elusive nature of that third species of feeling termed 'neutral' (adukkham-asukhā), or 'disinterested' (upekkhā)—the zero point, or line, as we should say, of hedonic quantity. The Cy. then gives the simile of selecting heads of cattle by elimination of the rest of the herd, which Hardy cites (*ibid.*, 177; East. Monachism, 270).

[2] Upekkhā-satiparisuddhiṃ. According to the Vibhanga, the mindfulness that is made pure stands for all the other elements present in consciousness, which have also been brought into clear relief, as it were, by the calm medium of equanimity. The simile is then adduced, given also in Hardy (*op. cit.*, 271), of the moon by day and by night. Upekkhā is latent in consciousness in the other stages of Jhāna, but rendered colourless by the radiance of intellectual and emotional exercise, as the crescent moon during the day, though present in the sky, is dimmed by the sun's splendour (Asl. 178).

ness and vitality, the right views, the right endeavour, etc. . . .

[*Continue as in* § 163.]

*   *   *   *   *   *

[Summary.]

[165*a*] Now, on that occasion
the skandhas are four,
the spheres are two,
the elements are two,
the nutriments are three,
the faculties are eight,
the Jhāna is twofold,[1]
the Path is fourfold,
the powers are seven,
the causes are three,
contact counts as a single factor,
etc., etc.

[*Continue as in* § 58, *etc.*]

*   *   *   *   *   *

[166] What on that occasion is the skandha of syntheses?

Answer as in § 164.[2]

*   *   *   *   *   *

[Here ends] the Fourfold System of Jhāna.

---

[1] Namely, 'disinterestedness' and 'self-collectedness' (Asl. 179). Else one would have looked to find ekangikaṃ Jhānaṃ.

[2] The printed text omits satindriyaṃ, though it is explicitly required by the context. K. gives it.

(*b*) The Fivefold System of Jhāna (pañcakanayo).][1]

[167] *The First Jhāna. Question and answer as in the fourfold course,* § 160.

[168] Which are the states that are good?

When, that he may attain to the heavens of Form, he cultivates the way thereto, and so, by earth-gazing, enters into and abides in the Second Jhāna (the second rapt meditation) wherein is no working of conception, but only of thought discursive—which is born of concentration, and is full of joy and ease—then the contact, the feeling, the perception, the thinking, the thought, the discursive inquiry, the joy, the ease, the self-collectedness, etc. . . .

[*Continue as for the Second Jhāna in* § 161.]

[Summary.]

[168*a*] Now, on that occasion
the skandhas are four,
the spheres are two,
the elements are two,
the nutriments are three,
the faculties are eight,

---

[1] Jhāna is usually alluded to in the Pitakas in the fourfold order. The fivefold division is obtained by the successive, instead of simultaneous, elimination of vitakko and vicāro. According to the Cy., it was optional to the teacher, after the example of the Buddha, to use either at his discretion, adapting himself to the particular mental state of his pupils, or having a view to the effectve flow of his discourse. A passage is quoted from the Pitakas—probably S. iv. 363 or A. i. 299, n. 2 (*cf.* K. V. 413; Mil. 337)—where samādhi is distinguished as (1) having vitakko and vicāro, (2) having only the latter, (3) having neither.

the Jhāna is fourfold,
the Path is fourfold,
etc., etc.

[*Continue as in* § 58.]

*　　*　　*　　*　　*　　*

[169] What on that occasion is the skandha of syntheses?

Contact, thinking, discursive thought, joy, etc. . . .

[*Continue as in* § 162.]

*　　*　　*　　*　　*　　*

[170-175] The Third, Fourth and Fifth Jhānas.

[*These are identical in formulation with the Second, Third and Fourth Jhānas of the Fourfold System. Questions and answers as in* §§ 161-166.]

[Here ends] the Fivefold System of Jhāna.

[(*c*) The Four Modes of Progress (catasso paṭipadā).][1]

[1] It has been seen that, before the several stages of Jhāna could be attained to, the student had to purge and discipline himself in specific ways—elimination of all attention to mundane matters, elimination of discursive cogitation, and so on. The special stage of Jhāna supervened after each act of self-control and intensified abstraction. In these processes there was an earlier and a subsequent stage called—at least in the later books—upacāra and appanā respectively. The effective cognition linking these two was an exercise of paññā which, in the text, is known as abhiññā ('intuition'), probably the intuitive or subconscious fetch of the mind to compass the desired appanā, or conception. Now, whether the preparatory abstraction was easy or difficult, and whether the constructive generalizing effort was sluggish or vigorous, depended on the moral temperament and the mental ability

[176] Which are the states that are good?

When, that he may attain to the heavens of Form, he cultivates the way thereto, aloof from sensuous appetites, aloof from evil ideas, and so, by earth-gazing, enters into and abides in the First Jhāna . . . progress being painful and intuition sluggish—then the contact[1] . . . the balance that arises—these . . . are states that are good.

[177][2] . . . [*or*] when . . . he . . . so enters into and abides in the First Jhāna . . . progress being painful, but intuition quick . . .

[178] . . . [*or*] when . . . he . . . so enters into and abides in the First Jhāna . . . progress being easy, but intuition sluggish . . .

[179] . . . [*or*] when . . . he . . . so enters into and abides in the First Jhāna . . . progress being easy and intuition quick—then the contact, etc. . . . the balance that arises—these . . . are states that are good.

---

respectively of the individual student (Asl. 182-184). See the double explanation in A. ii. 149-152, where the swiftness or sluggishness of intuition in both accounts depends on the acuteness or flabbiness of the five faculties of faith, energy, mindfulness, concentration, wisdom. The ease or difficulty in self-abstraction depends, in the first explanation, on whether the student is by nature passionate, malignant, dull, or the reverse of these three. In the second account progress is painful if he have filled his consciousness with the disciplinary concepts of the Foul Things (*vide* below, § 263), Disgust with the World, Impermanence and Death; easy if he simply work out the Four Jhānas.

On the varying import of abhiññā (which occurs in no other connexion in the present work), see 'Dialogues of the Buddha,' i. 62. On upacāra and appanā, see 'Yogāvacara's Manual,' p. xi. We shall probably learn more about the whole procedure when the Visuddhi Magga and the Vibhanga are edited.

[1] *Cf.* § 1.

[2] The same question is to be understood as repeated in each section.

[180] *These four combinations are repeated in the case of the 2nd to the 4th Jhānas on the Fourfold System, and of the 2nd to the 5th on the Fivefold System.*

[Here end] the Four Modes of Progress.

[(*d*) The Four Objects of Thought (cattāri ārammaṇāni).][1]

[181] Which are the states that are good?

When, that he may attain to the heavens of Form, he cultivates the way thereto, and so, aloof from sensuous appetites, aloof from evil ideas, by earth-gazing, enters into and abides in the First Jhāna (the first rapt meditation), wherein conception works and thought discursive, which is born of solitude, and is full of joy and ease, but which is limited, and has a limited object of thought—then the contact[2] . . . the balance that arises—these . . . are states that are good.

[182] . . . [*or*] when . . . the First Jhāna[3] . . . is limited, but has an object of thought capable of infinite extension . . .

[183] . . . [*or*] when . . . the First Jhāna . . . is capable of infinite extension, but has a limited object of thought . . .

[184] . . . [*or*] when . . . the First Jhāna . . . is capable of infinite extension, and has an object of thought capable of infinite extension—then the contact, etc. . . . the balance that arises, these . . . are states that are good.

---

[1] That is to say, the percepts or concepts on which the student, in seeking to induce Jhāna, fixes his attention are here classified as having the potentiality to induce a weak or a lofty mood of rapt contemplation. Buddhaghosa describes the former kind of object as having the shallowness of a mere basket or dish (Asl. 184). See also below, §§ 1019-1024.

[2] *Cf.* § 1.

[3] In the following condensed passages the question and answer in the text respectively coincides with and commences like the precedent given in § 181.

[185] *These four combinations are repeated in the case of the 2nd to the 4th Jhānas on the Fourfold System, and of the 1st to the 5th*[1] *Jhānas on the Fivefold System.*

[Here end] the Four Objects of Thought.

[(*e*) (=*c* and *d*) The Sixteenfold Combination (soḷasakkhattukaṃ).]

[186] Which are the states that are good?

When, that he may attain to the heavens of Form, he cultivates the way thereto, aloof from sensuous appetites, aloof from evil ideas, and so, by earth-gazing, enters into and abides in the first Jhāna . . .

where progress is painful and intuition sluggish, which is limited, and has a limited object of thought . . .

[187] . . . [*or*] which is limited, but has an object of thought capable of infinite extension . . .

[188] . . . [*or*] which is capable of infinite extension, but has a limited object of thought . . .

[189] . . . [*or*] which is capable of infinite extension, and has an object of thought capable of infinite extension . . .

[190] . . . [*or*] where progress is painful, but intuition is quick, which is limited, and has a limited object of thought . . .

[191] . . . [*or*] . . . etc.

[*Continue for* §§ 191-193 *as in* §§ 187-189.]

---

[1] In the text, § 185, after paṭhamaṃ jhānaṃ read . . . pe . . . pañcamaṃ jhānaṃ. So K. *Cf.* § 180. Again, after avikkhepo hoti supply . . . pe . . .

[194] . . . [*or*] where progress is easy, but intuition sluggish, which is limited,[1] and has a limited object of thought . . .

[195] . . . [*or*] . . . etc. [*Continue for* §§ 195-197 *as above.*]

[198] . . . [*or*] where progress is easy and intuition quick, which is limited, and has a limited object of thought . . .

[199] [*Continue for* §§ 199-201 *as above.*]

[202] [*These sixteen combinations are repeated in the case of the 2nd to the 4th Jhānas on the Fourfold System, and of the 1st to the 5th Jhānas on the Fivefold System.*]

[Here ends] the Sixteenfold Combination.

[2. The Remaining Seven Artifices *which may also be developed in* sixteenfold combination (aṭṭhakasiṇaṃ soḷasakkhattukaṃ).][2]

---

[1] In the text supply parittaṃ before parittārammaṇaṃ.

[2] The first artifice for the induction of Jhāna having been that of earth-gazing (see above, *passim*). In the Sutta Pitaka—viz., in the Mahā Sakuludāyi-Sutta (M. ii., p. 14), and in the Jhāna Vagga (A. i. 41)—ten kasiṇas are enumerated, those omitted in the Dhammasangaṇi being the kasiṇas of intellection (viññāṇa) and space (ākāsa). The fact of the omission and the nature of the two omitted kasiṇas are commented on by Buddhaghosa (Asl. 186). He explains the omission of the former by its being identical with the second of the four Aruppajhānāni given in §§ 265-268, and that of the latter through its ambiguity. For either it amounts to the 'yellow' kasiṇa (sun-lit space), or it amounts to the first Aruppajhāna (§ 265). The Ceylon tradition has ten kasiṇas also, but admits āloka (light) instead of viññāṇa. And it includes yet another quasi-kasiṇa in the shape of a bhūta-kasiṇa, or the four elements taken collectively, after each has been

[203] Which are the states that are good?

When, that he may attain to the heavens of Form, he cultivates the way thereto, aloof from sensuous appetites, aloof from evil ideas, and so, by the artifice of

water . . .
fire . . .
air . . .
blue-black . . .
yellow . . .
red . . .
white . . .

enters into and abides in the First Jhāna . . . then the contact, etc., that arises—these . . . are states that are good.

[Here ends] the Sixteenfold Combination in the case of the seven remaining artifices for induction.

[II.

The Stations of Mastery[1] (abhibhāyatanāni).

1. 'Forms as Limited' (rupāni parittāni).

(*a* and *b*) Fourfold and Fivefold Jhāna.]

[204] Which are the states that are good?

When, that he may attain to the heavens of Form, he

---

separately dwelt upon. See 'Yogāvacara's Manual, 1896,' pp. 48-52.

[1] Eight 'stations' or 'positions of mastery' are given in the Mahā-parinibbāna-Sutta (pp. 28, 29; see S. B. E. xi. 49, 50, and in A. iv. 305), but the formulæ of the first four differ slightly from those in our text. The Cy. draws attention to this discrepancy (Asl. 189). In the Suttanta the æsthetic aspect of the objects perceived is taken into account in all four stations, the specific difference replacing it in two of them being the conscious dwelling on some part of one's own bodily frame or rūpaskandha. In the Dhammasangaṇi this consciousness is excluded from all the stations. To teach by way of its inclusion and exclusion is called 'merely a *jeu d'esprit* in the Master's discourse' (desanā-vilasa-mattam eva). See following note.

cultivates the way thereto, and, unconscious of any part of his corporeal self,[1] but seeing external objects to be limited, gets the mastery over them with the thought 'I know, I see!'[2] and so, aloof from sensuous appetites, aloof from evil ideas, enters into and abides in the First Jhāna, etc. . . . then the contact, etc., that arises—these . . . are states that are good.

[205] [*Repeat in the case of the* 2*nd to the* 4*th Jhāna on the Fourfold System, and of the* 2*nd to the* 5*th Jhāna on the Fivefold System.*]

[(*c*) The Four Modes of Progress.]

[206-210] *Repeat the four combinations of* progress *as* painful *or* easy, *and of* intuition *as* sluggish *or* quick *set out in* §§ 176-180, *substituting for* 'earth-gazing' *the Mastery-formula just stated.*

---

[1] Ajjhattaṃ arūpasaññī (=na rūpasaññī). This rendering is in accordance with Buddhaghosa's comments (Asl. 188, 189, 191). The student, either because he has tried and failed, or because he did not wish to try, has not induced Jhāna by way of fixing attention on his own hair or the rest. *Cf.* the Mahā Rāhulovāda-Sutta (M. i. 62), where the individual's rūpa-skandha is fully set forth with reference to the four elements, ajjhattikā paṭhavīdhātu, etc., beginning with 'hair' and the rest. *Cf.* § 248 n.

[2] The external objects in question are contemplated on the kasiṇa system (Asl. 188). And just as a man of vigorous digestion bolts a spoonful of rice, so the aspirant after sublime truth swiftly and easily transcends the initial act of external perception when the object is insignificant, and brings forth the desiderated concept (appanā). The judgments by which he registers the consciousness of intellectual mastery have reference, according to Buddhaghosa, to past experience of enlightenment, and indicate simply a recognition, or, in terms of syllogism, a minor premise identified. But he states that, in the Siṇhalese commentary on the Nikāyas, they are interpreted as implying a present access of new light, a fresh moral attainment, gained after the thinker transcends perceptual consciousness (*ibid.*).

[(*d*) The Two Objects of Thought.]

[211-213] *Repeat, substituting for* 'earth-gazing' *the Mastery-formula,* § 181, *where the Jhāna* 'is limited, and has a limited object of thought,' *and* § 183, *where the Jhāna* 'is capable of infinite extension, but has a limited object of thought.'[1]

[(*e*=*c* and *d*) The Eightfold Combination (aṭṭhakkhattukaṃ.][2]

[214-221] *Repeat, with the same substitution,* §§ 186, 188, 190, 192, 194, 196, 198, *and* 200 *of the Sixteenfold Combination.*

[222] *Repeat these eight combinations in the case of each of the remaining Jhānas.*

[2. 'Forms as limited and as beautiful or ugly'[3] (rūpāni parittāni suvaṇṇa-dubbaṇṇāni).

---

[1] The 'objects of thought' are here the kasiṇas, essentially discerned to be 'limited' or insignificant. Hence two, not four varieties; and hence eight, not sixteen combinations. The term appamāṇaṃ connoting merely a *relative,* not an absolute infinitude, there is only a difference of degree in the depth, purifying efficacy, or what not, of the Jhāna attained to. The same illustrative figure is accordingly used, varied in degree. The *gourmand,* discontented with a small dish of rice, demands more and more. So the aspirant (now ñāṇuttaro, not ñāṇuttariko), aiming at perfect self-concentration, refuses to call that infinite which seems so (*ibid.*).

[2] So K.

[3] The general æsthetic designations of suvaṇṇaṃ and dubbāṇaṃ are in the Cy. paraphrased by parisuddhaṃ and its negative. Just as the limited nature of visible things was held to be an efficacious consideration for conceptual efforts, and the notion of 'infinite' helpful for dulness, so the beautiful and the ugly were prescribed for inimical conduct and for indulgence in passion respectively. The appropriateness of it all is said to be discussed in the Cariyā-niddesa of the Visuddhi Magga (Asl. 189).

(*a*) and (*b*)]

[223] Which are the states that are good?

When, that he may attain to the heavens of Form, he cultivates the way thereto, and, unconscious of any part of his corporeal self, but seeing external objects to be limited, and to be beautiful or ugly, gets the mastery over them with the thought, 'I know, I see!' and so, aloof from sensuous appetites, aloof from evil ideas, enters into and abides in the First Jhāna, etc. . . . then the contact, etc., that arises—these . . . are states that are good.

[224] *Repeat in the case of each of the remaining Jhānas.*

Develop in eightfold combination.

[3. 'Forms as infinite' (rūpāni appamāṇāni).[1]

(*a*) and (*b*)]

[225] Which are the states that are good?

When, that he may attain to the heavens of Form, he cultivates the way thereto, and, unconscious of any part of his corporeal self, but seeing external objects to be infinite, gets the mastery over them with the thought, 'I know, I see!' and so, aloof from sensuous appetites, etc.

[*Continue as in* § 204.]

[226] *Repeat in the case of each of the remaining Jhānas.*

[(*c*) The Four Modes of Progress.]

[227-231] *Repeat* §§ 206-210, *substituting* 'infinite' *for* 'limited.'

---

[1] See note on §§ 211-213. Taken in order, Buddhaghosa's comment there reproduced applies to that part of the text. According to the context, it might better apply here, where the external forms or kasiṇa-objects are now contemplated as 'infinite.' The reflection, however, applies to either passage.

[(*d*) The Two Objects of Thought.]

[232-234] *Repeat, with the same substitution as in* (*c*), §§ 211-213.

[(*e*=*c* and *d*) The Eightfold Combination.]

[235-242] *Develop, with the same substitution as in* (*c*) *and* (*d*), *after the manner of* §§ 187, 189, *and so on to* § 201.

[243] *Repeat these eight combinations in the case of each of the remaining Jhānas.*

[4. 'Forms as infinite and as beautiful or ugly' (rūpāni appamāṇāni suvaṇṇa-dubbaṇṇāni).

(*a*) and (*b*)]

[244] *Repeat* § 223, *substituting* 'infinite' *for* 'limited.'

[245] *Repeat in the case of each of the remaining Jhānas.*

Develop in eightfold combination.

[5. 'Forms as blue-black,' etc. (rūpāni nīlāni).[1]

---

[1] It is well known that it is as difficult to determine the range of colour indicated by nīlaṃ as to decide the colour-value of the word γλαυκός. Like the latter term, nīlaṃ may originally have referred more to lustre than to tinge, meaning darkly lustrous, jetty, or nigrescent. Any way, it is not plausible to render the term by 'blue' when one is referred to human hair or bile (pittaṃ) as instances of it in the human body. See note 2 to § 248. In Jāt. iii. 138 hair-dye or hair-wash is called nīliyaṃ—much, perhaps, as we speak of 'blacking' or 'russet polish' for shoes. This implies that the colour called nīlaṃ was, if not the usual, at least the desiderated colour of human hair.

If it were what we understand by a typical blue, the term would be applied to sky and sea, or the violet band of the rainbow, which is, I believe, never the case. Possibly our own colour-parallels in these respects are a modern development. *Cf.* Havelock Ellis in *Contemporary Review*, vol. lxix., p. 727. Modern Hindu colour-terms are, I am told, largely of Persian origin.

(*a*)]

[246] Which are the states that are good?

When, that he may attain to the heavens of Form, he cultivates the way thereto, and, unconscious of any part of his corporeal self, but seeing external objects which are blue-black, blue-black in colour, blue-black in visible expanse,[1] blue-black in luminousness, gets the mastery over them with the thought, 'I know, I see!' and so, aloof from sensuous appetites, etc.

[*Continue as in* § 204.]

* * * * * *

[6-8. 'Forms as yellow,' etc. (rūpāni pītāni).

[247] *Repeat* § 246, *substituting for* 'blue-black, blue-black in colour,' etc., 'yellow,' 'red,' *and* 'white'[2] *successively.*

Develop these Stations of Mastery in the Sixteenfold Combination.

[III.

The Three First Deliverances (tīni vimokkhāni.[3]]

1.

[248] When, that he may attain to the heavens of Form, he cultivates the way thereto, and, conscious of his bodily

---

[1] Nīlanidassanaṃ, indicating, according to the Cy. (190), a uniform sheet of blue without break. The colours in this and following sections may reside in a flower, a piece of cloth, or some other basis.

[2] The remaining three English colour-names may match the Pali terms as loosely as in the previous case. *Cf.* S. B. E. xi., *loc. cit.* In the Sutta there translated instances of the colours are given, and, curiously enough, 'white' is illustrated, not by milk, or the distant Himâlaya snows, but by the morning star.

[3] Followed by four more of the Eight Deliverances in the next chapter, §§ 265-268. The eighth alone is not given in the present work. See Mahā Parinibbāna Sutta, p. 30; A. iv. 306. According to the Cy. (190), the term 'deliverance' (vimokkhaṃ, or adhimuccanaṃ) is used

form,[1] sees bodily forms, and so, aloof from sensuous appetites, aloof from evil ideas, enters into and abides in the First Jhāna, etc. . . . then the contact, etc., which arises, these . . . are states that are good.

2.

[249] When, that he may attain to the heavens of Form, he cultivates the way thereto, and, unconscious of his corporeal self, sees external bodily forms, and so, aloof from sensuous appetites, etc.

[*Continue as in preceding section.*]

3.

[250] When, that he may attain to the heavens of Form, he cultivates the way thereto, and, with the thought, 'How fair it is!'[2] aloof from sensuous appetites, etc.

---

to denote the being set free from 'adverse conditions' and their seductive fascinations, so that the attention is sustained with all the detachment and confidence that the child feels who is borne on his father's hip, his little limbs dangling, their clutch unneeded.

[1] Rūpī. Judging by the Cy. (190), this is equivalent to ajjhattaṃ rūpasaññī—that is, to the opposite of the term 'unconscious of any part of his corporeal self,' the attitude prescribed in the Stations of Mastery, *supra*, § 204 *et seq*. The parikammaṃ selected is 'one's own hair and the rest.' If a nīla-parikammaṃ is sought, attention is fixed on the hair or bile (pittaṃ) or the pupil of the eye. If the induction is to be by way of yellow, fat or skin may be taken; if red, flesh, blood, or the tongue, or the palms of the hands or feet, etc.; if white, the teeth, nails, or white of the eye. At the same time 'he sees external bodily forms in the nīla or other kasiṇa *with the Jhāna-vision*' (jhānacakkhunā passati).

How this dual effort of intense attention was effected I do not pretend to understand, but Buddhaghosa more than once refers us for a more detailed account to the Visuddhi Magga.

[2] That is to say, says the Cy. (191), not the conscious acquirement of the concept (appanā), but the consciousness

[*Continue as in the first Deliverance.*]

These three Deliverances may also be developed in Sixteenfold Combination.

[IV.

The Four Jhānas of the Sublime Abodes (cattāri brahmavihārajhānāni).[1]

1. Love (mettā).

(*a*) Fourfold Jhāna.]

[251] Which are the states that are good?

When, that he may attain to the heavens of Form, he

of the perfection or purity of colour or lustre in the particular kasiṇa is here meant. (The reading should, of course, be subhan ti.) And this æsthetic consciousness is declared by Buddhaghosa to quicken the sense of emancipation from morally adverse conditions analogously to that perception of moral beauty which may be felt in the Sublime Abodes of the following sections. According to the Paṭisambhidā-magga, here quoted, when, on pervading the whole world with heart of love, pity, etc., all feeling of aversion from living beings is rooted out, the student is struck with the glory of the idea, and works his deliverance.

[1] On these four great exercises, see Rhys Davids, S. B. E. xi. 201, n.; and, on their emancipating efficacy, M. i. 38. Buddhaghosa again refers the reader to his Visuddhi Magga for a more detailed commentary (*vide* chap. ix., and *cf.* Hardy, 'Eastern Monachism,' p. 243 *et seq.*). The four are set out here only under the 'Suddhika' formulæ—that is, under heads (*a*) and (*b*). But (*c*), or the Modes of Progress, as well as (*d*) and (*e*), are understood to follow in each case (Asl. 192). The object of thought (ārammaṇaṃ) in this connexion will be 'limited' if the student dwells in love, etc., on but a restricted number of beings; 'infinite' if his heart embrace vast numbers.

The commentator has not a little to say in the present work, however, on the nature and mutual relations of the 'Abodes' (pp. 193-195). First, the characteristics of each

cultivates the way thereto, and so, aloof from sensuous appetites, aloof from evil ideas, enters into and abides in the First Jhāna (the first rapt meditation), wherein conception

---

are fully set forth, together with their false manifestation (vipatti). Clinging (sinehasambhavo) is the vipatti of love, the essential mark of which is the carrying on of beneficent conduct, etc. Tears and the like are less truly characteristic of pity than is the bearing and relieving the woes of others. Laughter and the like are less genuine expressions of sympathy (muditā, which is strictly *συγχαιροσύνη*, *Mitfreude*) than is appreciation of what others have achieved. And there is a condition of disinterestedness (upekkhā) which is prompted by ignorance, and not by that insight into the karma of mankind which can avail to calm the passions.

He next designates the four antisocial attitudes which are to be extirpated by these ethical disciplines, taken in order—ill-will (vyāpādo), cruelty (vihesā), aversion (arati), and passion (rāgo)—and shows how each virtue has also a second vice opposed to it. This he terms its near enemy, as being less directly assailed by it than its ethical opposite, the latter resembling an enemy who has to lurk afar in the jungle and the hills. Love and vengeful conduct cannot coexist. To prevail in this respect, let love be developed fearlessly. But where love and its object have too much in common, love is threatened by lust. On this side let love be guarded well. Again, the near enemy to pity, more insidious than cruelty, is the self-pity pining for what one has not got or has lost—a low, profane melancholy. And the corresponding worldly happiness in what one has, or in consequence of obliviousness as to what one has lost, lies in wait to stifle appreciation of the good fortune of others. Lastly, there is the unintelligent indifference of the worldling who has not triumphed over limitations nor mastered cause and effect, being unable to transcend external things.

The remainder of his remarks are occupied with the necessary ethical sequence in the four Abodes, and the importance of observing method in their cultivation, and finally with their other technical appellation of Appamaññā, or Infinitudes. In this connexion he repeats the touching illustration given in Hardy (*op. cit.*, 249) of the

works and thought discursive, which is born of solitude, is full of joy and ease, and is accompanied by Love—then the contact, etc. . . . [? *continue as in* § 1] . . . the balance that arises—these . . . are states that are good.

[252] Which are the states that are good?

When, that he may attain to the heavens of Form, he cultivates the way thereto, suppressing the working of conception and of thought discursive, and so, by earth-gazing, enters into and abides in the Second Jhāna (the second rapt meditation), which is self-evolved, born of concentration, is full of joy and ease, in that, set free . . . the mind grows calm and sure, dwelling on high—and which is accompanied by Love—then the contact, etc.

[*Continue as in the foregoing.*]

[253] Which are the states that are good?

When, that he may attain to the heavens of Form, he cultivates the way thereto, and further, through the waning of all passion for joy, holds himself unbiassed, the while, mindful and self-possessed, he experiences in his sense-consciousness that ease whereof the Noble Ones declare: 'He

---

mother and her four children. Her desire for the growth of the infant is as Mettā; for the recovery of the sick child as Karuṇā; for the maintenance of the gifts displayed by the youth as Muditā; while her care not to hinder the career of her grown-up son is as Upekkhā.

It may be remarked, by the way, that when Hardy, with a foreigner's want of muditā, calumniates the Buddhist mendicant (p. 250) as one who thinks about the virtues of solidarity without practising them, he quite forgets that these exercises are but preparations of the will for that ministering to the intellectual needs of others to which the recluse's life was largely devoted, and the importance of which the Western, in his zeal for material forms of charity, does not even now appreciate at its real value. And Buddhism did not believe in giving the rein to good impulses unregulated by intellectual control.

that is unbiassed and watchful dwelleth at ease'—and so, by earth-gazing, enters into and abides in the Third Jhāna, which is accompanied by Love[1]—then, etc.

[*Continue as in the foregoing.*]

(*b*) Fivefold Jhāna.

[254-257] *Repeat question and answers in* §§ 167, 168, 170, 172, *adding in each answer, as in the foregoing section,* 'and which is accompanied by Love.'[2]

2. Pity (karuṇā).

[258, 259] *Repeat question and answers in the preceding sections* (*a*) *and* (*b*), *but substituting in each case* 'and which is accompanied by Pity' *for the clause on Love.*

3. Sympathy (muditā).

[260, 261] *Repeat question and answers in the preceding two sections, but substituting in each case* 'and which is accompanied by Sympathy' *for the clause on Pity.*

4. Disinterestedness (upekkhā).

[262] When, that he may attain to the heavens of Form, he cultivates the way thereto, and, by the putting away of ease and by the putting away of ill, by the passing away of the happiness and of the misery he was wont to feel, he thus, by earth-gazing, enters into and abides in the Fourth Jhāna (the fourth rapt meditation) of that utter purity of mindfulness which comes of disinterestedness, where no ease is felt nor any ill, and which is accompanied by Disinterestedness—then the contact, etc.

[*Continue as in* § 165.]

---

[1] Love necessarily involves happiness (somanassaṃ =cetasikaṃ sukhaṃ, § 10, n.), hence it cannot be cultivated by way of the Fourth—or, under (*b*), Fifth—Jhāna.

[2] Omitting the Fifth Jhāna. See preceding note.

The Four Jhānas of the Sublime Abodes may be developed in Sixteen Combinations.

[V.

The Jhāna of Foul Things (a s u b h a-j h ā n a ṃ.)]

[263] Which are the states that are good?

When, that he may attain to the heavens of Form, he cultivates the way thereto, and so, aloof from sensuous appetites, aloof from evil ideas, enters into and abides in the First Jhāna, wherein, etc. . . . and which is accompanied by the idea of a bloated corpse[1] . . .

[*or*] [264] of a discoloured corpse . . .
[*or*] of a festering corpse . . .
[*or*] of a corpse with cracked skin . . .
[*or*] of a corpse gnawn and mangled . . .
[*or*] of a corpse cut to pieces . . .
[*or*] of a corpse mutilated and cut in pieces . . .
[*or*] of a bloody corpse . . .
[*or*] of a corpse infested with worms . . .
[*or*] of a skeleton . . .

then the contact . . . the balance which arises—these . . . are states that are good.[2]

---

[1] The formula of the First Jhāna is understood to be repeated in the case of each of the ten Asubhas, but of the First only. For, in the words of the Cy. (p. 199), 'just as on a swiftly-flowing river a boat can only be steadied by the power of the rudder, so from the weakness (d u b b a-l a t t ā) of the idea (in this case) the mind can only be steadied in its abstraction by the power of conceptual activity (v i t a k k o).' And this activity is dispensed with after the First Jhāna.

[2] For a more detailed account of this peculiar form of moral discipline, the reader is again referred to the Visuddhi Magga (chap. vi.). Hardy ('East. Mon.'), who quotes largely from the Sinhalese commentary on the Visuddhi Magga, may also be consulted (p. 247 *et seq.*). In the Satipatthāna Sutta (D. 22. *Cf.* Warren, 'Buddhism in Transla-

The Jhāna of Foul Things may be developed in Sixteen Combinations.

[Here ends the Chapter on] Good in relation to the Universe of Form.

---

tion,' p. 353 *et seq.*; and M.I. 58) a system of nine Asubha-meditations is set out in terms somewhat different. In S. v. (pp. 129-131) five of the Asubhas, beginning with 'the skeleton' meditation, are prescribed in connexion with the sambhojjhangas of mindfulness and disinterestedness. And the same five are given in the Jhāna Vagga of A. i. 42 (*cf.* A. iii. 323). The ten here given are said in the Cy. (pp. 197-199) to be prescribed for such as were proved to be passionately affected by the beauty of the body—of the figure, skin, odour, firmness or continuity, plumpness, limbs and extremities, symmetry, adornment, identifying self with the body, or complacency in the possession of it (? kāye mamattaṃ; *cf.* S. N. 951), and teeth respectively. A dead body is not essential to this kind of mind-culture, the Cy. citing the cases of those Theras who obtained the requisite Jhāna by the glimpse of a person's teeth, or by the sight of a rājah on his elephant. The essential procedure lay in getting a clear and courageous grasp of the transience of any living organism.

[CHAPTER III.

Good in relation to the Universe of the Formless (a r ū p ā v a c a r a - k u s a l a ṃ).

The Four Jhānas connected with Formless Existence (c a t t ā r i a r ū p a j j h ā n ā n i).[1]

1. The Sphere of Unbounded Space (ā k ā s ā n a ñ c ā- y a t a n a ṃ).]

[265] Which are the states that are good?

---

[1] These often appear in the Nikāyas as the fourth to the seventh of the Eight Vimokhas or Deliverances (*cf.* §§ 248-250; Mahā Par. Sutta, p. 30; A. iv. 306). Though treated of in the Visuddhi Magga (chap. iii.), Buddhaghosa only makes comparison with the account of them given in the Vibhanga. In S. iii. 237, and frequently in the Majjhima, they occur in immediate sequence to the four Jhānas without any collective title, and not as concomitants of the Fourth Jhāna. There, too, the formulæ also have this slight variation from those in the present work, that the conscious attainment of each stage of abstraction is expressed by a brief proposition of identification, *e.g.*, a n a n t o ā k ā s o t i . . . n' a t t h i k i ñ c ī t i (It is boundless space! . . . There is nothing whatever!). The Cy. explains this by a curious quibble which is incidentally of interest (p. 204). It was the wish of the Buddha to carry out, as in previous procedure so in this, the study of the Four Objects of Thought [ā r a m m a ṇ ā n i; see above, *passim*, under (*d*)]. And the first of these is that one's object is 'limited.' But if the student, in attaining to an undifferentiated consciousness of unbounded space, *realize* its nature by the, so to speak, exclamatory thought, 'It is boundless!' he cannot logically proceed to consider it as limited. If I interpret Buddha-

When, that he may attain to the Formless heavens, he cultivates the way thereto, and so, by passing wholly beyond all consciousness of form, by the dying out of the consciousness of sensory reaction,[1] by turning the attention from any consciousness of the manifold,[2] he enters into and abides in that rapt meditation which is accompanied by the consciousness of a sphere of unbounded space—

---

ghosa aright, an interesting significance is hereby added to these parenthetical exclamations, which are not unfrequent in Buddhist philosophy. They seem to imply an act of conscious recognition.

[1] The student is to withdraw all interest in and attention to the world of rūpa, to cease so entirely to differentiate the *plenum* of external phenomena (including his own form) which impinge on his senses, that sensations cease, or resolve themselves into a homogeneous sense of extended vacuum. Paṭigho, rendered by sensory reaction, is explained to be sight-perception, sound-perception, smell, taste, and touch-perception. 'Thought is (here) not sustained by way of the five doors' (Asl. 201, 202). Hardest of all was it to abstract all attention from sounds. Āḷara Kālāma, one of Gotama's teachers, and proficient in these rapt states, at least so far as the sixth Vimokha (M. i. 164), was credited with the power of becoming so absorbed that he failed to see or hear hundreds of carts passing near him (Asl. 202). On the psycho-physiological use of paṭigho, see the theory of sense in the book on form, *infra*, § 597 *et seq*.

[2] Nānattasaññānaṃ amanasikārā. On the latter term, see above, p. 5, n. 1. Nānattaṃ is of rare occurrence in the Nikāyas; but see M. i. 3, where, in a series of concepts, it follows 'unity' and precedes 'the whole' (Neumann renders by *Vielheit*); also S. iv. 113, 114, where it is explained to refer to the various kinds of sensation, the corresponding viññāṇa, and the resulting feeling. In the Vibhanga, quoted by Buddhaghosa (p. 202), it is explained to mean cognition of the mutual diversity or dissimilarity (aññamaññaṃ asadisā) of nature in the eight kinds of good thoughts, the twelve bad thoughts (below, § 365), as well as in those ideas of good and bad results which are taken next to these. For cittāni, however, saññā is substituted, possibly limiting the application of the discernment of diversity to the sensuous basis.

even the Fourth Jhāna, to gain which[1] all sense of ease must have been put away, and all sense of ill must have been put away, and there must have been a dying out of the happiness and misery he was wont to feel—(the rapt meditation) which is imbued with disinterestedness, and where no ease is felt nor any ill, but only the perfect purity that comes of mindfulness and disinterestedness—then the contact, etc. . . . [*cf.* § 165] the balance that arises, these . . . are states that are good.

[2. The Sphere of Infinite Intellection (viññāṇañcāyatanaṃ).[2]]

[266] Which are the states that are good?

When, that he may attain to the Formless heavens, he cultivates the way thereto, and, having passed[3] wholly beyond the sphere of boundless space, enters into and abides in that rapt meditation which is accompanied by the

---

of all those 'thoughts.' The context, nevertheless, seems to point to a certain general, abstract, 're-representative' import in saññā as here applied. It is said to be the consciousness of one who is occupied with manodhātu or with manoviññāṇadhātu—with, let us say, representative or with re-representative cognition—with ideas or with cognition of those ideas. The ideation in this case is about sensuous phenomena as manifold, and the abstract nature of it lies, of course, in considering their diversity as such.

[1] In the text the formula of the Fourth Jhāna remains unaltered (*cf.* § 165). But it is sandwiched between the cumbrous adjectival compounds referring to space and to disinterestedness. Hence some modification was necessary to avoid uncouthness of diction.

[2] Strictly viññāṇānañcāyatanaṃ. The usually elided syllable (rūḷhi-saddo) is noticed in the Cy. (205).

[3] K., here and in the two following replies, has the gerund samatikkamma, following the usage in the Nikāyas (see, *e.g.*, D., M. P. S., 30; M. i. 174, 209; S. iii. 237, 238; A. iv. 306). Buddhaghosa apparently reads samatikkamā (205), as is the unvarying case in the first only of these four arūpajjhānas.

consciousness of a sphere of infinite intellection[1]—even the Fourth Jhāna, to gain which all sense of ease must have been put away, etc.

[*Continue as in previous section.*]

[3. The Sphere of Nothingness (ākiñcaññāyatanaṃ).]

[267] Which are the states that are good?

When, that he may attain to the Formless heavens, he cultivates the way thereto, and, having passed wholly beyond the sphere of infinite intellection, enters into and abides in that rapt meditation which is accompanied by the consciousness of a sphere of nothingness—even the Fourth Jhāna, to gain which all sense of ease must have been put away, etc.

[*Continue as in* § 265.]

[4. The Sphere where there is neither Perception nor Non-perception (neva-saññā-nāsaññāyatanaṃ).]

[268] Which are the states that are good?

When, that he may attain to the Formless heavens, he cultivates the way thereto, and, having passed wholly beyond the sphere of nothingness, enters into and abides in that rapt meditation which is accompanied by the consciousness of a sphere where there is neither perception nor non-perception[2]—even the Fourth Jhāna, to gain which all sense of ease must have been put away, etc.

[*Continue as in* § 265.]

---

[1] The only explanation given of a term on which one would gladly have heard Buddhaghosa expatiate is, 'There is no end for him in respect to that which has to be cogitated' (*lit.*, minded; manasikātabba-vasena) (Asl. 205). On the next stage, too (§ 267), no light at all is thrown (p. 206).

[2] Buddhaghosa explains this mental state as the cultivation of the functioning of the subtle residuum of conscious

The Four Jhānas connected with Formless Existence may be developed in sixteen combinations.

---

syntheses (saṅkhārāvasesa-sukhuma-bhāvaṃ). In so far as perception (presumably understood as being wholly introspective) has become incapable of effective functioning (paṭu-saññā-kiccaṃ), the state is non-perceptual. In so far as those faint, fine conscious reactions are maintained, the state is 'not non-perceptual.' This oscillation about a zero-point in consciousness is illustrated by the similes quoted (not from this Cy.) by Hardy (*op. cit.*, 264), namely, of the bowl containing just so much oil as suffices for cleansing purposes, but not to be poured out; also, of the little pool, sufficient to wet the feet, but too shallow for a bathe. Both oil and water exist, or do not exist, according to what action can be taken with respect to them. The Cy. adds that this liminal point obtains not only in saññā, but also in feeling, thought, and contact (208). The study of the 'threshold' of consciousness, and of the supra- and sub-liminal grades clustering about it, is familiar enough to the investigator in psychophysics. What is unfamiliar to us is the exploitation of the borderland of consciousness in the interests of ethical growth. Leibnitz might have found in the neva-saññā-nāsaññāyatanaṃ, had he had opportunity, the inspiration for his theory of *petites perceptions*.

[CHAPTER IV.

Degrees of Efficacy in Good relating to the Three Realms.

1. Good in relation to the Universe of Sense (kāmāvacarakusalaṃ).]

[269] Which are the states that are good?

When a good thought concerning the sensuous universe has arisen, which is (I.) accompanied by happiness and associated with knowledge—a thought which is

of inferior, or
of medium, or
of superlative efficacy,[1]

or the dominant influence in which is

desire, or
energy, or

---

[1] The effective power or karma of all the foregoing thoughts and exercises to modify the individual's existence in one universe or another for good seems to have been, for practical purposes, distinguished under three grades of efficacy. So I gather, at least, from the comment on this curious section (pp. 211, 212): '"inferior" (hīnaṃ) must be understood to mean paltry in respect of heaping up.' 'Heaping up' is in later books almost always associated with karma. Meaning to toil, more specifically to dig up, pile up, it is used to express the metaphorical notion of ever accumulating merit or demerit constituting the individual's potentiality in the way of rebirth. *Cf.* Mil. 109; also below, § 1059, n. 9, on 'she who toils.' The Paṭṭhāna may throw more light on the subject (Asl., *ibid.*).

[another] thought, or
investigation ;[1]
or the dominant influence in which is
desire of inferior,
of medium, or
of superlative efficacy ;
or the dominant influence in which is
energy of inferior,
of medium, or
of superlative efficacy ;
or the dominant influence in which is
[another] thought of inferior,
of medium, or
of superlative efficacy ;

---

[1] An explanation is also needed, it seems to me, for this association of the Four Iddhipādas (M. i. 103 ; A. iii. 82 ; S. v. 264-266) with this special aspect of karma ; for they lead to Arahatship rather than to rebirth in some other plane. The Cy. only states that when anyone, in the act of accumulating, relinquishes desire or the rest, 'that' is called inferior [in efficacy]; that when these four states are moderately or superlatively efficacious they are called accordingly ; and that 'when anyone has accumulated, having made desire (chando), *i.e.*, the wishing-to-do, his sovereign, chief and leader,' then the procedure is said to be under the dominant influence of desire. So for the other three.

It is to be regretted that the Cy. does not discuss the term vīmaṃsā (investigation), or the propriety of its position in this series of four. It would be interesting to have learnt its psychological import in relation to vitakko and vicāro. There is a suggestion of dual symmetry about the series: as chando is to viriyaṃ (conation passing into action), so is cittaṃ (the idea) to the discursive re-representative intellection of vīmamsā. I have rendered cittādhipateyyaṃ by the influence of *another* thought in accordance with the Cy. (213), where it is said to be an associated thought, or states associated with the original 'good thought.'

There is another brief comment on the adhipateyyas below, § 1034, n. 2.

or the dominant influence in which is
investigation of inferior,
of medium, or
of superlative efficacy,[1]
then the contact . . . the balance that arises—these . . . are states that are good.

[270] Which are the states that are good?

When a good thought concerning the sensuous universe has arisen which is (II.) accompanied by happiness, associated with knowledge, and prompted by a conscious motive . . .
or (III.) accompanied by happiness, and disconnected with knowledge . . .
or (IV.) accompanied by happiness, disconnected with knowledge, and prompted by a conscious motive . . .
or (V.) accompanied by disinterestedness, and associated with knowledge . . .
or (VI.) accompanied by disinterestedness, associated with knowledge, and prompted by a conscious motive . . .
or (VII.) accompanied by disinterestedness, and disconnected with knowledge . . .
or (VIII.) accompanied by disinterestedness, disconnected with knowledge, and prompted by a conscious motive—a thought which is of inferior . . .
or of medium . . .
or of superlative efficacy . . .

---

[1] The tabulated form adopted in this and following replies is intended not only to facilitate a conspectus of the system, but also to indicate the elision in the Pali (expressed by . . . p e . . .) of the repetition of the unvarying framework of the reply before and after each tabulated term. The Roman numerals in this and the next reply refer to the original statement of the 'Eight Main Types of Thought' in Chapter I. Apparently the sensuous basis of the ārammaṇaṃ of each thought is not intended to be here rehearsed.

or the dominant influence in which is
desire, or
energy, or
another thought;
or the dominant influence in which is
desire of inferior,
of medium, or
of superlative efficacy;
or the dominant influence in which is
energy of inferior,
of medium, or
of superlative efficacy;
or the dominant influence in which is
[another] thought of inferior,
of medium, or
of superlative efficacy;
then the contact . . . the balance that arises—these . . . are states that are good.[1]

2. Good in relation to the Universe of Form.

[271] Which are the states that are good?

When, that he may attain to the heavens of Form, he cultivates the way thereto, and, aloof from sensuous appetites, aloof from evil ideas, by earth-gazing enters into and abides in the First Jhāna (the first rapt meditation) . . . which is
of inferior.
or of medium,
or of superlative efficacy;

---

[1] In accordance with the usual procedure in the Dhamma Sangaṇi, when combining several subjects in one sentence, the final details apply only to the last subject in the series. Hence 'investigation' is omitted in connexion with Thought VIII., because, presumably, the latter is 'disconnected with knowledge.' And it would likewise have been omitted in connexion with Thoughts III., IV. and VII., but *not* in connexion with the others.

or the dominant influence in which is
desire, or
energy, or
a thought, or
investigation;
or the dominant influence in which is
desire . . . energy . . . a thought . . . investigation
of inferior,
of medium,
or of superlative efficacy—
then the contact . . . the balance that arises—these . . . are states that are good.

[272] *Repeat in the case of the other Jhānas, both of (a) and (b).*

3. Good in relation to the Formless Universe.

[273] Which are the states that are good?

When, that he may attain to the Formless heavens, he cultivates the way thereto, and so, by passing wholly beyond all consciousness of form, by the dying out of the consciousness of sensory reaction, by turning the attention from any consciousness of the manifold, he enters into and abides in that rapt meditation which is accompanied by the consciousness of a sphere of unbounded space—even into the Fourth Jhāna, to gain which all sense of ease must have been put away, etc.—(the rapt meditation) where there is neither ill nor ease, but only the perfect purity that comes of mindfulness and disinterestedness, and which is of
inferior . . .
medium . . .
or superlative efficacy . . .
or the dominant influence in which is
desire . . .
or energy . . .
or a thought . . .
or investigation . . .

or the dominant influence in which is
desire . . . energy . . . a thought . . . investigation
of inferior . . .
medium . . .
superlative efficacy—
then the contact . . . the balance that arises—these . . . are states that are good.

[274-276] *Here follow the three remaining* 'Jhānas connected with Formless Existence,' *each modified by the characteristics enumerated in the foregoing answer. Cf.* §§ 266-268.[1]

[1] In § 275 the text inadvertently omits majjhimaṃ . . . pe . . . panītaṃ . . . pe . . . before vīmaṃsādhipateyyaṃ.

[CHAPTER V.

Thought engaged upon the Higher Ideal (lokuttaraṃ cittaṃ).

I. THE FIRST PATH (paṭhamo maggo.)[1]

The Twenty Great Methods (vīsati mahānayā).

1. *Rapt Meditation* (jhānaṃ).

(i.) The Four Modes of Progress in Purification (suddhika-paṭipadā).]

[277] Which are the states that are good?

When he cultivates the Jhāna of the Higher Ideal (the rapt meditation), whereby there is a going forth and onward, making for the undoing of rebirth[2]—and when, that he

[1] That is to say, the first stage of the way or course of life leading to Arahatship or Nirvana. In the answers, bhūmi (Stage) is substituted for Path. And the 'First Bhūmi' is declared in the Cy. (pp. 214, 215) to be equivalent to the first-fruits (or fruition) of recluseship (*cf.* D. i., second sutta); in other words, to the fruit of sotāpatti, or of 'conversion,' as it has been termed.

[2] The special kind of Jhāna which he who has turned his back on the three lower ideals of life in the worlds of sense, form, or the formless, and has set his face steadfastly toward Arahatship, must 'practise, bring forth and develop,' is described by Buddhaghosa as being ekacittakkhaṇikaṃ appanā-jhānaṃ—rapt meditation on a concept induced by the momentary flash of a thought (*cf.* K. V., pp. 620, 458)—and by the text itself as niyyānikaṃ apacayagāmiṃ. The former of these two last terms is thus commented upon: 'It is a going forth (down from) the world, from the cycle of rebirth. Or, there is a going

may attain to the First Stage, he has put away views and opinions,[1] and so, aloof from sensuous appetites, aloof from evil ideas, enters into and abides in the First Jhāna, wherein conception works and thought discursive, which is born of solitude, is full of joy and ease, progress thereto being difficult and intuition sluggish—then there is contact, feeling, perception, thinking, thought, conception, discursive thought, joy, ease, self-collectedness, the faculties of faith, energy, mindfulness, concentration, wisdom, ideation, happiness, vitality, and *the faculty of believing, 'I shall come to know the unknown,'*[2] right views, right intention, *right speech, right action, right livelihood,*[3] right endeavour, right

---

forth by means of it. The man who is filled with it, comprehending Ill, goes forth, putting away the uprising (of Ill) goes forth, realizing the cessation (of Ill) goes forth, cultivating the path (leading to that cessation) goes forth.' And the latter term: This is *not* like that heaping together and multiplying of rebirth effected by the good which belongs to the three worlds of being. *This* is even as a man who, having heaped up a stockade eighteen cubits high, should afterwards take a great hammer and set to work to pull down and demolish his work. For so it, too, sets about pulling down and demolishing that potency for rebirth heaped up by the three-world-good, *by bringing about a deficiency in the causes thereof.*

[1] Diṭṭhigatāni, lit. resorting to views. All traditions or speculations adhered to either without evidence or on insufficient evidence, such as are implied in the states called 'theory of individuality, perplexity, and the contagion of mere rule and ritual' (Asl. 214; *infra*, §§ 1002-1005).

[2] The italics show those constituents of consciousness wherein this Jhāna differs from that mentioned in § 160, the constituents of which are identical with those of the First Type of Good Thought, § 1.

[3] These three factors of the 'Eightfold Path,' which were not explicitly included in the Eight Types of Good Thoughts, were, according to the Cy., included implicitly in the 'or-whatever-states.' See above, p. 5, n. 1. Here the Cy. only remarks that, whereas these three are now 'included in the Pali' because the Eightfold Path has Nirvana for its goal,

mindfulness, right concentration; the powers of faith, energy, mindfulness, concentration, wisdom, conscientiousness, the fear of blame; the absence of lust, hate, dulness, covetousness and malice, right views, conscientiousness, the fear of blame, serenity, lightness, plasticity, facility, fitness and directness in both sense and thought, mindfulness, intelligence, quiet, insight, grasp and balance.

Now these—or whatever other incorporeal, causally induced states there are on that occasion—these are states that are good.

[278-282] 'Contact,' 'feeling,' 'perception,' 'thinking,' *and* 'thought' *are described as in* §§ 2-6.

[283] What on that occasion is conception?

The ratiocination, the conception, which on that occasion is the disposition, the fixation, the focussing, the application of the mind, right intention, 'Path-component,' 'contained in the Path'[1]—this is the conception that there then is.

[284] 'Discursive thought' *is described as in* § 8.

[285] What on that occasion is joy?

The joy which on that occasion is gladness, rejoicing at, rejoicing over, mirth, merriment, felicity, exultation, transport of heart, the joy which is a factor in the Great Awakening[2]—this is the joy that there then is.

'pity' and 'sympathy' are not included because they have living beings for their object, and not Nirvana.

[1] The Path being the 'Eightfold Path,' 'conception' (vitakko) is reckoned as included in it, in virtue of its being approximately equivalent to 'intention' (sankappo).

[2] Pīti-sambojjhango. The seven Sambojjhangas are enumerated in A. iv. 23; S. v. 110, 111; and also in Mil. 340, where they are termed 'the jewel of the sevenfold wisdom of the Arahats.' On the state called sambodhi, see Rhys Davids, 'Dialogues of the Buddha,' i., pp. 190-192. It is in the Cy. (217) described as the harmony of its seven constituent states, and as forming the opposite to the detrimental compound consisting of the accumulations of adhesion (līnaṃ) and excitement, indulgence in the pleasures and satiety of sensuality, and addiction to the speculations of Nihilism and Eternalism (below, § 1003).

[286] 'Ease' *is described as in* § 10.

[287] What on that occasion is self-collectedness?

The stability, solidity, absorbed steadfastness of thought which on that occasion is the absence of distraction, balance, imperturbed mental procedure, quiet, the faculty and the power of concentration, right concentration, the concentration which is a factor in the Great Awakening, a 'Path-component,' 'contained in the Path'—this is the conception that there then is.

[288] 'Faith' *is described as in* § 12.

[289] What on that occasion is the faculty of energy?

The mental inception of energy which there is on that occasion, the striving and the onward effort, the exertion and endeavour, the zeal and ardour, the vigour and fortitude, the state of unfaltering effort, the state of sustained desire, the state of unflinching endurance, the solid grip of the burden, energy, energy as faculty and as power, right energy, the energy which is a factor in the Great Awakening, a Path-component, contained in the Path—this is the energy that there then is.

[290] What on that occasion is the faculty of mindfulness?

The mindfulness which on that occasion is recollecting, calling back to mind the mindfulness[1] which is remembering, bearing in mind, the opposite of superficiality and of obliviousness; mindfulness, mindfulness as faculty and as power, right mindfulness, the mindfulness which is a factor in the Great Awakening, a Path-component, contained in the Path—this is the mindfulness that there then is.

[291] 'Concentration' *is described in the same terms as* 'self-collectedness,' § 287.

The verb bujjhati is thus paraphrased: He arises from the slumber of vice, or discerns the four Noble Truths, or realizes Nirvana.

[1] Sati, repeated as in § 14, has dropped out of the printed text. K. repeats it.

[292] What on that occasion is the faculty of wisdom?

The wisdom which there is on that occasion is understanding, search, research, searching the Truth, discernment, discrimination, differentiation, erudition, proficiency, subtlety, criticism, reflection, analysis, breadth, sagacity, leading, insight, intelligence, incitement, wisdom as faculty and as power, wisdom as a sword, as a height, as light, as glory, as splendour, as a precious stone; the absence of dulness, searching the Truth, right views, that searching the Truth which is a factor in the Great Awakening,[1] a Path-component, contained in the Path—this is the wisdom that there then is.

[293-295] *The faculties of* 'ideation,' 'happiness,' *and* 'vitality' *are described as in* §§ 17-19.

[296] What on that occasion is the faculty of believing, 'I shall come to know the unknown' (anaññātaññassāmītindriyaṃ)?[2]

The wisdom that makes for the realization of those Truths[3] that are unrealized, uncomprehended, unattained

---

[1] Under the name of Dhammavicayo, searching the truth, or doctrine, or religion.

[2] According to Buddhaghosa (216), the inspiring sense of assurance that dawns upon the earnest, uncompromising student that he will come to know the doctrine of the great truths—that Ambrosial Way unknown in the cycle of worldly pursuits and consequences where the goal is not ambrosial—is to him as the upspringing of a new faculty or moral principle.

[3] Tesaṃ dhammānaṃ . . . sacchikiriyāya paññā, etc., which may more literally be rendered the wisdom (or understanding, etc.) of, for, or from, the realization of, etc. 'Bringing right opposite the eyes' is the paraphrase (Asl. 218). The student while 'in the First Path' learns the full import of those concise formulæ known as the Four Noble Truths, which the Buddha set forth in his first authoritative utterance. Previously he will have had mere second-hand knowledge of them; and as one coming to a dwelling out of his usual beat, and receiving fresh garland and raiment and food, realizes that he is encountering new

to, undiscerned, unknown—the wisdom that is understanding, search, research, searching the Truth, etc.

[*Continue as in* § 292.]

[297] What on that occasion are right views?

Answer as for 'wisdom,' § 292.

[298] 'Right intention' *is described in the same terms as* 'conception,' § 283.

[299] What on that occasion is right speech (sammā-vācā)?

To renounce on that occasion, abstain and refrain from, and feel averse to, the four errors of speech,[1] to leave them uncommitted and undone, to incur no guilt, nor to trespass nor transgress with respect to them, to destroy the causeway leading to them[2]—right speech, a Path-component, contained in the Path—this is the right speech that there then is.

[300] What on that occasion is right action (sammā-kammanto)?

To renounce on that occasion, abstain and refrain from, and feel averse to, the three errors of conduct,[3] to leave them uncommitted and undone, to incur no guilt, nor to trespass nor transgress with respect to them, to destroy the causeway leading to them—right conduct, a Path-component, contained in the Path—this is the right conduct that there then is.

[301] What on that occasion is right livelihood (sammā-ājīvo)?

To renounce on that occasion, abstain and refrain from, and feel averse to, wrong modes of livelihood, to leave them

---

experiences, so are these truths, not known hitherto by him, spoken of as 'unknown' (Asl. 218).

[1] That is, lying, slander, rude speech and frivolous talk. See the Cūla Sīla, *e.g.*, in D. i. 4.

[2] Setughāto, *i.e.*, the cause or condition of evil speaking—namely, lust, hate and dulness (Asl. 219). The metaphor occurs in A. i. 220, 221, 261; ii. 145, 146.

[3] That is, murder (of *any* living thing), theft and unchastity. D. i. 4.

unpractised and undone, to incur no guilt, nor to trespass nor transgress with respect to them, to destroy the causeway leading to them—right livelihood, a Path-component, contained in the Path—this is the right livelihood that there then is.

[302-304] 'Right endeavour,' 'right mindfulness,' 'right concentration,'[1] *are described as in* §§ 289-291.

[305-311] *The* 'powers' *of* 'faith,' 'energy,' 'mindfulness,' 'concentration' *and* 'wisdom' *are described as in* §§ 288-292; *those of* 'conscientiousness' *and* 'the fear of blame' *as in* §§ 30, 31.

[312-319] 'The absence of lust' *and* 'the absence of hate' *are described as in* §§ 32, 33; 'the absence of dulness' *as in* § 309 ('wisdom'); 'the absence of covetousness' *and* 'the absence of malice' *are described as in* §§ 35, 36; 'conscientiousness' *and* 'the fear of blame' *as in* §§ 38, 39; 'right views' *as in* § 292 *or* 309 ('wisdom').

[320] What on that occasion is serenity of sense?

The serenity, the composure which there is on that occasion, the calming, the tranquillizing, the tranquillity of the skandhas of feeling, perception and syntheses, the serenity which is a factor in the Great Awakening—this is the serenity of sense that there then is.

[321] What on that occasion is serenity of thought?

The serenity, the composure which there is on that occasion, the calming, the tranquillizing, the tranquillity of the skandha of intellect, the serenity which is a factor in the Great Awakening—this is the serenity of thought that there then is.

[322-331] *The remaining five attributes characterizing both sense and thought* 'on that occasion':—'buoyancy,' 'plasticity,' etc.—*are described as in* §§ 42-51.

[332-337] 'Mindfulness,' 'intelligence,' 'quiet,' 'insight,' 'grasp' and 'balance' *are described as in* §§ 290, 292 ('wisdom'), 291, 292, 289 ('energy') *and* 291 *respectively.*

---

[1] Samādhi, before sambojjhango, has dropped out of the printed text.

These, or whatever other incorporeal, causally induced states there are on that occasion—these are states that are good.

[Summary.]

[337*a*] Now at that time
the skandhas are four,
the spheres are two,
the elements are two,
the nutriments are three,
the faculties are nine,
the Jhāna is fivefold,
the Path is eightfold,
the powers are seven,
the causes are three,
contact,
feeling,
perception,
thinking,
thought,
} are each single [factors];
the skandhas of
feeling,
perception,
syntheses,
intellect,
} are each single [factors];
the sphere of ideation,
the faculty of ideation,
the element of representative intellection,
the sphere of a [representative] state,
the element of a [representative] state,
} are each single [factors].

These, or whatever other incorporeal, causally induced states there are on that occasion—these are states that are good.

* * * * * *

[*Here the questions and answers concerning the first two of the four skandhas enumerated are to be understood to follow as in* §§ 59-61.]

[338] What on that occasion is the skandha of syntheses?

Contact,
thinking,[1]
conception,
discursive thought,
joy,
self-collectedness,
the faculties of
faith, concentration,
energy, wisdom,
mindfulness, vitality,
believing 'I shall come to know the unknown;'
right views, right livelihood,
right intention, right endeavour,
right speech, right mindfulness,
right action, right concentration;
the seven powers;[2]
the absence of
lust, hate and dulness;
the absence of
covetousness and malice,
right views;
conscientiousness, the fear of blame;
serenity, wieldiness,
buoyancy, fitness,
plasticity, directness
of sense and thought;
mindfulness and intelligence;
quiet and insight;
grasp and balance.

---

[1] The printed text has vedanā instead of cetanā, which is obviously wrong.
[2] These are set out in the original as in § 277.

These, or whatever other incorporeal, causally induced states there are on that occasion, exclusive of the skandhas of feeling, perception and intellect—these are the skandha of syntheses.

* * * * * *

[*Questions on the remaining items in the* 'Summary' *are understood to follow.*]

[340][1] Which are the states that are good?

When he cultivates the Jhāna of the Higher Ideal (the rapt meditation), whereby there is a going forth and onward, making for the undoing of rebirth—and when, that he may attain to the First Stage, he has put away views and opinions, and so, aloof from sensuous appetites, aloof from evil ideas, enters into and abides in the First Jhāna . . . progress thereto being difficult, but intuition quick . . .

[*or*] [341] . . . progress thereto being easy, but intuition sluggish . . .

[*or*] [342] . . . progress thereto being easy and intuition quick—then the contact . . . the balance that arises—these . . . are states that are good.

[343] *Repeat the Four Modes in the case of the 2nd to the 4th Jhāna on the Fourfold System, and of the 1st to the 5th Jhāna on the Fivefold System.*

[Here end] the Modes of Progress in Purification.

[(ii.) The Section on Emptiness (suññataṃ).[2]]

(*a* and *b*.)

[344] Which are the states that are good?

When he cultivates the Jhāna of the Higher Ideal (the

---

[1] The answer marked [339] in the text is merely a repetition of lokuttara-jhānaṃ as dukkhāpaṭipadaṃ dandhābhiññaṃ, *i.e.*, of the first 'Mode of Progress' given in [277]. I have therefore omitted it. No repetition is noticed in this connexion by the Cy. K. has no such repetition.

[2] Called in the Cy. (221) suññata-vāro, with the subsections suddhika-suññatā, or 'Emptiness applied to

rapt meditation), whereby there is a going forth and onward, making for the undoing of rebirth—and when, that he may attain to the First Stage, he has put away views and opinions, and so, aloof from sensuous appetites, aloof from evil ideas, enters into and abides in the First Jhāna, wherein conception works and thought discursive, which is born of solitude, is full of joy and ease, and which is EMPTY—then the contact . . . the balance that arises—these . . . are states that are good.

[345] *Repeat the 2nd to the 4th Jhanas on the Fourfold System, and the 1st to the 5th on the Fivefold System, with the addition in each case of the phrase* 'and which is EMPTY.'

[Here ends] the 'Emptiness' Section.

---

the purification-formula,' *i.e.*, the group marked (*a* and *b*), and suññata-paṭipadā, or 'the Modes of Progress taken in connexion with Emptiness,' *i.e.*, the group marked (*c*).

On the technical term 'emptiness,' see above, § 121, and Rhys Davids, 'Yogāvacara's Manual,' pp. xxvii, xxviii. Of the three 'riddles' there discussed—'the empty, the aimless and the signless'—only the first two are here prescribed for cultivation. Buddhaghosa argues on the subject at some length (Asl. 221-225). He explains that the three terms are so many names for the way to the Ideal (lokuttara-maggo), each throwing a special *aspect* of it into greater relief than the other two, while yet no advance can be made without all three concepts. The advent of the Path as a conscious ideal is especially characterized by insight into the fact that the sanskāras are *void* of a permanent soul, and of all that conduces to happiness. The virtue or quality of the Path, again, is wholly *empty* of lust, hate and dulness. So also is its object, namely, Nirvana. But the chief import of 'empty' is said to relate to the fact first named—the nonentity of any substratum or soul in anything. The 'aimless' applies chiefly to the insight into dukkhaṃ, or the nature of pain or ill. All aspiration or hankering after sanskāras withers up under the penetration of such insight. By it, too, the path of the Ideal becomes revealed. The third 'riddle,' the 'signless'—*i.e.*, the path conceived as free from the three signs or false tenets of Permanence, Sorrow and Soul—comes up for meditation later (§§ 506, 511, etc.).

[(*c*) The Modes of Progress, with 'Emptiness' as the Basis (suññata-mūlaka-paṭipadā).]

[346] Which are the states that are good?

When he cultivates the Jhāna of the Higher Ideal . . . and when, that he may attain to the First Stage, he . . . enters into and abides in the First Jhāna . . . progress thereto being difficult and intuition sluggish, the method being the concept of EMPTINESS—then the contact . . . the balance that arises—these . . . are states that are good.

[347-349] *Repeat the same formula, substituting in succession the three remaining Modes of Progress* (§§ 176-179), *with the addition in each case of the phrase* 'the method being the concept of EMPTINESS.'

[350] *Repeat the same formula, substituting in succession the remaining Jhānas on the Fourfold System and those on the Fivefold System, and applying in each case the Four Modes of Progress, with the additional phrase on* 'Emptiness.'

[(ii.) The Aimless (appaṇihitaṃ).

(*a* and *b*)].[1]

[351] Which are the states that are good?

When he cultivates the Jhāna of the Higher Ideal . . . and when, that he may attain to the First Stage, he . . . enters into and abides in the First Jhāna . . . which is born of solitude, is full of joy and ease, and which is AIMLESS—then the contact . . . the balance that arises—these . . . are states that are good.

[352] *Repeat the same formula, substituting the remaining three, and the five Jhānas in succession, with the addition in each case of the phrase* 'and which is AIMLESS.'

---

[1] As in the foregoing, the Cy. (*ibid.*) co-ordinates this, and the following section, with the two on 'emptiness,' calling (*a* and *b*) suddhika-appaṇihitā, and the next group appaṇihita-paṭipadā.

[(*c*) The Modes of Progress, with Aimlessness as the Basis (appaṇihita-mūlaka-paṭipadā).]

[353] When he cultivates the Jhāna of the Higher Ideal . . . and when, that he may attain to the First Stage of it, he . . . enters into and abides in the First Jhāna . . . progress whereto is difficult and intuition sluggish, the method being the concept of AIMLESSNESS—then the contact . . . the balance that arises—these . . . are states that are good.

[354-356] *Repeat the same formula, substituting in succession the three remaining Modes of Progress, with the addition in each case of the phrase* 'the method being the concept of AIMLESSNESS.'

[357] *Repeat the same formula, substituting in succession the remaining three, and the five Jhānas, and applying in each case the Four Modes of Progress, with the additional phrase on* 'Aimlessness.'

[2-20. The Remaining Nineteen Great Methods.]

[358] Which are the states that are good?

Here follow nineteen concepts, each of which can be substituted for 'the Jhāna of the Higher Ideal' *in the preceding* 81 *answers* [§§ 277-357], *as a vehicle in training the mind for Arahatship. They are as follows:*

2. The Path of the Higher Ideal.
3. The Advance in Mindfulness[1] toward the Higher Ideal.
4. The System of Right Efforts[2] toward the Higher Ideal.
5. The Series of Mystic Potencies[3] applied to the Higher Ideal.
6. The Faculty relating to the Higher Ideal.
7. The Power relating to the Higher Ideal.

---

[1] Satipaṭṭhāna. M. i. 56.
[2] Sammappadhāna. See below, § 1367.
[3] Iddhipāda. See above, § 273 *et seq.*

8. The Great Awakening to the Higher Ideal.
9. The Truth of the Higher Ideal.
10. The Peace[1] of the Higher Ideal.
11. The Doctrine of the Higher Ideal.
12. The Skandha related to the Higher Ideal.
13. The Sphere of the Higher Ideal.
14. The Element of the Higher Ideal.
15. The Nutriment of the Higher Ideal.
16. Contact with the Higher Ideal.
17. Feeling relating to the Higher Ideal.
18. Perception relating to the Higher Ideal.
19. Thinking relating to the Higher Ideal.
20. Thought relating to the Higher Ideal.

[The Dominant Influences in the Modes of Progress (adhipaṭi).]

[359] Which are the states that are good?

When he cultivates the Jhāna of the Higher Ideal . . . and when, that he may attain to the First Stage, he . . . enters into and abides in the First Jhāna . . . progress whereto is painful and intuition sluggish, and the dominant influence in which is desire, energy, a thought, or investigation, then the contact . . . the balance that arises—these are states that are good.

[360] *Repeat this formula in the case of the remaining three and five Jhānas.*

[361] *Repeat the foregoing* [§§ 359, 360] *in the case of each of the nineteen remaining* 'Great Methods.'

[Here ends] the First Path.

II. The Second Path.

[362] Which are the states that are good?

When he cultivates the Jhāna of the Higher Ideal (the rapt meditation), whereby there is a going forth and onward, making for the undoing of rebirth—and when, that he may

[1] Samatho. See above, § 54.

attain to the Second Stage, he has diminished the strength of sensual passions and of malice,[1] and so, aloof from sensuous appetites, aloof from evil ideas, enters into and abides in the First Jhāna . . . progress whereto is difficult and intuition sluggish—then the contact . . . the faculty of knowledge made perfect[2] . . . the balance that arises—these . . . are states that are good.

* * * * * *

[Here ends] the SECOND PATH.

III. THE THIRD PATH.

[363] Which are the states that are good?

When he cultivates the Jhāna of the Higher Ideal (the rapt meditation), whereby there is a going forth and onward, making for the undoing of rebirth—and when, that he may attain to the THIRD STAGE, he has put away the entire residuum of sensual passions and of malice,[3] and so,

---

[1] *Cf.* D. i. 156 and M. P. S. 16, 17. It is striking that here and in the following answer no diminution of moho (dulness) is included. *Cf.*, however, below, § 1134. Ignorance (=dulness) is only really conquered in the Fourth Path. The diminution is described (Asl. 238) as coming to pass in two ways: vicious dispositions arise occasionally and no longer habitually, and when they do arise it is with an attenuated intensity. They are like the sparse blades of grass in a newly-mown field, and like a flimsy membrane or a fly's wing.

[2] *Cf.* § 296. The faith and hope of the Sotāpatti, or student of the First Path, while struggling with the limitations of his stage of knowledge (ñātamariyādaṃ, the Cy. calls them, p. 239), are now rewarded by his attainment, as a Sakadagāmī, of that deepening philosophic insight into the full implication of the 'Four Truths' termed aññā, or knowledge *par excellence*, and applied, in Buddhist writings, only to evolving or evolved Arahatship. *Cf.* below, § 555.

[3] These, which the Cy., in connexion with the Second Path, termed collectively kilesā, are now referred to as saññojanāni. See § 1229 *et seq.* and § 1113 *et seq.*

aloof from sensuous appetites, aloof from evil ideas, enters into and abides in the First Jhāna . . . progress whereto is difficult and intuition sluggish—then the contact . . . the faculty of knowledge made perfect . . . the balance that arises—these . . . states that are good.

[Here ends] the THIRD PATH.

IV. THE FOURTH PATH.

[364] Which are the states that are good?

When he cultivates the Jhāna of the Higher Ideal (the rapt meditation), whereby there is a going forth and onward, making for the undoing of rebirth, and when, that he may attain the FOURTH STAGE, he has put away absolutely and entirely all passion for Form, all passion for the Formless, all conceit, excitement and ignorance, and so, aloof from sensuous appetites, aloof from evil ideas, enters into and abides in the First Jhāna . . . progress whereto is difficult and intuition sluggish—then the contact . . . the faculty of knowledge made perfect . . . the balance that arises—these . . . are states that are good.

[364*a*] What on that occasion is the faculty of knowledge made perfect (a ñ ñ i n d r i y a ṃ)?

The wisdom that makes for the realization of those truths that have been realized, comprehended, attained to, discerned and known—the wisdom that is understanding, search, research, searching the Truth, etc.

[*Continue as in* § 292.]

* * * * * *

These, or whatever other incorporeal, causally induced states there are on that occasion, these are states that are good.

[Here ends] the FOURTH PATH.

[Here ends] Thought engaged upon the Higher Ideal.

[PART II.—BAD STATES OF CONSCIOUSNESS.

Chapter VI.

The Twelve Bad Thoughts (dvādasa akusalacittāni).]

I.

[365] Which are the states that are bad?[1]

When a bad thought has arisen, which is accompanied by happiness, and associated with views and opinions,[2] and has as its object a sight, a sound, a smell, a taste,[3] a touch, a [mental] state, or what not, then there is

contact,
feeling,
perception,
thinking,
thought,
conception,
discursive thought,
joy,

---

[1] In this connexion those constituents of the twelve thoughts which in themselves are ethically neutral are to be understood as unchanged in the connotation assigned them in connexion with good thoughts. There being for bad thoughts no other sphere of existence save the sensuous universe, this is to be understood throughout (Asl. 247).

[2] Diṭṭhigata-sampayuttaṃ. *Cf.* p. 83, n. 1, with §§ 381, 1003.

[3] Rasārammaṇaṃ vā is inadvertently omitted in the printed text.

ease,
self-collectedness;[1]
the faculties of
energy,
concentration,[2]
ideation,
happiness,
vitality;
wrong views,
wrong intention,
wrong endeavour,
wrong concentration;
the powers of
energy,
concentration,
unconscientiousness,
disregard of blame;
lust, covetousness,
dulness,[3] wrong views,
unconscientiousness,
disregard of blame,

---

[1] See following note.

[2] Concentration of mind is essential to the higher life of Buddhism; nevertheless, so far is it from constituting excellence, that it is also an essential to effective evil-doing. If the mind be undistracted, says Buddhaghosa, the murderer's knife does not miss, the theft does not miscarry, and by a mind of single intent (lit., of one taste) evil conduct is carried out (Asl. 248). *Cf.* the Hebrew idiom rendered by 'the heart being set'—to do good or evil (Eccles. viii. 11; Ps. lxxviii. 8).

[3] Hate (doso) and malice (vyāpādo) do not find a place among the factors of Bad Thoughts (corresponding to the place occupied by their opposites in the Good Thoughts, § 1) till we come to the last four types of bad thoughts. Whereas these are accompanied by melancholy (domanassaṃ), the subject of the first and the following three types of thought is a cheerful sinner. Joy, ease, happiness, were held to be incompatible with hate.

quiet,
grasp,[1]
balance.

Now, these—or whatever other incorporeal, causally induced states that there are on that occasion—these are states that are bad.[2]

[366-370] What on that occasion is contact . . . feeling . . . perception . . . thinking . . . thought?

Answers as in §§ 2-6 *respectively.*

[371] What on that occasion is conception?

Answer as in § 7, *substituting* 'wrong intention' (micchāsankappo) for 'right intention.'

[372-374] What on that occasion is discursive thought . . . joy . . . ease?

Answers as in §§ 8-10 *respectively.*

[375] What on that occasion is self-collectedness?

Answer as in § 11, *substituting* 'wrong concentration' *for* 'right concentration.'

[376] What on that occasion is the faculty of energy?

Answer as in § 13, *substituting* 'wrong endeavour' *for* 'right endeavour.'

[377] What on that occasion is the faculty of concentration?

Answer as in § 375.

---

[1] Vipassanā (insight) has been erroneously included in the text. Moral insight was as incompatible with immoral thoughts to the Buddhist as it was to Socrates and Plato. Hence also 'wisdom' and 'mindfulness' are excluded, as well as 'faith.' The Cy. rules that the followers of heretical dogmas and mere opinion can have but a spurious faith in their teachers, can only be mindful of bad thoughts, and can only cultivate deceit and delusion. Nor can there possibly be that sixfold efficiency of sense and thought which is concomitant with good thoughts (§§ 40-51). Asl. 249.

[2] Kusalā in the text is, of course, a slip. There are in all these Bad Thoughts ten 'whatever-other' states: desire, resolve, attention, conceit, envy (issā, or read icchā, longing), meanness, stolidity, torpor, excitement, worry (Asl. 250). See above, p. 5, n. 1.

[378-380] What on that occasion is the faculty of ideation . . . happiness . . . vitality?

Answers as in §§ 17-19 respectively.

[381] What on that occasion are wrong views (micchādiṭṭhi)?[1]

The views which on that occasion are a walking in opinion, the jungle of opinion,[2] the wilderness of opinion,[3] the puppet-show of opinion,[4] the scuffling of opinion,[5] the Fetter of opinion,[6] the grip[7] and tenacity[8] of it, the inclination towards it,[9] the being infected by it, a by-path, a wrong road, wrongness, the 'fording place,'[10] shiftiness of grasp—these are the wrong views that there then are.

---

[1] Micchādiṭṭhi is defined in the Cy. (p. 248) as ayāthāvadassanaṃ, seeing things as they are not. (On diṭṭhi, see § 1003, n.) Sixty-two kinds of this perverted vision, or ill-grounded speculation are distinguished in the Brahmajāla Sutta (D. i.), all of them being theories of existence, and are alluded to by the commentator (p. 252). *Cf.* Rhys Davids, 'American Lectures,' p. 27 *et seq.*

[2] Because of the difficulty of getting out of it, as out of a grass, forest, or mountain jungle (Asl., *ibid.*).

[3] Because of the danger and fearsomeness of indulging in such opinions, as of a desert beset with robbers and snakes, barren of water or food (*ibid.*).

[4] Buddhaghosa does not derive this term from visūkaṃ, but from visu-kāyikaṃ = antithetically constituted—*i.e.*, to sammādiṭṭhi.

[5] The disorder and struggle through some being Annihilationists, some Eternalists, etc. (Asl. 253).

[6] See § 1113.

[7] The obsession by some object of thought, like the grip of a crocodile (Asl. 253).

[8] The text of the Cy. reads patiṭṭhāho for paṭiggāho. K., however, reads patiggāho.

[9] *I.e.*, towards the fallacious opinion of Permanence, etc. (Asl. 253).

[10] Titthāyatanaṃ. It is impossible to get an English equivalent for this metaphor, which literally means only a standing-place, but which is usually, in its first intention, associated with a shallow river-strand or seashore, and, in

[382-384] What on that occasion is wrong intention . . wrong endeavour . . . wrong concentration?

Answers as in §§ 371, 376, 375 *respectively.*

[385, 386] What on that occasion is the power of energy . . . the power of concentration?

Answers as in §§ 383, 384 *respectively.*

[387] What on that occasion is the power of unconscientiousness (ahirikabalaṃ)?

The absence which there is on that occasion of any feeling of conscientious scruple when scruples ought to be felt, the absence of conscientious scruple at attaining to bad and evil states—this is the power of unconscientiousness that there then is.

[388] What on that occasion is the power of disregard of blame (anottappabalaṃ)?

The absence which there is on that occasion of any sense of guilt where a sense of guilt ought to be felt, the absence[1] of a sense of guilt at attaining to bad and evil states—this is the power of disregard of blame that there then is.

[389] What on that occasion is lust?

The lust, lusting, lustfulness which there is on that occasion, the infatuation, the feeling and being infatuated, the covetousness, the lust that is the root of badness—this is the lust that there then is.

[390] What on that occasion is dulness?

The lack of knowledge, of vision, which there is on that occasion; the lack of co-ordination, of judgment, of wakefulness,[2] of penetration; the inability to comprehend, to grasp thoroughly; the inability to compare, to consider,

---

its second, with sectarian speculative beliefs and the teaching of them. Buddhaghosa himself gives an alternative connotation: (*a*) 'where the foolish, in the course of their gyrations (? *i.e.*, samsāra) cross over'; (*b*) the region or home of sectarians (titthiyā). *Cf.* the use of the term in M. i. 483.

[1] Na has here dropped out of the printed text.

[2] Sambodho. *Cf.* § 285.

to demonstrate; the folly, the childishness, the lack of intelligence; the dulness that is vagueness, obfuscation, ignorance, the Flood[1] of ignorance, the Bond of ignorance, the bias of ignorance, the obsession of ignorance, the barrier of ignorance; the dulness that is the root of badness—this the dulness that there then is.

[391-397] What on that occasion is covetousness . . . are wrong views . . . is unconscientiousness . . . disregard of blame . . . quiet . . . grasp . . . balance?

Answers as in §§ 389, 381, 387, 388, 375, 376, *and, again,* 375 *respectively.*

Or whatever other incorporeal, causally induced states there are on that occasion—these are states that are bad.

[Summary.]

[397*a*] Now, on that occasion
the skandhas are four,
the spheres are two,
the elements are two,
the nutriments are three,
the faculties are five,
the Jhāna is fivefold,
the Path is fourfold,
the powers are four,
the causes are two,[2]
contact, } are each single [factors];
etc. } etc.

[*Continue as in* § 58.]

* * * * * *

---

[1] On ignorance as a Flood and as a Bond, see below, §§ 1151, 1151*a*.

Whereas the mark (lakkhanaṃ) of lust is the seizing on an object in idea, it is the essence (raso) of dulness to cover up the real nature of that object, with the result that the attention devoted to it is of a superficial nature (ayoniso). Asl. 249.

[2] Namely, 'lust' and 'dulness.'

[398] What on that occasion is the skandha of syntheses?

Contact,
thinking,
conception,
discursive thought,
joy,
self-collectedness;
the faculties of
energy,
concentration,
vitality;
wrong views,
wrong intention,
wrong endeavour,
wrong concentration;
the powers of
energy,
concentration,
unconscientiousness,
disregard of blame;
lust, covetousness,
dulness; wrong views;
unconscientiousness,
disregard of blame;
quiet,
grasp,
balance.

These, or whatever other incorporeal, causally induced states there are on that occasion, exclusive of the skandhas of feeling, perception and intellect—these are the skandha of syntheses.

[*Continue as in* § 58.]

* * * * * *

II.

[399] Which are the states that are bad?

When a bad thought has arisen which is accompanied

by pleasure, associated with views and opinions, and prompted by a conscious motive,[1] and which has as its object a sight . . . or what not, then there is contact . . . balance . . .

[*Continue as in the First Thought,* § 365.]

III.

[400] Which are the states that are bad?

When a bad thought has arisen which is accompanied by happiness and disconnected with views and opinions, and which has as its object a sight, a sound, a smell, a taste, a touch, or what not, then there is contact, etc.

[*Continue as in the first Bad Thought, but omitting the single, twice enumerated item* 'wrong views.'][2]

[Summary.]

[400*a*] Now, at that time
the skandhas are four,
the spheres are two,

---

[1] The Cy. instances the case of a young man who, being refused the hand of the daughter of some false doctrinaire on the ground of his being of a different communion, is prompted by his affections to frequent the church of the girl's people and to adopt their views, thus gaining his reward (Asl. 255).

[2] Somanassindriyaṃ, bracketed in the text, must, of course, be included. The Cy. instances the frame of mind of those who are indulging in 'worldly pleasures,' such as public sports and dances, and at village festivals (ṇatasamajjādīni). *Cf.* 'Dialogues of the Buddha,' I., p. 7, n. 4.

It is difficult to interpret the concisely and obscurely worded double illustration given in the Cy. (p. 257) of this type of thought. The same circumstances are supposed as in the Third Thought, with the added low-class delights of horse-play and vulgar curiosity.

the elements are two,
the nutriments are three,
the faculties are five,
the Jhāna is fivefold,
the Path is threefold,
etc., etc.

[*Continue as in* § 58.]

* * * * * *

[401] What on that occasion is the skandha of syntheses?

Answer as in § 398, *omitting* 'wrong views.'

IV.

[402] Which are the states that are bad?

When a bad thought has arisen which is accompanied by pleasure, disconnected with views and opinions, and prompted by a conscious motive, and which has as its object a sight . . . or what not, then there is contact . . . balance . . .

[*Continue as in the Third Thought,* § 400.]

V.

[403] Which are the states that are bad?

When a bad thought has arisen which is accompanied by disinterestedness, and associated with views and opinions, and has as its object a sight, a sound, a smell, a taste, a touch, a [mental] state, or what not, then there is

contact, thought,
feeling, conception,
perception, discursive thought,
thinking, disinterestedness,
self-collectedness;
the faculties of
energy,

concentration,
ideation;
disinterestedness,
vitality;
wrong views,
wrong intention,
wrong endeavour,
wrong concentration;
the powers of
energy,
concentration,
unconscientiousness,
disregard of blame;
lust, covetousness,
dulness; wrong views;
unconscientiousness,
disregard of blame,
composure,
grasp,
balance.

These, or whatever other incorporeal, causally induced states there are on that occasion—these are states that are bad.

[404-407] *Questions and answers on* 'contact,' 'feeling,' 'disinterestedness,' *and* 'the faculty of disinterestedness' *identical with those in* §§ 151-154.

* * * * * *

[Summary.]

[407*a*] Now, at that time
the skandhas are four,
etc.,
the faculties are five,
the Jhāna is fourfold,[1]

---

[1] *Cf.* § 154*a*.

the Path is fourfold,
etc.
[*Continue as in* § 58.]

* * * * * *

[408] What on that occasion is the skandha of syntheses?

Contact,
thinking,
conception,
discursive thought,
self-collectedness,
etc.

[*Continue as in* § 398, 'joy' *having been omitted as incompatible with* 'disinterestedness.']

* * * * * *

VI.

[409] Which are the states that are bad?

When a bad thought has arisen which is accompanied by disinterestedness, associated with views and opinions, and prompted by a conscious motive, and which has as its object a sight . . . or what not, then there is contact, etc.

[*Continue as in Thought V.*]

* * * * * *

VII.

[410] Which are the states that are bad?

When a bad thought has arisen which is accompanied by disinterestedness, and disconnected with views and opinions, and which has as its object a sight . . . or what not, then there is contact, etc.

[*Continue as in Thought V., omitting* 'wrong views.']

* * * * * *

[Summary.]

[410*a*] Now at that time
the skandhas are four,
etc.,
the faculties are five,
the Jhāna is fourfold,
the Path is threefold,
etc.

[*Continue as in* § 397*a*.]

* * * * * *

[411] What on that occasion is the skandha of syntheses?

Answer as in § 398, *omitting both* 'joy' *and* 'wrong views.'

* * * * * *

VIII.

[412] Which are the states that are bad?

Answer as in Thought VII., with the additional factor, inserted as in Thoughts II., IV., VI., of 'prompted by a conscious motive.'[1]

IX.

[413] Which are the states that are bad?

When a bad thought has arisen which is accompanied by melancholy and associated with repugnance,[2] and which has as its object a sight, a sound, a smell, a taste, a touch, a mental state, or what not, then there is
contact,
feeling,
perception,

---

[1] The Cy. gives no illustrations of this or the three preceding types of thought.

[2] Paṭigho, used (§ 1060) to describe doso, and again (§ 597 *et seq.*) in connexion with sense-stimulation, as 'reaction.'

thinking,
thought,
conception,
discursive thought,
distress,
self-collectedness;
the faculties of
energy,
concentration,
ideation,
melancholy,
vitality;
wrong intention,
wrong endeavour,
wrong concentration;
the powers of
energy,
concentration,
unconscientiousness,
disregard of blame;
hate,
dulness;
malice;
unconscientiousness,
disregard of blame,
quiet,
grasp,
balance.

These, or whatever other incorporeal, causally induced states there are on that occasion—these are states that are bad.

[414] *The question and answer on* 'contact,' § 2.

[415] What on that occasion is feeling?

The mental pain, the mental distress (d u k k h a ṃ), which, on that occasion, is born of contact with the appropriate element of representative intellection; the painful, distressful sensation which is born of contact with thought;

the painful, distressful feeling which is born of contact with thought—this is the distress that there then is.

[416, 417] What on that occasion is distress (dukkhaṃ) . . . the faculty of melancholy (domanassindriyaṃ)?

Answers as for 'feeling' *in* § 415, omitting 'with the appropriate element of representative intellection.'

* * * * * *

[418] What on that occasion is hate?

The hate, hating, hatred which on that occasion is a disordered temper, the getting upset,[1] opposition, hostility, churlishness,[2] abruptness,[3] disgust of heart—this is the hate that there then is.

[419] What on that occasion is malice?

Answer as for 'hate.'

* * * * * *

Or whatever other incorporeal, causally induced states there are on that occasion—these are states that are bad.

---

[1] Vyāpatti, vyāpajjanā. *Cf.* § 1060, n. 5. Here the comment is pakatibhāva-vijahanaṭṭhena = throwing off a normal state (Asl. 258). 'Like gruel that has gone bad' (Sum., l. 211).

[2] Caṇḍikkaṃ. See J. P. T. S., 1891, p. 17; P. P. ii. 1 (= ii. 11). Smp. 297. Morris thinks caṇḍittaṃ is the right spelling. I incline to hold that the *lectio difficilior* is more likely to be correct. The Cy. in four passages spells with kk. K., by an oversight, has caṇḍittaṃ in the present passage, but kk in §§ 1060, 1314.

[3] Asuropo. Refers, according to the Cy. (258), to the broken utterance of a man in a rage.

It is not a little curious that such constituents as 'self-collectedness,' 'quiet' and 'balance' should not be found incompatible with hate as described above. 'Concentration' is less incompatible, and it must be remembered that all three states are described in the same terms. Hence, if one stands, the others cannot fall. But see under Thoughts X. and XII.

[Summary.]

[419*a*] Now, on that occasion
the skandhas are four,
etc.,
the faculties are five,
the Jhāna is fourfold,
the Path is threefold,
the powers are four,
the causes are two,[1]
etc.

[*Continue as in* §§ 58-61.]

* * * * * *

[420] What on that occasion is the skandha of syntheses?

Contact,
thinking,
conception,
discursive thought,
self-collectedness;
the faculties of
energy,
concentration,
vitality;
wrong intention,
wrong endeavour,
wrong concentration;
the powers of
energy,
concentration,
unconscientiousness,
disregard of blame;
hate,
dulness;

---

[1] Namely, doso and moho.

malice;
unconscientiousness,
disregard of blame,
quiet,
grasp,
balance.

These, or whatever other incorporeal, causally induced states there are on that occasion, exclusive of the skandhas of feeling, perception and intellect—these are the skandha of syntheses.

* * * * * *

X.

[421] Which are the states that are bad?

When a bad thought has arisen which is accompanied by melancholy, associated with repugnance, and prompted by a conscious motive, and which has as its object a sight . . . or what not, then there is contact, etc.

[*Continue as in Thought IX.*]

* * * * * *

XI.

[422] Which are the states that are bad?

When a bad thought has arisen which is accompanied by disinterestedness and associated with perplexity, and which has as its object a sight, a sound, a smell, a taste, a touch, a mental state, or what not, then there is

contact,
feeling,
perception,
thinking,
thought,
conception,

8

discursive thought,
disinterestedness,
self-collectedness;
the faculties of
energy, disinterestedness,
ideation, vitality;
wrong intention,
wrong endeavour;
the powers of
energy,
unconscientiousness,
disregard of blame;
perplexity;
dulness;
unconscientiousness,
disregard of blame,
grasp.

These, or whatever other incorporeal, causally induced states there are on that occasion—these are states that are bad.

[423] What on that occasion is contact?

The usual formula.

* * * * * *

[424] What on that occasion is self-collectedness?

The sustaining of thought which there is on that occasion[1]—this is the self-collectedness that there then is.

* * * * * *

[1] Buddhaghosa says on this passage (Asl. 259): 'Inasmuch as this weak form of thought has only the capacity of keeping going, or persisting (pavatti ṭhitimattakaṃ'), none of the other features of 'self-collectedness' are here applied to it. It is clear, therefore, that the '. . . pe . . .' after ṭhiti in the text is a mistake. And *cf.* K. 'Concentration,' it will be noticed, as well as 'quiet' and 'balance,' are entirely omitted.

[425] What on that occasion is perplexity (vicikicchā)?[1]

The doubt, the hesitating, the dubiety, which on that

---

[1] It is tempting to render vicikicchā by 'doubt.' It would not be incorrect to do so. The dual state of mind which is the etymological basis of *dou-bt* is shown in two of the terms selected to describe the word. Again, the objects of vicikicchā, as given in § 1004, are those to which the term 'doubt,' in its ethico-religious sense, might well be applied. But there are features in which the Buddhist attitude of vicikicchā does not coincide with doubt as usually understood in the West. Doubt is the contrary of belief, confidence, or faith. Now, the approximate equivalents of the latter—saddhā and pasādo—are not alluded to in the answer, as they might be, for the purpose of contrast. Again, though this by itself is also no adequate ground for not matching the two terms in question, the etymology of the words is very different. There is nothing of the dual, divided state of mind in the structure of vicikicchā as there is in that of 'doubt.' Cikit is the desiderative or frequentative of cit, to think; vi, the prefix, indicating either intensive or distracted thinking. Thus, the etymology of the Indian word lays stress on the dynamic rather than the static, on the stress of intellection rather than the suspense of inconclusiveness. When the term recurs (§ 1004), Buddhaghosa refers it to kiccho—to 'the fatigue incurred through inability to come to a decision'—a position nearer, psychologically, to 'perplexity' than to 'doubt.' It is quite true that, on etymological ground, neither is kankhā a match for our term 'doubt.' Kānks is to desire. The word would seem to give the emotional and volitional complement of the intellectual state implied in vicikicchā, the longing to escape into certainty and decision attendant on the anxious thinking. Kankhā, however, is not one of any important category of ethical terms, as is vicikicchā; besides, its secondary meaning—namely, of a matter *sub judice*, or of the state of mind connected therewith (see Jāt. i. 165; M. i. 147)—seems to have superseded the primary meaning, which is retained in ākankhati (*cf.* Ākankheyya Sutta, M. i. 33). Hence, it can be fairly well rendered by 'doubt.' I do not, then, pretend that 'per-

occasion is puzzlement,[1] perplexity; distraction, standing at cross-roads;[2] collapse,[3] uncertainty of grasp; evasion, hesitation;[4] incapacity of grasping thoroughly,[5] stiffness of mind,[6] mental scarifying[7]—this is the perplexity that there then is.

* * * * * *

---

plexity' is etymologically the equivalent of vicikicchā, but I use it (1) to guard against a too facile assimilation of the latter to the implications of 'doubt' as used by us, and (2) to throw emphasis on the 'mortal coil' and tangle of thought in one who, on whatever grounds, is sceptically disposed.

[1] Vimati, almost an exact parallel to vicikicchā, connoting as it does either intense or distraught mind-action.

[2] Dveḷhakaṃ, dvedhāpatho. Here we get to the etymological idea in our own 'doubt.' The Cy. has, for the one, 'to be swayed or shaken to and fro'; for the other, 'as a path branching in two, this being an obstacle to attainment' (259).

[3] Samsayo, the etymological equivalent of 'collapse.' To succumb to one's inability to be persistently carrying on such problems as, Is this permanent or impermanent? etc., says the Cy. (*ibid.*).

[4] Asappanā, parisappanā. According to the Cy., these mean, respectively, 'to relinquish' (or slip down from—osakkati; *cf.* Trenckner's 'Miscellany,' p. 60) 'an object of thought through inability to come to a decision,' and 'to slip' (or run—sappati [*vide* sarp]) 'about on all sides from inability to plunge in.' Asl. 260.

[5] Apariyogāhaṇā, employed to describe moho. See § 390.

[6] I should not have hesitated to adopt, for thambhitattaṃ, chambhitattaṃ (vacillation), the alternate reading in the Cy. (Asl. 260), were it not that the latter paraphrases the term by saying 'the meaning is a condition of denseness (or rigidity, thaddho). For when perplexity arises, one makes one's mind stiff (stubborn, dense, thaddhaṃ).' K. also reads thambhitattaṃ. Both terms, however, though opposed in connotation, are derived from the root stambh, to prop; and both are used to

---

[7] See note on p. 117.

[Summary.]

[425*a*] Now, at that time
the skandhas are four,
etc.,
the faculties are four,
the Jhāna is fourfold,
the Path is twofold,
the powers are three,
the cause is one,[1]
etc.

[*Continue as in* § 58.]

* * * * * *

[426] What on that occasion is the skandha of syntheses?

Contact,
thinking,
conception,
discursive thought,
self-collectedness;
the faculties of
energy,
vitality;

---

describe the gaseous element, which, though it is vacillating, holds solids apart. See below, § 965. There is the further comment (Asl., *ibid.*) that, 'in respect of certainty, inability to *carry on the idea* in the mind is meant.' Vicikicchā, then, though it implies active racking of the brain, impedes progress in effective thinking, and results in a mental condition akin to the denseness and apariyogāhanā of moho.

[7] Manovilekho. 'When perplexity arises, seizing the object of thought, it scratches the mind, as it were' (*ibid.*). When the term is used to describe kukkuccaṃ, or worry (§ 1160), it is illustrated in the Cy. by the scaling of a copper pot with an awl (āraggaṃ). Asl. 384.

[1] Namely, moho.

wrong intention,
wrong endeavour;
the powers of
energy,
unconscientiousness,
disregard of blame;
perplexity,
dulness;
unconscientiousness,
disregard of blame,
grasp.[1]

Or whatever other, etc.

[*Continue as in* § 420.]

* * * * * *

XII.

[427] Which are the states that are bad?

When a bad thought has arisen which is accompanied by disinterestedness and associated with excitement, and which has as its object a sight, a sound, a smell, a taste, a touch, a mental state, or what not, then there is

contact,
feeling,
perception,
thinking,
thought,
conception,
discursive thought,
disinterestedness,
self-collectedness,
the faculties of
energy,
concentration,
ideation,

---

[1] On the omission of 'balance,' *cf.* below, § 429, n.

disinterestedness,
vitality;
wrong intention,
wrong endeavour,
wrong concentration;
the powers of
energy,
concentration,
unconscientiousness,
disregard of blame;
excitement;
dulness;
unconscientiousness,
disregard of blame,
quiet,
grasp,
balance.

These, or whatever other incorporeal, causally induced states there are on that occasion—these are states that are bad.

[428] *Usual question and answer on* 'contact.'

* * * * * *

[429] What on that occasion is excitement (uddhaccaṃ)?

The excitement of mind which on that occasion is disquietude, agitation of heart, turmoil of mind—this is the excitement that there then is.[1]

* * * * * *

---

[1] Yaṃ cittassa uddhaccaṃ avūpasamo, cetaso vikkhepo, bhantattaṃ cittassa—idaṃ vuccati uddhaccaṃ. It seems clear that, whether or no uddhaccaṃ can elsewhere be rendered by terms indicative of a puffed-up state of mind (see Rhys Davids, 'Buddhism,' p. 109; Warren, 'Buddhism in Translations,' p. 365; Neumann, 'Die Reden,' etc., I., *passim*), the specific meaning in this connexion (TATTHA katamaṃ uddhaccaṃ) is the antithesis of vūpasamo, and the equivalent of vikkhepo,

[429*a*] Now, at that time
the skandhas are four,
etc.,
the faculties are five,

---

both of which are expressions about the meaning of which there is little or no uncertainty. In Sanskrit auddhatya is only found twice in later works, one of them Buddhist (*v.* Böthl. and Roth., *s.v.*), and there means wrestling, a word used by ourselves for certain agitated, perfervid mental states. That the term should be yoked with kukkuccaṃ (worry) in the Nīvaraṇas (see §§ 1158-1160; and *cf.* the cognate meaning in another allied pair, thīnamiddhaṃ, §§ 1155-1157) goes far to rob it of implications of vanity or self-righteousness. (In 'Dialogues of the Buddha,' i. 82, the former pair are rendered 'flurry and worry.') Buddhaghosa gives little help; but he distinguishes uddhaccaṃ, as a struggling over *one* object of thought (ekārammaṇe vipphandati), from perplexity as a struggling over *divers* objects of thought. The Buddhists were apparently seeking for terms to describe a state of mind antithetical to that conveyed by the designation thīṇamiddhaṃ—stolidity and torpor. In the latter there is excessive stability—the immobility not of a finely-adjusted balance of faculties and values, but of an inert mass. In the former (uddhacca-kukkuccaṃ) there is a want of equilibrium and adjustment. From some cause or another the individual is stirred up, agitated, fussed; in American idiom, 'rattled.'

What I have rendered 'turmoil' (bhantattaṃ; more literally, wavering, rolling, staggering) Buddhaghosa calls vibhanti-bhāvo (*sic lege*), bhantayāna-bhantagonādīnam viya (Asl. 260).

Whatever the exact meaning of uddhaccaṃ may be, there is enough to show that it is in great part antithetical to some of the other constituents enumerated under the Bad Thought in question—at least, when these are taken in their full intention. I refer to the approximately synonymous group: 'self-collectedness,' 'concentration,' 'quiet' and 'balance.' The last, indeed (avikkhepo), is a contradiction in terms to the phrase which describes uddhaccaṃ as cetaso vikkhepo! The text actually omits it, but this is through mere inadvertence (*cf.* § 430).

the Jhāna is fourfold,
the Path is threefold,
the powers are four,
the cause is one,
etc.

[*Continue as in* § 58.]

*   *   *   *   *   *

It is given in K., and the Cy. explicitly states (p. 260) that there are *twenty-eight* constituents enumerated, fourteen of them being described in terms of one or other of the other fourteen. (If the reader will compare § 427 with the corresponding descriptions given in §§ 2-57, he will prove this to be correct.) Nor is there a word to comment on, or explain away any apparent incongruity in the inclusion. There is only a short discussion, alluded to already, on the relation of uddhaccaṃ and vicikicchā. Thoughts XI. and XII., as departing from the symmetrical procedure of I. to IX., are said to be miscellaneous items, and to be concerned with persistent attending to the idea (ārammaṇe pavaṭṭanaka-cittāni). And just as, if a round gem and a tetragonal gem be sent rolling down an inclined plane, the former's motion is uniform, while that of the latter is from one position of rest to another, so vicikicchā connotes a continual working of thought, while uddhaccaṃ works on one given basis at a time.

There being, then, as it would appear, this fairly close analogy between 'perplexity' and 'excitement,' it is fair to assume that 'self-collectedness' and its synonyms are to be understood in Thought XII., as present in the feeble degree to which they, or at least the first of them, is present in Thought XI. (see § 424, n.). The compilers were thus between two fires as to their logic. Either avikkhepo must go to admit of the use of vikkhepo—in which case the synonyms of avikkhepo (samādhi, etc.) must go too—or it and its synonyms must be retained with a highly attenuated import. Possibly the subject was conceived as agitated on some one point only, but calm as to things in general.

[430] What on that occasion is the skandha of syntheses?

Contact,
thinking,
conception,
discursive thought,
self-collectedness;
the faculties of
energy,
concentration,
vitality;
wrong intention,
wrong endeavour,
wrong concentration;
the powers of
energy,
concentration,
unconscientiousness,
disregard of blame;
excitement;
dulness;
unconscientiousness,
disregard of blame,
quiet,
grasp,
balance.

Or whatever other, etc.

[*Continue as in* § 62.]

* * * * * *

[Here end] the Twelve Bad Thoughts.

[*PART III.—INDETERMINATE STATES OF CONSCIOUSNESS.*[1]

Chapter I.

On Effect, or Result (vipāko).

A. Good Karma.

1. In the sensuous universe.

(*a*) The Five Modes of Cognition considered as effects of good (kusalavipākāni pañca-viññāṇāni).]

(i.) [431] Which are the states that are indeterminate?

When, as the result of good karma[2] having been wrought, having been stored up in connexion with the sensuous universe, visual cognition has arisen, accompanied by disinterestedness,[3] and having as its object something seen, then there is

contact,	thinking,
feeling,	thought,
perception,	disinterestedness,

self-collectedness;

---

[1] Dhammā avyākatā. The term and its treatment are discussed in my Introduction. *Cf.* Vis. Magga, ch. xiv.

[2] Kammaṃ; literally, action, work, deed.

[3] In this and the two following sections (2 and 3) upekkhā is apparently used as a psychological term only, without ethical implication, and signifies simply neutral feeling.

the faculties of
ideation,
disinterestedness,
vitality.

These, or whatever other[1] incorporeal, causally induced states there are on that occasion—these are states that are indeterminate.

[432] *Question and answer on* 'contact' *as above, passim.*

[433] What on that occasion is feeling?

The mental [condition], neither pleasant nor unpleasant, which on that occasion is born of contact with the appropriate element of visual cognition; the sensation, born of contact with thought, which is neither easeful nor painful; the feeling, born of contact with thought, which is neither easeful nor painful—this is the feeling that there then is.

[434] What on that occasion is perception?

The perception, the perceiving, the state of having perceived, which on that occasion is born of contact with the appropriate element of visual cognition—this is the perception that there then is.

[435] What on that occasion is thinking?

The thinking, the cogitating, the reflection which on that occasion is born of contact with the appropriate element of visual cognition—this is the thinking that there then is.

[436] What on that occasion is thought?

The thought which on that occasion is ideation, mind, heart, that which is clear, ideation as the sphere of mind, the faculty of ideation, intellect, the skandha of intellect, the appropriate element of visual cognition—this is the thought that there then is.

[437] What on that occasion is disinterestedness?

Answer as for 'feeling,' § 436, *omitting the phrase* 'which is born of contact with the appropriate element of visual cognition.'

---

[1] There will be but one of these, viz., attention (Asl. 262).

[438] What on that occasion is self-collectedness?

The persistence of thought[1] which there is on that occasion—this is the self-collectedness that there then is.

[439] What on that occasion is the faculty of ideation?

Answer as for 'thought,' § 436.

[440] What on that occasion is the faculty of disinterestedness?

Answer as in § 437.

[441] What on that occasion is the faculty of vitality?

Answer as in § 19.

Or whatever other incorporeal, causally induced states there are on that occasion—these are the states that are indeterminate.

[Summary.]

[441*a*] Now, on that occasion
the skandhas are four,
the spheres are two,
the elements are two,
the nutriments are three,
the faculties are three,[2]
contact counts as a single factor,
etc.
[*Continue as in* § 58],

---

[1] In the text omit . . . pe . . . after ṭhiti, as in § 424, and for the same reason (Asl. 262).

[2] Jhāna and the Path, says the Cy. (262), are not included in the summary; and why? Jhāna at its extremity has conception (vitakko), and the Path at its extremity has cause (hetu). Hence, it is not consistent to include Jhāna in a thought that has no conceptual activity, or the Path, when the thought is not causally effective.

This remark throws a little light on to the problem of indeterminate states. In vitakko the mind is working towards an end good or bad; in the Path the first factor (right views) is synonymous with 'absence of dulness,' which is the cause or root of good (§ 1054). Neither vitakko nor amoho is, therefore, a possible constituent in a cognition which is inefficacious to produce good or bad karma.

the faculty of ideation counts as a single factor,
the element of visual cognition counts as a single factor,
the sphere of [mental] states counts as a single factor,
etc.

[*Continue as in* § 58.]

* * * * * *

[442] What on that occasion is the skandha of syntheses?

Contact,
thinking,
self-collectedness,
the faculty of vitality,

or whatever other incorporeal, causally induced states there are on that occasion, exclusive of the skandhas of feeling, perception and intellect—these are the skandha of syntheses.

* * * * * *

(ii.-v.) [443] Which are the states that are indeterminate?

When, as the result of good karma having been wrought, having been stored up in connexion with the sensuous universe,

auditory cognition,
olfactory cognition, or
gustatory cognition

has arisen, accompanied by disinterestedness, and having as its object

a sound,
a smell, or
a taste

respectively . . . or
cognition of body

has arisen, accompanied by ease, and having as its object something tangible,[1]

then there is

contact, thinking,
feeling,[2] thought,
perception, ease,
self-collectedness;
the faculties of
ideation,
ease,
vitality.

Now, these, or whatever other incorporeal, causally induced states there are on that occasion—these are states that are indeterminate.

[444] *Question and answer on* 'contact' *as above, passim.*

[445] What on that occasion is feeling?

The bodily pleasure, the bodily ease, which on that occasion is born of the appropriate element of the cognition of body; the pleasurable, easeful sensation which

---

[1] Or 'a touch' (*v.* p. 2, n. 2). The view that the cognition of something tangible has a positive hedonic concomitant—pleasant or, if the karma be bad (§ 556), unpleasant—as compared with the neutral feeling attending other kinds of sense-cognition (under the given circumstances), is of psychological interest. And the comment it evokes is not less so. Touch, or body-sensibility, is, the Cy. explains (263), the one sense through which the four elements without and within the individual come into direct contact. Other cognition is secondary, inasmuch as the other senses are *derived* (upādā). They are as balls of cotton-wool on four anvils, deadening the impact of the hammer. In touch the wool is beaten through, and the reaction is stronger. *Cf.* this with the theory of sense below, §§ 596-632. Nevertheless, the ease or the distress is so faintly marked, that the cognition remains 'indeterminate.'

The constituent states, contact, etc., refer only to the last-named species of cognition. In the case of the other four 'disinterestedness' would have to be substituted for 'ease.'

[2] Vedanā has dropped out of the printed text.

is born of contact with the body; the pleasurable, easeful feeling which is born of contact with the body—this is the feeling that there then is.

[446] What on that occasion is perception?

The perception, the perceiving, the state of having perceived, which on that occasion is born of contact with appropriate element of the cognition of body—this is the perception that there then is.

[447] What on that occasion is thinking?

The thinking, the cogitating, the reflection, which on that occasion is born of contact with the appropriate element of the cognition of body—this is the thinking that there then is.

[448] What on that occasion is thought?

The thought which on that occasion is ideation, mind, heart, that which is clear; ideation as the sphere of mind, the faculty of ideation, intellect, the skandha of intellect, the appropriate element of the cognition of body—this is the thought that there then is.

[449] What on that occasion is ease?

The bodily pleasure, the bodily ease which on that occasion is the pleasant, easeful sensation born of contact with the body; the pleasant, easeful feeling born of contact with the body—this is the ease that there then is.

[450-453] What on that occasion is self-collectedness[1] . . . the faculty of ideation[2] . . . of ease . . . of vitality?

Answers as in §§ 438, 448, 449 *and* 441 *respectively.*

Or whatever other incorporeal, causally induced states there are on that occasion—these are states that are indeterminate.

---

[1] In § 450 omit . . . pe . . . in the text after ṭhiti.

[2] In § 451 supply kāya- before viññāṇadhātu. The state manindriyaṃ is, it is true, one of representative cognition only, but it is occupied, under the given circumstances, with a kāya-viññāṇaṃ. The 'door of mano' has as its object any or all of the objects of the five senses.

[Summary.]

[453*a*] Now, on that occasion
the skandhas are four,
etc.

[*Continue as in* § 441*a*, *substituting* 'the element of the cognition of body' *for* 'the element of visual cognition.']

*   *   *   *   *   *

[454] What on that occasion is the skandha of syntheses?

Answer as in § 442.

*   *   *   *   *   *

[(*b*) Good (karma) taking effect in ideation (kusalavipākā manodhātu).]

[455] Which are the states that are indeterminate?

When, as the result of good karma having been wrought, having been stored up in connexion with the sensuous universe, an element of ideation[1] has arisen, accompanied by disinterestedness, and having as its object a sight, a sound, a smell, a taste, something tangible, or what not, then there is

contact,	thought,
feeling,	conception,

[1] Once more the Cy. points out (263) the significance of the affix -dhātu (element), as meaning the absence of entity (nissatta), the 'emptiness' or phenomenal character of the ideational faculty. *Cf.* above, p. 33, n. The characteristics of mano are here set out. See Introduction (Theory of Intellection). The theory of a *sensorium commune* here alluded to is practically identical with that adopted by Aristotle in the 'De Sensu.' 'The basis (or site, vatthu) of this kind of thought is a constant, namely, the heart; the objects of the "doors" (or of the idea-door) are not constants. Whereas they come in one after another, this is the *locus* (ṭhānaṃ), which has the function of receiving them into unity' (ekasampaṭicchanakiccaṃ).

The process of cognition is completed by manoviññāṇadhātu (see below).

perception, discursive thought,
thinking, disinterestedness,
self-collectedness;
the faculties of
ideation,
disinterestedness,
vitality.

These, or whatever other[1] incorporeal, causally induced states there are on that occasion—these are states that are indeterminate.

[456] *Question and answer on* 'contact' *as above, passim.*

[457] What on that occasion is feeling?

The mental [condition], neither pleasant nor unpleasant, which on that occasion is born of contact with the appropriate element of ideation; the sensation, born of contact with thought, which is neither easeful nor painful; the feeling, born of contact with thought, which is neither easeful nor painful—this is the feeling that there then is.

[458-460] What on that occasion is perception . . . thinking . . . thought?

Answers as in §§ 446-448, *substituting* 'element of ideation' *for* 'element of the cognition of body.'

[461] What on that occasion is conception?

The ratiocination, the conceiving which on that occasion is the disposition, the fixation, the focussing, the application of the mind[2]—this is the conception that there then is.

[462] What on that occasion is discursive thought?

The process, the sustained procedure, the progress and access [of the mind] which on that occasion is the continuous adjusting and directing of thought—this is the discursive thought that there then is.

---

[1] These (Asl. 264) include two others, resolve and attention. *Cf.* above, p. 5, n. 1.

[2] Inasmuch, says the Cy. (264), as this thought is neither good nor bad (in its effect), intention (*sankappo*), either right or wrong, is not included in the connotation of its component vitakko. *Cf.* §§ 7 and 371, also p. 125, n. 2.

[463-467] What on that occasion is disinterestedness . . . self-collectedness . . . the faculty of ideation . . . of disinterestedness . . . of vitality?

Answers as in §§ 437, 438, 460, 440,[1] 441 *respectively.*

[Summary.]

[467*a*] Now, on that occasion
the skandhas are four,
the spheres are two,
the elements are two,
the nutriments are three,
the faculties are three,
contact counts as a single factor,
etc.

[*Continue as in* § 58.]

the faculty of ideation counts as a single factor,
the element of ideation counts as a single factor,
etc.

* * * * * *

[468] What on that occasion is the skandha of syntheses?

Contact,	discursive thought,
thinking,	self-collectedness,
conception,	the faculty of vitality.

Or whatever other incorporeal, causally induced states there are on that occasion, exclusive of the skandhas of feeling, perception and intellect—these are the skandha of syntheses.

* * * * * *

---

[1] The references given in the text will prove, on examination, to be for the most part misleading.

(*c*) Good (karma) taking effect in representative intellection (kusala-vipākā manoviññāṇadhātu).

(i.) *When accompanied by happiness.*

[469] Which are the states that are indeterminate?

When, as the result of good karma having been wrought, having been stored up in connexion with the sensuous universe, an element of representative cognition[1] has arisen, accompanied by happiness and having as its object

---

[1] The function of the manoviññāṇadhātu is discussed in the Introduction (Theory of Intellection). As a resultant state, it is here said (Asl. 264), when 'accompanied by happiness,' to eventuate in two sets of circumstances: 'Standing in the doors of the five senses, it accomplishes the task (or function, kiccaṃ) of deciding (santīrana) as to that idea (or percept) which the element of ideation, just expired, received on the expiry of that sense-cognition which constituted the result of good karma.' Again: 'When the action of the six doors (senses and ideation) results in a more impressive idea, this becomes what is called *the* idea' (tad-ārammaṇaṃ), *i.e.*, 'the object of the *impulse*' (javanaṃ), and the element of representative cognition is drawn away to fix itself on that object. So a vessel crossing a strong current avails to turn the latter aside for a moment, though its natural course is a flowing downward. The normal flow of the intellect is, so to speak, down the stream of the individual life (bhavaṅgam ev' otarati). And it is this normal functioning of the intellect which alone is here taken into account.

The further stage of cognition immediately preceding any outgoing or conative impulse such as seems to be meant by the word javanaṃ (*cf.* Sum. 194; Abh. S. iii. 3)—I allude to that of 'establishing' (or full assimilation, as we might say—voṭṭhappanaṃ)—is not here explicitly mentioned. But it is probably implied in the phrase santīranādi, 'deciding *and the rest.*' And it is discussed a few pages further on (Asl. 269, 272).

a sight, a sound, a smell, a taste, something tangible, the idea [of any of these], or what not, then there is

contact,	conception,
feeling,	discursive thought,
perception,	joy,
thinking,	ease,
thought,	self-collectedness;

the faculties of
ideation,
happiness,
vitality.

These, or whatever other, etc.

[*Continue as in* § 455.]

[470-482] *These thirteen constituent states are described as in* §§ 2-11 *and* 17-19, *with the exception of* 'conception' (vitakko) *and* 'self-collectedness' (cittass' ekaggatā), *which are described with the restricted connotation used in* §§ 461, 464.

[Summary.]

[482*a*] *Identical with* § 467*a*, *but* 'the element of representative cognition' (manoviññāṇadhātu) *must be substituted for* 'the element of ideation.'[1]

* * * * * *

[483] What on that occasion is the skandha of syntheses?

Contact,	discursive thought,
thinking,	joy,
conception,	self-collectedness;

the faculty of vitality.

Or whatever incorporeal, causally induced states there are on that occasion, exclusive of the skandhas of feeling,

---

[1] The reference to [58] in the text is again incorrect, for there is to be no rehearsal of either Jhāna or Path. *Cf.* p. 125, n. 2, and Asl. 264.

perception and intellect—these are the skandha of syntheses.

* * * * * *

(ii.) *When accompanied by disinterestedness.*

[484] Which are the states that are indeterminate?

When, as the result of good karma having been wrought, having been stored up in connexion with the sensuous universe, an element of representative cognition[1] has arisen, accompanied by disinterestedness, and having as its object a sight, etc. (*cf.* above, § 469] . . . then there is

contact, thought,
feeling, conception,
perception, discursive thought,
thinking, disinterestedness,
self-collectedness;
the faculties of
ideation,
disinterestedness,
vitality.

These, or whatever other, etc.

[*Continue as in* § 469.]

---

[1] This sort of resultant cognition is said to take effect or occur on five sorts of occasions: (i.) The conception of infirm offspring, viz., blind, deaf, imbecile or insane, hermaphrodite or neuter; (ii.) during the span of one individual lifetime (bhavangaṃ); (iii.) in the decision (santīranaṃ) respecting an idea where the object causes neither pleasure nor pain; (iv.) when the 'that-object' (tadārammaṇaṃ) of absorbing impressiveness arises (*cf.* § 469, n.); (v.) when death opens the way to renewed existence (cuti). It will be seen that these five correspond to the first, second, tenth, thirteenth and fourteenth occasion on which viññāṇas occur, according to the Visuddhi Magga (chap. xiv.; see Warren's 'Table of Contents,' J. P. T. S., 1891-93, p. 130). It is possible that the absence of explanatory matter in our Cy. is due to the existence of a full treatment by Buddhaghosa in the former earlier work.

[485-496] *These thirteen states are described as in the foregoing section* (i.), *except that the questions and answers on* 'feeling' *and* 'disinterestedness,' *as given in* §§ 152-154, *must be substituted for those on* 'feeling,' 'joy,' *and the* 'faculty of happiness' *given in* §§ 471, 477, *and* 481. 'Ease' *is omitted.*

[Summary.]

[496*a*] *Terms identical with those in* § 482*a*.

*   *   *   *   *   *

[497] *The skandha of syntheses is identical with the content stated in* § 483, *but with the omission of* 'joy.'

*   *   *   *   *   *

[(*d*) The Eight Main Types of Results (a ṭ ṭ h a m a h ā-v i p ā k ā).]

[498] Which are the states that are indeterminate?

When, as the result of good karma having been wrought, having been stored up in connexion with the sensuous universe, an element of representative cognition has arisen,

(i.) accompanied by happiness and associated with knowledge . . .

(ii.) accompanied by happiness, associated with knowledge, and prompted by a conscious motive . . .

(iii.) accompanied by happiness and disconnected with knowledge . . .

(iv.) accompanied by happiness, disconnected with knowledge, and prompted by a conscious motive . . .

(v.) accompanied by disinterestedness and associated with knowledge . . .

(vi.) accompanied by disinterestedness, associated with knowledge, and prompted by a conscious motive . . .

(vii.) accompanied by disinterestedness and disconnected with knowledge . . .

(viii.) accompanied by disinterestedness, disconnected

with knowledge, and prompted by a conscious motive, and having as its object a sight, a sound, a smell, a taste, something tangible, or what not, then there is contact[1] . . . balance. These, or whatever other incorporeal, causally induced states there are on that occasion—these are states that are indeterminate.

[498*a*] That absence of lust which is the root of indeterminateness . . . that absence of hate which is the root of indeterminateness . . . that absence of dulness which is the root of indeterminateness . . . these are states that are indeterminate.[2]

[2. In the universe of Form.]

[499] Which are the states that are indeterminate?

When, that he may attain to the heavens of Form, he cultivates the way thereto, and aloof from sensuous appetites, etc.,[3] enters into and abides in the First Jhāna . . . then there is contact, etc.[4] Now, these . . . are states that are good. But when, as the result of just this

---

[1] It is difficult in the present stage of knowledge respecting the Buddhist (academic) theory of the Indeterminate and of Vipāko to supply any safe reference for the elided states here supposed to be rehearsed. The following section (see note) seems to indicate that at least *three* more states than those enumerated in the kinds of indeterminates just discussed are to be included, namely, the absence of lust, of hate, and of dulness. But the Cy. is not at all lucid (pp. 265, 266), and breaks away into a long rambling discussion on casuistical views respecting vipāko.

[2] This highly elliptical paragraph, in which I have supplied the third 'root,' inadvertently omitted in the text, but required by the context (see above, §§ 32-34; K., Asl. 267, 268), is presumably intended to show wherein the niddesa, or descriptive exposition of certain of the constituent states of each of the Eight Types of Result differ from those given in each of the corresponding Eight Types of Good Thoughts (§§ 1-159).

[3] See § 160.

[4] Continue as in § 160.

good karma having been wrought, having been stored up in connexion with the universe of Form, he, aloof from sensuous appetites, etc., enters into and abides in the First Jhāna . . . then there is contact, etc. And these . . . are states that are indeterminate.

[500] *Repeat, substituting the formulæ of the remaining Jhānas on the Fourfold System, and of all the Jhānas on the Fivefold System.*

[3. In the universe of the Formless.]

[501] Which are the states that are indeterminate?

When, that he may attain to the heavens of the Formless, he cultivates the way thereto, and so, by passing wholly beyond all consciousness of form, by the dying out of the consciousness of sensory reaction, by turning the attention from any consciousness of the manifold, he enters into and abides in that frame of mind which is accompanied by the consciousness of a sphere of unbounded space—even the Fourth Jhāna, to gain which all sense of ease must have been put away, etc. [*continue as in* § 265]—then the contact . . . the balance that arises, these . . . are states that are good.[1]

But when, as the result of just this good karma having been wrought, having been stored up in connexion with the universe of the Formless, he, by passing wholly beyond all consciousness of form, by the dying out of the consciousness of sensory reaction, by turning the attention from any consciousness of the manifold, enters into and abides in that rapt meditation which is accompanied by the consciousness of a sphere of unbounded space—even the Fourth Jhāna, to gain which all sense of ease must have been put away, etc. [*continue as above*] . . . then the

---

[1] In the printed text the . . . pe . . . here should be omitted, as is done in §§ 503, 504. Omit likewise in § 502.

contact[1] . . . the balance that arises, these . . . are states that are indeterminate.

[502-504] *Here follow in succession the other three* 'Jhānas connected with Formless Existence' (§§ 266-268), *namely*, 'the Sphere of Infinite Intellection,' 'the Sphere of Nothingness,' *and* 'the Sphere where there is neither Perception nor Non-perception,' *each having the Fourth Jhāna as its* 'result,' *as in the formula stated in* § 501.

[4. In the pursuit of the Higher Ideal (lokuttara-vipāko).

I. The First Path.

The Twenty Great Methods.

1. *Rapt Meditation.*

(i.) The Four Modes of Progress in Purification.]

[505] Which are the states that are indeterminate?

When he cultivates the Jhāna of the Higher Ideal (the rapt meditation), whereby there is a going forth and onward, making for the undoing of rebirth, and when, that he may attain to the First Stage, he has put away views and opinions, and so, aloof from sensuous appetites, aloof from evil ideas, he enters into and abides in the First Jhāna . . . [*continue as in* § 277] progress thereto being difficult and intuition sluggish—then there is contact . . . balance. Now these . . . are states that are good.

But when, as the result of just this good Jhāna having been wrought, having been cultivated[2] in pursuit of the

---

[1] On the difficulty of determining which constituent dhammas are to be here understood, see § 498, n.

[2] The word 'karma' and its *proprium*, 'storing up' (upacitattaṃ), are now superseded respectively by lokuttaram jhānam and cultivation or practice (bhāvitattaṃ) (Asl. 289).

Higher Ideal, he, aloof from sensuous appetites, aloof from evil ideas, enters into and abides in the First Jhāna . . . progress whereto is painful, intuition wherein is sluggish, and which is EMPTY—then there is contact . . . the faculty of knowledge made perfect[1] . . . balance. And these . . . are states that are indeterminate.

[506] Which are the states that are indeterminate?

When he cultivates the Jhāna of the Higher Ideal (the rapt meditation) whereby there is a going forth and onward, making for the undoing of rebirth, and when, that he may attain to the First Stage, he has put away views and opinions, and so, aloof from sensuous appetites, aloof from evil ideas, he enters into and abides in the First Jhāna . . . [*continue as in* § 277] progress thereto being difficult and intuition sluggish — then there is contact . . . balance. Now these . . . are states that are good.

But when, as the result of just this good Jhāna having been wrought, having been cultivated in pursuit of the Higher Ideal, he, aloof from sensuous appetites, aloof from evil ideas, enters into and abides in the First Jhāna . . . progress whereto is painful, intuition wherein is sluggish, and which is SIGNLESS[2] . . .

[*or*] [507] (*repeating all the foregoing*) which is AIMLESS[3] —then there is contact . . . the faculty of knowledge made perfect . . . balance. And these . . . are states that are indeterminate.

[508] Which are the states that are indeterminate?

---

[1] *Cf.* above, § 362. No comment is given on the development of this faculty, in the case of indeterminate states, *before* the First Path is left behind. But the reason is presumably that, in the quest of the Ideal, the *result* implies the attainment of a higher path, or at least of the 'fruition' of the First Path. The faculty is not expressly stated in the corresponding passages of §§ 508, 509, either in the printed text or in K.; but there can, by the context, be no doubt that it is to be taken as read.

[2] See above, p. 91, n. 2. [3] *Ibid.*

When he cultivates the Jhāna of the Higher Ideal (the rapt meditation), whereby there is a going forth and onward, making for the undoing of rebirth, and when, that he may attain to the First Stage, he has put away views and opinions, and so, suppressing the working of conception and of thought discursive, enters into and abides in the Second Jhāna . . .

[*or*] . . . in the Third Jhāna . . .

[*or*] . . . in the Fourth Jhāna . . .

[*or*] . . . [*continue in the same way for fivefold Jhāna*] . . . progress whereto is painful and intuition sluggish, then this constitutes good (karma).[1]

But when, as the result [*of this or that Jhāna the corresponding Jhāna is attained*] progress whereto is painful, intuition wherein is sluggish,

and which is Empty,
Signless,
[*or*] Aimless,

then the contact . . . the balance that arises—these . . . are states that are indeterminate.

[509] *Repeat the two foregoing sections, substituting in order the three remaining Modes of Progress:* 'progress whereto is painful, but intuition quick,' 'progress whereto is easy, but intuition sluggish,' *and* 'progress whereto is easy, and intuition quick' (§§ 176-180).

[(ii.) The Notion of Emptiness applied to Purification (suddhika-suññataṃ).]

[510] Which are the states that are indeterminate?

When he cultivates the Jhāna of the Higher Ideal (the rapt meditation), whereby there is a going forth and onward, making for the undoing of rebirth, and when, that he may

---

[1] The compilers would appear, here and in certain subsequent answers, to have made an attempt at condensation otherwise than by the usual . . . pe . . . This is, I believe, a very rare instance.

attain to the First Stage, he has put away views and opinions, and so, aloof from sensuous appetites, aloof from evil ideas, he enters into and abides in the First Jhāna . . . which is EMPTY—then there is contact . . . balance. Now these . . . are states that are good.

But when, as the result of just this good Jhāna having been wrought, having been cultivated in pursuit of the Higher Ideal, he, aloof from sensuous appetites, aloof from evil ideas, enters into and abides in the First Jhāna . . . which is EMPTY . . .

[*or*] [511] which is SIGNLESS . . .

[*or*] [512] which is AIMLESS—then there is contact . . . balance. And these . . . are states that are indeterminate.

[513] *Repeat in the case of each of the remaining Jhānas on the Fourfold System, and of all the Jhānas on the Five-fold System.*

[(iii.) The Four Modes of Progress taken in connexion with the Notion of Emptiness (suññata[1]-paṭipadā).

The First Mode.]

[514] Which are the states that are indeterminate?

When he cultivates the Jhāna of the Higher Ideal (the rapt meditation), whereby there is a going forth and onward, making for the undoing of rebirth, and when, that he may attain to the First Stage, he has put away views and opinions, and so, aloof from sensuous appetites, aloof from evil ideas, he enters into and abides in the First Jhāna . . . progress whereto is painful and intuition sluggish,

and which is EMPTY,

then there is contact . . . balance. Now these . . . are states that are good.

But when, as the result of just this good Jhāna having been wrought, having been cultivated in pursuit of the Higher Ideal, he, aloof from sensuous appetites,

---

[1] *Sic lege.*

aloof from evil ideas, enters into and abides in the First Jhāna . . .

progress whereto is painful and intuition sluggish,

and which is EMPTY . . .

. . . [*or*] [515] which is SIGNLESS . . .

. . . [*or*] [516] which is AIMLESS,

then there is contact . . . balance. And these . . . are states that are indeterminate.

[517] *Repeat in the case of each of the remaining Jhānas on the Fourfold System, and of all the Jhānas on the Five-fold System.*

[*The Second, Third and Fourth Modes.*]

[518] Which are the states that are indeterminate?

When he cultivates the Jhāna of the Higher Ideal (the rapt meditation), whereby there is a going forth and onward, making for the undoing of rebirth, and when, that he may attain to the First Stage, he has put away views and opinions, and so, aloof from sensuous appetites, aloof from evil ideas, he enters into and abides in the First Jhāna . . .

—progress whereto is painful, but intuition quick,

and which is EMPTY . . .

—progress whereto is easy, but intuition sluggish,

and which is EMPTY . . .

—progress whereto is easy and intuition quick,

and which is EMPTY . . .

[*Repeat, substituting each of the remaining Jhānas in the case of each of the three Modes*] . . .

then these constitute good (karma).

But when, as the result [of this or that Jhāna in any the three Modes], he enters into and abides in any of the Jhānas taken in order, which is in any of the three Modes,

and which is EMPTY . . .

. . . [*or*] which is SIGNLESS . . .

. . . [*or*] which is AIMLESS,

then there is contact . . . balance. And these . . . are states that are indeterminate.

[(iv.) The Notion of Aimlessness applied to Purification (suddhika-appaṇihitaṃ).]

[519] Which are the states that are indeterminate?

When he cultivates the Jhāna of the Higher Ideal (the rapt meditation), whereby there is a going forth and onward, making for the undoing of rebirth, and when, that he may attain to the First Stage, he has put away views and opinions, and so, aloof from sensuous appetites, aloof from evil ideas, he enters into and abides in the First Jhāna . . .

which is AIMLESS,

then there is contact . . . balance. Now these . . . are states that are good.

But when, as the result of just this good Jhāna having been wrought, having been cultivated in pursuit of the Higher Ideal, he, aloof from sensuous appetites, aloof from evil ideas, enters into and abides in the First Jhāna . . .

. . . which is AIMLESS . . .

. . . [*or*] [520] which is SIGNLESS . . .

. . . [*or*] [521] which is EMPTY,

then there is contact . . . balance. And these . . . are states that are indeterminate.

[522] *Repeat in the case of each of the remaining Jhānas on the Fourfold System, and of all the Jhānas on the Fivefold System.*

[(v.) The Four Modes of Progress taken in connexion with the Notion of Aimlessness (appaṇihita-paṭipadā).]

[523] Which are the states that are indeterminate?

When he cultivates the Jhāna of the Higher Ideal (the rapt meditation), whereby there is a going forth and onward, making for the undoing of rebirth, and when, that he may attain to the First Stage, he has put away views and opinions, and so, aloof from sensuous appetites, aloof from evil ideas, enters into and abides in the First Jhāna . . . progress whereto is difficult and intuition sluggish,

and which is Aimless,

then there is contact . . . balance. Now these . . . are states that are good.

But when, as the result of just this good Jhāna having been wrought, having been cultivated in pursuit of the Higher Ideal, he, aloof from sensuous appetites, aloof from evil ideas, enters into and abides in the first Jhāna . . . progress whereto is difficult and intuition sluggish,

and which is Aimless . . .

. . . [*or*] [524] which is Signless . . .

. . . [*or*] [525] which is Empty,

then there is contact . . . balance. And these . . . are states that are indeterminate.

[526] Which are the states that are indeterminate?

When he cultivates the Jhāna of the Higher Ideal (the rapt meditation) whereby there is a going forth and onward, making for the undoing of rebirth, and when, that he may attain to the First Stage, he has put away views and opinions, and so, suppressing the working of conception and of thought discursive,[1] he enters into and abides in the Second Jhāna, or into [*any of the remaining Jhānas, both on the Fourfold and the Fivefold System*] . . . progress whereto is difficult and intuition sluggish,

and which is Aimless,

then this constitutes good (karma).

But when, as the result [*of this or that Jhāna the corresponding Jhāna is attained*], progress whereto is difficult and intuition sluggish,

and which is Aimless,

[*or*] which is Signless,[2]

---

[1] For vivicceva kāmehi read vitakkavicārānaṃ vūpasamā.

[2] For appaṇihitan ti vipāko repeated read animittan ti vipāko.

[*or*] which is EMPTY,[1]

then there is contact . . . balance. And these . . . are states that are indeterminate.

[527] *The Second, Third and Fourth Modes are now substituted in turn, as was done in* § 518.

[The Remaining Nineteen Great Methods.]

[528] Which are the states that are indeterminate?

Here follow nineteen concepts, each of which can be substituted for 'the Jhāna of the Higher Ideal' *in the preceding exercises* (§§ 505-528), *the exercise to which they are actually applied in this paragraph being the* 'Modes of Progress in Purification' *given in* §§ 505-509. *These nineteen concepts are enumerated in* § 358.

[(vi.) The Modes of Progress in Purification taken in connexion with the Dominant Influence of Desire (chandādhipateyya-suddhika-paṭipadā).][2]

[529] Which are the states that are indeterminate?

When he cultivates the Jhāna of the Higher Ideal (the rapt meditation), whereby there is a going forth and onward, making for the undoing of rebirth, and when, that he may attain to the First Stage, he has put away views and opinions, and so, aloof from sensuous appetites, aloof from evil ideas, enters into and abides in the First Jhāna . . . progress whereto is difficult and intuition sluggish, and the dominant influence in which is Desire—then there is contact . . . balance. Now these . . . are states that are good.

But when, as the result of just this good Jhāna having been wrought, having been cultivated in pursuit of the Higher Ideal, he, aloof from sensuous appetites, aloof from evil ideas, enters into and abides in the First Jhāna . . . progress whereto is difficult and intuition sluggish,

[1] Suññataṃ has been inadvertently omitted from the text. [2] Omitted in K.

—which is EMPTY . . .
. . . [*or*] [530] which is SIGNLESS[1] . . .
. . . [*or*] [531] which is AIMLESS,

and the dominant influence in which is Desire—then there is contact . . . balance. And these . . . are states that are indeterminate.

[532] *Repeat in the case of each of the remaining Jhānas on both systems.*

[533] *Repeat in the case of each of the three remaining* 'Modes of Progress' *applied to each Jhāna.*

[(vii.) The Notion of Emptiness applied to Purification, and taken in connexion with Desire as the Dominant Influence (chandādhipateyyaṃ suddhika-suññataṃ).][2]

[534] Which are the states that are indeterminate?

When he cultivates the Jhāna of the Higher Ideal (the rapt meditation), whereby there is a going forth and onward, making for the undoing of rebirth, and when, that he may attain to the First Stage, he has put away views and opinions, and so, aloof from sensuous appetites, aloof from evil ideas, enters into and abides in the First Jhāna . . . which is EMPTY, and the dominant influence in which is Desire—then there is contact . . . balance. Now these . . . are states that are good.

But when, as the result of just this good Jhāna having been wrought, having been cultivated in pursuit of the Higher Ideal, he, aloof from sensuous appetites, aloof from evil ideas, enters into and abides in the First Jhāna . . .

which is EMPTY . . .
. . . [*or*] [535] which is SIGNLESS . . .
. . . [*or*] [536] which is AIMLESS,

and the dominant influence in which is Desire—then there is contact . . . balance. And these . . . are states that are indeterminate.

---

[1] Read in the printed text animittaṃ for appanimittaṃ.

[2] Omitted in K.

[537] *Repeat in the case of each of the remaining Jhānas on both systems.*

(viii.)[1]

[538] Which are the states that are indeterminate?

When he cultivates the Jhāna of the Higher Ideal (the rapt meditation), whereby there is a going forth and onward, making for the undoing of rebirth, and when, that he may attain to the First Stage, he has put away views and opinions, and so, aloof from sensuous appetites, aloof from evil ideas, enters into and abides in the First Jhāna . . . progress whereto is difficult and intuition sluggish, which is EMPTY, and the dominant influence in which is Desire—then there is contact . . . balance. Now these . . . are states that are good.

But when, as the result of just this good Jhāna having been wrought, having been cultivated in pursuit of the Higher Ideal, he, aloof from sensuous appetites, aloof from evil ideas, enters into and abides in the First Jhāna . . . progress whereto is difficult and intuition sluggish,

—which is EMPTY . . .

. . . [*or*] [539] which is SIGNLESS[2] . . .

. . . [*or*] [540] which is AIMLESS,[3]

and the dominant influence in which is Desire—then there is contact . . . balance. And these . . . are states that are indeterminate.

[541] *Repeat in the case of each remaining Jhāna as passim.*

[542] *Repeat in the case of each of the three remaining* 'Modes of Progress' *applied to each Jhāna.*

---

[1] No title is appended to this group, but it will be seen that it is a repetition of group vi. (p. 145), with this additional feature, that the Jhāna which constitutes the Karma is EMPTY.

[2] Read animittaṃ for suññataṃ.

[3] Omit lokuttaro before phasso.

(ix.)

[543-546] *This group is identical with group* vii. [§§ 534-537], *except that the concept* Aimless *takes the place of the concept* Empty, *and conversely.*

(x.)

[547-551] *This group is identical with group* viii. [§§ 538-542], *except that the concept* Aimless *takes the place of the concept* Empty, *and conversely.*

[The Remaining Nineteen Great Methods.[1]]

[552] Which are the states that are indeterminate?

When he cultivates the Path of the Higher Ideal, the Advance in Mindfulness toward the Higher Ideal, the System of Right Efforts toward the Higher Ideal, etc. [*continue as in* § 358, *down to* 'Thought relating to the Higher Ideal'], whereby there is a going forth and onward, making for the undoing of rebirth, and when, that he may attain to the First Stage, he has put away views and opinions, and so, aloof from sensuous appetites, aloof from evil ideas, enters into and abides in the First Jhāna . . . progress whereto is difficult and intuition sluggish, and the dominant influence in which is Desire—then there is contact . . . balance. Now these . . . are states that are good.

But when, as the result of just this good Jhāna having been wrought, having been cultivated in pursuit of the Higher Ideal, he, aloof from sensuous appetites, aloof from evil ideas, enters into and abides in the First Jhāna . . . progress whereto is difficult and intuition sluggish, which is

Empty,
or Signless,
or Aimless,

and the dominant influence in which is

---

[1] *Cf.* above, p. 145.

Desire,
or Energy,
or a Thought,
or Investigation,

then there is contact . . . balance. And these . . . are states that are indeterminate.

[Here ends] Result in the FIRST PATH.

[II.—IV. THE REMAINING THREE PATHS. *Cf.* §§ 362-364*a*.]

[553] Which are the states that are indeterminate?

When he cultivates the Jhāna of the Higher Ideal (the rapt meditation), whereby there is a going forth and onward, making for the undoing of rebirth, and when, that he may attain to the SECOND STAGE, he has diminished the strength of sensual passions and of malice[1] . . . [*or*] when, that he may attain to the THIRD STAGE, he has put away the entire residuum of sensual passions and of malice . . . [*or*] when, that he may attain to the FOURTH STAGE, he has put away absolutely and entirely all passion for Form, all passion for the Formless, all conceit, excitement, and ignorance—and so, aloof from sensuous appetites, aloof from evil ideas, enters into and abides in the First Jhāna . . . progress whereto is difficult and intuition sluggish, then there is contact . . . the faculty of knowledge made perfect[2] . . . balance. Now these . . . are states that are good.[3]

---

[1] The passage which occurs here in the printed text, line 3 of the answer, viz., vivicc'eva . . . down to phasso hoti, seems to be a corrupt reading, presenting discrepancies with that symmetry both of construction and elision which usually marks Pitaka compilation. K. omits the phrase.

[2] This term (aññindriyaṃ hoti) is omitted in K. It belongs, however, to the attainment of the Second Path (see above, p. 96, n. 2), and is only superseded by the intellectual climax of aññātavindriyaṃ (§ 555). I do not think, therefore, that it is a wrong reading.

[3] Avyākatā here in the printed text should of course be kusalā.

But when, as the result of just this good Jhāna having been wrought, having been cultivated in pursuit of the Higher Ideal, he, aloof from sensuous appetites, aloof from evil ideas, enters into and abides in the First Jhāna . . . progress whereto is difficult and intuition sluggish, and which is EMPTY, then there is contact . . . the faculty of one whose knowledge is made perfect . . . balance. And these . . . are states that are indeterminate.

[554] *Question and answer on* 'contact' *as above passim.*

[555] What on that occasion is the faculty of one whose knowledge is made perfect (aññātavindriyaṃ)?[1]

The perfected knowledge, the science, the understanding of the doctrines of those whose knowledge is made perfect, their searching, research, searching the Truth; discernment, discrimination, differentiation; erudition, proficiency, subtlety; criticism, reflection, analysis; breadth, sagacity, leading; insight, intelligence, incitement; wisdom as faculty and as power; wisdom as a sword, as a height, as light, as glory, as splendour, as a precious stone; the absence of dulness, searching the Truth, right views, that searching the truth which is a factor in the Great Awakening; a Path-component, contained in the Path—this is on

---

[1] I am not up to the present aware whether this term occurs anywhere else in the Three Pitakas. By Buddhaghosa (Asl. 291) it is defined as the distinctive 'faculty of the aññātāvī (lit., the holder of things known), of him who, in the philosophy of the Four Truths, has completed what was to be done.' And the 'doctrines' mentioned in the answer are defined as the associated or constituent doctrines, 'within' which the subject has attained proficiency, or which he has mastered inwardly (sampayuttadhammānaṃ . . . thitānaṃ dhammānaṃ abbhantare).

Possibly, however, dhammānaṃ refers to those intellectual states as mastered and controlled by the aññātāvin, which are comprised in the answer.

that occasion the faculty of one whose knowledge is made perfect.

* * * * * *

Or[1] whatever other incorporeal, causally induced states there are on that occasion, these are states that are indeterminate.

[Here ends] result in connexion with the Higher Ideal.

[B—Bad Karma.[2]

(a) The Five Modes of Sense-Cognition.]

[556] Which are the states that are indeterminate?

When, as the result of bad karma having been wrought, having been stored up, visual cognition has arisen, accompanied by disinterestedness and having as its object a sight . . . auditory cognition has arisen, accompanied by disinterestedness and having as its object a sound . . . olfactory cognition has arisen, accompanied by disinterestedness and having as its object a smell . . . gustatory cognition has arisen, accompanied by disinterestedness and having as its object a taste . . . cognition of body has arisen, accompanied by distress and having as its object something tangible, then there is

---

[1] Avikkhepo hoti . . . pe . . . as included in the printed text, is omitted in K. It is, however, not incorrect, since a description of constituent states, beginning with 'contact' and ending with 'balance,' similar to that given in §§ 278-337, and only differing by the substitution of 'the faculty of one whose knowledge is made perfect' for 'the faculty of believing that I shall come to know the Unknown,' is here supposed to be fully rehearsed. As it stands, however, it is a little misleading.

[2] With section B, and its three subdivisions *a* to *c*, compare the co-ordinate results of good karma described above, §§ 431-468 and 484-497. Under B *happy* results are out of the question, the determining antecedents having been evil.

contact, feeling, perception, thinking, thought, distress,
self-collectedness;
the faculties of
ideation,
distress,
vitality.[1]

Now these, or whatever other incorporeal, causally induced states there are on that occasion—these are states that are indeterminate.

[557] *Question and answer on* 'contact' *as above passim.*

[558] What on that occasion is feeling?

The bodily pain, the bodily distress which, on that occasion, is born of contact with the appropriate element of cognition of body; the painful, distressful sensation which is born of contact with the body; the painful, distressful feeling which is born of contact with the body—this is the feeling that there then is.

[559] What on that occasion is distress?

The bodily pain, the bodily distress which, on that occasion, is the painful, distressful sensation born of contact with the body; the painful, distressful feeling born of contact with the body—this is the distress that there then is.

[560] What on that occasion is the faculty of distress?

Answer as in § 559.

* * * * * *

---

[1] Judging by the corresponding answer respecting good karma in § 443, the . . . pe . . . here appended in the printed text is erroneous. K. omits it.

This list and the following sections (557-560) apply to the last-named mode of sense-cognition, namely, that of body. In the case of the other modes, 'disinterestedness' instead of 'distress' would occasion to certain questions different answers.

Or whatever other incorporeal, causally induced states there are on that occasion, these are states that are indeterminate.

[Summary.]

[560*a*] Now at that time

the skandhas are four,
the spheres are two,
the elements are two,
the nutriments are three,
the faculties are three,
contact,
etc.

[*Continue as in* § 58.]

the faculty of ideation counts as a single factor,
the element of the cognition of body[1] counts as a single factor.
the sphere of [mental] states counts as a single factor,
etc.

[*Continue as in* §§ 58-61.]

*　*　*　*　*　*

[561] What on that occasion is the skandha of syntheses?

Contact,	discursive thought,
thinking,	self-collectedness;
conception,	the faculty of vitality.

Or whatever other incorporeal, causally induced states there are on that occasion, exclusive of the skandhas of feeling, perception and intellect—these are the skandha of syntheses.

*　*　*　*　*　*

[*Continue as in* § 63, etc.]

---

[1] For mano-viññāṇadhātu in the printed text read kāya-viññāṇadhātu.

[(*b*) *The Element of Ideation.*]

[562] Which are the states that are indeterminate?

When, as the result of bad karma having been wrought, having been stored up, an element of ideation has arisen, accompanied by disinterestedness, and having as its object a sight, a sound, a smell, a taste, something tangible or what not, then there is

contact, thought,
feeling, conception,
perception, discursive thought,
thinking, disinterestedness,
self-collectedness;
the faculties of
ideation,
disinterestedness,
vitality.

Now these, or whatever other incorporeal, causally induced states there are on that occasion—these are states that are indeterminate.

* * * * * *

[Summary.]

[562*a*] *This, including the description of the appropriate* skandha of syntheses [563], *is identical with the corresponding Summary*, §§ 467*a*, 468.

[(*c*) *The Element of Representative Intellection.*]

[564] Which are the states that are indeterminate?

When, as the result of bad karma having been wrought, having been stored up, an element of representative intellection has arisen, accompanied by disinterestedness, and having as its object a sight, etc.,[1] or what not, then there is

contact, thought,
feeling, conception,

[1] *Cf.* § 562.

perception, discursive thought,
thinking, self-collectedness;
the faculties of
ideation,
disinterestedness,
vitality.

Now these, or whatever other incorporeal, causally induced states there are on that occasion—these are states that are indeterminate.

* * * * * *

[*Continue as in* §§ 485-496.]

[Summary.]

[564*a*, 565] *This, including the description of the appropriate* skandha of syntheses, *is identical with* §§ 496*a*, 497.

[Here end] the Indeterminates which are the result of Bad [Karma].

[CHAPTER II.

Action-thoughts.[1]

A. In connexion with the Sensuous Universe.

(*a*) *On occasion of Ideation* (kāmāvacara-kiriyā).]

[566] Which are the states that are indeterminate? When an element of ideation of the kind termed *kiriyā*

[1] I have borrowed for a title the term kiriya-cittaṃ from Asl. 293. The later form is kriyā-cittaṃ (see Abh. S., p. 2 *et seq.*; Bastian's 'Buddhistische Psychologie,' Anhang). Kiriyā is discussed in my Introduction. The Cy. has the following on the term: 'Kiriyā here means simply *doing* (karaṇa-mattaṃ). In all kiriyā-thoughts those in which the stage of javanaṃ is attained are like wind-blown blossoms, but those in which that stage is not attained are like blossoms where the tree has been felled, barren of fruit. But when this or that is kept going in the performance of function, then there is "doing" pure and simple. Hence the term kiriyā is used.' Now, javanaṃ, according to Buddhaghosa (Sum. I., 195), is the effective outcome of an act of cognition, the stage when the mind or character of the percipient subject is modified (ethically) in one way or another. But in the species of indeterminate thoughts termed kiriyā there can be no practical outcome for good or bad, no karma can be set free. Hence the simile of the sterile blossoms. The Abh. S. gives also three species of non-causative kriyā-thoughts as connected with the sensuous universe—reflection on sense-impressions, reflection on ideas, and the genesis of mirth (hasituppāda-cittaṃ). These correspond fairly well to the three given in the Dh. S., if the two modes of representative intellection be taken in inverted order.

has arisen,[1] which is neither good nor bad nor the result of karma, which is accompanied by disinterestedness, and which has as its object a sight, a sound, a smell, a taste, something tangible, or what not, then there is

contact, thought,
feeling, conception,
perception, discursive thought,
thinking, disinterestedness,
self-collectedness ;[2]
the faculties of
ideation,
disinterestedness,
vitality.

Now these, or whatever other incorporeal, causally induced states there are on that occasion—these are states that are indeterminate.

* * * * * *

[Summary.]

[566*a*] Now, at that time
the skandhas are four,

---

[1] According to the Cy., the ideation which is kiriyā differs from the ideation which is *result* only in the mode of its arising (upattiṭṭhānaṃ). The latter arises immediately after the act of sense-cognition. The former arises while sensation is actually proceeding, while the organism is being turned towards the object (Asl. 294). Again (*ibid.*), that the thought is 'neither good nor bad' means the absence of that cause of good or of bad which is termed the root of the one or of the other; it means the absence of those conditions of good or of bad which are termed considering things by way of their causes (yoniso-manasikārā), or not so considering them. 'Nor the result of karma' means the absence of the generative cause (janakahetu), known as good or bad (as the case may be). Asl. 293. The marginal reading in the last sentence is obviously right.

[2] With its minimum connotation, *i.e.*, as in § 438 and elsewhere (Asl. 293).

the spheres are two,
the elements are two,
the nutriments are three,
the faculties are three,
contact,
etc.

* * * * * *

[567] *The* skandha of syntheses (*as well as the remainder of the foregoing summary*) *is identical with the corresponding passages in* Chapter I., viz., §§ 467*a*, 468.

* * * * * *

(*b*) *On occasion of Representative Intellection.*

1.

[568] Which are the states that are indeterminate ?

When an element of representative intellection of the kind termed *kiriyā* has arisen, which is neither good nor bad nor the result of karma, which is accompanied by happiness,[1]

---

[1] The Cy. (p. 294) pronounces this species of thought not common to men, but peculiar to the arahat. 'It is obtained in the six doors,' *e.g.*, when an arahat sees a spot (ṭhānaṃ) favourable to one of those prescribed spiritual wrestlings termed padhānāni [*sic lege; cf.* below, § 1366, (v.)], 'by this thought he is gladdened.' When he comes to a market-place, 'hears the uproar of the bargaining, and thinks, "I have done with all this thirst for gain," by this thought he is gladdened. When he has made an offering of fragrant odours or flowers at the shrine, by this thought he is gladdened. When he is tasting the food he has received as ordained, and thinks, "Verily I have carried out the doctrine incumbent upon me," by this thought he is gladdened. When he is carrying out minor rules concerning the body, and thinks, "I have fulfilled the rules concerning the door of the body," by this thought he is gladdened. Such is this kind of intellection when obtained in connexion with the "fivefold door." In connexion with the door of *ideation*, it arises with reference to the

and which has as its object a sight, a sound, a smell, a taste, something tangible, or what not, then there is

contact,	conception,
feeling,	discursive thought,
perception,	joy,
thinking,	ease,
thought,	self-collectedness;
the faculties of	
energy,	ideation,
concentration,	happiness,
vitality.	

Now these, or whatever other incorporeal, causally induced states there are on that occasion—these are states that are indeterminate.

[569] *Question and answer on* 'contact' *as above passim.*

* * * * * *

[570] What on that occasion is self-collectedness?

The stability, solidity, absorbed steadfastness of thought which on that occasion is the absence of distraction, balance, imperturbed mental procedure, quiet, the faculty and the power of concentration[1]—this is the self-collectedness that there then is.

* * * * * *

[571] What on that occasion is the faculty of energy . . . [572] of concentration?

Answers as in § 13 *and* § 570 *respectively.*

* * * * * *

---

past and the future.' As, for instance, when the Buddha smiled at the recollection of occurrences in certain of his former births, or, again, when he foresaw this and that.

[1] It might have been expected that this 'power' as well as that of 'energy' would have found a place in the enumeration of the constituent states. The Cy. (p. 295) explains that 'concentration' and 'energy' are not present in full strength. It follows that no 'powers' are included in the summary.

[Summary.]

[572*a*] Now at that time
the skandhas are four,
the spheres are two,
the elements are two,
the nutriments are three,
the faculties are five,
contact,
etc.

[*Continue as in* § 482*a*.]

* * * * * *

[573] What on that occasion is the skandha of syntheses?

Contact,
thinking,
conception,
discursive thought,
joy,
self-collectedness,
the faculties of
energy,
concentration,
vitality.

Or whatever other incorporeal, causally induced states there are on that occasion, exclusive of the skandhas of feeling, perception, and intellect—these are the skandha of syntheses.

* * * * * *

2.

[574] Which are the states that are indeterminate?

When an element of representative intellection of the kind termed *kiriyā* has arisen, which is neither good, nor bad, nor the result of karma, which is accompanied by disinterestedness,[1] and which has as its object a sight, a sound, a smell, a taste, something tangible, or what not, then there is

contact, thought,
feeling, conception,
perception, discursive thought,
thinking, disinterestedness,
self-collectedness ;
the faculties of
energy, ideation,
concentration, disinterestedness,
vitality.

Now these, or whatever other incorporeal, causally induced states there are on that occasion—these are states that are indeterminate.

* * * * * *

[Summary.]

[574*a*] *Identical with* 572*a*.

* * * * * *

[575] *The* skandha of syntheses *is identical with that in* § 573, *but* 'joy' *must be omitted.*

* * * * * *

3-

[576] Which are the states that are indeterminate?

When an element of representative intellection of the

[1] This kind of thought, unlike the last, is, says the Cy. (295), common to all intelligent (sacittaka) beings; in fact, there is none such who does not experience it. (The marginal reading is here evidently the more correct.) If it arise in connexion with the 'five doors,' it is an act of establishing; if in connexion with the door of ideation, it is an act of reflection. By it the six specific channels of cognition lay hold of their several objects.

kind termed *kiriyā* has arisen that is neither good, nor bad, nor the result of karma—(I.)[1] which is accompanied by happiness and associated with knowledge . . . (II.) which is accompanied by happiness, associated with knowledge, and prompted by a conscious motive . . . (III.) which is accompanied by happiness and disconnected with knowledge . . . (IV.) which is accompanied by happiness, disconnected with knowledge and prompted by a conscious motive . . . (V.) which is accompanied by disinterestedness and associated with knowledge . . . (VI.) which is accompanied by disinterestedness, associated with knowledge and prompted by a conscious motive . . . (VII.) which is accompanied by disinterestedness and disconnected with knowledge . . . (VIII.) which is accompanied by disinterestedness, disconnected with knowledge and prompted by a conscious motive —and which has as its object a sight, a sound, a smell, a taste, something tangible, or what not—then there is contact . . . balance. Now these . . . are states that are indeterminate.

* * * * * *

[576*a*] That absence of lust which is the root of the indeterminate . . .

that absence of hate which is the root of the indeterminate . . .

that absence of dulness which is the root of the indeterminate . . .

these are states that are indeterminate.[2]

* * * * * *

[B. In connexion with the Universe of Form (rūpāvacara-kiriyā).]

---

[1] The Latin numerals refer to the Eight Main Types of Thought set forth in the first 159 sections of this work. In this connexion, however, they are no longer effective as 'good,' *i.e.*, as producing good karma.

[2] See above, § 498*a*.

[577] Which are the states that are indeterminate?

When he cultivates rapt meditation in connexion with the universe of Form, and of the kind termed *kiriyā* which is neither good, nor bad, nor the result of karma, and which is concerned with easeful living under present conditions[1]—and so, aloof from sensuous appetites, aloof from evil ideas, by earth-gazing, enters into and abides in the First Jhāna . . . then there is contact . . . balance. Now these . . . are states that are indeterminate.

[578] *Repeat in the case of each remaining Jhāna on the Fourfold, and of those on the Fivefold System.*

[C. In connexion with the Universe of the Formless (arūpāvacara-kiriyā).]

[579] Which are the states that are indeterminate?

When he cultivates rapt meditation in connexion with the universe of the Formless, of the kind termed *kiriyā*, which is neither good, nor bad, nor the result of karma, and is concerned with easeful living under present conditions—and when, by passing wholly beyond all consciousness of form, by the dying out of the consciousness of sensory reaction, by turning the attention from any consciousness of the manifold, he enters into and abides in that rapt meditation which is accompanied by the consciousness of a sphere of unbounded space—even the Fourth Jhāna, to gain which all sense of ease must have been put away, etc. . . . then there is contact . . . balance. Now these . . . are states that are indeterminate.

---

[1] *Diṭṭha-dhammasukha-vihāraṃ.* In this individual existence (imasmiṃ attabhāve), explains the Cy. (296. On this term, *cf.* below, p. 175, n. 1). In Sum. I., 121 the paraphrase runs, 'that state of existence one happens to have got.' *Cf.* 'Dialogues of the Buddha,' I. 50, n. The passage there commented upon (D. I. 37) is the heresy which holds that Jhāna constituted an equivalent for Nirvāna.

[580-582] *Here follow, with the same opening formula as in the foregoing answer, the three remaining* 'Jhānas connected with Formless Existence.' *See* §§ 266-268.

* * * * * *

[582*a*] That absence of lust which is the root of the indeterminate . . . that absence of hate which is the root of the indeterminate . . . that absence of dulness which is the root of the indeterminate . . . these . . . are states that are indeterminate.[1]

* * * * * *

[Here ends] the DIVISION ON THE GENESIS OF THOUGHTS.

---

[1] In K. a footnote is here appended, drawing attention to the apparent discrepancy in the fact that this passage, hitherto given under the universe of sense [§§ 498*a*, 576*a*], is here associated with the universe of the Formless. This, it adds, should be accepted after due deliberation.

[BOOK II.

FORM (rūpakandaṃ).

Introductory.]

[583] Which are the states that are indeterminate?[1]

The results of good and bad states taking effect in the universe of sense, in that of form, in that of the formless or in [the life] which is Unincluded,[2] and as connected with the skandhas of feeling, perception, syntheses, and intellect;[3] as well as those states known as *kiriyā* which are neither good, nor bad, nor the result of karma; all form, moreover;

---

[1] The subject of the Ethically Indeterminate has not been exhausted by the inquiry into Vipāko and Kiriyā. It includes two other species: Form (or External Phenomena) and Nirvāna (Uncompounded Element). (Asl. 296.) Hence it is that the following inquiry into 'Form' as objective and subjective phenomenon is led up to by a question connecting it with the foregoing inquiry into the genesis of 'thought,' which is presented from the point of view of a-rupino dhammā, or formless (incorporeal) states of consciousness.

[2] Apariyāpannā. This term, which is often employed in Book III., and which is intended to convey a sense of the 'apartness' of the pursuit of the Highest from all lower aims, is dealt with below (§ 992).

[3] I follow, here as often elsewhere, the punctuation of K. In this identical answer later on, however, K. is self-inconsistent, placing a colon before, and a comma after, the enumeration of the skandhas. See § 983. One or the other is probably an inadvertency.

and [finally] Uncompounded Element[1]—these are states that are indeterminate.

[584] In this connexion what is 'all form' (sabbaṃ rūpaṃ)?

The four great phenomena[2] and that form which is derived from the four great phenomena—this is what is called 'all form.'[3]

[584-594] *Here follows the Mātikā, or table of contents of the following analysis of Form, considered under quantitative categories—the usual Buddhist method. That is to say, Form is considered, first, under a number of single, uncorrelated qualities, then under dichotomized qualities, then under*

---

[1] Asankhatā ca dhātu. This term, which both Buddhaghosa and the original Atthakathā (see § 1,376 in printed text of Dh. S.) identify with Nirvāna, occurs often in this connexion with its opposite 'all form' (*v.* p. 168, n. 3) in Book III. I do not know whether this, so to speak, cosmological conception of the Ethical Ideal occurs in the older books of the Pitakas, or whether, indeed, the commentators have not laid upon the physical term more than it was intended to bear—a connotation that derives perhaps from the 'scholastic' ages of Buddhism. For example, in §§ 1016-1018 of the present work, to identify uncompounded element with Nirvāna, just after it has been opposed to the 'topmost fruit of arahatship,' would apparently land the compilers in a grave inconsistency. I have yet to meet with a passage in the first two Pitakas which establishes the identification. In the *Milinda-pañho*, giving the traditional doctrine of an age half-way between Pitakas and Commentaries, we can see the theory of Nirvāna as the one *asankhataṃ* developing. See pp. 268 *seq.* *Cf.* also K. V. 317-30.

[2] *Mahābhutāni*, that is, the four elements, literally, the things-that-have-become, *die grossen Gewordenen*, τὰ γιγνόμενα—a far more scientific term than elements or στοιχεῖα. See further below, §§ 597, 647 *et seq.*

[3] The various implications of the term *rūpaṃ*, such as objective phenomena, concrete or compound, the object of the sense of sight, material existence without sensuous appetite, etc., are discussed in my Introduction (ii.).

qualities which, taken singly, give inclusion, inclusion under the opposite, or exclusion from both ; or which, taken in pairs, afford three combinations. We then get pairs of qualities taken together, affording four *combinations. After that comes consideration of Form under more inductive classifications, e.g., the four elements and, fifthly, their derivatives, and so on, as given below.*

[Chapter I.

Exposition of Form under Single Concepts (ekaka-niddeso).]

[595] All form is that which is
not a cause,
not the concomitant of a cause,
disconnected with cause,[1]
conditioned,[2]
compound,[3]
endowed with form,[4]
mundane,[5]
co-Intoxicant,[6]

---

[1] Na hetum eva. On the Commentator's analysis of the meanings of 'cause,' see under § 1053. The special connotation here is that 'form' as such is not the ground or 'root,' or psychical associate of any moral or immoral result. Asl. 303. The two following terms are dealt with under §§ 1074, 1076.

[2] Sappaccayaṃ. *Cf.* § 1083.

[3] Sankhataṃ. This quality is involved in the preceding quality. See § 1085. See also above, p. 166, n. 1.

[4] Rūpiyaṃ, or rūpam eva. The table of contents (§ 584) gives the former; K. has here the latter. Either the one or the other has been omitted from the present section of the printed text. The Cy. gives the latter term —Rūpam evā ti rūpino dhammā, etc. Asl. 304.

[5] Lokiyaṃ; the antithesis of lokuttaraṃ. *Cf.* § 1093.

[6] Sāsavaṃ. See § 1096 *et seq.*

favourable to
the Fetters,[1]
the Ties,
the Floods,
the Bonds,
the Hindrances;
infected,[2]
favourable to grasping,[3]
belonging to corruption,[4]
indeterminate,
void of idea,[5]
neither feeling, nor perception, nor synthesis,[6]
disconnected with thought,
neither moral result, nor productive of moral result,[7]
uncorrupted yet belonging to corruption,[8]
not that 'where conception works and thought discursive,[9]
not that 'wherein is no working of conception, but only of thought discursive,'
void of 'the working of conception and of thought discursive,'

---

[1] Saññojaniyaṃ, etc. This and the four following terms are severally discussed in connexion with the ethical metaphors of Fetters and the rest. See § 1113 *et seq.*

[2] Parāmaṭṭhaṃ. See § 1174 *et seq.*

[3] Upādāniyaṃ. See § 990 and § 1213 *et seq.*

[4] Sankilesikaṃ. See § 993 and § 1229 *et seq.*

[5] Anārammaṇaṃ, the idea or mental object belonging, of course, to the arūpa-dhammo.

[6] Acetasikaṃ. See § 1022.

[7] See § 989.

[8] See § 994.

[9] Na savitakka-savicāraṃ. This and the two following technical terms mark off 'form' from the *mental* discipline of Jhāna, even though Jhāna may be practised for the sake of passing from a sensuous existence to the 'universe of Form.' *Cf.* §§ 160, 168, 161, and 996-998.

not 'accompanied by joy,'
not 'accompanied by ease,'
not 'accompanied by disinterestedness,'[1]
not something capable of being got rid of either by insight or by cultivation,
not that the cause of which may be got rid of either by insight or by cultivation,
neither tending to, nor away from, the accumulation involving re-birth,
belonging neither to studentship nor to that which is beyond studentship,
limited,[2]
related to the universe of sense,
not related to the universe of form,[3]
nor to that of the formless,
included,
not of the Unincluded,[4]
not something entailing inevitable retribution,[5]
unavailing for (ethical) guidance,
cognizable when apparent[6] by the six modes of cognition,

---

[1] *Cf.* §§ 999-1001. These are all mental states, characterizing the other four skandhas, not the rūpakkhandho. Similarly, the four following doctrinal expressions are only applicable to mental and moral categories. *Cf.* §§ 1007-1118.

[2] Parittaṃ. See § 1019.

[3] Read na rūpāvacaraṃ.

[4] See p. 165, n. 2.

[5] This and the following term belong to ethical, immaterial categories of thought. See §§ 1028-1030 and 1291; also 1288, 1289, and 277.

[6] *I.e.*, remarks the Commentator, when it is present (in consciousness). 'For, strictly speaking, with reference to visual and other sense-cognition, they (*read* na hi tāni) do not cognize the past and future; that is the function of representative cognition (manoviññāṇaṃ)' (Asl. 304).

impermanent,[1]
subject to decay.

Such is the category of Form considered by way of single attributes.[2]

---

[1] Aniccaṃ, 'inasmuch as, having fallen into this stream of sense-cognition it ('form') has become mere flotsam, has become something gone, something that is not' (*ibid.*). This shows well the idealist or psychological standpoint of the Buddhist tradition. Form is impermanent for the individual perceptive consciousness.

[2] The Cy. gives as the reason for there being no catechism on each of the foregoing attributes the fact that there is no correlated opposite, as in the next category, from which each term is to be differentiated (Asl. 303). This, in view of the procedure in Book I., is scarcely adequate. However, every term is examined in the sequel, as the foregoing notes will have indicated.

[CHAPTER II.

The Category of Form considered by way of dual attributes—positive and negative (duvidhena rūpa-sangaho).

'There is form which is derived.'][1]

[596] What is that form which is derived?

The sphere[2] of

vision, smell,
hearing, taste,
body-sensibility;[3]

the sphere of

sights, odours,
sounds, tastes;

the faculties of

femininity, masculinity,
vitality;

---

[1] This and the following italicised headings are quoted from the table of contents, § 585, etc.—atthi rūpaṃ upādā, and again, atthi rūpaṃ no upādā. The ablative resembles our idiom '*quâ* derived'—form as derived. In § 584 and in § 597, etc. the gerund upādāya is employed. Depending on, not released from, is the paraphrase (Asl. 300, 305). 'Grounded in' were an approximate rendering, the literal meaning being 'taking hold of.'

[2] Āyatanaṃ. The word means (see my Introduction) simply 'field,' locus, range, *Gebiet*.

[3] Lit. body. The Upanishads use 'skin.' *Cf.* our modern term 'skin-sensibility,' in extension of 'touch,' 'tactile sense.' The corresponding objective 'sphere of the tangible' is classed among things *un*derived. See § 647.

intimation
by act,
by speech;
the element of space;

buoyancy, plasticity, wieldiness, integration, maintenance, decay, impermanence,	of form.

solid nutriment.

[597] What is that form which is the sphere of vision (cakkhāyatanaṃ)?

The eye,[1] that is to say the sentient organ,[2] derived from

---

[1] Cakkhu, which stands for vision, sense of sight and eye. 'Eye,' however, is always in the present work to be understood as the seeing faculty or visual sense, and not as the physical organ or 'eye of flesh' (maṃsa-cakkhu). The Cy. gives an account of the eye, of which the following is the substance: First the aggregate organism (sasambhāra-cakkhu). A ball of flesh fixed in a cavity, bound by the socket-bone beneath and by the bone of the eyebrow above, by the angles of the eye at the sides, by the brain within and by the eyelashes without. There are fourteen constituents: the four elements, the six attributes dependent on them, viz., colour, odour, taste, sap of life, form (saṇṭhānaṃ), and collocation (sambhavo); vitality, nature, body-sensibility (kāyappasādo) and the visual sentient organ. The last four have their source in karma. When 'the world,' seeing an obvious extended white object fancies it perceives the eye, it only perceives the basis (or seat—vatthu) of the eye. And this ball of flesh, bound to the brain by nerve-fibres, is white, black and red, and contains the solid, the liquid, the lambent and the gaseous. It is white by superfluity of humour, black by superfluity of bile, red by superfluity of blood, rigid by superfluity of the solid, exuding by superfluity of the liquid, inflamed by

---

[2] See note on p. 174.

the Great Phenomena, forming part of the nature of the self,[1] invisible and reacting[2]—by which eye, invisible and

---

superfluity of the lambent, quivering by superfluity of the gaseous. But that sentient organ (pasādo) which is there bound, inherent, derived from the four great principles—this is the visual sense (pasādacakkhu). Placed in the midst and in the front of the black disc of the composite eye, the white disc surrounding it (*note that the iris is either not distinguished or is itself the 'black disc'*) and in the circle of vision, in the region where the forms of adjacent bodies come to appear (*there seems here some omission in the text*), it permeates the seven ocular membranes as sprinkled oil will permeate seven cotton wicks. And so it stands, aided by the four elements, sustaining, binding, maturing, moving (samudīranaṃ)—like an infant prince and his four nurses, feeding, bathing, dressing and fanning him—maintained by nutriment both physical (utu) and mental, protected by the (normal) span of life, invested with colour, smell, taste and so forth, in size the measure of a louse's head—stands duly constituting itself the door of the seat of visual cognitions, etc. For as it has been said by the Commander of the Doctrine (Sāriputta):

> The visual sense by which he beholds forms
> Is small and delicate, comparable to a louse's head.

The elaborate architectonics of this paragraph in the original is a fine effort of the Commentator's style. I am not clear to what the 'etc.' after 'cognitions' alludes. But the expression occurs in the description of each sense. *Cf.* the description in Hardy, 'Man. of Buddhism,' p. 419.

[3] Pasādo. By selecting this term, continues the Cy., he (the Buddha) rejects the other (physical) eye. So far as I know, the as yet unidentified verses quoted in the previous note are the only early instance of the word pasādo, meaning literally clearness, brightness, serenity, faith, being used to denote the receptive reacting sense-agency. It is not easy to divine exactly how the Buddhists came to use the word in this connexion. It is used co-ordinately for all the other senses, hence the sensuous signification had nothing to do with the specific nature of sight (unless this was

---

[1] See note [1] on p. 175. [2] See note [2] on p. 175.

reacting, one[3] has seen, sees, will, or may see form that is visible and impingeing—this that is sight, the sphere of sight, the element of vision, the faculty of vision, this that is 'a world,'[4] 'a door,' 'an ocean,' 'lucent,' 'a field,' 'a

---

made the Type of all other sensation). Taken causatively it may conceivably have meant either that which makes clear—a revealer, as it were (*cf.* Böthl. and Roth—prasādana), or that which gratifies or satisfies (*Beruhigen*), both meanings emphasizing psychological *process*, rather than 'product' or 'seat.'

[1] Attabhāva-pariyāpanno. 'The body and the five skandhas are here termed nature of the self, after the usage of foolish folk who say, "This is myself"' (Asl. 308). Thus the usage of attabhāvō was a concession on the part of the Great Teacher to animistic phraseology.

[2] '*I.e.*, impact and reaction are set up in the eye' (*ibid.*).

[3] Paraphrased by ayaṃ satto, any given individual (*ibid.*).

[4] This and the following similes will be quotations of metaphors applied to the senses in the Sutta Pitaka. *E.g.*, that of the 'empty village' occurs in S. iv. 174—Suñño gamo ti kho, bhikkhave, channam ajjhattikānam [? āyatanānam] adhivacanaṃ. That of a 'door,' which in the age of the Commentaries was the regular term for sense-organ, is, I believe, seldom used in the Sutta Pitaka, and then only as a poetical figure, not as a technical term. *Cf.*, *e.g.*, indriyesuguttadvāro (D I., 63, 250). Buddhaghosa simply paraphrases the various metaphors—'world,' by reason of wasting and decay; 'door,' by reason of customary resort; 'ocean,' by reason of its insatiableness; 'lucent,' by reason of its purity; 'field,' by reason of the springing up (growth) of contact, etc.; 'base,' by reason of its fixed seat; 'guide,' 'guidance,' by reason of its leading the nature-of-the-self showing agreements and differences; 'hither shore,' by reason of its being included in the 'body of this life' (or individuality, sakkāyaṃ); 'empty village,' because it is common to many, because there is no headman (*i.e.*, Ego or soul. 'Many' must mean the individual considered as an aggregate of constituents.) The metaphors, it will be seen, are applied equally, with the sole exception of 'guide' and 'guidance,' to each remaining sense. By the explanation of these two figures given in the Cy., they should have been

basis,' 'a guide,' 'guidance,' the 'hither shore,' an 'empty village'—this is that form which constitutes the sphere of vision.

[598] What is that form which is the sphere of vision?

The eye, that is to say the sentient organ, derived from the four Great Phenomena, forming part of the nature of the self, invisible and reacting, and against which eye, invisible and reacting, form that is visible and impingeing, has impinged,[1] impinges, will, or may impinge—this that is sight, the sphere of sight, the constituent element of sight, etc. [*continue as in* § 597].

[599] What is that form which is the sphere of vision?

The eye, that is to say the sentient organ, derived from the four Great Phenomena, forming part of the nature of the self, invisible and reacting, which eye, invisible and reacting, has impinged, impinges, will, or may impinge on form[2] that is visible and impingeing—this that is sight, the sphere of sight, etc. [*continue as in* § 597].

[600] What is that form which is the sphere of vision?

The eye, that is to say the sentient organ, derived from the four Great Phenomena, forming part of the nature of the self, invisible and reacting, (i.) depending on which eye, in consequence of some visible form,[3] there has arisen, arises, will, or may arise

visual contact;[4] . . .

---

left to stand for each sense. Buddhaghosa, however, is of course not responsible for the expressions used in the Pitakas. Yet it is slightly disappointing that he makes no effort to account for an omission which is not without psychological justification.

[1] In this answer, according to the Cy. (p. 309), involuntary visual sensation is described, as when lightning flashes on the sight of one not looking for it.

[2] Here (Asl. 309) we have *voluntary* sense-impression described—the process in the case of one 'who, by his own desire, seeking to look at some object, concentrates his vision.'

[3] Cakkhum nissāya, rūpaṃ ārabbha.

[4] Here there should be in the text . . . pe . . . as in

(ii.) and depending on which eye, in consequence of some visible form, there has arisen, arises, will, or may arise—born of that visual contact—

a feeling . . .
[*or* iii.] a perception . . .
[*or* iv.] thinking . . .
[*or* v.] a visual cognition[1] . . .

[further, vi.] depending on[2] which eye, and having a visible form as its object, there has arisen, arises, will, or may arise

visual contact,

(vii.) and depending on which eye, and having a visible form as its object, there has arisen, arises, will, or may arise, born of that visual contact,

a feeling . . .
[*or* viii.] a perception . . . .

---

the corresponding passage for the other four senses. *Cf.* note 4. In K. it is also inadvertently omitted here.

[1] Cakkhuviññāṇaṃ here replaces the fourth mode of consciousness, cittaṃ, or thought, in the series invariably stated as aroused by 'contact' in connexion with the Eight Types of Thought given in Book I, chap. i. Thinking (cetanā) may stand for a train of ideas set going by the sensation having no special reference to the visible object as such. Visual cognition, on the other hand, would take special account of the thing seen. Or possibly the two are to be considered as corresponding approximately to process and product. *Cf.* what has been said above on both terms, p. 8, n. 1.

[2] Judging by the corresponding passages in §§ 604, 608, 612, 616, by K. and by the comments of Buddhaghosa, I find that the following passage has been erroneously omitted in the text before the words cakkhum p'etaṃ:— . . . pe . . . yaṃ cakkhuṃ nissāya rūpārammaṇo cakkhusamphasso uppajji vā uppajjati vā uppajjissati vā uppajje vā, yam cakkhuṃ nissāya rūpārammaṇā cakkhusamphassajā vedanā . . . pe . . . saññā . . . pe . . . cetanā . . . pe . . . cakkhuviññāṇam uppajji vā uppajjati vā uppajji vā uppajje vā. *Cf.* also § 620.

[*or* ix.] thinking . . .
[*or* x.] visual cognition—
this that is sight, the sphere of sight, etc. [*continue as in* § 597].[1]

[601-604] What is that form which is the sphere of hearing?

The ear, that is to say the sentient organ,[2] derived from the four Great Phenomena, forming part of the nature of the self, invisible and reacting,—

(*a*) by which ear, invisible and reacting, one has heard, hears, will, or may hear sound that is invisible and impingeing;—

(*b*) against which ear, invisible and reacting, sound that is invisible and impingeing, has impinged, impinges, will, or may impinge;—

(*c*) which ear, invisible and reacting, has impinged, impinges, will, or may impinge on sound that is invisible and impingeing;—

(*d*) depending on which ear, in consequence of a sound, there has arisen, arises, will, or may arise
auditory contact; . . .
and, depending on which ear, in consequence of a

---

[1] According to the Cy. (310), this reply, when rehearsed in full, reveals ten distinct answers, each commencing with the refrain: 'The eye, that is to say,' etc., to 'self, invisible and reacting.' They may be summarized and generalized thus: (i.) Sense-impression or contact, as conditioned by sense-organ and sense-*stimulus*. (ii.) Resultant feeling. (iii.-v.) Resultant intellectual states. (vi.) Sense-impression or contact, as conditioned by sense-organ and idea of sense-*object*. (vii.-x.) Resultant states as in (ii.-v). What was precisely the difference between the processes named as (i.) and (vi.) it is not yet easy to determine with certainty.

[2] This, situated within the cavity of the aggregate organism of the ear, and well furnished with fine reddish hairs, is in shape like a little finger-stall (anguli-veṭhanaka). (Asl. 310.) *Cf.* Hardy, *loc. cit.*

sound, there has arisen, arises, will, or may arise, born of that auditory contact,

a feeling . . .
[*or*] a perception . . .
[*or*] thinking . . .
[*or*] auditory cognition ;—

[further] depending on which ear, and having a sound as its object, there has arisen, arises, will, or may arise

auditory contact,

and, depending on which ear, and having a sound as its object, there has arisen, arises, will, or may arise, born of that auditory contact,

a feeling . . .
[*or*] a perception . . .
[*or*] thinking . . .
[*or*] auditory cognition ;—

this that is hearing, the sphere of hearing, the constituent element of hearing, the faculty of hearing, this that is 'a world,' 'a door,' 'an ocean,' 'lucent,' 'a field,' 'a basis,'[1] 'the hither shore,' 'an empty village'—this is that form which is the sphere of hearing.

[605-608] What is that form which is the sphere of smell?

The nose, that is to say the sentient organ,[2] derived from the four Great Phenomena, forming part of the nature of the self, invisible and reacting,—

(*a*) by which nose, invisible and reacting, one has smelt, smells, will, or may smell odour that is invisible and impingeing ;—

(*b*) against which nose, invisible and reacting, odour that is invisible and impingeing, has impinged, impinges, will, or may impinge ;—

---

[1] On the omission of 'a guide,' etc., see p. 175, n. 4.

[2] This is situated 'inside the cavity of the aggregate nasal organism, in appearance like a goat's hoof.' (Asl. 310). *Cf.* Hardy, *loc. cit.* Probably the hoof is imagined as regarded from below.

(*c*) which nose, invisible and reacting, has impinged, impinges, will, or may impinge on odour that is invisible and impingeing;—

(*d*) depending on which nose, in consequence of an odour . . . depending on which nose, and having an odour as its object, there has arisen, arises, will, or may arise

olfactory contact,

and, depending on which nose, in consequence of an odour . . . depending on which nose, and having an odour as its object, there has arisen, arises, will or may arise, born of that olfactory contact,

a feeling . . .
[*or*] a perception . . .
[*or*] thinking . . .
[*or*] olfactory cognition;—

this that is smell, the sphere, the constituent element, the faculty, of smell, this that is 'a world,' etc. [*continue as in* § 604].

[609-612] What is that form which is the sphere of taste?

The tongue, that is to say the sentient organ,[1] derived from the four Great Phenomena, forming part of the nature of the self, invisible and reacting;—

(*a*) by which tongue, invisible and reacting, one has tasted, tastes, will, or may taste sapids that are invisible and impingeing;—

(*b*) against which tongue, invisible and reacting, sapids that are invisible and impingeing, have impinged, impinge, will, or may impinge;—

(*c*) which tongue, invisible and reacting, has impinged,

---

[1] This is situated 'above the middle of the aggregate gustatory organism, in appearance like the upper side of the leaf of a lotus.' (Asl., *ibid.*) *Cf.* Hardy, *loc. cit.* The palate apparently was not included in the gustatory apparatus.

impinges, will, or may impinge on sapids that are invisible and impingeing ;—

(*d*) depending on which tongue, in consequence of a sapid . . . depending on which tongue, and having a sapid as its object, there has arisen, arises, will, or may arise

gustatory contact,

and depending on which tongue, in consequence of a sapid . . . depending on which tongue, and having a sapid as its object, there has arisen, arises, will, or may arise, born of that gustatory contact,

a feeling . . .
[*or*] a perception . . .
[*or*] thinking . . .
[*or*] gustatory cognition ;—

this that is taste, the sphere, the constituent element, the faculty of taste, this that is 'a world,' etc. [*continue as in* § 604].

[613-616] What is that form which is the sphere of body [-sensibility] ?

The body, that is to say the sentient organ,[1] derived

---

[1] The sphere of kāyo—so runs the comment (Asl. 311)—is diffused over the whole bodily form just as oil pervades an entire cotton rag. With the exception of this quality of relatively undifferentiated organ, the sense is co-ordinate with the other senses. To the objection that, if the sensitive surface be indeed so general it would convey confused impressions, it is counter-asserted that, if it were not so general, tactile impressions could not be adequately differentiated. Strictly speaking the body-sense is both everywhere and not everywhere. *Not* everywhere to the extent of being in things *as* seen or *as* tasted. We cannot segregate and analyze sensations as we can grains of sand, and hence qualities are said to coalesce in the object. Nevertheless each mode of sense conveys its specific messages.—Such seems to me the substance of what I have clothed to a slight extent in terms of Western psychology. The Com-

from the four Great Phenomena, forming part of the nature of the self, invisible and reacting;—

(*a*) by which body-sensibility, invisible and reacting, one has touched, touches, will, or may touch the tangible that is invisible and impingeing;—

(*b*) against which body-sensibility, invisible and reacting, the tangible, which is invisible and impingeing, has impinged, impinges, will, or may impinge;—

(*c*) which body-sensibility, invisible and reacting, has impinged, impinges, will, or may impinge on the tangible that is invisible and impingeing;—

(*d*) depending on which body-sensibility, in consequence of something tangible . . . depending on which body-sensibility, and having something tangible as its object, there has arisen, arises, will, or may arise

tactile contact,[1]

and depending on which body-sensibility, in consequence of something tangible . . . depending on which body-sensibility, and having something tangible as its object, there has arisen, arises, will, or may arise, born of that tactile contact,

a feeling . . .
[*or*] a perception . . .
[*or*] thinking . . .
[*or*] tactile cognition;—[2]

this that is body-sensibility, the sphere, constituent element, faculty of body-sensibility, this that is 'a world,' etc. [*continue as in* § 604].

---

mentary is of course tentative and groping, as elsewhere in its theory of sense; yet it must not be forgotten that it was not till about fifty years ago that Ernst Weber's 'Der Tastsinn und das Gemeingefühl' appeared, containing the positive results of a comparison of different skin-areas from the standpoint of their varying ability to convey clear or vague tactile impressions.

[1] Literally, body-contact.

[2] Literally, cognition of body, so rendered in § 443 *seq.*

[617] What is that form which is the sphere of [visible] form?

The form which, derived from the great principles, is visible under the appearance of colour and produces impact[1]—is blue,[2] yellow, red,[3] white, black,[4] crimson,[5] bronze,[6] green-coloured,[7] of the hue of the mango-bud;[8] is long, short,[9] big, little, circular, oval, square, hexagonal, octagonal, hekkaidecagonal; low, high, shady, glowing, light, dim, dull, frosty,[10] smoky, dusty; like in colour to the

---

[1] Sappaṭighaṃ, here paraphrased as *producing* (janakaṃ) reaction and impact. Asl. 317.

[2] Compared to the ummāpupphaṃ, or flax-blossom. *Cf.* my remark on nīlaṃ above, under § 246. Here the term is illustrated by an azure flower, such as we ourselves might quote as a type of blue. And yet even here the wide range and indefiniteness of the word find expression. For according to Böthl. and Roth, on the authority of Hemachandra, umā is applied to *night.*

[3] Like the blossom of *Pterospermum acerifolium* and *Pentapetro phœnicea* respectively (*ibid.*). I give these on Childers' authority.

[4] Like the morning star and charcoal respectively (*ibid.*).

[5] Like the reddish buds of the *Vitex negundo* and *kaṇavīra* trees (*ibid.*).

[6] Hari, omitted in the text, but given in K. and the Cy. (*ibid.*). 'Whereas, in the verse

Harittacahemavaṇṇaṃ kāmaṃ sumukkhapakamā,

hari is spoken of as golden (suvaṇṇaṃ), by its being elsewhere taken in conjunction with coined gold (jātarūpaṃ), it is here meant as dark (sāmaṃ)' (*ibid.*). *Cf.* Jat. V. 216, sāmā ti suvaṇṇa-sāmā.

[7] The colour of green grass (*ibid.*).

[8] K. and the Cy. read ambankuravaṇṇaṃ.

[9] See my Introduction, on 'long,' short, as only indirectly objects of sight. 'The foregoing seven visibles are set forth without reference to any base (vatthu); the following according to common usage' (*ibid.*).

[10] Paraphrased as cloudy and as himaṃ—which may be frosty, snowy or dewy—respectively. As the allusion is only to lustre-contrast, the sparkle of hoar-frost is probably implied.

disc of moon,[1] sun, stars, a mirror,[2] a gem, a shell, a pearl, a cat's eye,[3] gold[4] or silver;[5] or whatever other form there is which, derived from the four Great Phenomena, is visible and productive of impact—form which, visible and productive of impact, one has seen, sees, will, or may see with the eye that is invisible and reacting—this which is visible form, this which is the sphere of visible form, the constituent element of visible form—this is that form which is the sphere of visible form.

[618] What is that form which is the sphere of visible form?

That form which, derived from the Great Phenomena, is visible under the appearance of colour and produces impact . . .[6] on which form, visible and productive of impact, the eye, invisible and impingeing, has impinged, impinges, will, or may impinge—this that is visible form, etc. [*continue as in* § 617].

[619] What is that form which is the sphere of visible form?

---

[1] The following terms, says the Cy. (*ibid.*), illustrate varieties of lustre. A little gratuitous astronomy is then thrown in. The orb of the moon, viz., the mansion of the moon-god, is 49 yojanas in extent, is made of gold and roofed with silver. That of the sun is 50 yojanas, is made of gold and roofed with crystal. The constellations, the mansions of different gods, are 7, 8, or 10 yojanas in extent, and are made of the seven jewels. Between the moon below and the sun above is 1 yojana. The constellations take two years in their orbit. They and the sun go (*sic*) swiftly, the moon slowly. At times the moon leads, at times she is behind.

[2] Is of bronze (Asl. 318).

[3] Is not a gem; is the colour of the bamboo (*ibid.*).

[4] 'The Master's colour' (*ibid.*).

[5] Under kahāpaṇo, *i.e.*, silver coin, māsakas of copper, wood, and lac are to be included (*ibid.*). Quoted from Vin. iii. 238.

[6] In this and the next two answers, according to K., the list of typical forms given in § 617 is to be rehearsed each time in full.

That form which, derived from the Great Phenomena, is visible under the appearance of colour and produces impact —which form, visible and producing impact, has impinged, impinges, will, or may impinge on the eye that is invisible and reacting—this which is visible form, etc. [*continue as in* § 617].

[620] What is that form which is the sphere of visible form?

That form which, derived from the four Great Phenomena, is visible and produces impact—in consequence of which form, and depending on the eye, there has arisen, arises, will, or may arise

visual contact . . .

in consequence of which form and depending on the eye, there has arisen, arises, will, or may arise, born of that visual contact,

a feeling . . .
[*or*] a perception . . .
[*or*] thinking . . .
[*or*] visual cognition . . .

[further] having which visible form as its object,[1] and depending on the eye there has arisen, arises, will, or may arise

visual contact,

---

[1] In the printed text, for rūpārammaṇaṃ read rūpārammaṇo, and, two lines later, rūpārammaṇā. So for the other senses, § 624, etc. I follow the reading in K., making the word adjectival to sakkhusamphassajo. and then to vedanā, saññā, etc. *Cf.* the analogous passage in § 600 (in the passage I have restored to the text), in § 604, and so on. I confess I do not see what is gained by shifting cakkhuṃ nissāya, so that by K.'s reading it is sandwiched between adjective and noun, beyond the symmetry in these sense-object answers, of giving precedence everywhere to the object. But this does not invalidate the reading in K. Ārammaṇaṃ is a term of mental procedure, not of bare sense-function, such as is indicated by the relation of rūpaṃ : cakkhu.

and, having which visible form as its object, and depending on the eye, there has arisen, arises, will, or may arise

a feeling . . .
[*or*] a perception . . .
[*or*] thinking . . .
[*or*] visual cognition . . .

this which is visible form, the sphere, the constituent element of visible form—this is that form which is the sphere of visible form.

[621] What is that form which is the sphere of sound?

That sound which is derived from the four Great Phenomena, is invisible and produces impact, such as the sound of drums, of tabors, of chank-shells, of tom-toms, of singing, of music;[1] clashing sounds,[2] manual sounds,[3] the noise of people,[4] the sound of the concussion of substances,[5] of wind,[6] of water,[7] sounds human and other than human, or whatever other sound[8] there is, derived from the Great Phenomena, invisible and producing impact—such a sound, invisible and producing impact, as, by the ear, invisible and reacting, one has heard, hears, will, or may hear . . .

[622] . . . and on which sound, invisible and producing impact, the ear, invisible and reacting, has impinged, impinges, will, or may impinge . . .

[623] . . . which sound, invisible and producing impact,

[1] *I.e.*, the sound of lutes and other stringed instruments (Asl. 319).

[2] *E.g.*, of gongs and castanets (*ibid.*).

[3] *I.e.*, of hand-clapping (*ibid.*).

[4] *I.e.*, of a crowd when words and syllables have become indistinguishable (*ibid.*).

[5] *I.e.*, of trees rubbing against each other, or of the knocking of blocks (*ibid.*). Vin. Texts, iii. 213, n.

[6] *I.e.*, of wind as wind (*ibid.*).

[7] *I.e.*, either of beaten or flowing water (*ibid.*).

[8] *I.e.*, of splitting reeds, tearing cloth, and the like (*ibid.*).

has impinged, impinges, will, or may impinge on the ear that is invisible and reacting . . .

[624] . . . in consequence of which sound and depending on the ear, there has arisen, arises, will, or may arise

auditory contact . . .

. . . and[1] . . . born of that auditory contact,

a feeling . . .

[*or*] a perception . . .

[*or*] thinking . . .

[*or*] auditory cognition . . .

. . . [further] having a sound as its object and depending on the ear, there has arisen, arises, will, or may arise,

auditory contact,

. . . and . . . born of that auditory contact,

a feeling . . .

[*or*] a perception . . .

[*or*] thinking . . .

[*or*] auditory cognition ;

this that is sound, the sphere and constituent element of sound—this is that form which is the sphere of sound.

[625] What is that form which is the sphere of odour?

That odour which is derived from the four Great Phenomena, is invisible and produces impact, such as the odour of roots, sap, bark, leaves, flowers, fruit; verminous odours, putrid odours, pleasant and unpleasant odours,[2] or

---

[1] Continue as for visible forms in § 620.

[2] Sugandho, duggandho — these, says Buddhaghosa, namely, desired odour and undesired odour, exhaust all odour. He predicates the same of good and bad tastes (sādu, asādu, § 629). In § 648 we find, classed among the tangibles, pleasant contact and painful contact. But we do not find the commentator making the same comprehensive claim for hedonistic values in touches as in odours and tastes. Nor, as we have seen, does the text predicate anything hedonistically of sight or touch. This is interesting as bringing the psychology of Buddhism, with its acute if incipient intuition, in 'touch' with our modern

whatever other odour there is, derived from the four Great Phenomena, invisible and producing impact; such an odour, invisible and producing impact, as one has smelt, smells, will, or may smell with the nose, that is invisible and impingeing . . .

[626] . . . on which odour, invisible and producing impact, the nose, invisible and impingeing, has impinged, impinges, will, or may impinge . . .

[627] . . . such an odour, invisible and producing impact, as has impinged, impinges, will, or may impinge on the nose, invisible and reacting . . .

[628] . . . in consequence of which odour and depending on the nose, there has arisen, arises, will, or may arise

olfactory contact . . .

and[1] . . . born of that olfactory contact,

a feeling . . .

[*or*] a perception . . .

[*or*] thinking . . .

[*or*] olfactory cognition . . .

. . . [further] having an odour as its object and depending on the nose, there has arisen, arises, will, or may arise

olfactory contact,

. . . and . . . born of that olfactory contact,

a feeling . . .

[*or*] a perception . . .

[*or*] thinking . . .

[*or*] olfactory cognition ;

---

psychology. For we say that the more our knowledge of the external world is built up by a given sense, the more is that sense connected with *neutral* feeling. And it is precisely sight, touch, and hearing that give us most of that knowledge.

Aristotle remarks, with reference to the sense of smell only, that our never discriminating an odour without associating therewith an impression of something painful or pleasant, seems to reveal the imperfection of this sense in humans. Imperfect, *i.e.*, in delicacy of discrimination, touch being herein the most perfect sense (De. An. II. ix.).

[1] See § 624, note.

this that is odour, the sphere and constituent element of odour—this is that form which is the sphere of odours.

[629] What is that form which is the sphere of taste?

That taste which is derived from the four Great Phenomena, is invisible and produces impact, such as the taste of roots, stems, bark, leaves, flowers, fruits, of sour, sweet,[1] bitter,[2] pungent,[3] saline,[4] alkaline,[5] acrid,[6] astringent,[7] nice and nauseous sapids,[8] or whatever other taste there is, derived from the four Great Phenomena, invisible and producing impact — such tastes, invisible and producing impact, as with the tongue, invisible and reacting, one has tasted, tastes, will, or may taste . . .

[630] . . . against which taste, invisible and producing impact, the tongue, invisible and impingeing, has impinged, impinges, will, or may impinge . . .

[631] . . . a taste which, invisible and producing impact, has impinged, impinges, will, or may impinge on the tongue, invisible and reacting . . .

[632] . . . in consequence of which taste and depending on the tongue, there has arisen, arises, will, or may arise gustatory contact . . .

---

[1] Buttermilk (takkambilaṃ) is given as a typical sour sapid, ghee from cow's milk (gosappi) as the type of a sweet sapid. But, adds the Cy., sweet added to astringent (kasāvaṃ) and kept standing will lose all its sweetness, and so with raw sugar and alkaline substance. Ghee, however, kept standing, while it loses colour and smell, does not lose its taste. It therefore is the absolute sweet (ekanta-madhuraṃ) (Asl. 320).

[2] *E.g.*, as nimb-tree fruit (*ibid.*).

[3] *E.g.*, as ginger and pepper (*ibid.*).

[4] *E.g.*, as sea-salt (*ibid.*).

[5] *E.g.*, as the egg-plant (vātingaṇakaṭīraṃ), or as green palm sprouts (cocoanut cabbage) (*ibid.*).

[6] *E.g.*, as the jujube, or the *Feronia elephantum*, etc. (*ibid.*).

[7] *E.g.*, as the yellow myrobalan (harīṭakaṃ). I am, as before, indebted to Childers' Dictionary for all this botanical knowledge.

[8] Sādu asādu. See § 625, n. 1.

. . . and[1] . . . born of that gustatory contact,
a feeling . . .
[*or*] a perception . . .
[*or*] thinking . . .
[*or*] gustatory cognition,

[further] having a taste as its object and depending on the tongue, there has arisen, arises, will, or may arise
gustatory contact,
. . . and . . . born of that gustatory contact,
a feeling . . .
[*or*] a perception . . .
[*or*] thinking . . .
[*or*] gustatory cognition;

this that is taste, the sphere and constituent element of taste—this is that form which is the sphere of taste.[2]

[633] What is that form which is femininity (itthindriyaṃ)?

That which is of the female, feminine in appearance, feminine in characteristics, in occupation, in deportment, feminine in condition and being—this is that form which constitutes femininity.[3]

---

[1] See § 624, n.

[2] For the sphere of the tangible, see below, § 648.

[3] Literally the indriyaṃ—the faculty, potentiality of the female. Under 'appearance,' which the Cy. (321) rules to be here the import of liṅgaṃ (=saṇṭhānaṃ, *cf.* Mil. 133, 134), he indicates the physical proportions in which the woman, generally speaking, differs from the man—smaller hands, feet, and face, upper trunk less broad, lower trunk broader. Characteristics (nimittaṃ) are that by which she is recognisable (sanjānanaṃ), both external bodily marks (no beard, *e.g.*, nor tusks, which would seem to include certain animals) and modes of dressing. Under 'occupation' (kuttaṃ=kiriyā) there is an allusion to girls' distinctive amusements—playing with baskets, pestles [and mortars], and dolls (? literally, little daughters, dhītalikāya kīlanti), and spinning thread with a mattikavākaṃ, whatever that may be. Under 'deportment,' the 'absence of breadth' (avisa-

[634] What is that form which is masculinity (purisindriyaṃ)?

That which is of the male, masculine in appearance, masculine in characteristics, in occupation, in deportment, masculine in condition and being—this is that form which constitutes masculinity.[1]

---

daṃ) in women's walking, standing, sitting, lying, and eating is specified, all these being done more mincingly, less assertively by women. If a man so deport himself, it is said of him, 'He goes like a woman!' The 'condition and being' of the female, constituting her essential nature, are 'born of karma, and take their source at conception.' The other female characteristics are evolved by her 'potentiality' in the course of existence, just as the tree with all its appurtenances is evolved in time from the seed. This 'indriyam' is discernible, not by the eye, but by the mind (mano. It is an abstract idea). And it is not to the one sex just what the faculties of sight and so forth are to the other.

[1] The priority of place given to the female is a form of statement as characteristically Buddhist (not to say Indian) as that of saying 'moon and sun.' Both no doubt have their source very deep in the history, or prehistory, of humanity. The Commentator gives the correlative opposites in describing male characteristics, down to the 'swash-buckling and martial air,' which if a woman affect she is said to 'go like a man.' Boys are said to occupy themselves with their characteristic games of playing at carriages and ploughs, and at making sand-banks round puddles and calling them reservoirs.

He then remarks that these sexual distinctions have been evolved during the course of life in primeval ages; since when, originating by way of conception and, some of them, in the individual life, it happens that they get interchanged. He then quotes cases of hermaphroditism, said to have occurred in the members of the Order.

He is mindful also, as we might expect, to appreciate the sex to which he belongs, and makes a curious application to it of the doctrine of karma. 'Of the two, the male sex-marks are superior (uttamaṃ), those of the female inferior (hīnaṃ). Therefore the former disappear by means of a very bad karma, while the latter are established

[635] What is that form which is vitality (jīvitindriyaṃ)?

The persistence of these corporeal states, their subsistence, their going on, their being kept going on, their progress, continuance, preservation, life, life as faculty—this is that form which is vitality.[1]

[636] What is that form which is bodily intimation (kāyaviññatti)?

That tension, that intentness, that state of making the body[2] tense, in response to a thought, whether good, bad, or indeterminate, on the part of one who advances, or recedes, or fixes the gaze, or glances around, or retracts an arm, or stretches it forth—the intimation, the making known, the state of having made known—this is that form which constitutes bodily intimation.[3]

---

by a karma indifferently good. The latter, on the other hand, disappear by means of a karma indifferently bad, while the former are established by means of a very good karma. 'Thus, both disappear by badness and are *acquired* by goodness.'

Thus, our Commentator approximates more to Plato's position than to that of the typical religious celibate, finding woman not stronger to do evil, but rather the weaker in heaping up either good or evil.

[1] 'What there is to say, has been said already in connexion with the faculty of vitality as related to incorporeal (formless) states' (Asl. 323. See § 19).

[2] Kāyo is said to = sarīraṃ; possibly to distinguish it from kāyo as used for 'body-sensibility,' or the tactile sense (Asl. 324), or again from sense-experience generally (p. 43, n. 3).

[3] Kāyaviññatti is analyzed in a somewhat rambling style by the Commentator. The gist of his remarks amounts, I gather, to the following: In any communication effected by bodily action—which includes communications from animals to men, and *vice versâ*—that which is made known is one's condition (bhāvo) at the time, one's self (sayaṃ), and one's intention (adhippāyo); in other words, the *how*, the *who* or *what*, and the *what for*. And this is wrought by a bodily suffusion (vipphandanena).

He then classifies the kinds of thoughts which tend to

[637] What is that form which is intimation by language (vacīviññatti)?

That speech, voice, enunciation, utterance, noise, making noises, language as articulate speech, which expresses a thought whether good, bad, or indeterminate—this is called language. And that intimation, that making known, the state of having made known by language—this is that form which constitutes intimation by language.[1]

[638] What is that form which is the element of space (ākāsa-dhātu)?

That which is space and belongs to space, is sky and

'produce an intimation,' no others having this tendency. They are—

The eight good thoughts relating to the sensuous universe (§§ 1-159), and
the thought concerning intuition (abhiññā cittaṃ).
The twelve bad thoughts (§§ 365-430).
The eight great kiriyā-thoughts,
the two limited kiriyā-thoughts,
the one kiriyā-thought relating to the universe of form which has attained to intuition,
making eleven indeterminate thoughts.

Finally he refers us to his theory of 'Doors' (dvāra-kathā). See my Introduction. (Asl. 323-4.)

[1] Vacīviññatti is dealt with *verbatim* as bodily intimation was, 'vocal noise' being substituted for 'bodily suffusion.' 'Making noises' is to be understood as making a noise in a variety of ways. 'Articulate speech' (*lit.*, broken-up speech) is no mere jangle (bhango), but is vocal utterance so divided as to serve for communication (Asl. 325).

It is interesting to note in connexion with the problem as to whether communication or registration of thought is the historically prior function of language, that Buddhaghosa, for all his aptness to draw distinctions, does not make any allusion here to intimation by language forming only one of the functions of speech.

Still more curious, as being more germane to this specific aspect of language, is it that he does not take into account the oral communication of the registered ideas of the race.

belongs to sky,[1] is vacuum and belongs to vacuum, and is not in contact[2] with the four Great Phenomena—this is that form which is the element of space.

[639] What is that form which is lightness of form (rūpassa lahutā)?[3]

That lightness of form which is its capacity for changing easily, its freedom from sluggishness and inertia—this is that form which is lightness of form.

[640] What is that form which is plasticity of form?

---

[1] Buddhaghosa's etymology (Asl. 325) derives ākāso from 'unploughed'—what may not be ploughed, cut, or broken—which recalls Homer's *ἀτρύγετος αἴθηρ* and *ἀτρυγέτη θάλασσα* as well as the *ἀκάρπιστα πεδία* of Euripides (Asl. 326). 'Sky' he connects with striking—agham, a-ghaṭṭanīyaṃ—what is not strikable.

Ākāso, he continues, is that which delimitates, or sets bounds to forms, environing them and making them manifest. Through it, in forms thus bounded, we get the notions—hence above, hence below, hence across.

[2] Asamphuṭṭhaṃ catūhi mahabhūtehi. Although space is in this work treated of apart from the four elements, and does not, as a rule, count as a fifth element, in the Pitakas, yet, in the Mahā Rāhulovāda Sutta (M. i. 423), when Gotama is discoursing to his son of the distribution of the elements in the composition of the human body, he co-ordinates ākāsadhātu with the four other dhātus, to all appearance as though it should rank as a fifth element. In the older Upanishads it is usually coordinated with the four elements, though not, as such, in a closed list. In the Taittirīya Up., however, it appears as the one immediate derivative from the Âtman; wind, fire, water, earth, plants, etc., proceeding, the first from ākāça, the rest, taken in order, from each other.

The word asamphuṭṭhaṃ is paraphrased by nijjaṭakaṃ (or nissaṭaṃ), and may mean that space does not commingle with the four elements as they with each other.

'Belongs to' is, in the Pali, -gataṃ.

[3] *Cf.* above, §§ 42-47, with this and the two following answers. Supremely well-dressed hide is given as an illustration of the plasticity of matter (Asl. 326).

That plasticity of form which is its softness, smoothness, non-rigidity—this is that form which is plasticity of form.

[641] What is that form which is wieldiness of form?

That wieldiness of form which is its serviceableness, its workable condition—this is that form which is wieldiness of form.[1]

[642] What is that form which is the integration (upacayo) of form?

That which is accumulation of form is the integration of form[2]—this is that form which is the integration of form.

[643] What is that form which is the subsistence of form (rūpassa santati)?

That which is integration of form is the subsistence of form. This is that form which is the subsistence of form.

[644] What is that form which is the decay of form (rūpassa jaratā)?

That decay of form which is ageing, decrepitude, hoariness, wrinkles, the shrinkage in length of days, the hypermaturity of faculties—this is that form which is the decay of form.[3]

---

[1] Gold which is suddhanta (? sudhanta, well-blown) is given as typically 'wieldy' material (*ibid.*).

[2] Buddhaghosa evidently reads so rūpassa upacayo here (for yo), and in the next section sā rūpassa (for yā) (Asl. 327). This is only adopted by the text in §§ 732, 733. K. reads so and sā.

This and the following section formularize the coming into being of things. Integration is paraphrased (Asl. 327) as the cumulative effect of the spheres (āyatanānaṃ ācayo) as they are reproduced over and over again. The import of the term is vaḍḍhi, fulness of growth. Ācayo, or nibbatti, is to upacayo or vaḍḍhi as the welling up of water in a reservoir by a river's bank is to the brimming over of the water, while santati or pavatti (subsistence or persistence) is as the overflow and running of the water. All are expressions for the phenomenon of birth and growth (jātirūpassa).

[3] This is a stock formula, and occurs at M. i. 49; S. ii. 2, and 42. The Cy. points out (Asl. 328) that the three terms,

[645] What is that form which is the impermanence of form (rūpassa aniccatā)?

The destruction, disease, breaking-up, dissolution of form, the impermanence which is decline—this is that form which is the impermanence of form.[1]

[646] What is that form which is bodily (solid) nutriment (kabalinkāro āhāro)?[2]

Boiled rice, sour gruel, flour, fish, flesh, milk, curds, butter, cheese, tila-oil, cane-syrup, or whatever else[3] there is in whatever region that by living beings may be eaten, chewed, swallowed, digested into the juice[4] by which living

---

'decrepitude,' etc., show the phenomena that must take place in the lapse of time; the last two show the inference that is to be drawn from them. For just as a flood or a forest fire can be traced by the appearance of the grass and trees in its track, so can we infer respecting our life and faculties by the appearance of teeth, hair and skin.

[1] This and the preceding section formularize the waning and passing away of things. Birth-and-growth, decay and death are by the Commentator likened to three enemies of mankind, the first of whom leads him astray into a pit, the second of whom throws him down, the third of whom cuts off his head (Asl. 329).

[2] Literally, morsel-made food. 'Bodily' (or solid) suffices to distinguish it from the three immaterial nutriments. See p. 30.

[3] Under these come roots and fruits. Asl. 330.

[4] On this section, where 'form' is considered under the aspect of sustaining growth, etc., the Commentator gives a brief dissertation where an adumbration of physiological truth is humorously illustrated. Whereas, he says (Asl. 330-332), food is here first set out in terms of its embodiment, in ojā we have the evolved essence of it. Now whereas the former removes risk, the latter is a preservative. And the risk is this, that when no food is taken, the karma-born heat within feeds on the walls of the belly, making the owner cry out, 'I am hungry; give me something to eat!' and only setting his intestines free when it can get external food. The internal heat is likened to a shadow-demon who, having got the entry into a man's shadow, bites his head when hungry so that he cries out.

beings are kept alive—this is that form which is bodily nutriment.

[All] this is form which is derived.

[End of] the Section on Derivatives. First Portion for Recitation in the Division on Form.

[‘*There is form which is not derived*’ (n o u p ā d ā)].

[647] What is that form which is not derived?[1]

The sphere of the tangible, the fluid element—this is that form which is not derived.

[648] What is that form which is the sphere of the tangible (p h o ṭ ṭ h a b b ā y a t a n a ṃ)?

The earthy (solid) element, the lambent (calorific) element, the gaseous (aerial) element[2]; the hard and the

---

When other men come to help, the demon, quitting his hold, preys on them.

In the case of coarse food, *e.g.*, kudrūsa grain, ojā is said to be weak and sustains but a short time, while if a man drink ghee and the like he wants no other meal the whole day. Living beings are then classified in an order of increasing fineness in the food they live on, beginning with crocodiles, who, they say, swallow pebbles, continuing with peacocks, hyenas, and elephants, later with other birds, then with borderers, town-dwellers, kings, and ending with the Yāma and Paranimmitavasavatti gods, who enjoy food of supreme delicacy.

[1] ‘Just as derived form is derived in such and such a way and in no other, so, to say it is not derived, is equivalent to saying it is not derivable.’ Asl. 333.

Possibly the form of negative here employed (n o u p ā d ā) is a technical mark of the relatively unethical nature of this aspect of r ū p a ṃ. A n u p ā d ā, on the other hand, is used with a philosophical import. *Cf.* D. i. 17 with M. i. 148—a n u p ā d ā v i m u t t o and a n u p ā d ā p a r i n i b- b ā n a t t h a ṃ. See also below, §§ 1210 and 1213.

[2] In keeping with the general psychological standpoint of the present work, the things which are not derived from (have no foothold or support in) other things are considered

soft; the smooth and the rough; pleasant (easeful) contact, painful contact; the heavy and the light[1]—such a tangible, invisible and producing impact,[2] as, with the

---

under the aspect of sense-percepts. They are tangibles or intangibles. Element (dhātu) is now substituted for the collective term used above, namely, great phenomena or beings (mahābhūtāni, § 584 *et seq*. Both terms occur together in A. i. 222. The latter term may be used to denote great or wondrous derivatives of the four elements, great either physically or ethically, as when (Vin. ii. 240) the ocean and its 'great creatures' serve to illustrate the Dhamma and those wondrous phenomena, the human beings who by way of it are seeking or have attained Nirvāna. Dhātu, on the other hand, as the Cy. with unflagging 'mindfulness' once more points out, indicates absence of substratum or soul. Asl. 332.

On the essential characters of the four elements, see below, §§ 962-965, also the following note.

[1] The first two and last of these four pairs are so many aspects or modes of the earth-element (Asl. 332), and are paraphrased respectively as rigid and non-rigid, polished and jagged (saw-like), weighty and non-weighty. These correspond almost exactly to our modern view of the modes of resistance, *i.e.*, of *active* touch, or of skin-sensibility with a co-efficient of muscular sense. The Buddhist view lacks, as all but recent psychology has lacked, insight into the presence of the muscular factor; on the other hand, it is logically more symmetrical in giving 'lightness' where Dr. Bain, *e.g.*, gives 'pressure'—another positive.

Pleasant contact is defined as a tangible which is desired on account of pleasant feeling; the opposite, in the case of painful contact. Each of the three elements furnishes instances of either: In connexion with solidity there is the pleasant contact felt when a soft-palmed attendant is doing massage to one's feet, and the opposite when his hands are hard. From 'caloric,' or the flame-element, we may get the pleasure of a warming-pan in winter, or the reverse, if it is applied in summer. From the aerial element, we may get the pleasure of fanning in summer, or the discomfort of it in winter. Asl. 332, 333.

[2] The Cy. here discusses a point of attention in sense-perception which is interesting as adumbrating modern

body-sensibility, invisible and reacting, one has touched, touches, will, or may touch . . .

[649] . . . against which tangible, invisible, and producing impact, the body-sensibility, invisible and reacting, has impinged, impinges, will, or may impinge . . .

[650] . . . such a tangible, invisible and producing impact, as has impinged, impinges, will, or may impinge against the body-sensibility, invisible and reacting . . .

European theories respecting consciousness and subconsciousness (Asl. 333). In a concrete object of sense, the three modes of the tangible, *i.e.*, the three elements (solid, hot, airy), may all of them be present. Now do they all come 'at one stroke' into the field of consciousness (āpāthaṃ)? They do. Thus come, do they impinge on the body-sense? They do. When it has thus made them a (mental) object, does cognition of body arise at one blow? It does not. Why? Thus: Mental objects are made either by deliberate sensing or by intrusion. (The latter term—ussado—is more literally extrusion, or prominence, but either word shows that involuntary, as contrasted with voluntary attention is meant.) Now when one is deliberately testing the hardness or softness of a ball of boiled rice by pressure, heat and vapour are present, but it is the solid to which one gives attention. If hot water be tested by the hand, though there is solid and vaporous (matter), it is heat that occupies the attention. If one lets the breeze blow on the body at the window in hot weather, solid and heat are present, but it is the aerial element that is attended to. Or take involuntary impressions: If you stumble, or knock your head against a tree, or bite on a pebble, heat and wind are present, but the intrusive object is *solid* matter. So analogously for walking on something hot, or being deafened by a hurricane. The three elements are not apprehended as such at the same instant. And with regard to the extended surface of the body-sentience, cognition of body arises only in that spot where the sentient surface is impinged upon, *e.g.*, when a shoulder-wound is bathed (? dressed; *cf.* Vin. ii. 115 and Transl.) with a quill, the kāya-pasādo of the shoulder is impinged upon, or intensified, and there cognition arises. And where the pasādo is most powerfully impressed, there cognition arises first.

[651] . . . in consequence of which tangible and depending on the body-sensibility, there has arisen, arises, will, or may arise

bodily contact . . .

and . . . born of that bodily contact,

a feeling . . .
[*or*] a perception . . .
[*or*] thinking . . .
[*or*] cognition of body . . .

[further,] having a tangible as its object and depending on the body(-sensibility), there has arisen, arises, will, or may arise

bodily contact . . .

and . . . born of that bodily contact,

a feeling . . .
[*or*] a perception . . .
[*or*] thinking . . .
[*or*] cognition of body;

this that is the tangible, the sphere and element of the tangible—this is that form which is the sphere of the tangible.[1]

[652] What is that form which is the fluid (aqueous) element (āpodhātu)?

That which is fluid and belongs to fluid, that which is

---

[1] Buddhaghosa goes on, with reference to the senses generally, to give a psychological account of the passing from one group of sensations or 'object of thought' to another in terms not far removed from what would now be used to describe the 'movement of attention' (Asl. 334). We pass from one object to another (*a*) from deliberate inclination, or (*b*) from a sensation of preponderating impressiveness (ajjhāsayato vā visayādhimattato vā). *E.g.*, (*a*) from saluting a shrine, a believer forms the intention of entering to do homage to a statue and contemplate the carvings and paintings. (*b*) While contemplating some vast tope, a man is struck by the sound of music, and is then affected by flowers and incense brought near.

viscid[1] and belongs to viscous, the cohesiveness of form[2] —this is that form which is the fluid element.

[All] this is that form which is not derived.

[653] What is that form[3] which is the issue of grasping (upādiṇṇaṃ)?[4]

---

[1] Literally, oil (sneho). *Cf.* the description with that of ākāsadhātu, § 638.

[2] This is the aspect of the moist or liquid element in an object compact of several elements. The one essential 'mark' of āpo-dhātu is paggharaṇaṃ, flowing. See § 963. But 'cohesiveness of form means the cohering condition of some concrete in which there is superfluity of solid' (Asl. 335). For it is by the cohesive force of the fluid element that lumps of iron or what not are made rigid. Similarly in the case of stones, mountains, palms, tusks, horns, etc.

Hence Buddhaghosa passes on to discuss the mutually related spheres of the elements and their apparent approximations to each other, as in viscous things, *e.g.*, or congealed liquid, or boiling water. Corrupt MSS., however, render parts of the disquisition hard to follow. His conclusion is that whereas the elements may vary in their condition as phenomena, their essential mark never alters, however latent it may be. And he quotes a yet unedited sutta (Aṭṭhānaparikappa sutta), but which is repeated in A. i. 222, that it is easier for the four elements to change their essential character, than for the seeker of Nirvana (the Noble Student) to alter his high estate (Asl. 336).

[3] Here follow the remaining pairs of correlated terms, making up the categories of form under the Dual Aspect.

[4] Literally, 'which has been grasped at' or 'laid hold of.' This and the cognate terms are discussed under the 'Group on Grasping,' § 1213 *et seq.* It is disappointing to find that, with the exception of two items in the list of things 'grasped at,' or come into being through the action of karma (the two phrases are approximately equivalent), the Cy. does not discuss the inclusion of any. One would have liked to hear, *e.g.*, why, of all sense-objects, sounds alone are 'not the issue of grasping' (*cf.* the heresy concerning sound as result [of karma, K. V. 466], and why the elements of space and of fluidity may and may not be the

The spheres of sight, hearing, smell, taste, body-sensibility, femininity, masculinity, vitality, or whatever form there exists through karma having been wrought, whether it be in the spheres of visible forms, odours, tastes, or the tangible; the element of space, the fluid element, the integration or the subsistence of form,[1] or bodily nutriment—this is that form which is the issue of grasping.

[654] What is that form which is not the issue of grasping?

The sphere of sound, bodily and vocal intimation, lightness, plasticity and wieldiness of form, decay and impermanence of form, or whatever other form exists which is not due to karma having been wrought, whether it be in the sphere of visible forms, smells, tastes, or the tangible; the element of space or that of fluidity; the integration or the subsistence of form, or bodily nutriment—this is that form which is not the issue of grasping.

[655] What is that form which is both the issue of grasping and favourable to grasping (u p ā d i ṇ ṇ 'u p ā d ā n i y a m)?

The spheres of the five senses, femininity, masculinity and vitality, or whatever other form exists through karma having been wrought, whether it be in the spheres of

---

issue of grasping, or what they have to do with it in any way.

Concerning the two items above mentioned, how is it, asks the Cy. (337), 'that "decay and impermanence" are classed with respect to what is due, and what is not due to the performance of karma? They are classed with what is not the issue of grasping. That which has sprung from conditions other than karma is included under "not due to the performance of karma. . . ." And as these two forms arise neither from karma, nor from form-producing conditions other than karma, they are therefore not classified with reference to karma. How they are acquired will become evident later.'

[1] For rūpasantati read rūpassa santati.

visible forms, odours, tastes or the tangible, in the elements of space or fluidity, in the integration or the subsistence of form or in bodily nutriment—this is that form which is both the issue of grasping and favourable to grasping.

[656] What is that form which is not the issue of grasping, but is favourable to grasping (anupādiṇṇ' upādāniyaṃ)?[1]

The sphere of sounds, bodily and vocal intimation, the lightness, plasticity, wieldiness, decay and impermanence of form, or whatever other form exists which is not due to karma having been wrought, whether it be in the sphere of visible forms,[2] smells, tastes, the tangible, in the element of space or of fluidity, in the integration, or the subsistence of form, or in bodily nutriment—this is that form which is not the issue of grasping but is favourable to grasping.

[657] What is that form which is visible?

The sphere of visible forms—this is that form which is visible.

[658] What is that form which is invisible?

The sphere of vision . . . and bodily nutriment—this is that form which is invisible.[3]

---

[1] The privative prefixed to the first half of this dvandva-compound does not apply to the latter half. *All* form is upādāniyaṃ—see § 595 and *cf.* Dh. S. § 1538. Hence to get, as we do, a positive answer would, if upādāniyaṃ were to be taken negatively, be a very patent infringement of the law of contradiction. The distributed negative is given by anupādiṇṇānupādāniyaṃ as in § 992.

[2] I have elided saddāyatanaṃ, and, on the next line, inserted āpodhātu, as consistent with § 654. *Cf.* §§ 747, 750, and K.

[3] The answer in § 658 recurs with its elided passage very often, but it is not easy to point out the foregoing answer of which it is an abbreviation. For §§ 653, 655 include 'visible form,' 'which is absurd.' And they do not include 'sound,' which is invisible. I suggest that

[659] What is that form which reacts and impinges[1] (sappaṭighaṃ)?

The spheres of vision, hearing, smell, taste, body-sensibility; the spheres of visible forms, sounds, smells, tastes, tangibles—this is that form which reacts and impinges.

[660] What is that form which does not react or impinge?

Femininity . . . and bodily nutriment—this is that form which does not react or impinge.

[661] What is that form which is faculty (indriyaṃ)?

The faculties (or personal potentialities)[2] of vision, hearing, smell, taste, body-sensibility, femininity, masculinity, vitality—this is that form which is faculty.

[662] What is that form which is not faculty?

The spheres of visible form . . . and bodily nutriment—this is that form which is not faculty.[3]

---

§ 596 is referred to, with the implication that 'the sphere of visible form' must be omitted. All the other terms in § 596, if understood as strictly abstract sensibility or sensation, or as abstract ideas, are inaccessible to sight. Even in kabalinkāro āhāro, it is only the vatthu, or embodiment of the concept of nutriment, that is visible. And similarly, whereas one's bodily gestures are visible, the 'intimation' given is a matter of inference, a mental construction.

[1] Both terms have been applied in the detailed theory of sense given in § 597 *et seq.*

[2] Keeping to § 596 as the norm for these abbreviated replies, we may assume that these two (§§ 659 and 660) divide out that answer between them. Impact and reaction, as here understood, belong exclusively to the sphere of sensation. The term paṭigho has an emotional and moral significance elsewhere in this work, and means repulsion, repugnance. See § 1060.

[3] § 596 would seem to be divided also and differently by the indriyaṃ sections. What is na indriyaṃ, not having δύναμις, are thus the five kinds of sense-objects, intimation, space, the three modes of form, and the course

[663] What is that form which is Great Phenomenon (m a h ā b h ū t a ṃ) ?

The sphere of the tangible and the element of fluidity—this is that form which is Great Phenomenon.

[664] What is that form which is not Great Phenomenon ?

The sphere of vision . . . and bodily nutriment—this is that form which is not Great Phenomenon.[1]

[665] What is that form which is intimation (v i ñ ñ a t t i)?

Bodily and vocal intimation[2]—this is that form which is intimation.

[666] What is that form which is not intimation ?

The sphere of vision . . . and bodily nutriment—this is that form which is not intimation.

[667] What is that form which is sprung from thought (c i t t a - s a m u ṭ ṭ h ā n a ṃ)[3] ?

---

of the evolving rebirth of form as represented in abstract idea.

[1] This pair of relatives coincides with the first pair of attributes taken inversely: forms underived and derived (pp. 172-97).

[2] See above, §§ 636, 637. The abbreviated answer concerning the other relative will presumably be the entire list given in § 596, with the exception of the two modes of intimation.

[3] *Cf.* below, §§ 1195, 1196, and above, § 636, note.

Here, after being silent over the last ten questions, the Cy. resumes its parable (p. 337), without, however, throwing much light on these to us obscure distinctions. This and the next two pairs of questions and answers refer to form of some kind as brought into relation with an intelligent agent. And the purest instance of this is those groups of phenomena which are brought into play when the agent is expressing himself. The expression or intimation *itself*, it says, does not spring *directly* from thought, but it is said nevertheless to have its source in thought because those phenomena (of gesture and speech) on which the intima-

Bodily and vocal intimation, or whatever other form exists that is born of thought, caused by thought, has its source in thought, whether it be in the sphere of visible forms, sounds, odours, tastes or tangibles, in the spatial, or the fluid element, in the lightness, plasticity, wieldiness, integration or subsistence of form, or in bodily nutriment—this is that form which is sprung from thought.

[668] What is that form which is not sprung from thought?

The sphere of the five senses, femininity, masculinity and vitality, the decay and the impermanence of form, or whatever other form exists that is not born of thought, not caused by thought, does not have its source in thought, whether it be in the sphere of visible forms, sounds, odours, tastes, or tangibles, in the spatial or fluid element, in the lightness, plasticity, wieldiness, integration or subsistence of form, or in bodily nutriment—this is that form which is not sprung from thought.

[669] What is that form which comes into being together with thought (citta-saha-bhū)?

[670] What is that form which does not come into being together with thought?

Answers as in the preceding pair of relatives.

[671] What is that form which is consecutive to thought (citt' ānuparivatti)?

[672] What is that form which is not consecutive to thought?

Answers as in the preceding pair of relatives.

---

tion depends are immediately prompted by thought, just as we say that old age and death 'are' impermanence (in virtue of their forming part of the content of that idea). While there is thought, there is also expression of thought. But the concomitance stated in § 669 is not to be understood like that arising between thought and feeling and other mental processes. He is probably referring to the mental complex indicated above in § 1 and the like.

[673] What is that form which belongs to the self (a j j h a t t i k a ṃ)?[1]

The spheres of the five senses—this is that form which belongs to the self.

[674] What is that form which is external (to the self—b ā h i r a ṃ)?

The sphere of the five kinds of sense-objects . . .[2] and bodily nutriment—this is that form which is external (to the self).

[675] Which is that form which is gross (o ḷ ā r i k a ṃ)?

The spheres of the five senses and of the five kinds of sense-objects—this is that form which is gross.

[676] Which is that form which is subtle (s u k h u m a ṃ)?

---

[1] See below, §§ 1044, 1045. It will already have been noted (p. 59, n. 1.), that ajjhattaṃ, ajjhattikaṃ does not run on all fours with our modern psychological term 'subjective,' or that which belongs to the *conscious experience* of the individual. It connotes anything belonging to an individual organism, physical or mental. Hence, too, the word 'self' must here be understood in no narrow metaphysical, or even psychological sense, but as equivalent to the concrete person or attabhāvo (see above, p. 175, n. 1). It is used in the sense of all but the last of the four constituents into which Professor W. James divides the Self, viz., the material Self (body, clothes, family, home, property: the Buddhist would only admit the first item, I fancy), the social Self (recognition from others), and the spiritual Self (psychic faculties or dispositions). ('Principles of Psychology,' 1892, i. 292-296.) Only the fourth constituent, the 'pure Ego,' was rejected by Buddhism, as it was, twenty-two centuries later, by Hume. *Cf.*, however, the apparently more 'subjective' use in §§ 161 and 1207.

I have felt equal reluctance to foist the (relatively) modern counterpart 'objective' on to bāhiraṃ or bahiddhā (see § 1045).

[2] Read in full, this should coincide with the latter part of § 596, beginning at 'the spheres of visible form.'

Femininity . . . and bodily nutriment—this is that form which is subtle.[1]

[677] What is that form which is remote (dūre)?

Femininity . . . and bodily nutriment—this is that form which is remote.

[678] What is that form which is near (santike)?

The spheres of the five senses and of the five kinds of sense-objects—this is that form which is near.[2]

---

[1] The Cy., paraphrasing oḷārikaṃ by thūlaṃ, explains that this has reference to the material embodiment of sense-objects and to the fact of sensuous impact, sukhumaṃ connoting the contrary. Under the latter class we have, according to my assumption (p. 203, n. 3), the indriyas of sex and vitality, intimation, space, the modes of form and the nutritive principle in food. The force of this effort at dichotomy is, to the modern Western mind, curious and not obvious. It is suggestive of tradition earlier than the date of the compiling of the Abhidhamma, as early as the earlier Upanishads—of a time when there was no definite antithesis between material and immaterial, extended and unextended. We have seen that the senses, though 'invisible,' were conceived as species of 'form'—nay, that the later Cy. preserved the tradition of their shape and size. And I incline to think that just as, in the older Upanishads, soul was a shadowy, impalpable, but 'physical double of the physical body,' and just as 'when an early Greek philosopher speaks of τὸ ὄν, he does not mean Being, but Body' (Burnet, 'Early Greek Philosophy,' 27), so the items in the list divided out in these two answers are all *physical* 'forms,' whether patent, impressive, and pervading, or latent, fine and mysterious.

[2] Dūre, the Cy. explains, refers to that which on account of its being difficult to apprehend or discriminate cannot be discerned by way of the sensuous impact, whether it be literally far or near at hand. Conversely, santike refers to things which are patent to sense, even though they may be distant. The content of each division agrees with that of the preceding division, and we see that, whereas the field of sense-perception is pronounced to be a relatively patent, as well as gross concern, the essence of sex, vitality, etc.,

[*Basis* (vatthu).][1]

[679] What is that form which is the basis of visual contact (cakkhusamphassassa vatthu)?

The sphere of vision—this is that form which is the basis of visual contact.

[680] What is that form which is not the basis of visual contact?

The sphere of hearing . . .[2] and bodily nutriment—this is that form which is not, etc.

---

down to the nutritive principle in food, is found to be as obscure, latent or relatively inaccessible, as it was subtle or minute. Asl. 337.

[1] From § 653 to § 961 the Commentator lapses into silence, dismissing the reader with the remark that in the exposition on 'spheres,' etc. (§§ 695-741), the method of treatment is more detailed than it was above, and, further, that the category of triplets (§ 742 *et seq.*) is easy to understand. To enable the reader to gather with more ease the drift of this part of the catechizing, I have inserted a few headings to indicate whenever there is a change in the *aspect* under which 'form' is considered. Thus we have form considered under the aspect of the *basis* (vatthu) in the subjective procedure of coming-to-know, of the *object* so apprehended, and so forth.

In all the answers, where lacunæ occur, except where otherwise specified, the formula appears to be the answer of § 596, with one or more terms omitted, and with the occasional insertion of 'the sphere of the tangible,' according to the sense required by each specific process of dichotomy.

[2] By referring to the standard answer, § 596, it will be seen that the negatives in the present answer include 'visible forms,' or the objects of the sense of vision. Now, vatthu means seat, embodiment, or what we might call physical basis. However, then, the process of sense-stimulation was ultimately conceived, the effective result was held to take place in the sense-organ (and heart). The sense-object was defined as the ārammaṇaṃ of the contact. See § 687.

[681] What is that form which is the basis of
the feeling . . .
the perception . . .
the thinking . . .
the visual cognition
which is born of visual contact?

The sphere of vision—this is that form which is the basis of the . . . visual cognition[1] which is born of visual contact.

[682] What is that form which is not the basis of the . . . visual cognition born of visual contact?

The sphere of hearing . . . and bodily nutriment—this is that form which is not the basis of the . . . visual cognition born of visual contact.

[683] What is that form which is the basis of
auditory . . .
olfactory . . .
gustatory . . .[2]
bodily
contact?

The sphere of . . .[3] body-sensibility—this is that form which is the basis of . . . bodily contact.

[684] What is that form which is not the basis of . . . bodily contact?

---

[1] No hiatus appears, in either the English or Siamese edition of the text, between rūpaṃ and cakkhuviññāṇassa, but by the context the answer is, of course, understood to deal in turn with all four mental processes stated in the question. As usual, only the last term gets an explicit answer. All four processes must also be understood in the lacuna in § 682 and in § 686.

[2] Jivhā samphassassa has dropped out of the printed text.

[3] Here, of course, understand the spheres of hearing, smell, and taste, and in the three following lacunæ the corresponding forms of contact. Proceed similarly in the next two answers.

The sphere of vision . . . and bodily nutriment—this is that form which is not the basis of . . . bodily contact.

[685] What is that form which is the basis of
the feeling . . .
the perception . . .
the thinking . . .
the . . . cognition of body
that is born of . . . bodily contact?

The sphere . . . of body-sensibility—this is that form which is the basis of the . . . cognition of body that is born of . . . bodily contact.

[686] What is that form which is not the basis of the . . . cognition of body born of . . . bodily contact?

The sphere of vision . . . and bodily nutriment—this is that form which is not the basis of the . . . cognition of body born, etc.

[*Mental object or idea* (ā r a m m a ṇ a ṃ).]

[687] What is that form which is the object in visual contact?

The sphere of visible forms—this is that form which is the object in visual contact.

[688] What is that form which is not the object in visual contact?

The sphere of vision . . . and bodily nutriment[1]—this is that form which is not, etc.

[689] What is that form which is the object in
the feeling . . .
the perception . . .
the thinking . . .
the visual cognition
that is born of visual contact?

---

[1] *I.e.*, as in § 596, omitting only 'the sphere of visible forms,' and inserting, presumably, 'the sphere of the tangible.'

The sphere of visible forms—this is that form which is the object in . . . the visual cognition that is born of visual contact.

[690] What is that form which is not[1] the object in the . . . visual cognition born of visual contact?

The sphere of vision . . . and bodily nutriment—this is that form which is not the object, etc.

[691] What is that form which is the object in
auditory . . .
olfactory . . .
gustatory . . .
bodily
contact?

The sphere of . . . the tangible—this is that form which is the object in . . . bodily contact.

[692] What is that form which is not the object in . . . bodily contact?

The sphere of vision . . . and bodily nutriment—this is that form which is not the object in . . . bodily contact.

[693] What is that form which is the object in
the feeling . . .
the perception . . .
the thinking . . .
the . . . cognition of body
that is born of . . . bodily contact?

The sphere of the tangible—this is that form which is the object in the . . . cognition of body that is born of . . . bodily contact.

---

[1] The negative particle must be supplied in the printed text. The lacunæ in this and following sentences must be filled up analogously with those in the preceding group. Thus, in this question, the three other mental processes named in the preceding question are to be understood; the answer will be identical with that in § 596, excluding only 'the sphere of visible forms,' but inserting 'the sphere of the tangible.' And so on.

[694] What is that form which is not the object in the . . . cognition of body that is born of bodily contact?

The sphere of vision . . . and bodily nutriment[1]—this is that form which is not the object, etc.

[*Sphere of sense* (ā y a t a n a ṃ).]

[695] What is that form which is the sphere of vision?

The eye, that is to say, the sentient organ which is derived from the four Great Phenomena . . . this that is 'an empty village'—this is that form which is the sphere of vision.[2]

[696] What is that form which is not the sphere of vision?

The sphere of hearing . . . and bodily nutriment—this is that form which is not the sphere of vision.

[697] What is that form which is the sphere of
hearing . . .
smell . . .
taste . . .
body-sensibility?

The body, that is to say, the sentient organ which is derived from the four Great Phenomena . . . this that is 'an empty village'—this is that form which is the sphere of . . . body-sensibility.

[698] What is that form which is not the sphere of . . . body-sensibility?

---

[1] *I.e.*, repeat § 596 (into which 'the sphere of the tangible' does not enter).

[2] The replies given here and to the four questions condensed in § 697 are apparently intended to be those set out in sets of four expounding the current theory of sense-reaction, §§ 597-616. Similarly, for the replies to the questions on sense taken objectively (§§ 699, 701), see §§ 617-632, 648-651.

The contradictories seem to be described in all four answers, by a repetition of § 596, with the omission in each case of the specific item named in the question on the corresponding positive term, and, presumably, with the insertion of 'the sphere of the tangible.'

The sphere of vision . . . and bodily nutriment—this is that form which is not, etc.

[699] What is that form which is the sphere of visible forms?

That form which, derived from the four Great Phenomena, is visible under the appearance of colour . . . this . . . which is the constituent element of visible form—this is that form which is the sphere of visible forms.

[700] What is that form which is not the sphere of visible forms?

The sphere of vision . . . and bodily nutriment—this is that form which is not, etc.

[701] What is that form which is the sphere of
sound,
odour,
taste,
the tangible?

The earthy (solid) element . . . this that is the . . . element of the tangible—this is that form which is the sphere of the tangible.[1]

[702] What is that form which is not the sphere of . . . the tangible?

The sphere of vision . . . and bodily nutriment—this is that form which is not, etc.

[*Element* (d h ā t u).]

[703] What is that form which is the element of vision?

The sphere of vision—this is that form which is the element of vision.

---

[1] In the printed text read rūpaṃ phoṭṭabbā-yatanaṃ. The answer is, of course, the last of the four several replies, the three first being understood.

[704] What is that form which is not the element of vision?

The sphere of hearing . . . and bodily nutriment[1]—this is that form which is not the element of vision.

[705] What is that form which is the element of visible form?

The sphere of visible form—this is that form which is the element of visible form.

[706] What is that form which is not the element of visible form?

The sphere of vision . . . and bodily nutriment—this is that form which is not, etc.

[707] What is that form which is the element of sound . . . of odour . . . of taste . . . of the tangible?

The sphere of . . .[2] the tangible—this is that form which is the element of . . . the tangible.

[708] What is that form which is not the element of . . . the tangible?

The sphere of vision . . . and bodily nutriment—this is that form which is not the element of . . . the tangible.

[*Faculty* (i n d r i y a ṃ).]

[709] What is that form which is the faculty of vision?

The eye, that is to say, the sentient organ which is derived from the four Great Phenomena . . . this that is 'an empty village'[3]—this is that form which is the faculty of vision.

[710] What is that form which is not the faculty of vision?

---

[1] Here supply the answer in § 596, omitting the first term, and inserting 'the sphere of the tangible.'

[2] Here, of course, supply the spheres of the other three senses.

[3] For the full formula, see § 597.

The sphere of hearing . . . and bodily nutriment[1]—this is that form which is not, etc.

[711] What is that form which is the faculty of hearing . . . smell . . . taste . . . body-sensibility?

The . . .[2] body, that is to say, the sentient principle, which is derived from the four Great Phenomena . . . this that is 'an empty village'—this is that form which is the faculty of . . . body-sensibility.

[712] What is that form which is not the faculty of . . . body-sensibility?

The sphere of vision . . . and bodily nutriment—this is that form which is not, etc.

[713] What is that form which is femininity (lit., the female faculty or potentiality)?[3]

That which is of the female, feminine in appearance, characteristics, occupation, and deportment, feminine in condition and being—this is that form which is femininity.

[713*a*] What is that form which is not femininity?

The sphere of vision . . . and bodily nutriment—this is that form which is not, etc.[4]

[714] What is that form which is masculinity?

That which is of the male, masculine in appearance, characteristics, occupation, and deportment, masculine in condition and being—this is that form which is masculinity.

[715] What is that form which is not masculinity?

Answer as in § 713*a*.[5]

---

[1] *I.e.*, answer as in § 596, omitting the first item, and inserting 'the sphere of the tangible.'

[2] See §§ 601, 605, 609, 613. [3] See §§ 633-635.

[4] [713*a*] is inadvertently omitted in the printed text.

[5] §§ 713*a*, 715, and 717 are presumably identical with § 596, with the successive omission of the term excluded by each question, and with the insertion always of 'the sphere of the tangible.'

[716] What is that form which is (the faculty of) vitality?

The persistence of these corporeal states, their subsistence, their going on, their being kept going on, their progress, continuance, preservation, life, life as faculty—this is that form which is (the faculty of) vitality.

[717] What is that form which is not (the faculty of) vitality?

Answer as in § 713*a*.

[*Intimation* (viññatti).]

[718] What is that form which is bodily intimation?

Answer as in § 636.

[719] What is that form which is not bodily intimation?

The sphere of vision . . . and bodily nutriment—this is that form which is bodily intimation.

[720] What is that form which is vocal intimation?

Answer as in § 637.

[721] What is that form which is not vocal intimation?

The sphere of vision . . . and bodily nutriment—this is that form which is not, etc.[1]

[*Space and fluid.*][2]

[722] What is that form which is the element of space?

That which is space and belongs to space, is sky, belongs to sky, is vacuum, belongs to vacuum, and is not in contact with the four Great Phenomena—this is that form which is the element of space.

---

[1] Again, in these two negative categories, § 596 is presumably followed with corresponding omissions and insertion. See p. 209, note 1.

[2] *Cf.* with §§ 638, 652.

[723] What is that form which is not the element of space?

Answer as § 721.

[724] What is that form which is the element of fluidity?

That which is fluid and belongs to fluid, that which is viscid and belongs to viscid; the cohesiveness of form—this is that form which is the element of fluidity.

[725] What is that form which is not the element of fluidity?

Answer as in § 721.

[*Modes of form.*]

[726] What is that form which is lightness of form?

That lightness of form which is its capacity for changing easily, its freedom from sluggishness and inertia—this is that form which is lightness of form.

[727] What is that form which is not lightness of form?

The sphere of vision . . . and bodily nutriment—this is that form which is not lightness of form.

[728-731] *Questions on the other two modes of form* 'plasticity' *and* 'wieldiness' *are answered by the descriptions given in* §§ 640, 641. *The corresponding contradictory terms are described in the same terms as in* § 727, *viz.: as in* § 596, *with the omissions and insertion as indicated on p.* 216, *n.* 5.

[*Evolution of form.*]

[732] What is that form which is the integration of form?

That which is accumulation of form is the integration of form—this is that form which is, etc.

[733] What is that form which is not the integration of form?

The sphere of vision . . . and bodily nutriment—this is that form which is not, etc.

[734-737] *Questions on the* 'subsistence,' 'decay,' *and* 'impermanence' *of form and their contradictories are answered analogously with those in the group on* 'Modes of form,' *the three positives being described as in* §§ 642-645.

[*Nutrition.*]

[740] What is that form which is bodily nutriment?
This is answered as in § 646.
[741] What is that form which is not bodily nutriment?
The sphere of vision . . . and the impermanence of form—this is that form which is not bodily nutriment.

Such are the Categories of Form under Dual Aspects.
[End of] the Exposition of the Pairs.

[Chapter III.

Categories of Form under Triple Aspects. Exposition of the Triplets.][1]

[742-744] What is that form which is

(i.) *personal[2] and derived?*

The spheres of the five senses.

(ii.) *external and derived?*

The sphere of visible form . . . and bodily nutriment.[3]

(iii.) *external and not derived?*

The sphere of the tangible and the fluid element.

[745-747] What is that form which is

(i.) *personal and the issue of grasping?*

The spheres of the five senses.

---

[1] To lighten the tedium to the reader of looking through this lengthy analysis of form considered as of the self or of the not-self taken in combination with the presence or absence of some other attribute, I have attempted a mode of grouping the triplets. I have also curtailed each answer of that constant feature, the concluding affirmation, termed in the Cy. (p. 55) the appanā. *Cf.* preceding answers.

[2] Ajjhattikaṃ. The word 'personal' corresponds more strictly perhaps to puggalikaṃ, but it is less cumbrous than 'of,' or 'belonging to, the self,' while it is, at the same time, not an incorrect rendering. See p. 207, n. 1.

[3] This presumably still refers to § 596, which these two first answers may be held to exhaust between them, without the insertion of 'the sphere of the tangible,' which comes under (iii.). *Cf.* the preceding chapter.

(ii.) *external and the issue of grasping ?*

Femininity, masculinity, vitality, or whatever other form exists through karma having been wrought, whether it be in the spheres of visible form, odour, taste, or the tangible, in the spatial or the fluid element, in the integration or subsistence of form, or in bodily nutriment.[1]

(iii.) *external and not the issue of grasping ?*

The sphere of sound, bodily and vocal intimation, the lightness, plasticity, wieldiness, decay, and impermanence of form, or whatever other form exists which is not due to karma having been wrought, whether it be in the spheres of visible form,[2] odour, taste, or the tangible, in the spatial or the fluid element, etc. [*continue as in* ii.].

[748-750] What is that form which is

(i.) *personal and both the issue of grasping and favourable to grasping ?*

(ii.) *external and both the issue of grasping and favourable to grasping ?*

(iii.) *external and not the issue of grasping but favourable to grasping ?*

The answers are identical with those in the preceding triplet, taken in order.[3]

[751-753] What is that form which is

(i.) *personal and invisible ?*

The spheres of the five senses.

(ii.) *external and visible ?*

The sphere of visible form.

(iii.) *external and invisible ?*

The sphere of sound . . . and bodily nutriment.[4]

---

[1] *Cf.* §§ 653, 654.

[2] Saddāyatanaṃ, here repeated in the printed text, is omitted in K.

[3] In § 750 read kammassa before katattā.

[4] Fill up from § 596 as before.

[754-756] What is that form which is

(i.) *personal and reacting (impingeing)* ?[1]

The spheres of the five senses.

(ii.) *external and impingeing* ?

The spheres of the five kinds of sense-objects.

(iii.) *external and non-impingeing* ?[2]

Sex[3] . . . and bodily nutriment.

[757-759] What is that form which is

(i.) *personal and a faculty* ?

The five faculties of sense.

(ii.) *external and a faculty* ?

Sex and vitality.

(iii.) *external and not a faculty* ?

The sphere of visible form . . . and bodily nutriment.[4]

[760-762] What is that form which is

(i.) *personal and not one of the Great Phenomena* ?

The spheres of the five senses.

(ii.) *external and belonging to the Great Phenomena* ?

The sphere of the tangible and the fluid element.[5]

(iii.) *external and not one of the Great Phenomena* ?

The spheres of the [other four kinds of sense-objects][6] . . . and bodily nutriment.

[763-765] What is that form which is

(i.) *personal and not intimation* ?

The spheres of the five senses.

(ii.) *external and intimation* ?

Bodily and vocal intimation.[7]

---

[1] See p. 175, n. 2, and p. 183, n. 1.

[2] For sappaṭighaṃ read appaṭighaṃ.

[3] This term is substituted as a convenient abbreviation for the indriyas of both sexes. *Cf.* § 596.

[4] Supply as before from § 596.

[5] See § 647 *et seq.*

[6] Actually 'of visible form . . .' See note 1.

[7] See §§ 636, 637.

(iii.) *external and not intimation?*

The spheres of the five kinds of sense-objects . . . and bodily nutriment.

[766-768] What is that form which is

(i.) *personal and sprung from thought?*[1]

The spheres of the five senses.

(ii.) *external and sprung from thought?*

Bodily and vocal intimation, or whatever other form exists which is born of thought, caused by thought, etc. [*continue as in* § 667].

(iii.) *external and not sprung from thought?*

Sex and vitality, the decay and impermanence of form, or whatever other form exists which is not born of thought, caused by thought, etc. [*continue as in* § 668].

[769-771] What is that form which is

(i.) *personal and does not come into being together with a thought?*

The spheres of the five senses.

(ii.) *external and comes into being together with a thought?*

Bodily and vocal intimation.

(iii.) *external and does not come into being, etc.?*

The spheres of the five kinds of sense-objects . . . and bodily nutriment.

[772-774] What is that form which is

(i.) *personal and not consecutive to a thought?*

(ii.) *external and consecutive to a thought?*

(iii.) *external and not consecutive to a thought?*

The answers are identical with those in the preceding triplet, taken in order.

[775-777] What is that form which is

(i.) *personal and gross?*[2]

The spheres of the five senses.

---

[1] See § 667 *et seq.*

[2] See § 675 *et seq.*

(ii.) *external and gross?*

The spheres of the five kinds of sense-objects.

(iii.) *external and subtle?*

Sex . . . and bodily nutriment.

[778-780] What is that form which is

(i.) *personal and near?*[1]

The spheres of the five senses.

(ii.) *external and remote?*

Sex . . . and bodily nutriment.

(iii.) *external and near?*

The spheres of the five kinds of sense-objects.

[781-783] What is that form which is

(i.) *external and not the basis of visual contact?*[2]

The spheres of the five kinds of sense-objects . . . and bodily nutriment.

(ii.) *personal and the basis of visual contact?*

The sphere of vision.

(iii.) *personal and not the basis of visual contact?*

The sphere of the other four senses.

[784-786] What is that form which is

(i.) *external and not a basis of*
the feeling . . .
the perception . . .
the thinking . . .
the visual cognition
that is born of visual contact?

(ii.) *personal and a basis of the feeling*[3] *. . . the visual cognition that is born of visual contact?*

(iii.) *personal and not a basis of the feeling . . . the visual cognition that is born of visual contact?*

Answers identical with those in the preceding triplet.

---

[1] See § 677 *et seq.* [2] See § 679 *et seq.*

[3] Concerning the lacunæ in this and the following sentences on 'basis,' *cf.* § 681 *et seq.* and notes.

[787-789] What is that form which is

(i.) *external and not a basis of*

auditory . . .

olfactory . . .

gustatory . . .

bodily contact ?

The spheres of the five kinds of sense objects . . . and bodily nutriment.

(ii.) *personal and a basis of . . . bodily contact ?*

The spheres of the other four senses respectively.

(iii.) *personal and not a basis of . . . bodily contact ?*

The sphere of . . . vision, hearing, smell, taste.

[790-792] What is that form which is

(i.) *external and not a basis of*

the feeling . . .

the perception . . .

the thinking . . .

the . . . cognition of body

that is born of . . . bodily contact ?

(ii.) *personal and a basis of . . . the cognition of body that is born of bodily contact ?*

(iii.) *personal and not a basis of . . . the cognition of body that is born of bodily contact ?*

Answers identical with those in the preceding triplet taken in order.

[793-795] What is that form which is

(i.) *personal and not the object apprehended on occasion of visual contact ?*

The spheres of the five senses.

(ii.) *external and the object apprehended on occasion of visual contact ?*

The sphere of visible form.

(iii.) *external and not the object apprehended on occasion of visual contact ?*

The spheres of the other four kinds of sense-objects . . . and bodily nutriment.

[796-798] What is that form which is

(i.) *personal and not the object of*

the feeling . . .
the perception . . .
the thinking . . .
the visual cognition

that is born of visual contact?

(ii.) *external and the object of . . . visual cognition?*

(iii.) *external and not the object of . . . . visual cognition?*

Answers identical with those in the preceding triplet, taken in order.

[799-801] What is that form which is

(i.) *personal and not the object apprehended on occasion of*

auditory . . .
olfactory . . .
gustatory . . .
bodily contact?

The spheres of the five senses.

(ii.) *external and the object apprehended on occasion of . . . bodily contact?*

The sphere of the tangible.

(iii.) *external and not the object apprehended on occasion of . . . bodily contact?*

The spheres of the five kinds of sense-objects . . . and bodily nutriment.

[802-804] What is that form which is

(i.) *personal and not the object of*

the feeling . . .
the perception . . .
the thinking . . .
the . . . cognition of body

that is born of . . . bodily contact?

The spheres of the five senses.

(ii.) *external and the object of the . . . cognition of body that is born of bodily contact?*

The sphere of . . . the tangible.

(iii.) *external and not the object of the . . . cognition of body that is born, etc.*

The spheres of the other four kinds of sense-objects . . . and bodily nutriment.

[805-807] What is that form which is

(i.) *external and not the sphere of vision?*

The spheres of the five kinds of sense-objects . . . and bodily nutriment.

(ii.) *personal and the sphere of vision?*

The eye, that is to say the sentient organ which is derived from the four Great Phenomena . . . this that is 'an empty village'—this, etc.[1]

(iii.) *personal and not the sphere of vision?*

The spheres of the other four senses.

[808-810] What is that form which is

(i.) *external and not the sphere of hearing, smell, taste, or body-sensibility?*

The spheres of the five kinds of sense-objects . . . and bodily nutriment.

(ii.) *personal and the sphere of . . . body-sensibility?*

The body, that is to say the sentient organ, which is derived from the Great Phenomena . . . this that is 'an empty village'—this, etc.

(iii.) *personal and not the sphere of . . . body-sensibility?*

The spheres of the other four senses.

[811-813] What is that form which is

(i.) *personal and not the sphere of visible form?*

The spheres of the five senses.

---

[1] For this and similar answers in following triplets see § 597 *et seq.*

(ii.) *external and the sphere of visible form?*

That form which, derived from the four Great Phenomena, is visible under the appearance of colour . . . this that is the element of visible form—this, etc.[1]

(iii.) *external and not the sphere of visible form?*

The spheres of the other four kinds of sense-objects . . . and bodily nutriment.

[814-816] What is that form which is

(i.) *personal and not the sphere of sound, or of odour, or of taste, or of the tangible?*

The spheres of the five senses.

(ii.) *external and the sphere of . . . the tangible?*

The earthy (solid) element, etc. . . . this that is the constituent element of the tangible—this, etc.[2]

(iii.) *external and not the sphere of . . . the tangible?*

The spheres of the other four kinds of sense-objects . . . and bodily nutriment.

[817-819] What is that form which is

(i.) *external and not the element of vision?*

The spheres of the five kinds of sense-objects . . . and bodily nutriment.

(ii.) *personal and the element of vision?*

The sphere of vision.

(iii.) *personal and not the element of vision?*

The other four senses.

[820-822] What is that form which is

(i.) *external and not the element of hearing, smell, taste, or body-sensibility?*

The spheres of the five kinds of sense-objects . . . and bodily nutriment.

(ii.) *personal and the element of . . . body-sensibility?*

The sphere of . . . body-sensibility.

---

[1] See § 617. [2] See § 648.

(iii.) *personal and not the element of . . . body-sensibility?*

The spheres of the other four senses.

[823-825] What is that form which is

(i.) *personal and not the element of visible form?*

The spheres of the five senses.

(ii.) *external and the element of visible form?*

The sphere of visible forms.

(iii.) *external and not the element of visible form?*

The spheres of the other four kinds of sense-objects . . . and bodily nutriment.

[826-828] What is that form which is

(i.) *personal and not the element of sound, odour, taste or the tangible?*

The spheres of the five senses.

(ii.) *external and the element of . . . the tangible?*

The sphere of the tangible.

(iii.) *external and not the element of . . . the tangible?*

The spheres of the five kinds of sense-objects . . . and bodily nutriment.

[829-831] What is that form which is

(i.) *external and not the faculty of vision?*

The spheres of the five kinds of sense-objects . . . and bodily nutriment.

(ii.) *personal and the faculty of vision?*

The sphere of vision.

(iii.) *personal and not the faculty of vision?*

The spheres of the other four senses.

[832-834] What is that form which is

(i.) *external and not the faculty of hearing, smell, taste, or body-sensibility?*

The spheres of the five kinds of sense-objects . . . and bodily nutriment.

(ii.) *personal and the faculty of . . . body-sensibility?*

The body, that is to say the sentient organ which is derived from the four Great Phenomena . . . this that is 'an empty village'—this, etc.

(iii.) *personal and not the faculty of . . . body-sensibility?*

The spheres of the other four senses.

[835-837] What is that form which is

(i.) *personal and not the potentiality of femininity?*

The spheres of the five senses.

(ii.) *external and femininity?*

That which is of the female, female in appearance, etc. [*continue as in* § 633].

(iii.) *external and not femininity?*

The spheres of the five kinds of sense-objects . . . and bodily nutriment.

[838-840] What is that form which is

(i.) *personal and not the potentiality of masculinity? etc.*

The questions and answers in this triplet are exactly analogous with those in the foregoing, § 634 *constituting the answer to* (ii.).

[841-843] *This triplet is on* 'vitality,' *and is also exactly analogous with that on* 'femininity,' § 635 *being substituted in* (ii.).

[844-846] What is that form which is

(i.) *personal and not bodily intimation?*

The spheres of the five senses.

(ii.) *external and bodily intimation?*

That tension, intension, tense state of the body, etc. [*continue as in* § 636].

(iii.) *external and not bodily intimation?*

The spheres of the five kinds of sense-objects . . . and bodily nutriment.

[847-849] *This triplet is on* 'vocal intimation,' *and similar to the foregoing,* § 637 *being quoted as the answer to the second question.*

[850-876] *Here follow ten triplets on the presence or absence, in form that is personal or external, of the ten following attributes—identical with those ending the categories according to Pairs* (§§ 722-741).

the element of space,	the integration of form,
the element of fluidity,	the subsistence of form,
the lightness of form,	the decay of form,
the plasticity of form,	the impermanence of form,
the wieldiness of form,	bodily nutriment.

Questions and answers in each of these triplets are identical with those in the triplet last set out on 'bodily intimation' (§§ 844-846), *the only varying elements being the specific kind of form inquired into and its definition in the second answer of each triplet. Thus the schema of the questions is*

(i.) *personal and not* . . .
(ii.) *external and* . . .
(iii.) *external and not* . . .[1]

Such are the Categories of Form under Threefold Aspects.
[End of] the Exposition of Triplets.

---

[1] There are several omissions in the printed text, breaking into the symmetry of the triplets, viz.: question and answer (iii.) on ākāsadhātu (following § 851); question and answer (iii.) on rūpassa upacayo (following § 865); question and answer (i.) on rūpassa santati (following § 865). These, if duly inserted, would bring the number of questions (and answers) at the end of this chapter up to 879, instead of 876. Had the triplets been grouped as such, the omissions would not have been possible.

[Chapter IV.

Categories of Form under Fourfold Aspects.][1]

[Derivation—Work of Karma.]

[877-880] What is that form which is

(i.) *derived and the issue of grasping?*

The spheres of the five senses; the potentialities of sex and vitality, or whatever other form exists through karma having been wrought, whether it be in the sphere of visible forms,[2] odours, or tastes, the element of space, the integration or subsistence of form, or bodily nutriment.

(ii.) *derived and not the issue of grasping?*

The sphere of sounds, bodily and vocal intimation, the lightness, plasticity, and wieldiness of form, or whatever other form exists which is not due to karma having been

---

[1] The logical method in this division is familiar enough, namely (where capitals represent positive, and uncials, negative terms), AB, Ab, aB, ab. The former term in the pair combined is, with its negative, a relative constant, there being a series of only six, namely, the concept of form as derived, as the product of karma, as that which breeds karma (literally, is karma-*ish* or karm-*ous*), as impressing the senses, as faculty, and as one of the elements (*i.e.*, the opposite of derived, conceived positively). The latter five of these six are in turn used as the relatively variable term, with the addition of three others: the concept of form with respect to grossness or delicacy, to distance, and to visibility.

[2] On sound and karma, see p. 201, n. 4.

wrought, whether it be in the spheres of visible forms, odours, or tastes, the element of space, the integration or subsistence of form, or bodily nutriment.

(iii.) *underived and the issue of grasping?*

[Form] due to karma having been wrought, which is in the sphere of the tangible and the fluid element.

(iv.) *underived and not the issue of grasping?*

[Form] not due to karma having been wrought, which is in the sphere of the tangible and the fluid element.

[Derivation—Production of Karma.]

[881-884] What is that form which is

(i.) *derived and both the issue of grasping and favourable to it?*

(ii.) *derived and not the issue of grasping but favourable to it?*[1]

(iii.) *underived and both the issue of grasping and favourable to it?*

(iv.) *underived and not the issue of grasping but favourable to it?*[2]

The four answers are respectively identical with those in the preceding group.

[Derivation—Impact.]

[885-888] What is that form which is

(i.) *derived and impingeing?*

The spheres of the five senses, and of visible form, sound, odour and taste.

(ii.) *derived and non-impingeing?*

Sex . . . and bodily nutriment.

(iii.) *underived and impingeing?*

The sphere of the tangible.

(iv.) *underived and non-impingeing?*

The fluid element.

---

[1] See § 656, n. 1.

[2] Read na before kammassa in the answer.

[Derivation—Bulk.]

[889-892] What is that form which is

(i.) *derived and gross?*

(ii.) *derived and subtle?*

(iii.) *underived and gross?*

(iv.) *derived and subtle?*

Answers respectively identical with those in the preceding group.

[Derivation—Proximity.]

[893-896] What is that form which is

(i.) *derived and remote?*

Sex . . . and bodily nutriment.

(ii.) *derived and near?*

The spheres of the five senses, and those of visible form, sound, odour and taste.

(iii.) *underived and remote?*

The fluid element.

(iv.) *underived and near?*

The sphere of the tangible.

[Work of Karma—Visibility.]

[897-900] What is that form which is

(i.) *the issue of grasping and visible?*

The sphere of visible form which is due to karma having been wrought.

(ii.) *the issue of grasping and invisible?*

The spheres of the five senses; sex and vitality, or whatever other form exists through karma having been wrought, whether it be in the spheres of odour, taste, or the tangible, the elements of space or fluidity, the integration or subsistence of form, or bodily nutriment.

(iii.) *not the issue of grasping*[1] *and visible?*

The sphere of visible form which is not due to karma having been wrought.

---

[1] In the printed text read anupādiṇṇaṃ.

(iv.) *not the issue of grasping and invisible?*

The sphere of sound, bodily and vocal intimation, the lightness, plasticity, wieldiness of form, the decay, or the impermanence of form, or whatever other form exists which is not due to karma having been wrought, whether it be in the spheres of odour, or of taste, or of the tangible, the elements of space, or of fluidity, the integration or subsistence of form, or bodily nutriment.

[Work of Karma—Impact.]

[901-904] What is that form which is

(i.) *the issue of grasping and impingeing?*

The spheres of the five senses, or whatever other form exists through karma having been wrought in the spheres of visible form, odour, taste or the tangible.

(ii.) *the issue of grasping and non-impingeing?*

Sex or vitality, or whatever other form exists through karma having been wrought in the elements of space or fluidity, in the integration, or subsistence of form, or in bodily nutriment.

(iii.) *not the issue of grasping and impingeing?*

The sphere of sound, or whatever other form exists which is not due to karma having been wrought in the spheres of the other four kinds of sense-objects.

(iv.) *not the issue of grasping and non-impingeing?*

Bodily and vocal intimation, the lightness, plasticity, wieldiness, decay, or impermanence of form, or whatever other form exists which is not due to karma having been wrought in the elements of space or fluidity, in the integration or subsistence of form, or in bodily nutriment.

[Work of Karma—Great Phenomena.]

[905-908] What is that form which is

(i.) *the issue of grasping and great phenomenon?*

The sphere of the tangible and the fluid element which are due to karma having been wrought.

(ii.) *the issue of grasping and not great phenomenon?*

The spheres of the five senses, sex, vitality, or whatever other form exists through karma having been wrought, in the element of space, in the integration or subsistence of form, or in bodily nutriment.

(iii.) *not the issue of grasping but great phenomenon?*

The sphere of the tangible and the fluid element which are not due to karma having been wrought.

(iv.) *not the issue of grasping nor great phenomenon?*

The sphere of sound, bodily and vocal intimation, the lightness, plasticity, wieldiness, decay and impermanence of form, or whatever other form exists which is not due to karma having been wrought, whether it be in the spheres of visible form, odour, or taste, in the element of space, in the integration or subsistence of form, or in bodily nutriment.

[Work of Karma—Bulk.]

[909-912] What is that form which is

(i.) *the issue of grasping and gross?*

(ii.) *the issue of grasping and subtle?*

(iii.) *not the issue of grasping and gross?*

(iv.) *not the issue of grasping and subtle?*[1]

Answers respectively identical with the four in the next preceding group but one (§§ 901-904).

[Work of Karma—Proximity.]

[913-916] What is that form which is

(i.) *the issue of grasping and remote?*

(ii.) *the issue of grasping and near?*

(iii.) *not the issue of grasping and remote?*

(iv.) *not the issue of grasping and near?*

Answers identical with those in the preceding group (*i.e., with those in* §§ 901-904), *but having the order of the first and second answers inverted, as well as that of the third and fourth.*

---

[1] In the answer to this question the printed text has omitted to insert apodhātu. *Cf.* §§ 892 and 880.

[917-936]

In the next five groups of four, form is considered as a combination of (*a*) 'the issue of grasping and favourable to grasping,' *and either* 'visible,'[1] 'impingeing,' 'a great phenomenon,' 'gross' *or* 'remote,' *or the opposites of these five taken successively;* (*b*) 'not the issue of grasping, but favourable to grasping,' *and the five above-named attributes and their opposites taken successively. Thus the questions are analogous to, and the answers identical with, those in the preceding five groups* (§§ 897-916).

[Impact—Faculty.]

[937-940] What is that form which is

(i.) *impingeing and faculty?*

The faculties of the five senses.

(ii.) *impingeing and not faculty?*

The five kinds of sense-objects.

(iii.) *non-impingeing and faculty?*

Sex and vitality.

(iv.) *non-impingeing and not faculty?*

Bodily and vocal intimation . . . and bodily nutriment.

[Impact—Great Phenomenon.]

[941-944] What is that form which is

(i.) *impingeing and a great phenomenon?*

The sphere of the tangible.

(ii.) *impingeing and not a great phenomenon?*

The spheres of visible form, sound, odour and taste.

(iii.) *non-impingeing and a great phenomenon?*

The fluid element.

(iv.) *non-impingeing and not a great phenomenon?*

Sex . . . and bodily nutriment.

---

[1] In the answer to the first question, § 917, read n a before kammassa.

[Faculty (Potentiality)—Bulk.]

[945-948] What is that form which is

(i.) *faculty and gross ?*

The faculties of the five senses.

(ii.) *faculty and subtle ?*

Sex and vitality.

(iii.) *non-faculty and gross ?*

The spheres of the five kinds of sense-objects.

(iv.) *non-faculty and subtle ?*

Intimation . . . and bodily nutriment.

[Faculty (Potentiality)—Proximity.]

[949-952] What is that form which is

(i.) *faculty and remote ?*

Sex and vitality.

(ii.) *faculty and near ?*

The faculties of the five senses.

(iii.) *non-faculty and remote ?*

Intimation . . . and bodily nutriment.

(iv.) *non-faculty and near ?*

The spheres of the five kinds of sense-objects.

[Great Phenomenon—Bulk.]

[953-956] What is that form which is

(i.) *a great phenomenon and gross ?*

The sphere of the tangible.

(ii.) *a great phenomenon and subtle ?*

The fluid element.

(iii.) *not a great phenomenon and gross ?*

The spheres of the five senses and of visible form, sound, odour and taste.

(iv.) *not a great phenomenon and subtle ?*

Sex . . . and bodily nutriment.

[Great Phenomenon—Proximity.]

[957-960] What is that form which is

(i.) *a great phenomenon and remote?*

The fluid element.

(ii.) *a great phenomenon and near?*

The sphere of the tangible.

(iii.) *not a great phenomenon and remote?*

Sex and vitality.

(iv.) *not a great phenomenon and near?*

The spheres of the five senses and of visible form, sound, odour and taste.

[Form as Seen, Heard, Imagined, Understood.]

[961] (i.) The sphere of visible form is Form Seen,
(ii.) The sphere of sound is Form Heard,
(iii.) The sphere of odour, taste and the tangible is Form Imagined,[1]

---

[1] Mutaṃ. I am under the impression that the first three members of this group are survivals of an older tradition, belonging to an age when the five senses had not been co-ordinated by psychological analysis comparable to that effected by the earlier Buddhist school, and when mano and its function, expressed here (in part) by this old past participle, were more vaguely conceived. In the Praçna Upanishad, *e.g.*, which may or may not be older than the Abhidhamma, either the five senses are grouped as above under manas, eye and ear, or the last two are alone held worthy to rank with the divine elements of life. If it be contended that the former interpretation is not plausible, it should be remembered that, in the far older Bṛihadāraṇyaka Upanishad (i., 5, 3), it is said that by manas we know when we are *touched* from behind. It is as though the tradition were endeavouring to say, Smell, taste, touching, *without* the aid either of sight or of hearing, require a greater effort of inference, of mental construction, of imagination, to realize the external cause, or potential concrete mental percept, than either sight or hearing.

(iv.) All form is Form Cognized by the mind.[1]

Such are the Categories of Form under Fourfold Aspects.
[End of] the Groups of Four.

Buddhaghosa, who here resumes his parable (Asl. 338), paraphrases mutaṃ by munitvā jānitabbaṭṭhena, and by phusitvā pi ñāṇuppattikāranato.

[1] Manasā viññātaṃ, that is, manoviññāṇena jānitabbaṃ. *Ibid.*

[CHAPTER V.

The Category of Form under a Fivefold Aspect (pañcavidhena rūpasangaho).]

[962-966] What is that form which is

(i.) *earth-element* (paṭhavī-dhātu)?[1]

That which is hard, rough, hardness, rigidity, whether it be of the self,[2] or external, or the issue of grasping,[3] or not the issue of grasping.

---

[1] The essential mark (lakkhaṇaṃ) of the earth-element is given as 'hardness' (kakkhaḷattaṃ, Asl., 332). This may very likely have conveyed to Buddhists what we understand by 'solid,' when the implication is density as opposed to what is liquid or gaseous, and it was tempting to use solidity in preference to hardness. But the former term is ambiguous, for it may mean the opposite of plane surface, and kakkhaḷattaṃ cannot be strained to mean that. Again, the opposite of the latter term is neither liquid nor flat, but soft or pliant. Further, compare its use in describing gravel or stone-food in Mil. 67, where we should certainly use 'hard.' The other characteristics of paṭhavīdhātu are said to be establishing a fulcrum or ποῦ στῶ, patiṭṭhānaṃ), and accepting (sampaṭicchanaṃ), the import of the latter term not being very clear.

[2] Ajjhattaṃ. See § 673, note, and § 742, note.

[3] In the Commentary, p. 338, where upādiṇṇaṃ is said to be na kammasamutthānaṃ eva, the negative particle must have crept in by some error, that which is upādiṇṇaṃ being essentially due to karma. See Dh. S., §§ 653, 654; Asl., pp. 46, 337 (§ 664), etc. Generally, says Buddhaghosa, the bony framework of the body (the most solid part of one's self, sarīraṭṭhakaṃ) is here

(ii.) *fluid-element* (āpodhātu)?

That which is fluid, belonging to fluid, viscid, belonging to what is viscid, the cohesiveness of form, whether it be of the self, or external, or the issue of grasping or not the issue of grasping.[1]

(iii.) *flame-element* (tejodhātu)?[2]

That which is flame, belonging to flame, heat, belonging to heat, hot, belonging to what is hot, whether it be of the self, or, etc. [*continue as in preceding*].

(iv.) *air-element* (vāyodhātu)?

That which is air, belongs to air [the fluctuation], the inflation,[3] of form, whether it be of the self, or, etc.

---

referred to. For this, while it may, or may not be upādiṇṇaṃ, is said to be wholly the issue of grasping when signifying that which is taken, laid hold of, infected.

[1] See § 652, note. The essential characteristics of āpodhātu are said to be flowing (paggharaṇaṃ), expansion or spreading (brūhanaṃ, *cf.* p. 12, note 3, Mil. 317) and congress (sangaho, Asl., *ibid.*). The last term may possibly be an attempt to express what we term, loosely enough, 'water always finding its own level.' The internal or personal āpo is distributed as bile, phlegm, pus, blood, sweat, serum, tears, and so on. M. i. 42.

[2] Never aggi or fire, in the Buddhist books. The essential characteristics are said to be (Asl., *ibid.*) heat, ripening, maturing (paripācanaṃ) and softening. By the heat within food and drink are digested. M., *loc. cit.*

[3] The text reads here both chambitattaṃ and thambhitattaṃ, fluctuation (quaking) and inflation. The former term, however, is not elsewhere in the Atthasālinī applied to vāyo; the latter, with the intensive vi-, is declared to be the characteristic mark of vāyo, other features of the element being onward movement (samudīranaṃ) and downward force (abhinīhāraṃ—*sic lege. Cf.* D. i. 76; M. i. 119; Asl. 332). Now Buddhaghosa passes over chambhitattaṃ in silence, but explains thambhitattaṃ. Again, though this is, of course, not conclusive, only the single term thambhitattaṃ rūpassa seems to be called for by the parallel, bandhanattaṃ rūpassa (cohesiveness), in the description of fluidity. It is significant also that K. omits chambhitattaṃ. On

(v.) *derived?*[1]

The spheres of the five senses . . . and solid nutriment.

Such is the Category of Form under a Fivefold Aspect.

[End of] the Group of Five.

---

these grounds taken together, I should be inclined to doubt the original inclusion of the term. The instance chosen to illustrate the inflating function characteristic of vāyo is that of the sheaths or stems of lotuses and reeds which are 'filled with air,' or wind (vātapuṇṇāni).

[1] 'Derived' (upādā) is the opposite of (i.) to (iv.). See §§ 647, 648.

[CHAPTER VI.

The Category of Form under a Sixfold Aspect.]

[967]

(i.) The sphere of visible forms is form cognizable by sight.
(ii.) The sphere of sounds is form cognizable by hearing.
(iii.) The sphere of odours is form cognizable by smell.
(iv.) The sphere of tastes is form cognizable by taste.
(v.) The sphere of the tangible is form cognizable by body-sensibility.
(vi.) All form is form cognizable by the mind.

Such is the Category of Form under a Sixfold Aspect.

[End of] the Group of Six.

[CHAPTER VII.

The Category of Form under a Sevenfold Aspect.]

[968]

(i.) The sphere of visible form is form cognizable by sight.

(ii.) The sphere of sound is form cognizable by hearing.

(iii.) The sphere of odour is form cognizable by smell.

(iv.) The sphere of taste is form cognizable by taste.

(v.) The sphere of the tangible is form cognizable by body-sensibility.

[969]

(vi.) The spheres of visible form, sound, odour, taste, and the tangible are form cognizable by the element of ideation.

(vii.) All form is form comprehensible by the element of representative intellection.

Such is the Category of Form under a Sevenfold Aspect.

[End of] the Group of Seven.

[Chapter VIII.

The Category of Form under an Eightfold Aspect.]

[970]

(i.) The sphere of visible form is form cognizable by the eye.

(ii.) The sphere of sound is form cognizable by the ear.

(iii.) The sphere of odour is form cognizable by the nose.

(iv.) The sphere of taste is form cognizable by the tongue.

(v.) Pleasurable agreeable contact obtainable by touch is form cognizable by the body.

(vi.) Unpleasant disagreeable contact obtainable by touch is form cognizable by the body.

(vii.) The spheres of the five kinds of sense-objects are form cognizable by ideation.

(viii.) All form is form comprehensible by representative intellection.

Such is the Category of Form under an Eightfold Aspect.

[End of] the Group of Eight.

[Chapter IX.

The Category of Form under a Ninefold Aspect.]

[971-973] What is that form which is

(i.) the faculty of vision?
(ii.) the faculty of hearing?
(iii.) the faculty of smell?
(iv.) the faculty of taste?
(v.) the faculty of body-sensibility?
(vi.) the potentiality of femininity?
(vii.) the potentiality of masculinity?
(viii.) the potentiality of vitality?

The eight answers are those given in the original descriptions of the eight faculties or potentialities enumerated (§§ 597, 601, 605, 609, 613, 633-535).

(ix.) What is that form which is not faculty?

The spheres of the five kinds of sense-objects . . .[1] and bodily nutriment.

Such is the Category of Form under a Ninefold Aspect.

[End of] the Group of Nine.

---

[1] That is to say, the *remainder* of § 596, but omitting, of course, the three 'indriyas' of the sexes and vitality, and presumably inserting 'the element of fluidity' (*cf.* p. 203, n. 3).

[CHAPTER X.

The Category of Form under a Tenfold Aspect.]

[974, 975] *The first eight questions and answers are identical with the first eight in the preceding group.*

[976, 977] What is that form which is

(ix.) *not faculty but impingeing?*

The spheres of the five kinds of sense-objects.

(x.) *not faculty and non-impingeing?*

Intimation . . .[1] and bodily nutriment.

Such is the Category of Form under a Tenfold Aspect.

[End of] the Group of Ten.

---

[1] That is to say, the remainder of § 596, beginning at bodily intimation, and presumably inserting 'the element of fluidity.'

[CHAPTER XI.

The Category of Form under an Elevenfold Aspect.]

[978, 979] What is that form which is
- (i.) the sphere of vision?
- (ii.) the sphere of hearing?
- (iii.) the sphere of smell?
- (iv.) the sphere of taste?
- (v.) the sphere of body-sensibility?
- (vi.) the sphere of visible form?
- (vii.) the sphere of sound?
- (viii.) the sphere of odour?
- (ix.) the sphere of sapids?
- (x.) the sphere of the tangible?

Answers as in §§ 597, 601, 605, 609, 613, 617, 621, 625, 629, 649 *respectively.*

[980]

(xi.) What is that form which is invisible, non-impingeing, and included in the sphere of [mental] states?[1]

Sex . . . and bodily nutriment.

Such is the Category of Form under an Elevenfold Aspect.

[End of] the Group of Eleven.

[End of] THE DIVISIONS OF FORM.

[End of] the Eighth Portion for Recitation.

---

[1] Dhammāyatana-pariyāpannaṃ. For the full content of the answer, see, as before, the last fourteen items in § 596.

[BOOK III.

THE DIVISION ENTITLED 'ELIMINATION'

(nikkhepa-kaṇḍaṃ).[1]

PART I.

CHAPTER I.

The Group of Triplets (tikaṃ).]

[981] Which are the states that are good?

The three roots of good (karma),[2] to wit, absence of lust, absence of hate, absence of dulness; the skandhas of

---

[1] Or rejection. According to the Cy. (344, 345), the various classes into which the states of the moral consciousness were distinguished (dhamma-vibhāgo) are now to be set forth by a method which, in its greater conciseness, is a rejection or discarding of the relatively more detailed exposition (vitthāra-desanaṃ) of Book I. 'Any intelligent person can recognise,' for instance, that in the concise terms in which the answer to question [984] is couched, the answer to question [1], among others, is involved. Relatively to the following Atthakathā, on the other hand (§ 1368 to end in the printed text), this method is in its turn less concise, more detailed.

[2] By 'root' is meant 'cause, condition, bringing to pass, generating, originating, producing.' And 'since there is no such thing as good detached from a root,' all good is hereby included. Asl. 344.

feeling, perception, syntheses and intellect when they are associated with those three roots; whatever action, bodily, vocal and mental,[1] springs from those three roots.

[982] Which are the states that are bad?

The three roots of bad (karma), to wit, lust, hate, dulness; the Corruptions that are united with them;[2] the skandhas of feeling, perception, syntheses and intellect when these are associated with them; whatever action, bodily, vocal and mental, springs from them.

[983] Which are the states that are indeterminate?

The results of good and bad states taking effect in the worlds of sense, form, or the formless, or in the [life that is] Unincluded;[3] the skandhas of feeling, perception, syntheses and intellect,[4] those states, moreover, known as kiriyā-thoughts,[5] which are neither good, nor bad, nor the results of karma; lastly, all form and uncompounded element.[6]

[984] Which are the states that are associated with a feeling of ease?

The skandhas of perception, syntheses and intellect[7] (the

---

[1] Manokammaṃ, inadvertently omitted in the printed text. *Cf.* § 982 and *passim*.

[2] Tad-ekaṭṭhā ca kilesā. Ekaṭṭhaṃ is defined (Asl. 345) as located in one and the same *thought* by virtue of a common origin, or in one and the same *person*, by virtue of a common exclusion, to wit here, of corrupt or faulty states. On kilesā, see § 1229 *et seq.*

[3] Apariyāpannā. See below, § 992, also § 583.

[4] To save much repetition throughout this division, *these* four skandhas are henceforward referred to as 'the four skandhas.'

[5] Dhammā kiriyā. *Cf.* § 566 *et seq.*

[6] In the printed text sankhatā should be asankhatā.

[7] The skandha of feeling is in this case the predominating factor, and not reckoned as merely an associate, or subordinate adjunct in consciousness. (Taṃ should be inserted before sampayutto in the text.)

feeling itself being excepted) are the states associated [with the consciousness arising] in an ease-yielding soil,[1] whether it belong to the worlds of sense or of form, or to the life that is Unincluded.

[985] Which are the states that are associated with distressful feeling?

The skandhas of perception, syntheses and intellect (the feeling itself being excepted) are the states associated [with the consciousness arising] in a distressful soil belonging to the sensuous universe.

[986] Which are the states that are associated with feeling that is neither painful nor pleasant?

The skandhas of perception, syntheses and intellect (the feeling itself being excepted) are the states associated [with the consciousness arising] in a neutral soil, whether it belong to the worlds of sense, form, or the formless, or to the life that is Unincluded.

[987] Which are the states that are results?

The results of good and bad states which take effect in the worlds of sense, form and the formless, and in the life that is Unincluded; [in other words] the four skandhas.[2]

---

[1] Sukha-bhūmiyaṃ. I have kept to the more literal rendering of bhūmi here, in preference to some such term as 'stage' (as in § 277 *et seq.*) or 'source,' because of the analogy drawn by the Cy. (p. 346):—just as by saying 'This is a sugar-soil' or 'a rice-land' we mean localities where these products thrive, so by sukha-bhūmi, etc., we mean a thought (or state of mind, cittaṃ), which is the place (or occasion, thānaṃ) for the uprising of ease (or happiness).

[2] K. invariably places a colon before that enumeration of four or more skandhas which is part of the usual procedure in these triplets. There is nothing explicit in the Cy. to justify my interpretation by the parenthesis 'in other words' of the somewhat amorphous construction of the answers thus punctuated. But I gather from its remarks that, in these concentrated replies, the skandha-list represents the preceding half of the answer, in which it occurs, *under*

[988] Which are the states that involve resultant states ?[1]

Good and bad states belonging to the worlds of sense, form and the formless, or to the life that is Unincluded ; [in other words] the four skandhas.

[989] Which are the states that neither are results, nor have the quality of involving resultant states ?

Those states concerning action which are neither good, nor bad, nor the results of karma ; all form, moreover, and uncompounded element.

[990] Which are the states that are both the issue of grasping and favourable to it ?[2]

The co-Intoxicant[3] results of good and bad states taking effect in the worlds of sense, form or the formless ; in other words, the four skandhas : such form, moreover, as is due to karma having been wrought.

[991] Which are the states that are not the issue of grasping but are favourable to grasping ?

Good and bad co-Intoxicant states taking effect in the worlds of sense, form, or the formless ; in other words, the four skandhas ; those states, moreover, known as kiriyā-thoughts, which are neither good, nor bad, nor the results of karma ; as well as such form as is not due to karma having been wrought.

[992] Which are the states that are neither the issue of grasping nor favourable to it ?

---

another aspect, viz., rāsaṭṭhena, or that of groups in consciousness. This is really the method followed in detail throughout Book I., but here in mere outline : first a reply in terms of dhammā, then the Summary, which is *mainly*, at least, in terms of skandha. *Cf.*, *e.g.*, §§ 431-441, 441*a*, 442. Also Asl. 152.

[1] Vipākadhamma-dhammā, paraphrased (Asl. 42) by vipāka-sabhāva-dhammā, states having a result-nature, or quality of result. See above, p. 164.

[2] See § 653 *et seq.*

[3] Sāsavā. See § 1096 *et seq.*

The Paths that are the Unincluded,[1] and the Fruits of the Paths,[2] and uncompounded element.

[993] Which are the states that are corrupt and baneful?[3]

The three roots of bad (karma), to wit, lust, hate, dulness; the Corruptions that are united with them; the four skandhas when these are associated with them; whatever action, bodily, vocal and mental, springs from them.

[994] Which are the states that are not corrupt but baneful?

Good and indeterminate co-Intoxicant states taking effect in the worlds of sense, form and the formless; in other words, the *five*[4] skandhas.

---

[1] See p. 165, note 2. The term apariyāpannā, when applied to dhammā and used in an ethico-psychological sense, is described as here in terms of path, fruit and uncompounded element. See § 1287. Its positive correlate is paraphrased, in Asl. 50, by 'contained in the threefold cycle of existence' (*i.e.*, the worlds of sense, form, etc.). I do not know whether apariyāpannaṃ with this lofty significance occurs in either of the older Pitakas. But it appears in K. V. 507, where it is declared a heresy to hold that any mere speculative opinion was of the Unincluded, and where the content of the latter concept is more amply set forth than in our manual.

[2] Read ca after maggaphalāni. The commentator vindicates the status of the arahat, here alluded to, as being free from all 'grasping' as follows: Although the skandhas (the temporary being) of the arahat may become a cause of grasping to those who say, Our mother's brother, the Thera! Our father's brother, the Thera! yet there is no grasping, no infection, attaching to the Paths, the Fruits and Nirvana. For just as there is no inducement to mosquitoes to alight on a ball of iron which has been heated all day, so these Things, by their excessive glory, do not attract the grasp of craving, pride or false opinion.

[3] Or corrupting. See § 1229 (note) *et seq.*

[4] Beginning with the skandha of material form.

[995] Which are the states that are neither corrupt nor baneful?

The Paths that are the Unincluded, and the Fruits of the Paths and uncompounded element.

[996] Which are the states 'wherein conception works and thought discursive'?[1]

The four skandhas (conception and discursive thought excluded)[2] which are associated[3] [with the consciousness arising] in a soil favourable to the working of conception and of discursive thought, whether it belong to the world of sense or of form, or to the life that is Unincluded.

[997] Which are the states 'wherein is no working of conception but only of thought discursive'?[4]

The four skandhas (discursive thought excluded) which are associated [with the consciousness arising] in a soil favourable to the working, not of conception, but only of discursive thought, whether it belong to the world of form, or to the life that is Unincluded.

[998] Which are the states that are 'void of the working of conception and of thought discursive'?[5]

The four skandhas which are associated [with the consciousness arising] in a soil void of conception and discursive thought, whether it belong to the world of sense, form, or the formless, or to the life that is Unincluded; all form, moreover, and uncompounded element.

---

[1] See § 160. Part of the formula for the First Jhāna. The world, universe, or heaven of the Formless is omitted, being a 'soil' where these mental processes could not grow. See §§ 265-268.

[2] They would else come under the skandha of syntheses. See § 62, and p. 251, n. 7.

[3] Read taṃ before sampayutto.

[4] See § 168—a phrase borrowed from the 'System of Fivefold Jhāna.'

[5] See § 162 *et seq.*

[999] Which are the states that are accompanied by joy?

The four skandhas (joy being excluded) which are associated [with the consciousness arising] in a soil yielding joy, whether it belong to the worlds of sense or form, or to the life that is Unincluded.

[1000] Which are the states that are accompanied by ease?

The skandhas of[1] perception, syntheses and intellect (ease being excluded) which are associated [with the consciousness arising] in an ease-yielding soil, whether it belong to the worlds of sense or form, or to the life that is Unincluded.

[1001] Which are the states that are accompanied by disinterestedness?

The skandhas of perception, syntheses and intellect (disinterestedness being excluded) which are associated [with the consciousness arising] in a soil favourable to disinterestedness, whether it belong to the worlds of form or the formless, or to the life that is Unincluded.

[1002] Which are the states that are to be put away by insight?[2]

---

[1] 'Joy' is not counted as a mode of feeling, but as a 'synthesis' (see p. 11, note 4); 'ease,' however, and 'disinterestedness' being two of the three modes of feeling, this skandha ceases to be merely an associated state.

[2] Dassanaṃ, lit., seeing or vision. In view of what *can* and can *not* be put away by 'insight,' it must be remembered that the term is here used in the technical sense it possesses for Buddhist ethics, and means the mental awakening, or intellectual conversion, by which one became a sotāpatti and entered the First Path—and no more. Asl. 356, 357; 43. It was the vehicle for breaking the three Fetters named here, and numbered as 4th, 5th and 6th in the list of ten named later (§§ 1113, 1123, note). It represented a certain vantage-point for mind and heart, from which the Promised Land of Nirvana was caught sight of, and the fact of impermanence first discerned (see the standard passage on this and ñāṇa-dassanaṃ, D. i. 76),

. The three Fetters,[1] to wit, the theory of individuality, perplexity, and the contagion of mere rule and ritual.

In this connexion

[1003] *What is the 'theory of individuality'?*[2]

---

as well as the futility of Substantialist theories, and the impotence of a religion of rules and works. Confidence in the new methods sprang up with the wider vision. Dassanaṃ was powerless to remove the cosmic processes of life and mind: the collocations of phenomena, the evolution of karma, the infinite mystery of the extra-sensuous (see § 1008 and note). On various ways of attaining this insight, see the interesting Kiṃsukā Sutta, S. iv. 191. Relatively to the higher standpoints to be gained it might rather, says Buddhaghosa, be called no-vision. For even as a man, bound on some mission to a king, if he saw the latter pass afar off on his elephant, would say, if questioned, that he had not seen him, he not having accomplished his mission, so the convert, though he have caught his first glimpse of Nirvana, yet because of all he has to do in the getting rid of evil, is said to have no vision. His knowledge consists in a contemplation of the Path.

[1] On the Fetters, see § 1113 *et seq.*

[2] Sakkāya-diṭṭhi, embodying one of the most dangerous of all delusions from the Buddhist point of view, is by the Cy. (p. 348) connected with kāyo, the phenomenal compound of five skandhas, and either with sat, in the sense of (noumenal) being, or with sayaṃ, one's own. *Cf.* S. N., verses 950, 951; Dhp., verse 367. The latter explanation —svakāya—is probably correct (*vide* E. Müller, 'Pāli Grammar,' p. 19). 'Individuality,' then, stands for this skandha-complex, which we should now speak of as 'body and soul' (or mind). Both term and theory are discussed by Dhammadinnā in M. i. 299 *et seq.* (See an article by the writer in J. R. A. S., 1894, p. 324.) The fourth Upādāna, or 'Grasping after a theory of soul,' is described in identical terms. See § 1217.

Diṭṭhi, which is here rendered by 'theory,' and which might with equal propriety be translated by 'speculation' or 'views'—all four terms having a common etymological basis in the notion of seeing, or things seen—is in the answer rendered by 'opinion,' as fitting better that 'mass of notions current among the mass of men' which in the

When in this world[1] the ignorant,[2] average[3] man who perceives not the Noble Ones,[4] who comprehends not, nor

---

case of the puthujjano does service for organized knowledge. Gotama might possibly have approved the Platonic description of δόξα as 'something more dusky than knowledge, more luminous than ignorance.' To translate by 'heresy' or 'delusion' has the disadvantage of necessitating the use of other terms in the case of sound diṭṭhi, such as that described, in M. P. S., Bh. I., as diṭṭhi ariyā niyyānikā. *Cf.* below, § 1366.

[1] Idha, a term, as the Cy. says, either of localization, or of instance in giving instruction; here used in the former sense, and meaning occurrence in the world. Asl. 348.

[2] Assutavā, lit., one who has not heard, *i.e.*, not been taught, who through lack of investigation, inquiry, acquiring, in such matters as skandhas, elements, spheres, conditions, constituents, meditations, is without proper tradition and attainment. *Ibid.*

[3] Puthujjano, the common worldling. The Cy. cites verses distinguishing *l'homme sensuel moyen* as either blind or amiable; of these the former is here meant. In another quotation (also as yet unverified) he is described as given to various common vices, governed by the individuality-theory, hanging on the lips of various ordinary preachers, immersed in every kind of re-birth; complicating life with various common complexities; carried away by divers vulgar currents; appeased or feverish with various low sources of gratification or of irritation; steeped in, greedy of, entangled in, infatuated with, involved in, sticking to, held fast and hampered by, the five low pleasures of sense; veiled, muffled, shrouded in, closed and cloaked and covered up by, the five low hindrances (§ 1152 *et seq.*); as absorbed among the countless folk in the past of low character and conduct opposed to noble doctrine; or, finally, as one separate and distinct from those noble folk who are given to virtue and learning.

[4] Ariyānaṃ adassāvī, referring either to the Buddhas, the Pacceka-buddhas and the disciples of the Buddhas, or to the Buddhas only. Buddhaghosa points out at some length that the inability to perceive, lit., see, holy persons is no mere visual shortcoming, but a lack of insight or of intelligent inference. The truly noble, as such, seen with

is trained according to[1] the doctrine of the Noble Ones, who perceives not good men,[2] who comprehends not, nor is trained according to, the doctrine of good men, regards (1) the self as bodily form, or (2) as having bodily form, or regards (3) bodily form as being in the self, or (4) the self as being in bodily form ;[3] or regards (5) the self as feeling, or (6) as having feeling, or regards (7) feeling as being in the self, or (8) the self as being in feeling; or regards (9) the self as perception, or (10) as having perception, or regards (11) perception as being in the self, or (12) the self as being in perception; or regards (13) the self as syntheses, or (14) as having syntheses, or regards (15) syntheses as being in the self, or (16) the self as being in syntheses ; or regards (17) the self as intellect, or (18) as having intellect, or regards (19) intellect as being in the self, or (20) the self as being in intellect—then this kind of opinion, this walking in opinion, this jungle of opinion, wilderness of opinion,

---

the bodily, or with the 'divine' eye, are not really seen. Their appearance (vaṇṇo) is apprehended, but not the area of their noble nature, even as dogs and jackals, etc., see them and know them not. Even the personal attendant of a Thera may not discern the hero in his master, so hard is it without insight and understanding to discern the standpoint attained by the saints, or the conditions of true nobility. 'What is to thee this vile body that thou seest, Vakkali? He who seeth the Doctrine, he it is who seeth Me!' S. iii., p. 120; Asl. 350.

[1] Avinīto. The Cy. enumerates, with examples, the five modes of the discipline (vinaya) of self-control, and of that of renunciation. These are given in Childers, *s.v.* vinayo.

[2] Sappurisā, meaning Pacceka-buddhas and the disciples of the Buddhas. (Asl. 349.)

[3] These four 'views' respecting the relation of each skandha to a conceivable central entity or attā are discussed in my Introduction. All, according to the Cy. (p. 354), are obstacles to the Paths, though not to heaven (maggāvaraṇā na saggāvaraṇā), and are overcome during progress through the First Path.

puppet-show of opinion, scuffling of opinion, this Fetter of opinion, the grip and tenacity of it, the inclination towards it, the being infected by it, this by-path, wrong road, wrongness, this 'fording-place,' this shiftiness of grasp—this is called the theory of individuality.

[1004] *What is 'perplexity'?*

To doubt, to be perplexed about, (1) the Master, to doubt, to be perplexed about, (2) the Doctrine, to doubt, to be perplexed about, (3) the Order, about (4) the Discipline, about (5) the past, the future, about both the past and the future, (6) as to whether there be an assignable cause[1] of states causally determined—it is this kind of doubt, this working of doubt, this dubiety, puzzlement, perplexity, distraction, standing at cross-roads; collapse, uncertainty of grasp; evasion, hesitation, incapacity of grasping thoroughly, stiffness of mind, mental scarifying, that is called perplexity.[2]

[1005] What is the contagion of mere rule and ritual?

The theory, held by recluses and Brahmins outside our doctrine,[3] that purification is got by rules of moral conduct, that purification is got by rites, that purification is got by rules of moral conduct and by rites[4]—this kind of opinion,

---

[1] Ida-paccayatā.

[2] See § 425. The specific forms of doubt are thus commented on (Asl. 354, 355): (1) As to whether or no the Teacher has the 32 major bodily marks, or the 80 minor bodily marks of a Buddha, or the requisite omniscience with respect to things past, future and present; (2) as to the adequacy of the Paths and their Fruits to lead indeed to the grand ambrosial Nirvana; (3) as to whether those of the Order are indeed at various stages of the path to salvation, or have rightly won their way so far; (4) as to whether the Training is helpful; (5) as to whether evolution by way of skandhas, dhātus and āyatanas has held in the past, or will hold in the future; (6) as to whether there is a twelve-graded cycle of causation, taking effect here and now or taking effect at all.

[3] Ito bahiddhā.

[4] I have ventured to adopt a reading differing slightly

this walking in mere opinion, this jungle of opinion, this wilderness of opinion, this puppet-show of opinion, scuffling of opinion, Fetter of opinion, the grip and tenacity of it, the inclination towards it, the being infected by it, this by-path, wrong road, wrongness, this 'fording-place,' this shiftiness of grasp—this is called the contagion of mere rule and ritual.

[1006] These three Fetters, and the Corruptions united with them,[1] and the four skandhas associated with them, as well as the action, bodily, vocal and mental, springing from them—these are the states which are to be put away by insight.

[1007] Which are the states that are to be put away by culture?[2]

---

from that both of the text and of K. The sense seems to demand it and the Cy. to imply it. The latter has: Sīlenā ti gosīlādinā, vatenā ti govatādinā va (*sic lege*), sīlabbatenā ti tadubhayena, suddhī ti kilesa-suddhi paramattha-suddhibhūtaṃ vā nibbānam eva. But it would not be in accordance with the methods of the Cy. to quote vatenā ti if suddhivatena stood in the text. (Asl. 355.)

As to the terms gosīla, govataṃ, it is not clear what were the practices and mode of life followed in the 'bovine morals,' etc., of those who were called govattikā, or in the 'canine (? Cynic) practices' of the kukkuravattikā. Both are named in M. i. 387. *Cf.* also Kh. P. Cy., p. 26.

Suddhi, it will be seen, is distinguished as, on the one hand, the mere renunciation of the Kilesas (see § 1229), on the other, perfect holiness or Nirvana.

On sīlabbataparāmaso, see Rhys Davids' 'American Lectures,' 146.

[1] These are said to be chiefly speculation and perplexity (regarded not as 'fetters,' but as plagues or evils), and, besides these, lust, hate, dulness, pride, stolidity, excitement, unconscientiousness, disregard of blame.

[2] Or practice: bhāvanā, the collective name for the systematized effort in self-training of the disciple who, having attained 'insight,' leaves 'the principles of the doctrine' that he may 'go on unto perfection' (Heb. vi. 1)—

Whatever lust, hate and dulness still remain, and any corruptions united with them; the four skandhas that are associated with them; whatever action, bodily, vocal or mental, springs from them.

[1008] Which are the states that are to be put away neither by insight nor by culture?

Good and indeterminate states relating to the worlds of sense, form or the formless, or to the life that is Unincluded; the four skandhas; all form, moreover, and uncompounded element.[1]

[1009] Which are the states the causes of which are to be put away by insight?[2]

The three Fetters, to wit, theory of individuality, perplexity, contagion of mere rule and ritual.

In this connexion

[1010] What is 'theory of individuality'? . . . [*continue as in* §§ 1003-1005].[3]

---

in other words, travel along the three higher Paths to Arahatship.

On the 'powers of bhāvanā,' see A. i. 52.

In A. i. 43, the 'one thing needful' for the perfecting of bhāvanā is said to be kāyagata-sati, mindfulness in what concerns the body, or bodily action.

[1] Hence only akusalā dhammā, 'bad states,' can be put away by insight and culture. Nor can even these two avail in mutual independence, for see §§ 1258, 1260. The rest of one's karma goes on accumulating. The good and the indeterminate, the modes of matter, and Simple Element:—these cannot cease for any individual until, according to Buddhaghosa, his abhisankhāra-viññāṇaṃ (Asl. 357)—his constructing, storing intellect, itself dies out with the extinction of his life as Arahat. See Sum. on the Kevaddha Sutta, D. i. 223; 'Dialogues of the Buddha,' i. 272 *et seq*.

[2] Pahātabba-hetukā, 'That is, the cause of them (hetu etesaṃ) is to be put away by insight.' Asl. 43.

[3] Here the reading in the text is obviously corrupt. I follow that in K., viz.: Tattha katamā sakkāyadiṭṭhi?

[1010*a*] These three Fetters, and the Corruptions united with them, and the four skandhas associated with them, as well as the action, bodily, vocal and mental, springing from them—these are the states the causes of which are to be put away by insight.

[1010*b*][1] The three Fetters:—theory of individuality, perplexity, contagion of mere rule and ritual—are the *states* that are to be put away by insight. The lust, hate and dulness united with them are the *causes* that are to be put away by insight. And the Corruptions united with them, the four skandhas associated with them, and the action, bodily, vocal and mental, springing from them, are the states *the causes of which* are to be put away by insight.

[1011] Which are the states the causes of which are to be put away by culture?

Whatever lust, hate and dulness still remain, these are *causes*[2] that are to be put away by culture. And the Corruptions united with them, the four skandhas associated with them, and the action, bodily, vocal and mental, springing from them—these are *states the causes of which* are to be put away by culture.

[1012] Which are the states the causes of which are to be put away neither by insight, nor by cultivation?

The afore-mentioned states excepted, all other states, good, bad and indeterminate, relating to the worlds of sense, form and the formless, and to the life that is Unincluded; in other words, the four skandhas; all form, moreover, and uncompounded element.

. . . pe . . . ayaṃ vuccati sakkāyadiṭṭhi—and so on.

[1] This paragraph, in which I again follow K., is not included in the text at all. Nevertheless, Buddhaghosa comments on it (p. 357).

[2] Here again I follow K. in reading pahātabba-hetū for hetukā. Buddhaghosa quotes the former reading (p. 358), as referring to the putting away of dulness accompanied by excitement.

[1013] Which are the states that make for the piling up [of rebirth]?[1]

Good and bad co-Intoxicant states relating to the worlds of sense, form and the formless; in other words, the four skandhas.

[1014] Which are the states that make for the undoing of rebirth?

The four Paths that are the Unincluded.

[1015] Which are the states that make neither for the piling up, nor for the undoing of rebirth?

The results of good and bad states taking effect in the worlds of sense, form or the formless, or in the life that is Unincluded; in other words, the four skandhas; those states, moreover, known as kiriyā-thoughts, which are neither good nor bad, nor the result of karma; all form also and uncompounded element.

[1015] Which are the states that appertain to studentship?[2]

The four Paths that are the Unincluded and the three lowest Fruits of the life of the recluse.

[1016] Which are the states not appertaining to studentship?

The topmost fruit[3]—the fruit that is Arahatship.

---

[1] Apacayagāmino. On its opposite, see p. 82, note 2. The latter is tantamount to going to Nirvana. The two processes are compared to the building up and pulling down of a wall. Asl. 44.

[2] Sekkhā, *i.e.* (Asl. 44), springing up in the three, or in the seven courses of training (*cf.* Childers, *s.v.*). Asekkhā implies that the student or probationer has perfected his studies and training and is become an adept, an Arahat. *Cf.* P. P., p. 14. On the term 'fruits of the life of the recluse,' see the Sāmaññaphala Sutta, D. i. 47.

[3] Uparitthimaṃ, a term used in P. P. i. 42 *et seq.*, where it is applied to the 'Fetters' which are put off *last.* *Cf.* below, § 1113, and p. 303. See also p. 166, n. 1.

[1017] Which are the states neither appertaining, nor not appertaining to studentship?

The afore-mentioned states excepted, all other states, good, bad and indeterminate, relating to the worlds of sense, form and the formless; all form also and uncompounded element.

[1018] Which are the states that are limited?[1]

All states, good, bad and indeterminate, which relate to the universe of sense; in other words, the *five* skandhas.

[1019] Which are the states that have a wider scope?[2]

States, good, bad and indeterminate, which relate to the worlds of form and the formless; in other words, the *four* skandhas.

[1021] Which are the states that are infinite?[3]

The Paths that are the Unincluded, and the Fruits of the Paths, and uncompounded element.

[1022] Which are the states that have limited objects of thought?

Those emotional, perceptual and synthetic states, as well as those of intellect applied to sense-impressions,[4] which arise in connexion with limited matters.

---

[1] Parittaṃ, understood as involving intellectual and ethical, as well as physical insignificance—the connotation of the French term *borné*. The illustration chosen is that of a lump of cowdung! The essential quality is appānubhāvatā, *i.e.*, of little importance or efficacy generally. Parittaṃ itself is ranked as an equivalent of the whole sphere of sense-experience. Asl. 44.

[2] Mahaggatā, *i.e.*, in respect of 'the ability to resist vice, of abundance of good result, of wide extension,' or of the attainment to a high pitch of will, energy, thought or wisdom. *Ibid.*

[3] Appamānā, or without measure. Asl. 45.

[4] This is a long and cumbersome periphrasis for citta-cetasikā dhammā, but a reference to §§ 1187-1190 will show that such is the content of the term. And Western

[1023] Which are the states that have enlarged[1] objects of thought?

Those emotional, perceptual and synthetic states, as well as those of intellect applied to sense-impressions, which arise in connexion with matters of wider scope.

[1024] Which are the states that have infinite objects of thought?

Those emotional, perceptual and synthetic states, as well as those of intellect applied to sense-impressions, which arise in connexion with matters of infinite importance.

[1025] Which are the states that are base?

The three roots of bad (karma)—lust, hate, dulness—the Corruptions united with them; the four skandhas associated with them; the action, bodily, vocal and mental, springing from them.

[1026] Which are the states that are of medium worth?

Co-Intoxicant states, good, bad and indeterminate, relating to the worlds of sense, form and the formless; in other words, the four skandhas.

[1027] Which are the states that are perfected?[2]

The Paths that are the Unincluded, and the Fruits of the Paths, and uncompounded element.

[1028] Which are the states the wrongfulness of which is fixed as to its consequences?[3]

---

psychology has not suggested to me any more compressed equivalent. *Cf.*, however, §§ 1282, 1284. 'Emotional' must be taken in its more limited sense, as the adjective to bare feeling or hedonic consciousness.

[1] See § 1021.

[2] The three subjects of this triplet of inquiry—dhammā hīṇā, majjhimā, paṇītā—are paraphrased (Asl. 45) as lāmakā (of poor quality, *cf.* Vin. ii. 76), midway between this and the third quality, and supramundane or ideal (lokuttarā).

[3] Micchattaniyatā, thus explained by the Cy. (*ibid.*): 'Wickedness' is that wrongful disposition which, in its

The five acts that have immediate results, and those wrong views that are fixed in their consequences.[1]

---

desire for happiness, sees benefit in things baneful and persists in this perversion. 'Fixed in its consequences' (lit., 'reaching down to') means yielding a result immediately on the disintegration of the skandhas (*i.e.*, after death). *Cf.* M. P. S. 17: asmi . . . niyato—I am fixed or sure (as to my future); also K. V. 609-612, and P. P. 13: katamo ca puggalo niyato? The answer to this question is practically identical with those given in these sections. It is the *persons* (puggalā) who are decisively good and bad that are called ānantarakā (incurring immediate destiny good or bad) instead of the 'acts' or the 'Paths,' as in the Dh. S.

These five acts, the Cy. says, refer to 'matricide, etc.,' as though the Abhithāṇas were here alluded to, whereas the five usually classed under this name appear to be murder, theft, impurity, lying and intemperance. *Cf.* §§ 1290, 1291. Compare the passage relating to lohituppādo, or the wounding of a Buddha, Vin. ii. 193, which is called an ānantarika-kammaṃ. I venture to think that, in the Mil., p. 25, the phrase kopañcānantariya-kammaṃ karoti is not intended, as the translator infers, to sum up the five offences previously specified, but is an allusion to five others, of which matricide was one and lohituppādo another. It only remains to ascertain whether or not the other three coincide with any other three of the six Abhithāṇas.

As to the immediacy of their consequences, whereas, from the Devadatta incident in the Cullavagga, the outrages entailed at least some of their retribution in this life, it will have been seen that, according to Buddhaghosa, the effect is experienced immediately after the cessation of the present life. The Cy. goes on: In the case of these acts, it is impossible for any other conduct to push off the karma of any one of them, so as to obtain room for the realization of its own consequences. Neither could the agent effect this if he were to build a golden sthūpa as big as Mt. Sineru, or a vihāra covered with gems and like a world-orb, or if he filled it with bhikkhus and their Buddha and found them in the four requisites during a whole lifetime. Asl. 358.

[1] The wrong views which are also niyatā are specified in the Cy. as those held by the Anti-causationists (ahetuka-

[1029] Which are the states the righteousness of which is fixed as to its consequences?[1]

The four Paths that are the Unincluded.

[1030] Which are the states that do not entail fixed consequences?

The afore-mentioned states excepted, all other states, good, bad and indeterminate, relating to the worlds of sense, form and the formless, or to the life that is Unincluded; in other words, the four skandhas; all form, moreover, and uncompounded element.

[1031] Which are the states that have the Path as their object of thought?[2]

Those emotional, perceptual and synthetic states, as well as those of intellect applied to sense-impressions, which arise in connexion with the Noble Path.

[1032] Which are the states that are causally dependent upon the Path?[3]

---

vādā, D. i. 53; M. i. 407), those who denied the efficacy of action (akiriya-vādā, D. i. 52; M. i. 404, 405), and the Nihilists (natthika-vādā, or uccheda-vādā, D. i. 55; M. i. 401-403). These are past praying for; more literally rendered, not a hundred, nor yet a thousand Buddhas would be able to enlighten them. *Ibid.*

[1] The reading should be sammatta-niyatā. *Cf.* Asl. 45; K.; K. V. 609.

[2] '"Path"' means the quest of Nirvana, or the progress in the destruction of the Kilesas.' (Asl. 45.)

[3] 'Maggahetukā, *i.e.*, the cause of those (states) in the sense of conditioning them is the Eightfold Path.' Asl. 45. Later (p. 359) the Cy. gives the purport of this triad as follows: 'In the first formula the kind of causal conjunction of the skandhas, in their connexion with the Path by way of cause, in the sense of condition, is set forth. In the second, the kind of causal conjunction of the other parts of the Path with Right Views, which are a constituent of the Path and are reckoned as cause (amoho; *cf.* §§ 16, 34, 1054); and in the third, the kind of causal conjunction of Right Views with those causes that are operative in the Path, is set forth.' Yet in the text it is the causal connexion of the

[Firstly] the four skandhas when associated with the stages of the Path as experienced by one who is conversant with the Path[1] (the stages being excepted).

[Secondly (1033)] the four skandhas when associated with the right views—these being both Path and Cause—of one who is conversant with the Path (the right views being excepted).

[Thirdly] the four skandhas when associated with the states of freedom from lust, hate and dulness peculiar to one who is conversant with the Path.

Now, these [last named] states are the 'Path-causes';[2] the former (the skandhas) are those states which are causally dependent upon the Path.

[1034] Which are the causes that are Path-governed?[3]

[Firstly] those emotional, perceptual and synthetic states, as well as those of intellect applied to sense-impressions, which in arising make the Noble Path their governor.

[Secondly] the four skandhas when associated with the investigation carried on by one who is conversant with the

---

four skandhas that is predicated about in all three formulæ. Does this implicate discrepant versions of the text?

[1] Ariyamaggasamangissa maggangāni.

[2] In the printed text, after amoho read ime dhammā magga-hetū. *Cf.* Cy. 45; K.; also above, § 1011.

[3] Maggādhipatino, *i.e.*, the Path, having them (those states) under its control in the sense of maintaining them, is their governor. Asl. 45. Later (p. 359) we get supplementary remarks showing that the relation of governor (or sovereign) and governed, in this connexion, resembles that between Christ and the believer who brings 'into captivity every thought to the obedience of Christ' (2 Cor. x. 5). All such thoughts or 'states' are insignificant (parittā) as compared with the one great object of devotion—the Path, the Fruit, Nirvana. Even to contemplate the progress of others in the Path, or to have seen the Tathāgata work a double miracle, is not precious to the student as is his own discernment and realization of what the Path means to *him*.

Path, and who is cultivating a way wherein investigation is the dominant factor.[1]

[1035] Which are the states that 'have arisen'?[2]

Those states that have been born, have become, have been gotten, created, re-created,[3] made manifest,—that have arisen, have come to pass, have happened, have supervened, have been caused to arise, are classed together among the things that have arisen, to wit, form, feeling, perception, syntheses, intellect.

[1036] Which are the states that have 'not arisen'?

Those states that are unborn, have not become, have not been gotten, nor created, nor re-created, nor made manifest; that have not arisen nor come to pass; nor happened, nor supervened; that have not been caused to arise, that are classed together among the things that have not arisen, to wit, forms, feelings, perceptions, syntheses, intellect.

[1037] Which are the states that are bound to arise?[4]

---

[1] The construction in this sentence is obscure. Vīmaṃsādhipateyyaṃ is apparently in the nominative case. The Cy., however (p. 359), substitutes, in quoting, the instrumental—which only makes the reading obscurer. Anyway, it proceeds to explain that the term shows a joint 'supremacy' between the Path and an adhipateyyaṃ to be only possible (*cf.* § 269) when the latter is either 'investigation' or 'energy.' When the latter is 'desire' or a 'thought,' then the Path yields its sway over the mind to the adhipateyyaṃ. But when the student makes either of the former his governing influence, both it and the Path are his joint governors.

[2] Uppannā, *i.e.*, which from the moment they came into being, and for as long as they had distinguishable being, have come to pass and been sustained. Asl. 45.

[3] Read nibbattā, abhinibbattā.

[4] Uppādino, *i.e.*, 'will certainly arise, from the fact that their efficient cause is in part completed' (Asl. 45). Later (pp. 360, 361) the potential happening of these resultant states is declared to be due to the enduring validity of their conditions (dhuvapaccayaṭṭhena), which cannot fail to produce their effects, even though

The results of those good and bad states related to the worlds of sense, form and the formless, or to the life that is Unincluded, the consequences of which are not yet matured,[1] to wit, the four skandhas and that form due to karma having been wrought which will arise.

[1038] Which are the states that are past?

Those states that are past are extinct, dissolved,[2] changed, terminated, exterminated; are past and classed among the things that are past; in other words, the five skandhas.

[1039] Which are the states that are future?

The states that are unborn, that have not become, not been gotten, nor created, nor re-created, nor made manifest; that have not arisen, nor come to pass, nor happened, nor supervened; that have not arrived, and are classed among the things that have not arrived.

[1040] Which are the things that are present?

Those states that have been born, have become, have been gotten, created, re-created,[3] made manifest; that have arisen, have come to pass, have supervened, have been caused to arise; that have arisen over against[4] and are classed among the things that have so arisen.

[1041-1043] Which are the states that have the past . . . future . . . present as their object of thought?

100,000 æons intervene. The gospel (lit., Path) of the future Buddha, Metteyya, is anuppanno, but his (or anyone's) fruition belongs to the uppādino dhammā.

[1] Avipakkavipākānaṃ. Inserted in K., but, as is stated in that edition, not inserted in the Burmese or the European text.

[2] The printed text reads niruddhangatā; the Cy., niruddhā vigatā; K., niruddhā pariṇatā (not vipariṇatā).

[3] Abhinibbattā is omitted in the printed text. *Cf.* § 1035; also K.

[4] Paccuppannā, the word rendered by 'present' in the question. *Cf.* our 'ob-vious,' 'ob-jective,' 'ob-ject,' in its most general psychological sense, as something present to the subject of the mental 'states.'

Those emotional, perceptual and synthetic states, as well as those of intellect applied to sense-impressions, which arise in connexion with states that are past . . . future . . . present.[1]

[1044] Which are the states that are personal ?[2]

Those states which, for this or that being, are of the self, self-referable, one's own,[3] individual, the issue of grasping; in other words, the five skandhas.

[1045] Which are the states that are external ?

Those states which, for this or that other being,[4] for other individuals, are of the self, self-referable, their own, individual, the issue of grasping;[5] in other words, the five skandhas.

[1046] Which are the states that are personal-external ?

States which are both [personal and external].[6]

[1047-1049] Which are the states that have an object of thought concerning the self . . . concerning that which is

---

[1] *Cf.* § 1022.

[2] On ajjhattā and bahiddhā *cf.* §§ 742, 743. The Cy. distinguishes four varieties in the connotation of ajjhattaṃ, namely, gocarajjhattaṃ, niyakajjhattaṃ, ajjhattajjhattaṃ and visayajjhattaṃ, two of which are identical with two of the three meanings cited by Childers. The specific meaning used here is said to be the second.

[3] For niyatā read niyakā.

[4] 'That is, all beings except one's self.' Asl. 361.

[5] Upādinnā is omitted in the printed text.

[6] Tad ubhayaṃ is the curt answer. It is to be regretted that Buddhaghosa's fertility in illustration was not applied to this species of dhammā. Incidentally one gathers that they alternate between self-reference and reference to other selves. For whereas the dhammā in the first and third questions are said to be either 'limited' or 'enlarged' (see §§ 1019-1021), and those in the second are said to be 'infinite,' states that are 'infinite' are said 'not to take as their object that which now relates to the external, now to the self.' (Asl. 361, 362.)

external [to the self] . . . concerning that which is 'personal-external'?

Those emotional, perceptual, synthetic states, as well as those of intellect applied to sense-impressions,[1] which arise in connexion with states of the self . . . states that are external . . . states that are personal-external.

[1050] Which are the states that are both visible and impingeing?[2]

The sphere of visible form.

[1051] Which are the states that are invisible, but impingeing?

The spheres of the five senses and the spheres of sound, odour, taste and the tangible.

[1052] Which are the states that are both invisible and non-impingeing?

The four skandhas; that form, moreover, which, being invisible and non-impingeing, is yet included in the sphere of [mental] states;[3] also uncompounded element.

[End of] the Triplets.

---

[1] *Cf.* § 1022 *et seq.*

[2] See § 597 *et seq.*, § 657 *et seq.*

[3] See § 980.

[CHAPTER II.

The Group on Cause (hetu-gocchakaṃ).][1]

I.

[1053] Which are the states that are causes?

(A) The three causes of good (karma).

---

[1] In connexion with the statement (§ 595) that form is 'that which is not a cause,' the Cy. distinguishes, as did Aristotle, four varieties of cause. The coincidence, however, scarcely extends beyond the number. Hetu is either (*a*) cause as cause (hetu-hetu); (*b*) cause as condition, or necessary antecedent 'wherewithal' (paccayahetu); (*c*) cause as ultimate or supreme (uttama-hetu); and (*d*) cause as an attribute held in common (sādhāranahetu). Asl. 303. These distinctions are shown to be applied as follows: (*a*) the trinity of threefold cause given in § 1053. Here the word is always paraphrased by 'root,' root, conversely, standing for productive agent in general (see the list in note to § 981), and, of course, for *moral* agency especially. (*b*) 'I have declared, bhikkhu, that the four great phenomena are the causes, are the conditions of the form-skandha.' When the paccayo is material, it may be said to coincide with Aristotle's second formal principle *ἡ ὕλη καὶ τὸ ὑποκείμενον*. Possibly paccayo was this conception so generalized as to include the immaterial wherewithal requisite for the effect. Colebrooke, however ('Life and Essays,' ii. 419), said that the Bauddhas distinguish between hetu as proximate cause and pratyaya (paccayo) as concurrent occasion. (*c*) 'When good (karma) takes effect, it is the object ultimately or supremely desired'—and the opposite, of course, in the case of bad karma. This may possibly approximate

(B) The three causes of bad (karma).

(C) The three causes of the indeterminate.

The nine causes operative in the sensuous universe.

The six causes operative in the universe of form.

The six causes operative in the universe of the formless.

(D) The six causes operative in the life that is the Unincluded.

(A) In this connexion,

[1054] Which are the three causes of good karma?

The absence of lust, hate and dulness.

In this connexion,

[1055] *What is the absence of lust?*

The absence of lust, lusting, lustfulness is the absence of infatuation, of raving, of passionateness; the absence of covetousness, that absence of lust which is the root of good (karma).[1]

[1056] What is the absence of hate?

The absence of hate, hating, hatred; love,[2] loving, loving disposition;[3] tender care, forbearance, considerateness;[4]

---

to Aristotle's final cause (τὸ οὗ ἕνεκα). (*d*) 'As the essence of the elements of earth and water (solid and liquid) are the condition of sweet or not-sweet, so is ignorance the common base-element of the syntheses (sanskāras). In our present connexion the term is said to be used in its first-named meaning.

[1] *Cf.* § 32. The Pali terms coincide in both answers. In the following answer, the terms differ considerably from those in § 33.

[2] The printed text has mettaṃ; the Cy. and K. read mettī.

[3] 'The mental condition of one who is possessed by love, and *through love is loosed from clinging.*' (Asl. 362.). *Cf.* note on p. 66.

[4] Anuddā, anuddāyanā, anuddāyitattaṃ. The Cy. paraphrases by rakkhati, showing the reference there is in these terms, usually rendered by 'pity,' 'compassion,' to the protective, shielding aspect of altruism and benevolence. *Cf.* its use in C. vii. 3, 13; S. ii., p. 218, where it

seeking the general good,[1] compassion; the absence of malice, of malignity; that absence of hate which is the root of good (karma).[2]

[1057] What is the absence of dulness?

Knowledge about ill, about the uprising of ill, about the cessation of ill, and about the way leading to the cessation of ill; knowledge about the former things, about the latter things, about both taken together; knowledge about the assignable causation of causally determined states—even that kind of wisdom which is understanding, search, research, searching the Truth, etc. [*continue as in* § 34].

These are the three causes of good (karma).

(B) In this connexion,

[1058] Which are the three causes of bad (karma)?

Lust, hate, dulness.

In this connexion,

[1059] *What is lust?*

That which is

passion (r ā g o),
infatuation (s a r ā g o),[3]
fawning (a n u n a y o),[4]
compliance (a n u r o d h o),[5]

---

is used to express that attitude of forbearance in the interests of the weaker brethren recommended by St. Paul to Roman and Corinthian adherents.

[1] Hitesitā. See C. ix. 5, 7.

[2] By all these words (*i.e.*, from 'love' to 'compassion'), concludes Buddhaghosa, the advance (upacāra) and conception (appanā) of love is described. Possibly the procedure in the induction of Jhāna was in his mind in using these technical terms. *Cf.* Rhys Davids, 'Yogāvacara's Manual,' p. xi.

[3] 'Meaning strong rāgo.' Asl. 362.

[4] This is opposed to paṭigho or repugnance in Mil. 44; *cf.* 122 and 322. The comment (Asl. 362)—visayesu sattānaṃ anunayanato—may indicate that the fawning is by way of pandering to the sensual appetites of others.

[5] This is opposed to virodho, paṭivirodho. See

delighting in (nandī),[1]
taking passionate delight in (nandī-rāgo),[1]
infatuation of mind (cittassa sarāgo),[2]
longing (icchā),
languishing (mucchā),
devouring (ajjhosānaṃ),[3]
greed (gedho),
omnivorous greed (paligedho),
cleaving to (saṇgo),
a slough (panko),[4]
seduction (ejā),[5]
trickery (māyā),[6]
genitrix (janikā),[7]

---

§ 1060. The Cy. (*ibid.*) paraphrases by kameti. *Cf.* S. i. 111; K. V. 485.

[1] Explained as the recurrence over and over again of that thirst for some object, the single occurrence of which constitutes the state called nandī. Asl. 363.

[2] Explained as qualifying the 'infatuation' already named by emphasizing the reference to a mental state or psychosis, and not to any personal entity. *Ibid.*

[3] '*I.e.*, grasping by swallowing, by putting a complete end to.' Asl. 363, 370. The term is probably formed from √sā, to bind (or to gain), and usually, by its context, signifies attachment. *Cf.* M. i. 109, 498; Mil. 74. Judging by the Commentary, however, there seems to be a homonym derived from the root aç, to eat, similar to the parallel evolution of jhāyati, from √dhyā and √kṣā. *Cf.* Rhys Davids, 'Dialogues of the Buddha,' i. 33, note 2. The passage in A. i. 66, 67, is the only one at present known to me where the word, occurring as it does in co-ordination with terms of attachment and also of greed, may be rendered equally well in either sense.

[4] Paraphrased by osīdanaṃ. Asl. 363.

[5] Paraphrased by ākaḍḍhanaṃ, used in the Dhp. Cy. (p. 412) to illustrate the magnetic power of the love of treasure and of family. *Ibid.*

[6] Paraphrased by vañcanaṃ. *Ibid.*

[7] Because lust causes beings to be reborn on the Wheel (of life). So for the following epithet. As it is written:

Taṇhā janeti purisaṃ, cittaṃ assa vidhāvati.

progenitrix (sañjananī),
seamstress (sibbanī),[1]
she who ensnares (jālinī),[2]
the river (saritā),[3]
she who is poisonous (visattikā),[4]
the thread (suttaṃ),[5]
diffusion (visaṭā),[6]
she who toils (āyūhanī),[7]
the consort (dutiyā),[8]
hankering (paṇidhi),

---

[1] The Cy. explains that lobho sews, or joins beings to sorrow by way of rebirth, just as a tailor joins one piece of cloth to another. *Ibid.*

[2] She=taṇhā, by the suffusion of which the manifold web of the senses becomes as a net. *Ibid.*

> Yassa jālinī visattikā
> taṇhā n'atthi kuhiñci netave.
> S. i. 107 ;=Dhp., ver. 180.

[3] From the swift current of lobho, or else from its glutinous tenacity, according to the Commentator, who quotes:

> Saritāni sinehitāni ca
> somanassāni bhavanti jantuno.
> Dhp., ver. 341.

[4] See above note 2.

[5] By reason of its chaining together destruction and misfortune as jars are arranged on a cord. Asl. 364.

[6] 'In the sense of spreading out over sensuous objects.' *Ibid.*

[7] '*I.e.*, she causes beings to toil after (āyūhapeti) this or that state.' *Ibid.* On āyūhati, see J. P. T. S., 1885, pp. 58, 59 ; 1886, pp. 155, 156 ; Mil. 108, 214.

[8] Lobho (or taṇhā) is likened to a dear *alter ego*, or wife, or travelling companion. The idea is found in Sutta Nipāta, verse 740, quoted by the Cy.:

> Tanhādutiyo puriso dīghaṃ addhānaṃ saṃsāraṃ
> Itthabhāvaññathābhāvaṃ saṃsāraṃ nātivattatī ti.

she who leads to renewed existence (bhavanettī),[1]
the jungle (vanaṃ),
the undergrowth (vanatho),[2]
intimacy (santhavo),[3]
unctuous affection (sineho),
affection (apekkhā),[4]
connexion (paṭibandhu),[5]
craving (āsā),
wanting (āsiṃsanā),
cupidity (āsiṃsitattaṃ),
craving for visual forms (rūpāsā, etc.),
craving for sounds,
craving for odours,
craving for tastes,
craving for the tangible,
craving for getting,
craving for wealth,
craving for children,
craving for life,
mumbling (jappā),[6]

---

[1] Cy.: Bhavanettī = the cord of existence. For by it beings are led, as cows by a cord bound about their necks, wherever they are wanted.

[2] The impenetrable, impassable nature of tropical forest growth often serves to illustrate the dangers of lobho or taṇhā. *Cf.* Dh., p. 283, quoted in the Cy. *Ibid.*

[3] 'Intimacy is of two kinds: it is either carnal (*i.e.*, of taṇhā) or friendly. Here the former is meant.' Asl. 365.

[4] 'Ālayakaraṇavasena apekkhatī ti apekkhā. *Ibid.* The quotation in the Cy. on this word is from the Mahāsudassana Sutta, 229, with which *cf.* S. iii. 144.

[5] 'As being constantly near to living beings there is no relative (or connexion) like taṇhā.' Asl. 365.

[6] The four following terms are all variants of jappā. 'Whenever anything is given to a greedy person, he will mutter, "This is mine, this is mine! This has been given me by so-and-so!"' Asl. 365. K. repeats jappā

mumbling on,
mumbling over,
muttering,
murmuring,
self-indulgence (loluppaṃ),[1]
self-indulging,
intemperateness,
agitation (puñcikatā),[2]
longing for the agreeable (sādhu kamyatā),[3]
incestuous passion (adhammarāgo),[4]
lawless lust (visamalobho),
appetite (nikanti),
hungering for (nikāmanā),
entreating (patthanā),
envying (pihanā),
imploring (sampatthanā),[5]
thirst for sensual indulgence (kāmataṇhā),
thirst for existence (bhavatanhā),
thirst for non-existence (vibhavatanhā),[6]
thirst for form,[7]
thirst for formlessness,
thirst for annihilation,
thirst for visible forms,[8]

---

after abhijappanā. *Cf.* C. iv. 14, 26: sakaṇṇa-jappakaṃ.

[1] See Jāt. i. 340; iv. 306. Buddhaghosa derives this from lumpati. *Cf.* Whitney's 'Roots,' etc., where it appears as the Intensive of lup, but belonging in meaning to lubh.

[2] The excitement or fluster produced by taṇhā is here, according to the Cy., likened to that shown by 'dogs wagging their tails' (read sunakhā) when seeking to find something. *Ibid.*

[3] The Cy. and K. read sādhu.

[4] For a mother, a mother's sister, etc. Asl. 366.

[5] *I.e.*, patthanā intensified. *Ibid.*

[6] *I.e.*, for a state of annihilation. *Ibid.*

[7] *I.e.*, for a state of pure (suddhe) form. *Ibid.*

[8] Before 'thirst for sounds' K. inserts rūpataṇhā for

thirst for sounds,
thirst for smells,
thirst for tastes,
thirst for the tangible,
thirst for mental states (dhammataṇhā),
a flood (ogho),
a yoke (yogo),
trammels (gantho),
attachment (upādānaṃ),
obstruction (āvaraṇaṃ),
hindrance (nīvaraṇaṃ),
counterfeiting (chadanaṃ),[1]
bondage (bandhanaṃ),[2]
depravity (upakkileso),
faltering (anusayo),[3]
pervading (pariyuṭṭhānaṃ),[4]
a creeper (latā),[5]
avarice (vevicchaṃ),[6]
root of pain,
source of pain (dukkhanidānaṃ),

---

the second time, the rūpāni craved for here being presumably 'sights,' 'perceptions of sight,' as distinguished from that supersensuous plane of being craved for under the former rūpataṇhā, and ranking next to the formless plane. The Cy., on the other hand, only notices between 'thirst for annihilation' and 'thirst for sounds,' the word diṭṭhirāgo, passion for speculation.

[1] So Asl. and K. *Cf.* Sutta Nip. i. 5, 7.

[2] *I.e.*, 'on the wheel' (of samsāra). *Ibid.*

[3] 'Through loss of strength.' *Ibid.*

[4] *I.e.*, the heart becomes possessed by lust, as a road by highwaymen. *Ibid.*

[5] . . . latā ubbhijjā tiṭṭhati. Dhp. 340. Quoted in the Cy. Greed or lust strangles its victim, as a creeper strangles a tree.

[6] See Sutta Nip. 1033. Buddhaghosa, however, paraphrases the term as 'multifarious wants,' Vielhaberei; 'vividhāni vatthūni icchati.' *Ibid.* At Asl., p. 375, he has a different explanation. *Cf.* S. N. ii., *s.v.* vevicchā.

production of pain (dukkhappabhavo),
Māra's trap (mārapāso),
Māra's fish-hook (mārabalisaṃ),
Māra's domain (māravisayo),
thirst,
thirst for delight (nandītaṇhā),
the fishing-net of thirst (jālaṃtaṇhā),[1]
the leash of thirst (gaddūlataṇhā),[2]
the ocean (samuddo),[3]
covetousness (abhijjhā),[4]
the lust that is the root of evil—

this is what is called lust.

[1060] *What is hate?*

When annoyance springs up at the thought: he has done me harm, is doing, will do me harm; he has done harm, is doing harm, will do harm to someone dear and precious to me; he has conferred a benefit, is conferring, will confer a benefit on someone I dislike and object to; or when annoyance springs up groundlessly[5]:—all such vexation of spirit,[6] resentment, repugnance, hostility;[7] ill-temper, irritation,

---

[1] Spread out like a net over the river. Asl. 367.

[2] *Cf.* Jāt. ii. 246; iii. 204. Taṇhā drags its victims about as dogs are drawn by a leash (Asl. 367).

[3] The thirst of lust is hard to satiate. *Ibid.* *Cf.* above, p. 175, note 4.

[4] See § 391.

[5] 'Aṭṭhāne vā pana āghāto ti akāraṇe kopo. *E.g.*, when one is vexed because it rains too much, or because it doesn't rain, or because the sun is too hot, or not hot enough, or because there is too much or too little wind, or because one cannot sweep away the Bo-tree-leaves, or because the wind prevents one from putting on one's robe, or because one has fallen over a tree-stump.' Asl. 367.

[6] Cittassa āghāto. Āghāto is rendered above by annoyance. The two next terms are paṭighāto and paṭighaṃ. The latter is the word used to express action and reaction in sense-activity. § 597 *et seq.*

[7] Paṭivirodho. *Cf.* Mil. 203, 402.

indignation;[1] hate, antipathy, abhorrence;[2] mental disorder,[3] detestation;[4] anger, fuming, irascibility; hate, hating, hatred; disorder, getting upset, derangement; opposition, hostility;[5] churlishness, abruptness, disgust of heart—this is what is called hate.

[1061] *What is dulness?*

Lack of knowledge about Ill, lack of knowledge about the uprising of Ill, lack of knowledge about the cessation of Ill, lack of knowledge about the way leading to the cessation of Ill; lack of knowledge about the former things, about the latter things and about both taken together; lack of knowledge about the assignable causation of causally determined states—even all that kind of lack of knowledge which is lack of insight, of understanding, of wakefulness, of enlightenment, of penetration, of comprehension, of sounding, of comparing, of contemplation, of perspicacity; impurity, childishness, unintelligence, the dulness that is stupidity, obtuseness, ignorance, a flood of ignorance, the yoke of ignorance, the dependence of ignorance, the being possessed by ignorance, the barrier of ignorance, the dulness that is the root of evil—this is called dulness.[6]

These are the three causes of bad [karma].

(C) In this connexion,

[1062] Which are the three causes of the indeterminate?

The absence of lust, hate and dulness coming to pass as

---

[1] Kopo, pakopo, sampakopo.

[2] Padoso, sampadoso.

[3] Cittassa vyāpatti; paraphrased as a *bouleversement*, or cataclysm of mind. Vyāpatti is used for the wrecking of a ship in Jāt. iv. 107. *Cf.* above, § 418.

[4] Manopadoso. *Cf.* Jāt. iv. 29; M. i. 377, where it means apparently curse or execration—the original sense of 'detesting.'

[5] See § 418.

[6] According to Asl. 368, this is 'thoroughly set out in the Commentary on the Vibhanga.'

the result of good states, or as the indeterminate states known as kiriyā-thoughts.[1]

[1063] Which are the nine causes operative in the sensuous universe (kāmavacarahetū)?

The three causes of good [karma], the three causes of bad [karma], the three causes of indeterminate [states]—these are the nine.

[1064] Which are the six causes operative in the universe of form?

The three causes of good [karma], the three causes of indeterminate [states]—these are the six.

[1065] Which are the six causes operative in the universe of the formless?

The three causes of good [karma], the three causes of indeterminate [states]—these are the six.

[1066] Which are the six causes operative in the Unincluded?

The three causes of good [karma], the three causes of indeterminate [states]—these are the six.

In this connexion,

[1067] Which are the three causes of good [karma]?

The absence of lust, hate and dulness.

In this connexion,

[1068-1070] What is the absence of lust . . . of hate . . . of dulness?

Answers as in §§ 1055-1057, *but omitting in* § 1056, *from* 'hatred' *to* 'the absence of malice,' *exclusively*.[2]

These are the three causes of good [karma].

(D) In this connexion,

---

[1] Kiriyāvyākatesu dhammesu. See above, § 566 *et seq.* The Cy. here is silent.

[2] Adoso has been inadvertently omitted in the text.

[1071] Which are the three causes of indeterminate [states]?

The absence of lust, hate and dulness coming to pass as the effect of good states—these are the three.

These are the six causes operative in the Unincluded.

These are the states which are causes.

[1072] Which are the states that are not causes?

Every state, good, bad and indeterminate, whether related to the worlds of sense, of form, of the formless, or to the life that is Unincluded, except the states enumerated above; in other words, the four skandhas; all form also and uncompounded element.

[1073] Which are the states that have causes as concomitants?[1]

---

[1] Sahetukā. The Cy. (p. 47) on this term has: Sampayogato pavattena saha hetunā ti sahetukā, and on the opposite: ahetukāth Taṭh'eva pavatto n'atthi etesaṃ hetū ti. This may be rendered: 'Sahetukā means, union in continuance with a cause.' And 'ahetukā means, there is for them no continuance of a cause.' The *sustaining* of a cause in concomitance with a given state is so much harped upon by the Cy. that one is tempted to surmise that the mediæval controversy, known by the formula, *Cessante causâ cessat et effectus*, was not unfamiliar to Buddhist scholastics. Have we here the categorizing of certain states, for the maintenance of which, as effects, the continuance of the cause is required? In that case the Buddhist would have agreed (see § 1075, n.) with a modern logician (J. S. Mill) that, in some cases only, 'The continuance of the condition which produced an effect is necessary to the continuance of the effect.' The coincidence, however, is extremely doubtful. The Pali even leaves it vague as to whether the concomitant cause is the cause of the state in question; sometimes, indeed, this is evidently not the case. *E.g.*, in § 1077 'dulness' is a hetu-dhammo, but not therefore the cause of the concomitant states, lust and hate. The compilers were, as usual, more interested in the psychology than in the logic of the matter, and were inquiring into the factors in cases of mental association.

Those states, to wit, the four skandhas, which have as concomitant causes the states enumerated above.[1]

[1074] Which are the states that have not concomitant causes?

Those states, to wit, the four skandhas, all form also, and uncompounded element, which have not as concomitant causes the states enumerated above.

[1075] Which are the states that are associated with a cause?[2]

The states, to wit, the four skandhas, which are associated with those states enumerated above.

[1076] Which are the states that are not associated with a cause?

The states, to wit, the four skandhas, all form also, and uncompounded element, which are not associated with the states enumerated above.

[1077] Which are the states that both are causes and have causes as their concomitants?

Lust with dulness is both. Dulness with lust is both. Hate with dulness is both. Dulness with hate is both.[3]

The absence of lust, the absence of hate, the absence of dulness—these also, taken one with the other, both are causes and have causes as their concomitants.

---

[1] Tehi dhammehi, *i.e.*, with one or other of the six causes of good or bad effects. Asl. 368.

[2] Hetu-sampayuttā. On the import of the term sampayutto, see p. 1, n. 4. This pair of opposites is further declared to be not different in meaning from the preceding pair (atthato nānattaṃ natthi), and the formulæ only differentiated for the purpose of adaptation to the various dispositions (ajjhāsayavasena) of the hearers. Asl. 48. This coincidence of meaning seems, however, to be applicable only in the sphere of hetu. In the next gocchakaṃ, the attribute of āsavavippayuttā is allowed to be compatible with the attribute sāsavā, § **1111**, and so for subsequent gocchakas.

[3] Dulness when accompanied by perplexity and excitement (uddhaccaṃ) is said to be a cause, but to have no cause as its concomitant. Asl. 368.

[1078] Which are the states that have causes as their concomitants, but are not causes?

The states, to wit, the four skandhas, which have as their concomitant causes those states [enumerated above as causes], the latter states themselves excepted.

[1079] Which are the states that are both causes and associated with a cause?

[1080] Which are the states that are associated with a cause, but are not causes?

Answers identical with those in the foregoing pair.[1]

[1081] Which are the states that are not causes, but have a cause as their concomitant?[2]

The states, to wit, the four skandhas, which are not the causes of those states enumerated above, but which have any of them as their concomitants.

[1082] Which are the states that are not causes and have not causes as their concomitants?

The states, to wit, the four skandhas, all form also, and uncompounded element, which neither are the causes of those states enumerated above, nor have any of them as their concomitants.

---

[1] *Cf.* § 1075, n. 2.

[2] Supplementary questions, says the Cy., dealing with the na-hetu states. Asl. 47.

[CHAPTER III.

The Short Intermediate Set of Pairs (cūḷantara-dukaṃ).]

[1083] Which are the states that are conditioned?[1]
The five skandhas, to wit, the skandhas of form, feeling, perception, syntheses and intellect.

[1084] Which are the states that are unconditioned?
'And uncompounded element.'[2]

[1085] Which are the states that are compound?[3]
Those states which are conditioned.

[1086] Which are the states that are uncompounded?
That state which is unconditioned.

[1087] Which are the states that have visibility?
The sphere of [visible] forms.

[1088] Which are the states that have no visibility?
The spheres of the senses and sense-objects; the four skandhas; that form also which, being neither visible nor impingeing, is included under [mental] states;[4] and uncompounded element.

---

[1] Sappaccayā, = attano nipphādakena, saha paccayena. Asl. 47.

[2] One would have expected the reading to be asankhatā va dhātu, instead of . . . ca dhātu, given both in the text and in K. The Cy. has asankhata-dhātuṃ sandhāya.

[3] Sankhatā is defined as 'made, come together by conditions.' Asl. 47.

[4] See § 1052.

[1089] Which are the states that impinge?[1]

The spheres of the senses and sense-objects.

[1090] Which are the states that are non-impingeing?

The four skandhas; that form also which, being neither visible nor impingeing, is included under [mental] states; also uncompounded element.

[1091] Which are the states that have [material] form?[2]

The four great principles as well as the form that is derived from the four great phenomena.[3]

[1092] Which are the states that have no material form?

The four skandhas, and uncompounded element.

[1093] Which are the states that are mundane?[4]

Co-Intoxicant[5] states, good, bad and indeterminate, relating to the worlds of sense, of form, or of the formless, to wit, the five skandhas.

[1094] Which are the states that are supra-mundane?

The Paths that are the Unincluded, and the Fruits of the Paths, and uncompounded element.

[1095] Which are the states that are cognizable in one way, and not cognizable in another way?

States that are cognizable by sight are not cognizable by hearing; conversely, states that are cognizable by hearing are not cognizable by sight. States that are cognizable by sight are not cognizable by smell . . . by taste . . . by body-sensibility, and conversely.

---

[1] Sappaṭighā. *Cf.* § 597, *et seq.*

[2] Rūpino, *i.e.*, they have a form which as such is devoid of discriminative consciousness (avinibhogavasena). Asl., p. 47, *cf.* p. 56; also Mil. 63; M. i. 293.

[3] *Cf.* § 597.

[4] Lokiyā = bound down to, forming a part of, the circle (of existence), which for its dissolving and crumbling away (lujjana palujjana) is called loko. To have got beyond the world, to be a non-conforming feature in it—in it, but not of it—is to be lokuttaro. Asl. 47, 48.

[5] See § 1103.

States that are cognizable by hearing are not cognizable by smell . . . by taste . . . by body-sensibility . . . by sight, and conversely.

So for states that are cognizable by smell, by taste, and by body-sensibility.[1]

---

[1] The Cy. meets the question, Why is there no couplet telling which states are cognizable or not cognizable by representative cognition or ideation (manoviññāṇaṃ)? by the answer, Such a distinction is quite valid, 'is not not-there,' but it is not stated explicitly, because of the absence of fixing or judging (vavatthānaṃ). 'There is none of this when, for instance, we judge, such and such things are not cognizable by visual intellection.' See Asl. 369. *Cf.* Mil. 87, where this intellectual process is more clearly set forth. Buddhaghosa's argument is to me less clear.

[CHAPTER IV.

The Intoxicant Group (ā s a v a - g o c c h a k a ṃ).]

[1096] Which are the states that are Intoxicants?[1]

The four Intoxicants, to wit, the Intoxicant of sensuality,

---

[1] 'Intoxicant' is but a *pis-aller* for ā s a v o, no adequate English equivalent being available (see Rhys Davids, 'Dialogues of the Buddha,' i., p. 92, n. 3). The choice of it here has been determined by Buddhaghosa's comment. This is as follows: 'Ā s a v ā means they flow on to. They are said to flow (*lege* s a v a n t i), to circulate about the senses and the mind. Or, they flow, in respect of mental states, right up to the elect, in respect of space, right up to the highest planes of becoming—I mean, their range embraces both states and space, this encompassing being denoted by the prefix *ā*. The Āsavas, moreover, are like liquors (ā s a v ā), such as spirits, etc., in the sense of that which may be kept a long time. For, in the world, spirits, etc., which have been laid down for a long period are called ā s a v a s. And if those spirits for this long storage are called ā s a v a s, these states deserve the name as well. For it is said: "The ultimate point of ignorance, brethren, before which ignorance has not existed, is not manifest" [alluding to the āsava of ignorance].' Asl. 48.

From this passage we gather that, to Buddhaghosa, the word ā s a v o, whatever other implications it may have had, typified mainly two notions, and these were *pervasion* and *length of growth of a potential and very potent effect*. The former metaphor—that of a flowing in, upon, and over —occurs with a cognate verb in the standard description of the guarded avenues of sensation—a n v ā s (s) a - v e y y u ṃ (*e.g.*, D. i. 70). The latter notion appears in the Intoxicant of renewed existence, the Intoxicant of speculative opinion, the Intoxicant of ignorance.

In this connexion

[1097] *What is the Intoxicant of sensuality?*

That sensual desire,[1] sensual passion, sensual delight,

Subhūti's opening remark on the term ('Abhidhānappadīpika-sūci,' *s.v. Asavo*): *māna-purisamadādayo yenāti*—that by which come pride and human madness [or infatuation]. No doubt the term also implied something that tainted, corrupted, *souillissait* as it flowed. But this is also part of the physiological and ethical import of the term I have selected in translating.

Later (p. 369) the Cy. considers the Intoxicants under numerical categories, according to the very usual Buddhist method. Thus, they are One, or undifferentiated, in virtue of their being, like liquor, long stored up. In the Vinaya they are treated of as Twofold:—the Intoxicants that have to be suppressed in this life and those that have to be eschewed in future lives (see V. iii. 21; V., pp. 143, 223). In the Suttanta, *e.g.*, in the Saḷāyatana-Sutta, they are distinguished under Three heads, diṭṭhāsava being omitted. (The Sutta referred to is not yet edited, but *v.* M. i. 55; S. iv. 256; A. i. 167; iii. 414; and *cf.* D. i. 84. In the Mahā-parinibbāna-sutta of the Dīgha Nikāya, however, all four Āsavas are mentioned (pp. 38, 40). Hence follows one of three possible conclusions. Either Buddhaghosa is for once in error, or the edition of the Sutta last named needs correcting, or it is a later work, contemporary, it may be, with the Abhidhamma.) In the passage on 'Penetration' (A. iii. 410-417) they are treated of as leading to Five different forms of rebirth. 'In the Āhuneyya-sutta of the Chakka nipāta' (*i.e.*, No. lviii. of that Nipāta, A. iii. 387) they are treated of under Six methods for overcoming them. In the Sabbāsava-discourse (M. i., pp. 7-11) Seven methods are given.

[1] 'Kāmachando ti kāmasankhāto chando na kattukamyatāchando na dhammachando.' Asl. 370. This carefully-drawn distinction between sensual desire and an ethically neutral state of bare conation, as well as the desire after the ideal, bears me out in the argument I ventured to put forward in J. R. A. S., January, 1898, and which is rediscussed in my Introduction.

sensual craving, sensual fondness, sensual thirst, sensual fever, sensual languishing, sensual rapacity, which is excited by the pleasures of the senses[1]—this is called the Intoxicant of sensuality.

[1098] *What is the Intoxicant of renewed existence?*

The desire, the passion for coming into being, delight in coming into being, craving, fondness for coming into being, the fever, the yearning, the hungering to come into being, which is felt concerning rebirths—this is called the Intoxicant of renewed existence.[2]

[1099] *What is the Intoxicant of speculative opinion?*[3]

To hold that the world is eternal, or that it is not eternal,[4] infinite or finite;[5] that the living soul is the body, or that the living soul is a different thing from the

---

[1] Pañcakāmaguniko rāgo kāmāsavo nāma (Asl. 369). The Cy. points out that to hanker after the mansions of the supreme gods or the wishing-trees of heaven or the craving for æsthetic luxuries (ābharaṇam) is not to be confounded with the Intoxicant of sensuality, since such desires are a step higher than the latter vice. But they are subsumed under the Tie of covetousness (§ 1136), and the Lust-cause (§ 1059). Asl. 371, 377.

[2] Literally, of becoming. 'That which is called bhavāsavo is the hoping for re-becoming, the passion connate with the Eternalist speculation (*v.* following answer and § 1003, n. 2), the craving for the state of Jhāna (jhānanikanti—*sic lege*), the passionate desire for re-births in the planes of form and of formlessness.' Asl. 369.

[3] Diṭṭhāsavo, '*i.e.*, the sixty-two theories.' *Ibid.* See D. i., Brahmajāla Sutta.

[4] *I.e.*, to hold that this five-skandha'd affair is permanent, fixed, a thing for all time—which is the Eternalist theory; or that it is annihilated, perishes—which is the Theory of Total Disintegration. Asl. 370, 371. *Cf.* §§ 1003, n. 3; 1315-16.

[5] Either of these theories is by the Cy. declared to be compatible with either of those in the preceding clause. And they are also said to be determined by the nature of the Jhāna practised by the adherent to one or the other. Asl. 371. See §§ 1317-18.

body;[1] or that he who has won truth[2] exists after death, or does not exist after death, or both exists and does not exist after death, or neither exists nor does not exist after death —this kind of opinion, this walking in opinion, this jungle of opinion, wilderness of opinion, puppet-show of opinion, scuffling of opinion, the fetter of opinion, the grip and tenacity of it, the inclination towards it, the being infected by it, this by-path, wrong road, wrongness, this 'fording-place,' this shiftiness of grasp[3]—this is called the Intoxicant of speculative opinion. Moreover, the Intoxicant of speculation includes all false theories.

[1100] *What is the Intoxicant of ignorance?*[4]

Answer as in § 1061 *for* 'dulness.'

These are the states that are Intoxicants.

[1102][5] Which are the states that are not Intoxicants?

Every state, good, bad and indeterminate,[6] which is not included in the foregoing (Intoxicants), whether relating to the worlds of sense, form or the formless, or to the life that is Unincluded, to wit, the four skandhas; all form also, and uncompounded element.

[1103] Which are the states that are co-Intoxicant?[7]

---

[1] *I.e.*, that the life (or living soul) is, or is not, annihilated on the dissolution of the body. *Ibid.*

[2] Tathāgato—in the Cy., satto ṭathāgato nāma. Clearly, therefore, not a reference to the Buddha only. See Robert Chalmers, 'Tathāgata,' J. R. A. S., January, 1898, pp. 113-115. The four speculations about such a person's future existence are named respectively Eternalist, Annihilationist, Semi-eternalist, Eel-wriggling (amarāvikkhepikā). *Ibid.*, see D. i. 3, §§ 58, 41, 59, 35.

[3] See under § 381.

[4] In the text, after dukkhudaye aññānaṃ, supply dukkhanirodhe aññānaṃ.

[5] '§ 1101' is apparently an erroneous interpolation. See § 1104, where it appears again and in its right place.

[6] In the text read kusalākusalavyākatā.

[7] Sāsavā, *i.e.*, states 'proceeding along with Asavas,' and which attānam ārammanaṃ katvā—'have made the Self their object.' Asl. 48.

Good, bad and indeterminate states, whether relating to the worlds of sense, form, or the formless ; in other words, the five skandhas.

[1104] Which are the states that are not co-Intoxicant?

The Paths that are the Unincluded, and the Fruits of the Paths, and uncompounded element.

[1105] Which are the states that are 'associated with Intoxicants'?

The states which are associated with those [Intoxicant] states,[1] to wit, the four skandhas.

[1106] Which are the states that are 'disconnected with Intoxicants'?

The states which are disconnected with those [Intoxicant] states, to wit, the four skandhas ; all form also, and uncompounded element.

[1107] Which are the states that are both Intoxicants and co-Intoxicant?

The Intoxicants themselves.[2]

[1108] Which are the states that are co-Intoxicant, but not Intoxicants?

The states which have the foregoing states (§ 1096) as their concomitants; that is to say, with the exception of the Intoxicants, all states whatever, good, bad and indeterminate, which are co-Intoxicant, whether they relate to the worlds of sense, of form or of the formless; in other words, the five skandhas.

---

[1] Answers of this form, which frequently occur in these 'Groups,' are not the mere repetitions of the question that they at first sight appear, but are, in logical idiom, analytic, or explicative propositions. The current term āsava-sampayuttā means or includes these four modes:—kāmāsava-sampayuttā, bhavāsava-sampayuttā, and so on.

[2] When mutally associated. *Cf.* the following pair of answers.

[1109] Which are the states that are both Intoxicants and associated with Intoxicants?

The Intoxicant of sensuality together with that of ignorance, and conversely. The Intoxicant of renewed existence together with that of ignorance, and conversely. The Intoxicant of speculative opinion together with that of ignorance, and conversely.

[1110] Which are the states that are associated with Intoxicants but are not Intoxicants?

The states which are associated with the foregoing states (§ 1096)—the latter themselves excepted—to wit, the four skandhas.

[1111] Which are the states that are disconnected with Intoxicants but co-Intoxicant?

The states which are disconnected with those abovenamed states (§ 1096), but which, good, bad, or indeterminate, have them as concomitants, whether they belong to the worlds of sense, of form, or of the formless, to wit, the five skandhas.

[1112] Which are the states that are disconnected with Intoxicants and are not co-Intoxicant?

The Paths that are the Unincluded and the Fruits of the Paths and uncompounded element.[1]

---

[1] In conclusion the Cy. declares (p. 372) that the Intoxicant of speculative opinion is put away during one's progress through the first (sotāpatti) path, the Intoxicant of sensuality in the third (anāgāmi) path, and the Intoxicants of renewed existence and ignorance in the fourth (arahatta) path.

[CHAPTER V.

The Group of the Fetters (saññojana-gocchakaṃ).]

[1113] Which are the states that are Fetters?

The ten Fetters, to wit, the Fetter of

sensuality,
repulsion,
conceit,
speculative opinion,
perplexity,
the contagion of mere rule and ritual,
the passion for renewed existence,
envy,
meanness,
ignorance.[1]

---

[1] Saññojanāni 'mean the things that bind, that fetter to the wheel of re-birth, the individual for whom they exist.' Asl. 48. This list differs in some items from the well-known dasa saññojanāni occurring so often in the Suttas, and enumerated in Childers. See Rhys Davids, 'American Lectures,' 141 *et seq.* That that older category was known to Buddhaghosa may be gathered from his naming the first three in order as 'states which are to be put away by insight,' § 1002 *et seq.* He proffers, however, no comment on the two lists as such. In M. i. 360-363, *eight* states of mind are enumerated and severally designated as a Fetter and a Hindrance, but they are quite different from either category habitually understood by these two titles. *Cf.* also M. i. 432; A. ii. 238; Div. S. 533, 553.

In this connexion,

[1114] *What is the Fetter of sensual passion?*

That sensual desire, sensual passion, sensual delight, sensual craving, sensual fondness, sensual fever, sensual languor, sensual rapacity, which is excited by the pleasures of the senses—this is called the Fetter of sensuality.[1]

[1115] *What is the Fetter of repulsion?*[2]

Answer as for 'hate,' § 1060.

[1116] *What is the Fetter of conceit?*[3]

---

[1] *Cf.* with § 1097. The single discrepancy is the omission in § 1114 of 'sensual thirst' (kāmapipāso), both in the P. T. S. text and in K.

[2] Paṭigha-saññojanaṃ, *cf.* §§ 413-421.

[3] Māna-saññojanaṃ—or pride. Conceit is etymologically more exact, though not so in any other respect. 'Lowly' is hīno. *Cf.* §§ 269, *et seq.*, 1025. 'Loftiness and haughtiness' are uṇṇati, uṇṇamo. '[Flaunting] a flag' is simply dhajo, the metaphor implying the pretensions conveyed by raising a flag over one's self or property, but answering better to our metaphor of a 'flourish of trumpets.' 'Assumption' is sampaggāho. The Cy. (p. 372) hereon has ukkhipanaṭṭhena cittaṃ sampaggaṇhātī ti—to grasp in the sense of tossing (puffing up) the mind. *Cf.* sīsaṃ ukkhipitvā, quoted by Childers, and the Hebrew figures for arrogance, etc.—lifting up head, horn, heel, or one's self on high; also paggāho, § 56. 'Desire of the heart for self-advertisement' is ketukamyatā cittassa. I can only make sense of the Cy. hereon by altering the punctuation followed in the text. Thus: Ketu vuccati bahūsu dhajesu accuggatadhajo. Māno pi punappuna uppajjamāno aparāpare upādāya accuggataṭṭhena ketum viyāti ketu. Ketuṃ icchatī ti ketukamyatassa bhāvo ketukamyatā. Sā pana cittassa, na attano, tena vuttaṃ:—ketukamyatā cittassā ti. 'A flag hoisted above many flags is called a ketu (sign, or standard); *cf.* Rāmāyaṇa i. 19, 16, quoted by Böthl. and Roth). By ketu is meant the conceit which arising again and again is like a signal in the sense of something set up on high. The state of ketu-desire, *i.e.*, to wish for self-advertisement, is ketukamyatā. But this means [a state of] mind, not of a self-entity, therefore the phrase is desire of the mind [or heart] for self-advertisement.'

Conceit at the thought 'I am the better man'; conceit at the thought 'I am as good [as they]'; conceit at the thought 'I am lowly'—all such sort of conceit, overweening, conceitedness, loftiness, haughtiness, flaunting a flag, assumption, desire of the heart for self-advertisement—this is called conceit.

[1117] *What is the Fetter of speculative opinion?*

Answer as for the 'Intoxicant of speculative opinion,' § 1099, *with this supplement:* And, with the exception of the 'Fetter of the contagion of mere rule and ritual,' all wrong views are included in the Fetter of speculative opinion.

[1118] *What is the Fetter of perplexity?*

Answer as for 'perplexity,' § 1004.

[1119] *What is the Fetter of the contagion of mere rule and ritual?*

Answer as for the 'contagion of,' etc., § 1005.

[1120] *What is the Fetter of the passion for renewed existence?*

Answer as for the 'Intoxicant of renewed existence,' § 1098.

[1121] *What is the Fetter of envy* (issāsaññojanaṃ)?

Envy, envying, enviousness—jealousy, the expression and mood of jealousy at the gifts, the hospitality, the respect, affection, reverence and worship accruing to others[1]—this is called the Fetter of envy.

[1122] *What is the Fetter of meanness* (macchari-saññojanaṃ)?

The Five Meannesses, to wit, meanness as regards dwelling, families, gifts, reputation, doctrine[2]—all this sort of

[1] In other words, discontent and murmuring at the success of one's neighbour, and complacency when bad luck overtakes him (*Schadenfreude*). Asl. 373. *Cf.* P. P., p. 19.

[2] Buddhaghosa is at some pains to distinguish genuine instances of want of magnanimity from such as are not. For example, it is macchariyaṃ when a bhikshu, enjoying the use of a lodging, grudges another a share of it, or when he grudges another intercourse with his own patrons

meanness, grudging, mean spirit, avarice and ignobleness,[1] niggardliness and want of generosity of heart[2]—this is called the Fetter of meanness.

---

and relatives, or gifts from the laiety for his piety, or that he should enjoy a reputation for physical or moral attractiveness, or that he should win proficiency in the letter, or the spirit of doctrine. On the other hand, it is not macchariyaṃ to deprecate the arrival at one's lodging of quarrelsome persons and the like, or the introduction to one's own social circle of peace-breakers, or the gifts made to selfish, miserly brethren instead of to the virtuous. Nor is it ungenerous in every case to withhold instruction from an inquirer. Reserve may be employed out of regard either for the doctrine, or for the inquirer. The latter may distort the imparted doctrine, or the doctrine may upset him. Nevertheless, it *is* an act of doctrinal illiberality to withhold the doctrine, if the inquirer is not a 'weak brother,' but one likely to prove hostile to 'our Cause' (amhākaṃ samayaṃ bhinditum samattho).

There then follows a mythological paragraph on the unpleasant rebirths awaiting those who err with respect to any one of these five forms of meanness. Asl. 374, 375.

[1] Veviccham kadariyaṃ. These terms are characterized (Asl. 375, 376) as respectively the soft (mudu) and hard (thaddha) varieties of meanness (*cf.* Childers, *s.v.* thaddho). We might name them the negatively and the positively anti-social. For the former is the spirit that says, spreading itself over all its own gettings, 'Mine be it, not another's!' (§ 1059). The latter (the anariyo) would even prevent another from giving to others.

[2] Kaṭukañcukatā aggahitattaṃ cittassa. There is doubt about the reading of the former term. K. has katakañcukatā, Buddhaghosa kaṭukañcukatā. The term is discussed by Morris, J. P. T. S., 1887, p. 161. Buddhaghosa's remark is as follows (Asl. 376): 'Kaṭukañcuko means that, on seeing a beggar, owing to one's styptic (kaṭuko) disposition, one's heart narrows or is bent (añcati—? $\sqrt{}$anh, or añc) and shrinks up.' He then, in offering an alternative explanation, relapses into characteristic etymology, deriving kaṭukañcukatā from kataccugāho—spoon-helps. When your rice-pot is full to the brim, one can only take niggling helps with the tip of

[1123] *What is the Fetter of ignorance?*

Answer as for the Intoxicant of ignorance, § 1100.

These are the states that are Fetters.

[1124] Which are the states that are not Fetters?

Every state, good, bad and indeterminate, which is not included in the foregoing [ten] states, whether it relates to the worlds of sense, or of form, or of the formless, or to the life that is Unincluded; in other words, the four skandhas; all form also, and uncompounded element.

Which are the states that are

[1125] (*a*) *favourable to the Fetters?*[1]

Co-Intoxicant states, good, bad and indeterminate, relating to the worlds of sense, form, or the formless; in other words, the five skandhas.

[1126] (*b*) *unfavourable to the Fetters?*

The Paths that are the Unincluded and the Fruits of the Paths, and uncompounded element.

Which are the states that are

[1127] (*a*) *associated with the Fetters?*

[1128] (*b*) *disconnected with the Fetters?*

Answers identical with those given to corresponding questions respecting the 'Intoxicants.' §§ 1105, 1106.

Which are the states that are

[1129] (*a*) *both Fetters and favourable to the Fetters?*

---

a spoon. And just as the heart of the niggard shrinks, so too is his body 'bent back on itself, thrown back on itself, obtains no peace' (he quotes from Mil., p. 297). Similarly aggahitattaṃ cittassa is a holding the heart fast, or back, preventing its expansion by way of gifts and service to others.

[1] Saññojaniyā. So the text and K. The Cy. reads saññojanīyā. But *cf.* ganthaniyā, oghaniyā, yoganiyā, Asl. 49. The Cy. explains the term, which is literally fetter-ish, as that which benefits the Fetters by developing them, once their inception has begun. Asl. 48.

The Fetters themselves are both

[1130] (*b*) *favourable to the Fetters but not themselves Fetters.*

The states which are favourable to those [ten] states afore-named; that is to say, with the exception of the Fetters themselves, all co-Intoxicant states whatever, good, bad and indeterminate, whether relating to the worlds of sense, form or the formless; in other words, the five skandhas.

Which are the states that are

[1131] (*a*) *both Fetters and associated with Fetters?*

The Fetter of sensuality in conjunction with the Fetter of ignorance, *and conversely*, is both. *So is any one of the remaining eight Fetters* when in conjunction with the Fetter of ignorance, *and conversely.*

[1132] (*b*) *associated with the Fetters but not a Fetter?*

The states which are associated with those ten states afore-named, with the exception of the Fetters themselves; in other words, the four skandhas.

Which are the states that are

[1133] (*a*) *disconnected with the Fetters yet favourable to them?*

The states which are disconnected with those afore-mentioned [ten] states, that is to say, good, bad and indeterminate states which are co-Intoxicant, whether they relate to the worlds of sense, or of form, or of the formless; in other words, the five skandhas.

[1134] (*b*) *disconnected with the Fetters and not favourable to them?*

The Paths that are the Unincluded and the Fruits of the Paths; all form also, and uncompounded element.[1]

---

[1] In quitting the subject of Fetters, the Cy. declares (pp. 376, 377) that the Fetters of sensuality and repulsion are put away during one's progress through the third (anagāmi) path, the Fetter of conceit in the fourth

(arahatta) path, the Fetters of speculative opinion, perplexity, and the contagion of mere rule and ritual, in the first (sotāpatti) path, the Fetter of the passion for renewed existence in the fourth path, the Fetters of envy and meanness in the first path, the Fetter of ignorance in the fourth path. Hence the second path seems, according to Buddhaghosa, to constitute an interim in the breaking of Fetters.

The following tables show how far the Dh. S. and its Cy. agree with the authorities quoted in Childers, *s.v.* samyojanaṃ (*cf.* D. i. 156):

Dh. S. and Asl.		*Childers.*
diṭṭhi vicikicchā sīlabbata-parāmāso	Removed by the First Path.	sakkāya-diṭṭhi vicikicchā sīlabbata-parāmāso
issā macchariyaṃ	Removed by the Second and Third Paths.	kāmarāgo paṭigho
kāmarago paṭigho	Removed by the Third Path.	
māno bhavarāgo avijjā	Removed by the Fourth Path.	rūparāgo arūparāgo māno uddhaccaṃ avijjā

On the work of the Fourth Path compare Dh. S., § 364, which is in agreement with the *right*-hand table. In the *first* edition (p. 452) of Dr. Oldenberg's 'Buddha' attention was called to discrepancies in this connexion.

[CHAPTER VI.

The Group of the Ties (gantha-gocchakaṃ).][1]

[1135] Which are the states that are Ties?

The four Ties, to wit, the bodily Tie of covetousness, the bodily Tie of ill-will, the bodily Tie of the contagion of mere rule and ritual, the bodily Tie of the inclination to dogmatize.

In this connexion,

[1136] *what is the bodily Tie of covetousness* (abhijjhā kāyagantho)?

Answer as for 'lust,' § 1059.[2]

[1137] *what is the bodily Tie of ill-will* (vyāpādo kāyagantho)?

Answer as for 'hate,' § 1060.

[1138] *what is the bodily Tie of the contagion of mere rule and ritual?*

Answer as in § 1005, *and,* § 1119, *for the Fetter so-called.*

---

[1] Gantho is defined as that which ties (or knots) or binds him for whom it exists on to the 'circle' of re-birth. And the term kāyagantho (body-tie) is used because the tying is effected through the body—that is, is got in conception and re-birth. Asl. 49, 377. The Ganthas are enumerated as in the present answer in S. iv. 59, and are frequently mentioned collectively, sometimes as Gandhas, throughout that volume. In the A. (ii. 24) I find only the general allusion sabba-gantha-pamocano.

[2] See also p. 293, n. 1.

[1139] *what is the bodily Tie of the inclination to dogmatize?*[1]

'"The world is eternal"—this is true, all else is false! "The world is not eternal"—this is true, all else is false! "The world is finite . . . is infinite"—this is true, all else is false! "The living soul is the body . . . is a different thing from the body"—this is true, all else is false! "He who has won truth exists after death . . . does not exist after death . . . both exists and does not exist after death . . . neither exists nor does not exist after death"—this is true, all else is false!'—this kind of opinion, this walking in opinion, this jungle of opinion, wilderness of opinion, puppet-show of opinion, scuffling of opinion, this Fetter of opinion, the grip and tenacity of it, the inclination towards it, the being infected by it, this by-path, wrong road, wrongness, this 'fording-place,' this shiftiness of grasp—this is called the bodily Tie of the inclination to dogmatize.

And, excepting only the bodily Tie of the contagion of mere rule and ritual, all wrong views are included under the bodily Tie of the inclination to dogmatize.

These are the states which are Ties.

[1140] Which are the states that are not Ties?

Every state, good, bad and indeterminate, which is not included in the foregoing [four] states, whether it relates to the worlds of sense or of form, or of the formless, or to the life that is Unincluded; in other words, the four skandhas; all form also, and uncompounded element.

Which are the states that

[1141] (*a*) *tend to become tied?*[2]

Good, bad and indeterminate states, relating to the worlds of sense, of form or of the formless, which are co-Intoxicant; in other words, the five skandhas.

[1] The sole comment on this species of spiritual hindrance is that it is the standpoint of those who have rejected the doctrines of the Omniscient. Asl. 377.

[2] Ganthaniyā. Ārammaṇakaraṇavasena ganthehi ganthitabbā ti ganthaniyā. Asl. 49.

[1142] (*b*) *do not tend to become tied?*

The Paths that are the Unincluded and the Fruits of the Paths, and uncompounded element.

Which are the states that are

[1143] (*a*) *associated with the Ties?*

The states connected with those four afore-named states; in other words, the four skandhas.

[1144] (*b*) *disconnected with the Ties?*

The states which are disconnected with those [four afore-named] states; in other words, the four skandhas; all form also, and uncompounded element.[1]

Which are the states that

[1145] (*a*) *are themselves Ties and tend to become tied?*

The Ties themselves are both.

[1146] (*b*) *tend to become tied, but are not Ties?*

The states which tend to become tied by those [four afore-named] states, that is, every state, good, bad and indeterminate, which is not included in the latter, whether it relates to the worlds of sense, of form, or of the formless; in other words, the five skandhas.

Which are the states that are

[1147] (*a*) *Ties themselves, and associated with the Ties?*

The bodily Tie of the contagion of mere rule and ritual in conjunction with the bodily Tie of covetousness, *and conversely*, is both. The bodily Tie of the inclination to dogmatize in conjunction with the bodily Tie of covetousness, *and conversely*, is both.[2]

[1148] (*b*) *associated with the Ties but not Ties?*

---

[1] Sabbañ ca rūpaṃ asankhatā ca dhātu is omitted in the text, but occurs in analogous passages (§§ 1124, 1167) and is given in K.

[2] It is not apparent to me why the Tie of ill will (vyāpādo) is omitted from these combinations, both in the text and in K. Buddhaghosa makes no comment.

The states which are associated with the four states afore-named (the Ties), the latter themselves excepted ; in other words, the four skandhas.

Which are the states that

[1149] (*a*) *are disconnected with the Ties, but tend to become tied?*

The states which are disconnected with the afore-named states, that is, good, bad and indeterminate states relating to the worlds of sense, of form, or of the formless, which are co-Intoxicant ; in other words, the five skandhas.

[1150] (*b*) *are disconnected with the Ties and do not tend to become tied?*

The Paths that are the Unincluded and the Fruits of the Paths, and uncompounded element.

[CHAPTER VII.

The Group of the Floods (o g h a - g o c c h a k a ṃ).]

[1151] Which are the states that are Floods?
. . . [*continue as in the* Group of Fetters.][1]

---

[1] This and the group in the next chapter are thus indicated to be taken as read, in both the text and K. By the table of contents, it can be seen that the same system of catechizing is followed as in the Groups of the Fetters and the Ties. In S. v., p. 59, may be seen the number and kind of 'states' included under Floods or under Bonds, the contents of either group being identical with the four Āsavas. These are the Flood or Bond of sensuality (k ā m a), renewed existence (b h a v a), speculative opinion (d i ṭ ṭ h i) and ignorance (a v i j j ā). The Atthasālinī only remarks that the Floods are states so called because they sink him for whom they exist into s a ṃ s ā r a, while the Bonds, like the Ties, chain him to the Circle (p. 49). Also that the adjectives, o g h a n i y ā and y o g a n i y ā, analogous to g a n t h a n i y ā, stand for that which can be engulfed by Floods and enchained by Bonds respectively.

[CHAPTER VIII.

The Group of the Bonds (yoga-gocchakaṃ).]

[1151*a*] Which are the states that are Bonds? . . . [*continue as in the* Group of Fetters].

[CHAPTER IX.

The Group of the Hindrances (nīvaraṇa-gocchakaṃ).]

[1152] Which are the states that are Hindrances?

The six Hindrances, to wit, the Hindrance of sensual desire, the Hindrance of ill will, the Hindrance of stolidity and torpor, the Hindrance of excitement and worry, the Hindrance of perplexity, the Hindrance of ignorance.[1]

In this connexion

[1153] *What is the Hindrance of sensual desire?*

Answer as for the 'Intoxicant of sensuality,' § 1097.[2]

[1154] *What is the Hindrance of ill will?*

Answer as for the 'Tie of ill will,' § 1137.

[1155] *What is the Hindrance of stolidity and torpor?*

First distinguish between stolidity and torpor.[3]

---

[1] In the Sutta Pitaka, the Hindrances form a category of five, ignorance (avijjā) being excluded. See the description in D. i. 71-74, and *cf.* D. i. 246; M. i. 60, 144, 181, 269, 294, etc.; A. iii. 63; S. v. 60, 94-98. This discrepancy is not noticed by Buddhaghosa. See also § 1112, etc. The Hindrances are to be understood as states which muffle, enwrap or trammel thought. States, again, which are nīvaraṇiyā are to be understood analogously to those which are saññojanīyā. Asl. 49.

[2] 'Sensual thirst' is again omitted, as in the description of the corresponding Fetter, § 1114.

[3] It is interesting to note that whereas the text calls thīnaṃ (stolidity) a morbid state of the cittaṃ and middhaṃ a morbid state of the kāyo, Buddhaghosa, in

In this connexion,

[1156] *What is stolidity?*

That which is indisposition,[1] unwieldiness[2] of intellect; adhering and cohering; clinging, cleaving to, stickiness; stolidity, that is, a stiffening, a rigidity of the intellect[3]—this is called stolidity.

[1157] *What is torpor?*[4]

That which is indisposition and unwieldiness of sense, a shrouding, enveloping,[5] barricading within[6]; torpor that

his Cy. on the Dīgha Nikāya (Sum. 211), speaks of thīnaṃ as citta-gelaññaṃ (sickness or affection of the mind), and of middhaṃ as cetasikagelaññaṃ. The apparent inconsistency, however, will vanish if the predominantly psychological standpoint of the Dhamma Sangaṇi be kept in mind. By kāyo, as Buddhaghosa reminds us (Asl. 378; see above, p. 43, n. 3), is meant 'the three skandhas' of feeling, perception and syntheses, that is to say, the three through which we have subjective experience of bodily states objectively conceived. And cetasiko is the adjective corresponding to kāyo taken in this sense (§ 1022). Hence stolidity is confined to the viññāṇa-skandha, which = cittaṃ = (approximately) representative intellection, while torpor is a corresponding affection of mind on its presentative and emotional side.

[1] Akalyatā, equivalent to gilānabhāvo, Asl. 377, where Mahā Vibhanga, i. 62, is quoted.

[2] See § 47.

[3] 'The (stolid) mind cannot be maintained in any required attitude or deportment. It is as inert as a bat hanging to a tree, or as molasses cleaving to a stick, or as a lump of butter too stiff for spreading' (Asl., *ibid.*). 'Attached to' (līnaṃ) is paraphrased by avipphārikatāya paṭikuṭitaṃ, lit., bent back without expansion, where the notion, as conceived by the Commentator, has something akin to kaṭukañcukatā or niggardliness. See § 1122, n. 2.

[4] Middhaṃ, derived by the Cy. from medhati ($\sqrt{}$med, 'be fat'); there is a cognate notion in our 'torpor,' *cf.* τέρπειν, to be sated, and $\sqrt{\text{tarp}}$.

[5] Onāho, pariyonāho. See Mil. 300; D. i. 246. In the latter work, the *a* is short. In the Cy. (Asl. 378) the

[6] See note on p. 312.

is sleep, drowsiness; sleep,[1] slumbering, somnolence—this is called torpor.

Now this is the stolidity and this is the torpor which are called 'the Hindrance of stolidity and torpor.'[2]

[1159] What is the Hindrance of excitement and worry?

First distinguish between 'excitement' and 'worry.'

In this connexion,

[1160] *What is excitement?*[3]

That excitement of mind which is disquietude, agitation of heart, turmoil of mind—this is called excitement.

[1161] What is worry?[4]

---

simile is 'enveloping the senses (kāyo) as a cloud the sky.' In Sum. i. 135 the latter of the two terms is applied to 'covering' a drum.

[6] Anto-samorodho. The Cy. explains that, as men cannot get out of an invested city, so dhammā, blockaded by torpor, cannot get out by expansion or diffusion).

[1] There is no comment on this repetition of soppaṃ.

[2] The Commentator in his general remarks on this Hindrance is at pains to point out that for the khīṇāsavo, or arahat, a periodical torpor or repose has ceased to engender bad karma. The Buddha allowed an after-dinner nap, for instance, at certain seasons (see M. i. 249), as not in itself conducive to a bemuddling of the mind. So powerful, however, is the Hindrance to the non-adept, that its influence is not rooted out till the arahat Path is gained. The arahat is fain to rest his frail body (lit., his fingernail-kāyo), but to him it is as *un*moral an act as the folding up of leaves and blossoms at night. On overcoming torpor see A. iv. 86.

[3] See § 429.

[4] In its primary meaning kukkuccaṃ is fidgeting, bad deportment of hands and feet. See Jāt. i. 119; ii. 142; also Sum. i. 1, 2. Hence mental fidget, the worry of *scruple* (lit., 'the little sharp stone in a man's shoe.' See Skeat's English Dictionary), the over-sensitive, over-scrupulous conscience. In the frequent cases of kukkuccaṃ, respecting the keeping of the rules of the Order, given in the Vinaya—'tassa kukkuccaṃ ahosi'—or kukkuccāyanto—no blame seems to have attached to the person in question. There was weakness in the anxiety

Consciousness of what is lawful in something that is unlawful; consciousness of what is unlawful in something that is lawful; consciousness of what is immoral in something that is moral; consciousness of what is moral in something that is immoral[1]—all this sort of worry, fidgeting, over-scrupulousness, remorse of conscience, mental scarifying[2] —this is what is called worry.

Now this is the excitement and this is the worry which are what is called 'the Hindrance of excitement and worry.'

[1162] *What is the Hindrance of ignorance?*
Answer as for 'dulness,' § 1061.

[1163] Which are the states that are not Hindrances?

Every state, good, bad and indeterminate, which is not included in the foregoing [six] states, whether it relates to the worlds of sense, of form, or of the formless, or to the life that is Unincluded; in other words, the four skandhas; all form also, and uncompounded element.

Which are the states that are
[1164] (*a*) *favourable to the Hindrances?*[3]

---

felt by the non-robust conscience as to the letter of the law; on the other hand, there was loyalty to the Master's decrees. Even the great Sāriputta was not above such scruples, when, on falling ill at a rest-house, he declined to take food, in accordance with the 31st Pācittiya rule (Vin. iv. 70). But Buddhaghosa quotes this as an instance of praiseworthy scruple, to be distinguished, as 'Vinaya-kukkuccam,' from the after-flush of burning anguish (anutāpo) accompanying the consciousness of having done amiss, a feeling that is no longer possible for an arahat. Asl. 384. *Cf.* below, § 1304.

[1] Things lawful (kappiyaṃ) and unlawful are explained as here referring merely to rules of routine in the Order, *e.g.*, to kinds of food, the dinner-hour, etc. By things moral and immoral (avajjam, etc.) are meant acts of virtue and of vice. Asl. 383.

[2] See p. 117, n. 7.

[3] Nīvaraṇiyā, to be understood as analogous to saññojanīyā. Asl. 49.

Co-Intoxicant states, good, bad and indeterminate, whether relating to the worlds of sense, form or the formless; in other words, the five skandhas.

[1165] (*b*) *unfavourable to the Hindrances?*

The Paths that are the Unincluded and the Fruits of the Paths, and uncompounded element.

Which are the states that are

[1166] (*a*) *associated with the Hindrances?*

[1167] (*b*) *disconnected with the Hindrances?*

Answers identical with those given to corresponding questions respecting the Intoxicants, §§ 1105, 1106.

Which are the states that are

[1168] (*a*) *Hindrances themselves and favourable to the Hindrances?*

The Hindrances themselves are both.

[1169] (*b*) *favourable to the Hindrances, but not themselves Hindrances?*

The states which are favourable to the Hindrances afore-named; that is to say, with the exception of the Hindrances, all co-Intoxicant states whatever, good, bad and indeterminate, whether they relate to the worlds of sense, form or the formless; in other words, the five skandhas.

Which are the states that are

[1170] (*a*) *both themselves Hindrances and associated with Hindrances?*

The following pairs are both themselves Hindrances and associated with Hindrances: Sensual desire in conjunction with ignorance, *and conversely.* Ill-will in conjunction with ignorance, *and conversely.*

Stolidity and torpor,
Excitement,
Worry,
Perplexity,
} *taken successively,* in conjunction with ignorance, *and conversely.*

Sensual desire,
Ill-will,
Stolidity and torpor,
Excitement,
Worry,
Perplexity,
} *taken successively*, in conjunction with ignorance, *and conversely*.

[1171] (*b*) *associated with Hindrances, but not themselves Hindrances?*

The states which are associated with the [six aforementioned] states, the latter themselves being excepted; in other words, the four skandhas.

Which are the states that are

[1172] (*a*) *disconnected with the Hindrances, but favourable to them?*

The states which are disconnected with those [six] states afore-named, that is to say, co-Intoxicant states, good, bad and indeterminate, whether they relate to the worlds of sense, form or the formless; in other words, the five skandhas.

[1173] (*b*) *disconnected with the Hindrances and unfavourable to them?*

The Paths that are the Unincluded, and the Fruits of the Paths, and uncompounded element.[1]

---

[1] Worry and perplexity are discarded in the First Path; sensual desire and ill-will in the Third Path; stolidity, torpor and ignorance in the Fourth. Asl. 384. Insight into the presence or absence of the (five) Hindrances is termed, in A. i. 272, manosoceyyaṃ.

[Chapter X.

The Group on Contagion (parāmāsa-gocchakaṃ).][1]

[1174] Which are the states that are contagious?

The Contagion of speculative opinion.

In this connexion,

[1175] What is the 'Contagion of speculative opinion'?

Answer as for the 'Intoxicant of speculative opinion,' *viz.*: 'To hold that the world is eternal, or that it is not eternal,' etc. (§ 1099).

[1176] Which are the states that are not a Contagion?

Answer as in the case of the 'states that are not Hindrances' (§ 1163).[2]

[1177, 1178] Which are the states that are

(*a*) *infected?*

(*b*) *uninfected?*

Answers as in the corresponding answers relating to the Hindrances (§§ 1164, 1165).

---

[1] The man, according to the Cy. (p. 49), who falls out of the right attitude toward dhammā, *i.e.*, who loses the belief in their impermanence, etc., lays himself open to the infectious touch of speculative views.

[2] The one kind of Contagion is always for the sake of symmetry referred to as plural, *e.g.*, the states afore-named (te dhammā ṭhapetvā). Asl. 385.

[1179, 1180] Which are the states that are

(*a*) *associated with the Contagion?*

(*b*) *disconnected with the Contagion?*

Answers as in the corresponding answers relating to the Hindrances (§§ 1166, 1167).

[1181, 1182] Which are the states that are

(*a*) *themselves Contagious and infected?*

The Contagion itself is both.

(*b*) *infected but not Contagious?*

The states which are infected by the states afore-named; that is to say, with the exception of the latter, all co-Intoxicant states whatever, good, bad and indeterminate, whether they relate to the worlds of sense, form, or the formless; in other words, the five skandhas.

[1183, 1184] Which are the states that are

(*a*) *disconnected with the Contagion, yet infected?*

(*b*) *disconnected with the Contagion and uninfected?*

Answers as in the corresponding sections on the Hindrances (§§ 1172, 1173).

[CHAPTER XI.

The Great Intermediate Set of Pairs (mahantara-dukam).][1]

[1185, 1186] Which are the states that have

(*a*) *a concomitant object of thought?*[2]

The four skandhas.

(*b*) *no concomitant object of thought?*

All form,[3] and uncompounded element.

[1187, 1188] Which are the states that are

(*a*) *of the intellect?*[4]

Cognition applied to sense-impressions; the element of ideation and the element of ideational cognition.

(*b*) *not of the intellect?*

The skandhas of feeling, perception and syntheses; all form, moreover, and uncompounded element.

[1189, 1190] Which are the states that are

(*a*) *involved in the life of sense?*[5]

---

[1] *Cf.* Chapter III. of this book. The Cy. refrains from any remarks on the answers in this chapter.

[2] Sārammaṇā.

[3] See p. 169: 'void of idea.' See K. V. 404.

[4] Cittā. See § 1022. 'Cognition applied,' etc., is in the original cakkhuviññāṇam and the rest. When 'sense' drops out of account in the following pairs, I have reverted to the approximately synonymous term 'thought.'

[5] Cetasikā. See § 1022.

The skandhas of feeling, perception and syntheses.

(*b*) *not involved in the life of sense?*

Intellect and all form and uncompounded element.

[1191, 1192] Which are the states that are

(*a*) *associated with thought?*

The skandhas of feeling, perception and syntheses.

(*b*) *disconnected with thought?*

All form and uncompounded element.

(Thought must not be described as associated or disconnected with itself.)[1]

[1193, 1194] Which are the states that are

(*a*) *conjoined with thought?*[2]

(*b*) *detached from thought?*

Answers as in §§ 1191, 1192 *respectively.*

(Thought must not be described as conjoined with, or detached from itself.)

[1195, 1196] Which are the states that are

(*a*) *sprung from thought?*[3]

The skandhas of feeling, perception and syntheses; bodily and vocal intimation; or whatever other form there be which is born of thought, caused by thought, sprung from thought, whether it be in the spheres of sights, sounds, smells, tastes,[4] or the tangible, the elements of space or fluidity, the lightness, plasticity or wieldiness of

---

[1] This refinement in the Buddhist Logic of Terms is usually expressed by the brief parenthesis governed by ṭhapetvā, excepting. See, *e.g.*, § 984 *et seq.*

[2] Citta-saṃsaṭṭhā. '*I.e.*, in a condition of continuity, immediate contiguity, with thought.' Asl. 49. The contrary -visaṃsaṭṭhā = 'not in the condition of continuity, immediate contiguity, with thought, although proceeding in unity with it.' *Ibid.*

[3] Citta-samuṭṭhānā. *Cf.* § 667.

[4] Rasāyatanaṃ has been omitted in the text, apparently by inadvertence.

form, the integration or subsistence of form, or bodily nutriment.

(*b*) *not sprung from thought?*

Thought; also every other kind of form, and uncompounded element.

[1197, 1198] Which are the states that

(*a*) *come into being together with thought?*[1]

The skandhas of feeling, perception and syntheses; bodily and vocal intimation.

(*b*) *do not come into being together with thought?*

Thought; also all other kinds of form,[2] and uncompounded element.

[1199, 1200] Which are the states that are

(*a*) *consecutive to thought?*[3]

(*b*) *not consecutive to thought?*

Answers as in the two foregoing answers respectively.

[1201, 1202] Which are the states that are

(*a*) *conjoined with and sprung from thought?*[4]

The skandhas of feeling, perception and syntheses.

(*b*) *not conjoined with and sprung from thought?*[5]

Thought itself; all form also, and uncompounded element.

---

[1] Citta-sahabhuno.

[2] *I.e.*, except the two modes of intimation, which are reckoned as 'form.' See § 596.

[3] Cittanuparivattinā.

[4] Citta-saṃsaṭṭha-samuṭṭhānā. The Cy. reads this and the terms in the two following pairs as dvandva compounds.

[5] The negative in the text is not distributed, and the compound of attributes qualifying 'states' must be taken conjunctively. This is borne out by the answer. *Cf.* §§ 1196, 1198, also p. 204, n. 1.

Saha-bhuno is parsed as saha bhavanti, not bhūtā. Asl. 49.

[1203, 1204] Which are the states that

(*a*) *are conjoined with and sprung from, and that come into being together with, thought?*

(*b*) *are not such as are conjoined with and sprung from and as come into being together with thought?*[1]

Answers as in the two foregoing answers respectively.

[1205, 1206] Which are the states that are

(*a*) *conjoined with and sprung from and consecutive to thought?*

(*b*) *not conjoined with, sprung from and consecutive to thought?*

Answers as in the two foregoing answers.

[1207, 1208] Which are the states that are

(*a*) *of the self?*

The spheres of the five senses and of ideation.

(*b*) *external?*

The spheres of the five objects of sense and of ideas.[2]

[1209, 1210] Which are the states that are

(*a*) *derived?*

The spheres of the five senses . . . and bodily nutriment.[3]

(*b*) *not derived?*

The four skandhas, the four great phenomena and uncompounded element.

[1211-1212] Which are the states that are

(*a*) *the issue of grasping?*[4]

Co-Intoxicant good and bad states, whether they relate to the worlds of sense, of form, or of the formless; in other words, the four skandhas, and such form as is due to karma having been wrought.

---

[1] See note 5, p. 320.

[2] Dhammāyatanaṃ.

[3] *Cf.* § 596.

[4] See M. i. 190.

(*b*) *not the issue of grasping?*

Co-Intoxicant good and bad states, whether they relate to the worlds of sense, of form, or of the formless; in other words, the four skandhas; also such kiriyā-thoughts as are neither good, nor bad, nor the effects of karma; the Paths, moreover, that are the Unincluded and the Fruits of the Paths, and uncompounded element.

[CHAPTER XII.

The Group on Grasping (upādāna-gocchakaṃ).]

[1213] Which are the states that have the attribute of Grasping?[1]

---

[1] Upādānā. This fundamental notion in Buddhist ethics is in the Cy. (pp. 450 and 385), paraphrased by the words 'they take violently, *i.e.*, they take hold with a strong grasp' (bhusaṃ ādiyanti . . . daḷhagāhaṃ gaṇhanti), the prefix upa being credited with augmentative import as in other terms, such as upāyāso and upakkuṭṭho. This shows that, in so far as Buddhaghosa gives the traditional sense, the word, in the Buddhism of his day, connoted rather the dynamic force of 'grasping' than the static condition of 'attachment' (*e.g.*, Warren, 'Buddhism in Translations,' p. 189 *et seq.*) or 'cleaving' (Hardy, 'Manual,' 394). Nor does his comment ratify such renderings as 'Hang' or 'Lebenstrieb' (Neumann, 'Die Reden Gotamo Buddhos,' pp. 104, 470). Fausböll's 'seizures' (S. N. in S. B. E., x., p. 138) and Oldenberg's 'Ergreifen' ('Buddha,' 3rd ed., 269), on the other hand, agree with Buddhaghosa.

The relation of the cognate term upādāniyo to upādānaṃ (*cf.* §§ 655, 881, 1219) is most clearly set forth in S. iv. 89; there the special senses are termed upādāniyā dhammā, and the passionate desire connected therewith the upādānaṃ. See also S. iv. 258. Buddhaghosa makes no comment on upādāniyaṃ when, as in § 1219, it is applied to dhammā; but when it is a question of rūpaṃ . . . upādāniyam (Dh. S., §§ 655, 881), he defines this as '*states* which are favourable to (hitā, lit., good for) the Graspings as objects by their

The four Graspings:—the Grasping after sense, the Grasping after speculative opinion, the Grasping after mere rule and ritual, the Grasping after a theory of soul.

In this connexion,

[1214] *What is the Grasping after sense?*

That sensual desire, sensual passion, sensual delight, sensual craving, sensual cleaving, sensual fever, sensual languishing, sensual rapacity, which is excited by the pleasures of the senses.[1]

[1215] *What is the Grasping after speculative opinion?*

'There is no such thing as alms, or sacrifice, or offering;[2] there is neither fruit, nor result of good, or of evil deeds; there is no such thing as this world, or the next;[3] there is no such thing as mother or father, or beings springing into birth without them;[4] there are in the world no recluses or brahmins who have reached the highest point, who have attained the height, who, having understood and

---

being bound up with grasping; in other words, phenomena which are the conditions of the mental objects of grasping' (upādānassa ārammaṇa-paccaya-bhūtāni). Asl. 42.

In the same connexion, rūpaṃ upādiṇṇaṃ (Dh. S., § 653) is by Buddhaghosa defined as [states] which have been got, laid hold of, taken (gahitā), by way of fruition—heaped up by karma having the property of craving. *Ibid.* None of the comments explains upādānaṃ in the sense of fuel, *i.e.*, as the basis of re-birth; each of the four Upādānas is paraphrased simply by to grasp at sense (kāmaṃ upādīyati), at speculation, etc.

[1] See § 1114 and § 1097; also § 1153.

[2] The Cy. explains these negations as merely meaning that none of the three has an efficacy, any fruition. Asl. 385.

[3] Ignoring any deeper metaphysic that may have here been implied, the Cy. explains these negations as held by the inhabitant of another world respecting this, or by an inhabitant here below respecting another world. *Ibid.*

[4] Beings so born, continues the Cy., he assumes there are none; nor have one's former lives any efficacy over one's subsequent parentage.

realized by themselves alone both this world and the next, make known the same"[1]—all this sort of speculation, this walking in opinion, wilderness of opinion, puppet-show of opinion, scuffling of opinion, this Fetter of opinion, the grip and tenacity of it, the inclination towards it, the being infected by it, this by-path, wrong road, wrongness, this 'fording-place,' this shiftiness of grasp[2]—this is what is called the Grasping after speculative opinion.

And with the exception of the Graspings after mere rule and ritual and after soul-theory, all wrong views are included in the Grasping after speculative opinion.

[1216] *What is the Grasping after mere rule and ritual?*

Answer as for the 'Contagion of mere rule and ritual,' § 1005.[3]

[1217] *What is the Grasping after soul-theory?*

Answer as for the 'Theory of individuality,' § 1003.

[1218] Which are the states that have not the attribute of Grasping?

All other states whatever, good, bad and indeterminate (except the foregoing), whether they relate to the worlds of sense, or of form, or of the formless, or to the life that is Unincluded; in other words, the four skandhas; all form also and uncompounded element.

[1219] Which are the states that are favourable Grasping?

Co-Intoxicant states, good, bad and indeterminate

---

[1] Buddhaghosa gives as typical forms of speculation grasped at, 'Both the soul (self) and the world are eternal.' These he calls the purimadiṭṭhiṃ uttaradiṭṭhiṃ (*sic lege*), terms which, whether they mean 'earlier and subsequent heresies,' or 'Eastern and Northern views,' or both, are equally interesting. The text, however, selects as a typical current speculation the views put forward by Ajita Kesakambali. See D. i. 55 and M. i. 402.

[2] *Cf.* § 381.

[3] The 'bovine morality and practices' noticed above (§ 1005, n. 3) are again instanced in the Cy. *Ibid.*

whether they relate to the worlds of sense, form or the formless ; in other words, the five skandhas.

[1220] Which are the states that are not favourable to Grasping?

The Paths that are the Unincluded, and the Fruits of the Paths ; and uncompounded element.

[1221-1224] Which are the states that are

(*a*) *associated with Grasping ?*

(*b*) *disconnected with Grasping ?*

(*c*) *Grasping and also favourable to Grasping ?*

(*d*) *favourable to Grasping but not Grasping ?*

Answers exactly analogous to those given to corresponding questions in other Groups, e.g., §§ 1125, 1141, 1164.

[1225-1228] Which are the states that are

(*a*) *both Grasping and associated with Grasping ?*

The Grasping after speculation in conjunction with that after sense is both, *and conversely.*

So is each of the other two Graspings in conjunction with that after sense, *and conversely.*

(*b*) *associated with Grasping but not Grasping ?*

(*c*) *disconnected with Grasping yet favourable to it ?*

(*d*) *disconnected with Grasping and not favourable to it ?*

Answers as in the Groups specified above, §§ 1125, 1141, 1164 *et seq.*[1]

---

[1] The First Path disposes of all forms of Grasping save the first, the extirpation of which is a task not finished till all the four Paths have been traversed. Asl. 386. Contrast with this §§ 1173 n., 1134 n., and 1112 n., where in every case 'sense,' 'sensuality' and 'sensual desire' are in the Cy. said to succumb in the Third or Anāgāmi's Path.

[CHAPTER XIII.

The Group on the Corruptions (kilesa-gocchakaṃ).]

[1229] Which are the states that have the attribute of corruption?[1]

---

[1] On the term kilesa the Cy. is silent. It is true that the word lies as near to the Buddhist believer as 'sin' to the Christian. As a rule, however, Buddhaghosa is too Socratic to accept familiar terms without examination. In this case he has confined his attention to the derivatives. Incidentally, however—in discussing the meaning of 'good' (above, § 1; Asl. 62)—he makes spiritual health to consist in the absence of kilesa-disease, showing that kilesa was co-extensive with evil or the absence of moral good. Of the derivatives, only sankiliṭṭha is made to convey the idea of impurity or foulness (see Childers, *s.v.* sankileso), bad butter being so termed (Asl. 319). Elsewhere it is paraphrased as 'possessed of sankileso,' while sankilesa (above, §§ 993-995; Asl. 42) is defined in close agreement with the description of sankleça in Böthl. and Roth (*quälen, belästigen*): 'the meaning is to trouble, to torment,' while the corresponding adjective is described as 'deserving sankilesa by persistently making self the object of one's thoughts . . . the term being an equivalent for those things which are the conditions (or objects) of sankilesa.' Corruption or impurity is, however, I believe, approximately what this group of terms represents to modern Buddhists; nor have I been able to select an English word adequate to render them in what seems to have been their first intention, viz., 'torment' (caused by moral unsoundness). 'Bases' or vatthūni are states so called because the Corruptions dwell (vasanti) in the (human) subject

The ten bases of corruption, to wit:

lust,	perplexity,
hate,	stolidity,
dulness,	excitement,
conceit,	unconscientiousness,
speculative opinion,	disregard of blame.

[1230-1237] In this connexion,

What is lust? . . . hate? . . . dulness? . . . conceit? . . . speculative opinion? . . . perplexity? . . . stolidity? . . . excitement?[1]

Answers as in §§ 1059-1061, 1116-1118, 1156, 1159.

[1238] *What is unconscientiousness?*

The absence of any feeling of conscientious scruple when scruples ought to be felt; the absence of conscientious scruple at attaining to bad and evil states.[2]

[1239] *What is disregard of blame?*

The absence of any sense of guilt where a sense of guilt ought to be felt, the absence of a sense of guilt at attaining to bad and evil states.

These are the states which have the attribute of corruption.

[1240] Which are the states that have not the attribute of corruption?

All other states whatever (*i.e.*, all except the afore-named ten), good, bad and indeterminate, whether they relate to the worlds of sense, form or the formless, or to the life that is Unincluded; in other words, the four skandhas, all form also and uncompounded element.

[1241, 1242] Which are the states that are

(*a*) *baneful?*

---

of them as immediate conditions (anantara-paccayā). Asl. 386.

[1] In the answer, vūpasamo in the text should be avūpasamo.

[2] See §§ 387, 388.

Co-Intoxicant states, good, bad and indeterminate, whether they relate to the worlds of sense, of form or of the formless;[1] in other words, the five skandhas.

(*b*) *harmless?*

The Paths that are the Unincluded, and the Fruits of the Paths, and uncompounded element.

[1243, 1243*a*] Which are the states that are

(*a*) *corrupt?*

The three roots of bad (karma), to wit, lust, hate, dulness, as well as the Corruptions united with them, the four skandhas associated with them, and the action, bodily, vocal and mental, springing from them.

(*b*) *not corrupt?*

Good and indeterminate states, whether they relate to the worlds of sense, form, or the formless, or to the life that is Unincluded; in other words, the four skandhas; all form also, and uncompounded element.[2]

[1244-1247] Which are the states that are

{ (*a*) *associated with the Corruptions?*
{ (*b*) *disconnected with the Corruptions?*

{ (*c*) *both Corruptions and baneful?*
{ (*d*) *baneful but not themselves Corruptions?*

Answers as in the corresponding pairs in the 'Graspings,' §§ 1221-1224.

[1248, 1249] Which are the states that are

(*a*) *both Corruptions and corrupt?*

The Corruptions themselves.

(*b*) *corrupt but not themselves Corruptions?*

The states which by those ten states are made corrupt, the ten themselves excepted; in other words, the four skandhas.

---

[1] Aparīyāpannā should, of course, be omitted from the printed text.

[2] This section is omitted, apparently inadvertently, in the printed text. *Cf.* the Mātikā.

[1250-1253] Which are the states that are

(*a*) *both Corruptions and associated with Corruptions?*

Lust, hate, conceit, speculative opinion, perplexity, stolidity, excitement, unconscientiousness and disregard of blame *taken severally* in conjunction with dulness, and dulness in conjunction with *each of them*. Lust, also, in conjunction with excitement, and conversely, *and so for the remaining eight bases*. Lust, also, in conjunction with unconscientiousness, *and conversely, and so for the remaining eight*. Lust, also, in conjunction with disregard of blame, *and conversely, and so for the remaining eight*.[1]

(*b*) *associated with Corruptions but not themselves Corruptions?*[2]

(*c*) *disconnected with Ills but baneful?*
(*d*) *disconnected with Ills and harmless?*

Answers to these three questions as in former groups. See §§ 1226-1228, 1171-1173, *etc.*[3]

---

[1] It is not very obvious, nor is any explanation volunteered by the Cy., why just the 3rd, 8th, 9th and 10th Bases of Corruption are selected as the constant of two factors in this connexion.

[2] In the answer, supply ye dhammā after Tehi dhammehi.

[3] The First Path witnesses the overcoming of speculative opinion and perplexity, the Third Path disposes of hate, but it requires the Fourth Path to overcome the remaining seven. Asl. 387.

[CHAPTER XIV.

The Supplementary Set of Pairs (piṭṭhidukaṃ).]

[1254] Which are the states that are to be put away by insight?

The Three Fetters, to wit: theory of individuality, perplexity and the contagion of mere rule and ritual.

[1255-1257] *Identical with* §§ 1003-1006.

[1258] Which are the states that are not to be put away by insight?

All states whatever, good, bad and indeterminate, except the three afore-mentioned, whether they relate to the worlds of sense, form or the formless, or to the life that is Unincluded; in other words, the four skandhas; all form also and uncompounded element.

[1259, 1260] Which are the states that are

(*a*) *to be put away by cultivation?*

All the remaining lust, hate and dulness as well as the Corruptions united with them, the four skandhas associated with them, and the action, bodily, vocal and mental, springing from them.

(*b*) *not to be put away by cultivation?*

Answer as for those states which are not to be put away by insight [§ 1258].

[1261] Which are the states the causes of which are to be put away by insight?

The Three Fetters, to wit: theory of individuality, perplexity and the contagion of mere rule and ritual.

[1262-1264] *Identical with* §§ 1003-1006.

[1265] Which are the states the causes of which are not to be put away by insight?

Answer as for those 'states which are not to be put away by insight,' § 1258.

[1266, 1267] Which are the states the causes of which are

(*a*) *to be put away by cultivation?*

All the remaining lust, hate and dulness: these are the causes that are to be put away[1] by cultivation. And the Corruptions united with them, the four skandhas associated with them, and the action, bodily, vocal and mental, springing from them, are the states the causes of which are to be put away by cultivation.

(*b*) *not to be put away by cultivation?*

Answer as for the 'states which are not to be put away by cultivation,' § 1260.

[1268-1271] Which are the states

(*a*) '*wherein conception works*'?

The four skandhas when associated with conception (the latter not being included), [which springs up] in a soil wherein conception works, either in the worlds of sense or form, or in the life that is Unincluded.[2]

(*b*) '*void of the working of conception*'?

The four skandhas when springing up in a soil void of conception, either in the worlds of sense, form or the formless, or in the life that is Unincluded; conception itself also, and all form and uncompounded element.

---

[1] In the text, for pahātabba-hetukā (first occurrence) read pahātabba-hetū.

[2] *Cf.* this and following pairs with §§ 996-998 and p. 252, n. 1. See also App. I., pp. 362, 363. In the text, arūpāvacare should be omitted, and apariyāpanne substituted for pariyāpanne.

(*c*) '*wherein works thought discursive*'?

(*d*) '*void of the working of thought discursive*'?

Answers (*substituting* 'discursive thought' *for* 'conception') *as in* §§ 1268, 1269 *respectively*.

[1272-1277] Which are the states that are

(*a*) *joyous*?[1]

(*b*) *not joyous*?

(*c*) *accompanied by joy*?

(*d*) *unaccompanied by joy*?

(*e*) *accompanied by ease*?

(*f*) *unaccompanied by ease*?

Answers to each pair of questions analogous to those in §§ 1268, 1269, 'joy' *or* 'ease' *being substituted in due order for* 'conception.'

[1278, 1279] Which are the states that are

(*a*) *accompanied by disinterestedness*?

The three skandhas of perception, syntheses and intellect,[2] when associated with disinterestedness (the latter not being included), [which springs up] in a soil congenial to it, either in the worlds of sense, form or the formless, or in the life that is Unincluded.

(*b*) *unaccompanied by disinterestedness*?

The four skandhas [when springing up] in a soil uncongenial to disinterestedness, either in the worlds of sense or form,[3] or in the life that is Unincluded; disinterestedness itself also, and all form and uncompounded element.

---

[1] Sappītikā. The term is used to qualify sukhaṃ, A. i. 81. How far, if at all, its connotation is distinguishable from that of pīti-sahāgatā (§ 1274) I cannot say.

In the answers to the positive terms arūpāvacare should be omitted from the printed text. *Cf.* § 265 *et seq.*

[2] Upekkhā (disinterestedness) is a mode of vedanā or feeling, and is therefore not said to be associated with itself.

[3] In the printed text omit arūpāvacare.

[1281-1287] Which are the states that

(*a*) *relate* (*belong*) *to the universe of sense?*[1]

Take from the waveless deep of woe beneath up to the heaven above of the Parinimittavasavatti gods inclusive—then whatever has there its range, and is therein included, whether it be skandha, element or sphere[2]—form, feeling, perception, syntheses, intellect: these are states that relate (belong) to the universe of sense.

(*b*) *do not relate* (*belong*) *to the universe of sense?*

The universe of form, that of the formless and the life that is Unincluded.

(*c*) *relate* (*belong*) *to the universe of form?*

Take from the Brahma-world below up to the heaven above of the Akaniṭṭha gods inclusive—then whatever states, both of sense and intellect, have therein their range and are therein included, whether they are states of one who has attained [Jhāna having potential good], or of one in whom [resultant Jhāna] has arisen, or of one living happily under present conditions.[3]

(*d*) *do not relate* (*belong*) *to the universe of form?*

The universe of sense, that of the formless and the life that is Unincluded.

(*e*) *relate* (*belong*) *to the universe of the formless?*

Take from the entrance among the gods of 'the sphere of infinite space'[4] as the lower limit, and up to the entrance

---

[1] Kāmāvacarā. The āvacaras are discussed in my Introduction (vi).

[2] Khandha-dhātu-āyatanā (*cf.* K.). I take this to be an adjectival dvandva compound qualifying dhammā, but the five following terms, the skandhas, to be in apposition to dhammā.

[3] The three terms rendered by the last three periphrases are samāpannassa, uppannassa and diṭṭhadhammasukhavihārissa. The Cy. (p. 388) explains them as referring to kusala-jhānaṃ, vipāka-jhānaṃ and kiriyā-jhānaṃ. The subject is further dealt with in my Introduction (viii).

[4] See pp. 71-75.

above among the gods of 'the sphere where there is neither perception nor non-perception'—then whatever states, both of sense and intellect, have therein their range and are therein included, whether they are states of one who has attained [Jhāna having potential good], or of one in whom [resultant Jhāna] has arisen, or of one living happily under present conditions: these are states that relate (belong) to the universe of the formless.

(*f*) *do not relate (belong) to the universe of the formless?*

The universe of sense,[1] that of form, and the life that is Unincluded.

(*g*) *belong to the Included?*

Co-Intoxicant states, good, bad and indeterminate, whether they relate to the worlds of sense, of form or of the formless; in other words, the five skandhas.

(*h*) *belong to the Unincluded?*

The Paths, and the Fruits of the Paths, and uncompounded element.

[1288, 1289] Which are the states by which

(*a*) *there is a going away?*[2]

The four Paths that are the Unincluded.

(*b*) *there is no going away?*

All states, good, bad and indeterminate, except those four, whether they relate to the worlds of sense, form or

---

[1] This is inadvertently omitted in the printed text.

[2] Niyyānikā. In § 277 *et seq.* the word has been rendered 'whereby there is a going forth and onward,' the Cy. leaving it somewhat vaguely defined, and the context, both in that connexion and this, showing that the expression imports rather the quest of the Ideal than its attainment. Here the Cy. is briefer and more emphatic (Asl. 50). The word is said to signify, 'They, cutting off the root of re-birth and making Nirvana their object, go down from (niyyanti) that round of transmigration.' The good states included under the opposite category will be those static stages of attainment in the upward progress termed the Fruits of the Paths.

the formless, or to the life that is Unincluded; in other words, the four skandhas; all form also, and uncompounded element.

[1290, 1291] Which are the states that are

(*a*) *fixed in their consequences?*[1]

The five acts that have immediate results, and those wrong views that are fixed in their consequences; the four Paths also that are the Unincluded.

(*b*) *not fixed in their consequences?*

Answer as in § 1289.

[1292, 1293] Which are the states that have

(*a*) *something beyond?*[2]

Co-Intoxicant states, good, bad and indeterminate, whether they relate to the worlds of sense, of form, or of the formless; in other words, the five skandhas.

(*b*) *no 'beyond'?*

The four Paths that are the Unincluded, and the Fruits of the Paths, and uncompounded element.

[1294, 1295] Which are the states that are

(*a*) *concomitant with war?*[3]

---

[1] See §§ 1028-1030.

[2] Sa-uttarā=capable of transcending, of rejecting self (or soul). Asl. 50. The term is applied to cittaṃ in D. i. 80. In the an-uttarā dhammā this transcending has been accomplished.

[3] Saraṇā, 'an equivalent for those passions, etc., overcome by which beings in divers ways incur weeping and misery' . . . '=together with fightings' (saha raṇehi). Asl. 50. 'Dulness associated with lust is co-warring (saraṇo) with lust, or, associated with hate, is co-warring with hate.' Asl. 388. One is reminded of the Christian parallel of 'fleshly lusts which war against the soul' and of τῶν ἡδονῶν τῶν στρατευομένων ἐν τοῖς μέλεσιν ὑμῶν, although the concomitance in assault is in this case not emphasized. In the Therīgāthā Subhā turns the tables—'wars a good warfare'—by fighting against the sensual desires hostile to her progress (vv. 358, 360).

The three roots of bad (karma): lust, hate and dulness —and the Corruptions united with them; the four skandhas associated with them; the action, bodily, vocal and mental, springing from them.

(*b*) *not concomitant with war?*

Good, bad and indeterminate states, whether they relate to the worlds of sense, form or the formless, or to the life that is Unincluded; in other words, the four skandhas; all form also, and uncompounded element.

[*PART II.*

The Suttanta Pairs of Terms (suttantika-dukaṃ).][1]

[1296, 1297] Which are the states that

(*a*) *partake of wisdom?*[2]

States which are the associates of wisdom.

(*b*) *partake of ignorance?*[3]

States which are the associates of ignorance.

[1298, 1299] Which are the states that have

(*a*) *the likeness of lightning?*[4]

---

[1] This title is discussed in my Introduction.

[2] Vījjābhāgino, *i.e.*, "they (the dhammā) partake (bhajanti) of wisdom by way of association with it, they *versantur* (vattanti) as parts or divisions of wisdom" (Asl. 50). Of the eight modes of Buddhist vijjā, viz.: knowledge born of insight (vipassanañāṇaṃ), the potency (iddhi) of the 'mental image,' and the six forms of intuition (abhiññā)—the first only is here referred to (*cf.* D. i., p. 76 *et seq.*, and Childers, *s.vv.*). The reader will remember that vijjā is a term borrowed by Buddhist ethics from Brahmanic doctrine. *Cf.* the expression tisso vijjā, p. 358. It is almost equivalent to our 'lore.' Six states are in the Anguttara (iii. 334) said to be vijjā-bhāgiyā.

[3] Ignorance respecting the Four Truths. Asl. 51.

[4] This and the following simile are gone into at some length (Asl. 388), as follows: Stage 1. The traveller sets out in the gloom. 2. He loses his way. 3. Lightning flashes out and illumines. 4. The road is made plain again. So to the 'noble' disciple there is: (1) the inception of insight making for the first (second or third) Paths; (2) the obliteration of truth by darkness; (3) the glory of

The science[1] of the three lowest of the Noble Paths.

(*b*) *the likeness of the thunderbolt ?*

The science of the topmost Path, the Path of Arahatship.

[1300, 1301] Which are the states that are

(*a*) *foolish ?*[2]

Unconscientiousness and disregard of blame. Besides, all bad states are foolish.

(*b*) *discreet ?*

Conscientiousness and fear of blame. Besides, all good states are discreet.

[1302, 1303] Which are the states that are

(*a*) *dark ?*[3]

Unconscientiousness and disregard of blame. Besides, all bad states are dark.

(*b*) *bright ?*

Conscientiousness and fear of blame. Besides, all good states are bright.

---

the Path is revealed; (4) the Four Truths are made plain. But in the thunderbolt of the might of Arahatship won we get the simile of (*a*) an all-penetrating power, (*b*) the mystery of its coming. *Cf.* that of the wind as applied to Regeneration, John iii. 8.

[1] Paññā, elsewhere rendered 'wisdom.' See § 17 and *cf.* n. 3. 'Science' is here to be understood, not so much in its modern sense of organized knowledge and organized methods of investigation and verification for the attaining and establishing that knowledge, as in the Platonic and Aristotelian sense of ἐπιστήμη, or the intellectual antithesis to *opinion*.

[2] Bālā, its opposite being paṇḍitā, which partakes of paññā. See § 16, where the substantival form, paṇḍiccaṃ, is rendered 'erudition,' and paraphrased (Asl. 147) as paṇḍitassa bhāvo, the state of a *wise* person, one who has discernment, discretion, one who has 'chosen that good part' as contrasted with the 'average sensual person' or foolish youth. With the answers *cf.* §§ 30, 31.

[3] On kaṇhā and sukkā, used with ethical significance, see M. i., 389; Dhp., ver. 87; Mil. 200. (*Cf.* 'Questions of King Milinda,' i. 284, n. 2.)

[1304, 1305] Which are the states that

(*a*) *conduce to remorse?*[1]

Misconduct in act, word and thought. Besides, all bad states conduce to remorse.

(*b*) *do not conduce to remorse?*

Good conduct in act, word and thought. Besides, no good states conduce to remorse.

[1306] Which are the states that are synonymous?[2]

---

[1] Tapaniyā. Whereas we, in 'remorse,' bring into relief the 'ayen*bite* of inwyt,' the Buddhist term refers to the flush of heat when the deed ill done is realized as such.

[2] This and the subjects of the two following questions are adhivacanā, nirutti and paññatti respectively. The three are said (Asl. 51) to 'converge in meaning' (atthato ninnakaraṇā), though their form is diverse. In the phrase 'An increaser of luck is an increaser of wealth' the terms are mutually delimitated. This is adhivacanaṃ. . . . In the phrase 'They construct (or combine, abhisankharonti), brethren, and are therefore "syntheses,"' there is a statement of fact together with the cause, as in discourse (abhilāpā). . . . In the phrase 'the ratiocination, conception, disposition [of the mind]' (see above, § 7), something is set out on this wise or that; and this is paññatti.

It seems inferable from the foregoing that by adhivacanaṃ a simple equipollence of terms is to be effected. 'Is' or 'are,' in translating, must be understood simply as =, and not as implying inclusion under a more general notion. The word occurs at every turn in the Cy., and has usually been rendered, in these footnotes, 'equivalent to.' *Cf.* a good instance in Jāt. i. 117; Div. 491.

The second example and the comment adumbrate what we mean by explanation. But in the absence of the context it is not easy to gather much respecting paññatti from the third passage cited. Coming to the answer common to all three questions, the Cy. instances as the things which are classed (sankhā), designated (samaññā), expressed, and current (vohāro) the names 'I,' 'another,'

That which is an enumeration, that which is a designation, an expression, a current term, a name, a denomination, the assigning of a name, an interpretation, a distinctive mark of discourse on this or that state.

[1306*a*] All states are processes of synonymous nomenclature.

[1307] Which are the states that are interpretative?
Answer as in § 1306.
[1307*a*] All states are processes of interpretation.

[1308] Which are the states that are expressions?
Answer as in § 1306.
[1308*a*] All states are processes of expression.

In this connexion,
[1309] *What is name?*[1]

'a man,' 'cattle,' 'Tisso,' 'a bed,' 'a house,' etc. *Name* is fourfold from the point of view of the grounds on which it is bestowed, viz.: (1) given by general consent on a special occasion (sāmañña-nāmaṃ), *e.g.*, that of the first King Mahāsammato; (2) given because of a personal quality (guṇa-nāmaṃ), *e.g.*, versed-in-the-Vinaya; (3) given because of a private wish or fancy (kittima-nāmaṃ), *e.g.*, naming of an infant; (4) not given; of primeval origin; primordially fortuitous (opapātika-nāmaṃ), *e.g.*, 'moon,' 'earth,' etc. See further § 1309, n.

Processes of nomenclature, etc.=adhivacanapathā, etc.

There is no being, no compound, concludes the Commentator, that is not somehow nameable. The very trees in desert and hill country will be named by country-folk. And if they admit to not knowing the name of any one kind, it will get the name of the 'nameless.' *Cf.* our *os innominatum*, or the Pic Sans-nom, and the like.

'Distinctive mark' is vyañjanaṃ.

[1] Here the Cy. makes use of its foregoing classification of name-kinds to show under which head to rank nāma when distinguished from rūpa. Nāma must, namely, be understood as opapātika-name, that is, all its constituents

The four skandhas and uncompounded element.

[1310] What is form?

The four great phenomena and the form which is derived from them.[1]

[1311] What is ignorance?

Answer as for 'dulness,' § 390 (*omitting* 'on that occasion').[2]

[1312] What is the craving for renewed existence?

Answer as for the 'Fetter of the passion for renewed existence,' § 1120.

[1313] What is speculative opinion about renewed existence?

Theories that both soul and world will be re-born, etc.

[1314] What is speculative opinion about existence not being renewed?

Theories that both soul and world will not be re-born, etc.

---

must be so understood. Feeling, *e.g.*, when it arises, is not named on the grounds on which a new individual, or an 'artificial kind'—table, etc.—might be named. 'One has not to take a name for it, saying, "Be thou called feeling!" The name has arisen together with it' (p. 392).

'Uncompounded element' is here spoken of again a Nirvana. *Ibid.* See above, p. 166, n. 1.

[1] *Cf.* § 584. The more concise form of question: tattha katamaṃ . . . is now sustained till the end. Hitherto it has only been used to cross-question the student on the details of a given answer, on 'name,' for instance, as part of the contents of the preceding answer. Hence the translation of tattha by 'in this connexion' (whatever the term in question may mean elsewhere). It is not clear, however, what is the force of tattha in these last fifty-seven questions, the greater part of the subjects not having occurred in the foregoing part of the manual.

[2] This pair of questions 'is included to show' how the mass of views in the following pairs is 'an upgrowth from the root of the Round of Re-birth.' Asl. 392.

[1315] What is the sort of speculation known as Eternalism?

That both soul and world are eternal, etc.

[1316] What is the sort of speculation known as Annihilation?

That both soul and world will be dissolved, etc.

[1317] What is the sort of speculation known as the Finite Theory . . . [1318] the Infinite Theory?

That both soul and world are finite . . . infinite, etc.

[1319] What is the sort of speculation known as the Theory of Origins . . . [1320] the Theory of the Hereafter?

Theories concerning the ultimate past . . . concerning futurity.

All this sort of opinion, walking in opinion, jungle of opinion, wilderness of opinion, puppet-show of opinion, scuffling of opinion, the Fetter of opinion, the grip and tenacity of it, the inclination towards it, the being infected by it, this by-path, wrong road, wrongness, this 'fording-place,' this shiftiness of grasp—this is what is called speculative opinion about renewed existence, and the rest.[1]

[1321] What is unconscientiousness? . . . [1322] disregard of blame?

Answers as for the ninth and tenth 'bases of corruption,' §§ 1238, 1239.

---

[1] This, the Diṭṭhi-formula (see §§ 381, 1099), is appended as well to each of the foregoing answers on speculative opinions. Of these, the first two (bhava and vibhava) are, in the Cy. (p. 392), connected with the next two respectively (*cf.* § 1099). All the eight are enumerated and discussed in the Brahmajāla Sutta. D. i. 13-40. The Cy. itself refers to this Sutta in connexion with the last two theories. See also 'Dialogues of the Buddha,' i. 26, n. 3.

[1323] What is conscientiousness?

The feeling of conscientious scruple when scruples ought to be felt, conscientious scruple at attaining to bad and evil states.

[1324] What is the fear of blame?

The sense of guilt where a sense of guilt ought to be felt, a sense of guilt at attaining to bad and evil states.[1]

[1325] What is contumacy?[2]

The being surly, refractious, contumacious when that which is in accordance with the Law has been said, contrariness, captiousness, want of regard, of consideration, of reverence, of deference.[3]

[1326] What is friendship with evil?

To follow after, to frequent the company of, and associate with,[4] such persons as are unbelievers, immoral, uneducated, mean-spirited[5] and witless;[6] to resort to and consort with

---

[1] See §§ 30, 31.

[2] Dovacassatā. For 'surly' the Cy. (p. 393) and K. read dovacassāyaṃ.

[3] The three first terms in the answer are in the original simply different forms of the same abstract noun, viz.: dovacassāyaṃ, dovacassiyaṃ, dovacassatā. The fourth term is literally 'taking the opposite side.' The fifth is literally 'gratification in antagonism.' The last is described as due to a lack of the habit of placing others before one's self. Asl. 393. The term in question the Cy. finally dismisses with the remark that, if persisted in in the foregoing fashion, it involves the four skandhas, especially that of syntheses. So for the complex generalizations in the following questions. They are not relatively simple states involving one skandha only. (The editing in the Cy. is here again very unfortunate.)

[4] Sevanā, nisevanā, saṃsevanā. The prefixes, according to the Cy., merely act as augmentatives.

[5] Maccharino; addicted to the five sorts of meanness. Asl. 394. See § 1122, n.

[6] Duppaññā.

them, to be devoted to them, enthusiastic about them,[1] and entangled with them.[2]

[1327] What is suavity?

The being gentle, tractable, amenable[3] when that which is in accordance with the Law has been said, the refraining from contradiction and from captiousness; the showing regard and consideration,[4] reverence and deference.

[1328] What is friendship with good?

To follow after, frequent the company of, and associate with, such persons as are believers, virtuous, well educated, generous and intellectual; to resort to and consort with them, to be devoted to them, enthusiastic about them, mixed up with them.

[1329-1332] What is skill in

(*a*) the Offences?
(*b*) restoration from the Offences?
(*c*) the Attainments?
(*d*) recovery from the Attainments?

That skill which is science, understanding, search, research, etc.,[5] when applied to

---

[1] Bhajana, sambhajanā, bhatti, sambhatti; all meaning originally 'forming a part of,' 'belonging to.' But the two former are paraphrased by upasankamanā. In the sense of devotion bhatti does not, I believe, occur in the Nikāyas. Perhaps its oldest appearance with this import is in Jāt. v. 340—where the Cy. gives as equivalent sineho—and in the Svet. Upanishad 6. 23.

[2] Taṃ sampavaṇkatā (so K. and the Cy.), *i.e.*, entanglement; lit., hooked along with them—with those persons, both in thought and deed. Asl. 394.

[3] Sovacassāyaṃ (*sic lege*), sovacassiyaṃ, sovacassatā.

[4] Ādariyaṃ, ādaratā; omitted in the text, but supplied in K. *Cf.* § 1325.

[5] The passage elided here and in the following sections is no doubt that in which science (paññā) is described, § 16 and *passim*. On 'skill' or 'proficiency' (kusalatā) see Introduction viii., on 'good.'

(*a*) the Offences termed the Five Groups of Offences and the Seven Groups of Offences;[1]
(*b*) restoration from [the effects of] those Offences;[2]
(*c*) a case of Attainment[3] where 'conception works and thought discursive,' a case of Attainment 'wherein is no working of conception, but only of thought discursive,' a case of Attainment 'void of the working of conception and of thought discursive';
(*d*) recovery from those Attainments.[4]

---

[1] That is, the group of 'Āpatti's termed Parājika, Saṇghādisesa, Pācittiya, Pāṭidesanīya and Dukkaṭa offences, and the group which, besides these, includes Thullaccaya and Dubbhāsita offences. Asl. 394; *cf.* Vin. v. 91. The scientific procedure is described in the Cy. as -pariccheda-jānana-paññā.

[2] Āpatti-vuṭṭhāna, or rising up from an offence. Buddhaghosa does not in this connexion explain the term, but in his Cy. on the passage, found in nearly identical words at Vin. iii. 112, and iv. 225 (which Cy. is found in Minayeff, Pāt. 69), he uses vuṭṭhāna as a general term covering all the three methods (parivāsa, mānatta, abbhāṇa) of expiation of, and release from, an offence committed by a member of the Order. *Cf.* Childers, *s.v.* sanghādiseso; Vin. v. 118. See also *infra*, § 1332.

[3] The Samāpattis, or various stages of self-concentration, include the Jhānas—as here—and other forms of samādhi, all pre-Buddhistic and all utilized in the body of Buddhist doctrine and culture. It is noteworthy that they are not here referred to as only eight in number—see Childers, *s.v.* (for that matter, neither do they find a place in the Aṭṭhaka-nipāta of the Anguttara). Neither is it clear that the three Samāpattis quoted in the answer coincide in all respects with the first three stages of *five*-fold Jhāna. If they do, and if we are to assume that the term includes more than those three stages, then, by Subhūti's inclusion of four Vimokhas, this would give us *nine* samāpattis. Again, in M. i. 301, a *fifth* Vimokha—the last—is spoken of as a Samāpatti, this bringing the number up to ten. *Cf.* M. i. 398-400.

[4] The kind of ability in emerging from (lit., rising out

[1333] What is proficiency in the Elements?[1]

That proficiency which is science, understanding, search, research, etc., when applied to the eighteen elements, viz.: sight, visual object and visual cognition, hearing, sound and auditory cognition, smell, odour and olfactory cognition, taste, sapid object and gustatory cognition, body-sensibility, the tangible and tactile cognition, mind, mental object and representative cognition.

[1334] What is proficiency in attention?[2]

That proficiency in attention which is science, understanding, etc., when applied to those elements.

[1335] What is skill in the spheres?[3]

That skill which is science, understanding, etc., when applied to the twelve spheres, namely, sight and visual form, hearing and sound, smell and odorous object, taste and sapid object, body-sensibility and the tangible, mind and mental object.[4]

---

of -vuṭṭhāṇa; see *supra*, § 1330) one or another kind of samādhi is, by the Cy., specified as a predetermination of the time when the subject wished to arouse himself, and the carrying out of this act of will—a time stated in terms of the motions of celestial bodies. 'When the moon, sun, constellations have gone to such and such a position I shall awake.' See, on this use of vuṭṭhāna, M. i. 302; A. iii. 311; S. iii. 270. On the modes of Jhāna here specified, see *supra*, § 160 *et seq.* Skill in the Attainment (samāpatti) itself is explained as the science of effecting discernment of the appanā or central concept (in Jhāna) as well as of the parikamma or preliminaries.

[1] Dhātuyo. The skill in this case is said to comprise acquisition, attention, hearing and remembering (instruction being entirely oral) and discrimination. Asl. 395.

[2] See p. 5, n. 1. [3] See § 597 *et seq.*

[4] In the last three modes of ability six factors common to all are distinguished: acquisition, attention, hearing, comparison (lit., measuring), penetration, contemplation. Of these, all but the fifth are exercised on mundane objects of thought; penetration is concerned with supramundane matters; attention and comparison can be exercised about

[1336] What is skill in the 'Conditioned Geneses'?

Science, understanding, etc., when applied to the formula: 'The syntheses come to pass because of ignorance; cognition comes to pass because of syntheses; name and form come to pass because of cognition; the sixfold sphere comes to pass because of name and form; contact comes to pass because of the sixfold sphere, feeling because of contact, craving because of feeling, grasping because of craving, renewed existence because of grasping, birth because of renewed existence, old age and death, grief, lamentation, distress, melancholy and despair come to pass because of birth. Such is the uprising of this whole mass of Ill.'[1]

[1337, 1338] What is skill in affirming . . . in negating [causal conjuncture]?

Science, understanding, etc., when applied to discerning that, in a given conjuncture, certain states are . . . are not, the cause and conditions of certain other states.[2]

[1339] What is upright?

Uprightness, without deflexion, twist, or crookedness.

[1340] What is soft?

That which is plasticity, gentleness, smoothness, pliancy, lowliness of heart.[3]

---

a mixture of both spheres of thought. Asl. 395. (To get this or any meaning out of the passage in question some emendation of the Cy. as edited has been necessary.)

[1] On this famous formula the Cy. merely remarks that 'it will appear in the Vibhanga on the Paṭiccasamuppāda.' Asl. 395.

[2] This species of skill (thāṇakusalatā, atthāṇakusalatā) constituted one of the Ten Powers of the Buddha. See M. i. 69. The Cy. (p. 395) takes for illustration sense-cognition as a series of specific results from specific processes; also cause and effect in the vegetable kingdom.

[3] Ajjavo and maddavo, the terms in this and the foregoing question, are synonymous with uj(j)ukatā and

[1341] What is patience?

That patience which is long-suffering, compliance, absence of rudeness and abruptness, complacency of heart.[1]

[1342] What is temperance?

That which is the absence of excess in deed, in word, and in deed and word together.[2]

Besides, all moral self-restraint is temperance.

[1343] What is amity?[3]

When all such speech as is insolent,[4] disagreeable, grating, harsh to others, vituperative to others, bordering

---

mudutā, §§ 50, 51, 44, 45. The one additional term—the last—is paraphrased as 'absence of conceit.' Asl. 395.

[1] Patience (khantī) is one of the ten Paramitās. Jāt. i., pp. 22, 23. See also A. iii. 254, 255. The last three synonyms are the opposites of the last three synonyms of 'hate.' See *supra*, §§ 418, 1060. Ajjavo, javano, maddavo, khantī and soraccaṃ are, in A. iii. 248, given as the dhammā of a thoroughbred horse.

[2] Temperance (soraccaṃ) is defined as 'to be well on the hither side of wickedness,' to avoid transgression in the three kinds in deed, in the four kinds in speech and in one's mode of livelihood. See Rhys Davids, 'Manual of Buddhism,' p. 142. The three transgressions of the mind are omitted, hence soraccaṃ applies apparently only to the self-expression of the individual. Asl. 396.

[3] Sākhalyaṃ, paraphrased by sammodaka and mudu. *Ibid.* *Cf.* the usual formula for the exchange of courtesies on greeting, *e.g.*, M. i. 16.

[4] Aṇḍakā. This and the following terms occur in M. i. 286. See Morris's Notes, J. P. T. S., 1884, 1886, 1889. Buddhaghosa's comment obviates the necessity either for Kern's hypothesis that the word, when applied to speech, should be read as kaṇḍaka, or for that of Morris, that it should be read as caṇḍaka. He says (Asl. 396): Just as in a defective (sadose) tree bosses (aṇḍakāni; excrescences, warts) protrude, so through faultiness, by words of bragging and insolence, are swellings (aṇḍakā) produced.

'Disagreeable' (asātā) is omitted in the M. i. 286.

upon anger, not conducive to concentration, is put away, and when all such speech as is innocuous,[1] pleasant to the ear,[2] affectionate, such as goes to the heart, is urbane,[3] sweet and acceptable to people generally—when speech of this sort is spoken—polished, friendly and gentle language —this is what is called amity.

[1344] What is courtesy?

The two forms of courtesy: hospitality towards bodily needs and considerateness in matters of doctrine. When anyone shows courtesy it is in one or other of these two forms.[4]

[1345] What is it to have the door of the faculties unguarded?[5]

'Grating'=kakkasā=(Asl. *ibid.*) pūtikā. By a somewhat forced figure grating or rasping speech is compared to the disagreeable sensation in the ear (sotaṃ not kaṇṇā!) by the entrance of the crumbling pulverous tissue of a rotten tree. 'Vituperative,' etc. (parābhisajjanī); as it were, a lurking branch of barbed thorns wounding the limbs and obstructing passage. *Ibid.*

[1] Innocuous=neḷā=niddosā. Asl. 397.

[2] *I.e.*, by varied sweetness.

[3] Porī, *i.e.*, town-conversation, either because it is full of good points (guṇa), or used by persons of breeding, or simply urban. For town-dwellers use fitting terms, calling a father a father and a brother a brother. *Ibid.*

[4] Paṭisanthāro, both āmisena and dhammena, is discussed at length by Buddhaghosa (Asl. 397-399). He takes, as usual, the etymology of the term—a spreading out or diffusion—and shows it as a covering or closing, through kindness and generosity, of the gap there may be between the having of the giver and the recipient of his attentions. Both are supposed to be members of the Order, and many of the hospitable and polite ministrations described occur in Vin. ii. 210, 211. See also Mil. 409.

[5] Aguttadvāratā. This and the contrary attitude in § 1347 constitute an important formula in Buddhist doctrine, and occur in D. i. 70, M. i. 180, 269, etc. It is also quoted K.V. 426, 464.

When a certain individual[1] sees an object with the eye[2] he is entranced with the general appearance, or in the details of it.[3] He does not set himself to restrain that which might give occasion for wicked states, covetous, dejected, to flow in over him, were he to dwell unrestrained as to the sense of sight. He keeps no watch over his faculty of sight, nor does he attain to mastery over it. And so in like manner when he hears a sound with the ear . . . smells an odour with the nose . . . tastes a sapid with the tongue . . . feels a tangible with the body . . . recognises a mental object with the mind, he is entranced with the general appearance and in the details of it. He does not set himself to restrain that which might give occasion for wicked states, covetous, dejected, to flow in over him, were he to dwell unrestrained as to the mental faculty. He keeps no watch over the mental faculty, nor does he attain to mastery over it. That these six faculties should be thus

---

[1] K. omits puggalo, given in the printed text. The latter omits it in the corresponding answer, § 1347.

[2] This is a passage naturally calling for psychological qualification from the Commentator (Asl. 399, 400). '"Eye" stands here for the total efficient cause (kārana-vasena), namely, for that visual cognition which is the generally accepted form-seeing capacity. As the Ancients have said: The eye does not see form, not being of the nature of intellect (cittaṃ); the intellect, not being of the nature of eye, does not see form (the Cy. has here been wrongly punctuated). One sees with the sense-embodied mind impingeing on the 'door-object' (dvārārammaṇe saṃghaṭṭanena pasādavatthukena cittena passati), that is, with the aggregate organism, or apparatus, as when we say, "he shoots with the bow."'

[3] On nimittagāhī and anuvyañjana-gāhi, see notes relating precisely to this passage in D. i. 70, in 'Dialogues of the Buddha,' i. 80. The former term is, in the Atthasālinī, defined as the act of one who, not content with simply beholding what is attractive and so forth, or what is characteristically female or male, grasps at it with passionate desire.

unguarded, untended, unwatched over, unrestrained, is what is called having the door of the faculties unguarded.

[1346] What is immoderation in diet?[1]

When anyone, through carelessness and without judgment, takes food[2] for purposes of sport,[3] sensual excess, personal charm and adornment, his insatiableness, immoderation, and want of judgment are what is called immoderation in diet.

[1347] What is it to have the doors of the faculties guarded?

When a certain individual sees an object with the eye he is not entranced with the general appearance or the details of it. He sets himself to restrain that which might give occasion for wicked states, covetous, dejected, to flow in over him, were he to dwell unrestrained as to the sense of sight. He keeps watch over this faculty of sight, and attains to mastery over it. And so in like manner, when he hears a sound with the ear . . . smells an odour with the nose . . . tastes a sapid with the tongue . . . feels a tangible with the body . . . recognises an idea with the mind, he is not entranced with the general appearance and the details of it. He sets himself to restrain that which might give occasion for wicked states, covetous, dejected, to flow in over him, were he to dwell unrestrained as to the mental faculty. He keeps watch over the mental faculty, and attains to mastery over it. That these six faculties should be thus guarded, tended, watched over,

---

[1] Bhojane amattaññutā = a sustained indulging without reflection . . . the ignoring of measure or bounds therein. Asl. 402.

[2] Āhāraṃ 'both edible and potable.' Asl. 401.

[3] Davāya, etc. That is to say, that he may be able to dance or do acrobatic feats, etc. Or like kings and courtiers who feed to swell their 'pride of life' and manhood, etc. Asl. 402, 403.

restrained, is what is called having the doors of the faculties guarded.

[1348] What is moderation in diet?

When anyone takes food with reflection and judgment, not for purposes of sport, excess, personal charm and attractions, but so as to suffice for the sustenance and preservation of the body, for allaying the pangs [of hunger][1] and for aiding the practice of the higher life,[2] and thinking the while, 'I shall subdue that which I have been feeling and shall cause no new feeling to arise,[3] and maintenance shall be mine, blamelessness also and comfort'—this content, moderation, judgment in diet is what is called moderation in diet.

[1349] What is forgetfulness?[4]

---

[1] Vihiṃsūparatiyā. Vihiṃsā=abhutta-paccayā uppajjanaka-khudā. Asl. 403.

[2] Brahmacariyānuggahāya.

[3] This formula (as Trenckner terms it, 'Pāli Misc.,' 74) of abstemious living occurs M. i. 355; S. iv. 104, 176, etc.; also Mil. 367. The comments in the Asl. reveal a more specific and less sublime interpretation of the vedanā in question than is taken by the translator of the last-named passage (Rhys Davids, 'Questions of King Milinda,' ii. 231). According to the former, purāṇañ ca vedanaṃ is simply that due to one's not having dined, and navañ ca vedanaṃ to one's having dined too much, or to one's having dined. Asl. 403, 404. Psychologically then, the ideal state of one relieved of the craving of appetite would seem to be, not the positive sensations of surfeit or of having well dined, but the relatively negative state of not-hungry, not-thirsty. Under 'comfort' (phāsuvihāro = bhojānisaṃso) gourmands, who fail to acquire the same, are described, with some gusto, under five current sobriquets —'Hold, waistcoat!' 'Gyrator' (because unable to rise after eating), etc. Abstemious procedure is also categorized otherwise and in detail. Asl. 404.

[4] In this answer (describing muṭṭhasaccaṃ) the text requires some emendation. Anussati should be asati, and the privative *a* should of course be dropped in a-pilāpanatā, a-sammussanatā. K. reads (here only)

Unmindfulness, lapse of memory, non-recollection, non-remembrance, not bearing in mind, superficiality, oblivion.

[1350] What is lack of intelligence?

Answer as for 'ignorance' *or* 'dulness,' § 1311, etc.

[1351] What is mindfulness?

Answer as in § 14, *omitting* 'on that occasion.'[1]

[1352] What is intelligence?

Answer as for 'wisdom' *or* 'science,' § 16. *And see* § 53.

[1353] What is the power of computation?[2]

Answer as for 'wisdom,' § 16.

[1354] What is the power of cultivation?

That which is the pursuing, the cultivating, the multiplying of good states.

Moreover, the seven factors in the Great Awakening[3] are the power of cultivation.

[1355] What is composure?

Answer as for 'quiet,' §§ 11, 54.[4]

[1356] What is insight?

Answer as for 'insight' *and* 'wisdom,' §§ 55, 16.

---

pamussanatā—not so the Cy.—and repeats asati after appaṭissati. See § 14 and footnote.

[1] K. reads for asammussanatā, appamussanatā. *Cf.* preceding note.

[2] Paṭisankhānabalaṃ. This is not included in any set of 'powers' enumerated in the present work (*cf.* § 1, etc.), nor does it form part of paññābalaṃ (§ 29). However, it is included in the eight very different kinds of powers given in A. iv. 223, ranking as the specific balaṃ of the erudite or bahussuto. *Cf.* the use of paṭisankhā in Vin. i. 213. In the present connexion it seems as a correlative term to have superseded dassanaṃ (insight); see above, §§ 1002-1012, 1254-1267.

[3] See §§ 285, 287, etc.

[4] In this and the following references the phrase 'on that occasion' must be understood to be omitted.

[1357] What is 'the mark of composure'?[1]
Answer as for 'quiet,' § 1357.
[1358] What is 'the mark of grasp'?
Answer as for 'grasp' *and* 'energy,' §§ 56, 13.

[1359] What is grasp?
Answer as for 'the mark of grasp,' § 1358.
[1360] What is balance?
Answer as for 'balance,' § 57.

[1361] What is moral failure?[2]
Excess in deed, excess in word, excess in both together. Moreover, all immorality is moral failure.
[1362] What is theoretic fallacy?[3]
'There is no such thing as alms, or sacrifice, or offering; there is neither fruit, nor result of good or evil deeds; there is no such thing as this world or the next; there is no such thing as mother, or father, or beings springing into birth without them; there are in the world no recluses or brahmins who have reached the highest point, who have attained the height, who, having understood and realized by themselves alone both this world and the next, make known the same'—all this sort of speculation . . . this is what is called theoretic fallacy. Moreover, all wrong views are theoretic fallacies.

[1363] What is moral progress?
Absence of excess in deed, in word, and in deed and word together.'[4]
[1364] What is progress in theory?
'There is such a thing as alms, sacrifice, and offering; . . . fruit, and the result of good and evil deeds; . . . this

---

[1] Samatha-nimittaṃ. Explained by Taṃ ākāraṃ gahetvā puna pavattetabbassa samathassa nimitta-vasena. Asl. 53.
[2] Sīlavipatti. *Cf.* §§ 1363, 1342.
[3] Diṭṭhivipatti. *Cf.* § 1215.
[4] Sīla-sampadā. *Cf.* § 1342.

world and the next; mother, father and beings springing into birth without them; . . . recluses and brahmins who have reached the highest, who have attained the height, who having understood and realized by themselves alone both this world and the other world, make known the same'—all this sort of science, understanding, etc.[1] . . . this is what is called progress in theory. Moreover, all right views are progress in theory.

[1365] What is purity in morals?

Absence of excess in deed, in word, and in deed and word together.[2]

[1366] What is purity in theory?

Knowledge of the specific nature of Karma;[3] knowledge

---

[1] Continue as in § 16.

[2] *Cf.* § 1363. Purity in theory would seem to indicate perfection relative to progress in theory, while in moral matters a similar distinction does not apparently hold. The Cy. only explains this want of distinction by saying that in § 1363 the sīla of restraint of the Pātimokkha is alluded to, while in § 1365 visuddhi-sīla is spoken of.

[3] K. reads here kammassakataṃ ñāṇaṃ—a curious phrase. Buddhaghosa, to judge by his exposition, reads kamma-ssakata-ñāṇaṃ (Asl. 406, 407) or -ssakatā-, or -ssakataṃ ñānaṃ (Asl. 406). The corresponding adjective to this sakatā or sakataṃ occurs in the passage quoted from the Sutta Pitaka by Nāgasena (Mil. i. 45; *cf.* Rhys Davids' trans., i. 101, n. 1; also Asl. 66), namely, kammassakā (sattā); *i.e.*, according to the translator's view, 'having each their own karma.' As this passage occurs in the yet inedited 135th Sutta of the Majjhima N., the Papañca Sūdanī may prove to have a more lucid commentary on it than that given in the Atthasālinī. The latter is to this effect: [This phrase means] the science of knowing that *this* karma (or action) is sakaṃ, *that* karma is not sakaṃ. In this connexion all bad karma, whether it be done by one's self or by another, is not sakaṃ. How so? Because it destroys utility and creates disutility. But good karma, which has the reverse effect, is named sakaṃ. Just as a man with a full purse in the course of a journey

of the Truths in their due order; the knowledge of him who holds the Path; the knowledge of him who holds the Fruit of the Path.

(i.)[1] The phrase 'Now purity of theory' is equivalent to that science, understanding . . . right theory (views) [*described above*, § 16].

(ii.) In the phrase 'And as the struggle of him who holds certain views,'[2] 'struggle' means that inception of energy etc. [*described above*, § 13].

---

may stop at various cities where festivals are going on and, determining what votive outlay he will make, takes part accordingly in those festivals as his inclination prompts, and safely emerges from the jungle, even so do beings who are established in this knowledge of the sakataṃ of karma, when they have heaped up much karma making for transmigration, safely and at ease attain arahatship, even to the extent of numbers innumerable.

Now if sakaṃ mean here, as it usually does, 'one's own,' that still seems no explanation of the assertion that one's bad actions are not one's own. And how does the parable bear out the assertion?

[1] With the foregoing question and answer the catechism proper of the 'Dhamma Sangaṇi' comes to an end. There follow eleven sundry phrases or terms, not made the subject of any part of the catechism, and appended here in the phraseology of a commentary. They are severally either referred to some reply in the catechism, or briefly expounded, and are probably all culled from the Sutta Pitaka as technicisms of Buddhist ethics. Very possibly they form one connected sentence, giving an eloquent and concise description of the nature of Wisdom and Emancipation. Buddhaghosa has nothing very enlightening on this fraction of ancient commentary included in the text, but promises an explanation of at least the division of the subject of 'agitation' in the Commentary on the 'Vibhanga.'

[2] Yathā diṭṭhissa ca padhānaṃ. It is just possible one should read Yathādiṭṭhissa; K., however, divides the two words. The Cy. merely remarks that the energy put forth is intelligent or scientific, and can be applied either to worldly or to higher things.

(iii.) The phrase 'agitation' implies dread of birth, dread of old age, dread of sickness, dread of death.

(iv.) The phrase 'occasion of agitation' means birth, old age, sickness, death.

(v.) The phrase 'And the earnest struggle of him who is agitated' refers to [the four Right Struggles]:—When a bhikkhu brings forth the desire (*a*) that bad and wicked states which have not arisen should not arise, (*b*) that bad and wicked states which have arisen should be put away, (*c*) that good states which have not arisen should arise, (*d*) that good states which have arisen should stand firm, should not get confused, should be frequently practised, made to abound, cultivated, and perfected—then he uses endeavour, sets energy a-going, reaches forward in thought and struggles.[1]

(vi.) The phrase 'And discontent in good states' means the longing for higher achievement in one who is dissatisfied over the cultivation of good states.[2]

(vii.) The phrase 'And the not shrinking back in the struggle' means the thorough and persevering and unresting performance, the absence of stagnation, the unfaltering volition, the unflinching endurance,[3] the assiduous pursuit, exercise and repetition which attend the cultivation of good states.

---

[1] See A. ii. 15, 16, 74. It will be seen that the four modes of will-culture described on p. 15 of A. ii. as the Sammapadhānāni (and quoted in the Dh. S.) are, on p. 74, termed respectively the Struggles for Self-control, for Renunciation, for Cultivation (or Development) and for Preservation. Yet on p. 16 a different connotation is given to each of these four terms.

[2] This and the next phrase (vii.) occur consecutively in A. i. 50. The progress of sublime discontent in a pious individual from giving small donations to the Order, then greater gifts till he personally enters the Order and finally wins the goal of Arahatship, is briefly described, Asl. 407. The last attainment gives the winner the title of the Greatly Content.

[3] *Cf.* § 13.

(viii.) The phrase 'Wisdom' means the threefold wisdom, namely (*a*) reminiscent knowledge of one's former births, (*b*) knowledge of the relapse and renascence of beings, (*c*) the knowledge that makes an end of the Intoxicants.

(ix.) The phrase 'Emancipation' means the twofold emancipation, namely, (*a*) detachment of thought,[1] and (*b*) Nirvana.[2]

(x.) The phrase 'knowledge in making an end' means the knowledge he has who holds the Path.

(xi.) The phrase 'knowledge in origins' means the knowledge he has who holds the Fruit of the Path.

End of the Division entitled 'Elimination.'

---

[1] Cittassa ca adhimutti=vimutti (emancipation). D. i. 174.

[2] This is, I believe, the only passage in the original Manual where the word occurs. This is interesting in view of the fact that it occurs in what appears to be an appendix of original Commentary, and also that the term occurs so frequently in the old digest which follows in the text. See Appendix I.

APPENDIX I.

The Digest, or Condensed Paraphrase of Book III. (§§ 981-1295), entitled Division of Exposition, or the Elucidation (a t t h u d d h ā r o).

Immediately following the text of the Dhammasangaṇi itself is a supplement of some 230 questions and answers. The questions are verbatim those of the 'Elimination' Division, or Book III., taken in order, but without the cross-questioning on the details of the various lists of ethical factors or defects, such as the varieties of cause (h e t u), or of the 'Intoxicants,' etc. The answers are for the most part more tersely worded than those in Book III., and couched in language more or less different, including several terms that came into technical use after the earliest ages of Buddhism.

No distinctive title is assigned to this supplement in the Manual itself. It is probable that the final announcement 'D h a m m a - s a n g a ṇ i - p p a k a r a ṇ i s a m a t t ā' refers, not to it, but to the entire work. In the 'Atthasālinī,' however (p. 409 *et seq.*), this section is pronounced to be commentary, not text, and is termed the A ṭ ṭ h a k a t h ā-k a ṇ ḍ a ṃ, or expositional division; and in an earlier passage it was termed the fourth V i b h a t t i comprising the a t t h u d d h ā r o (Asl. 6). The tradition is related that it is the work of Sāriputta, and was compiled by him with the object of making clearer the contents of the 'N i k-k h e p a - k a ṇ ḍ a ṃ' (Book III., *i.e.*, virtually the whole Manual) to a pupil who could not otherwise understand it.

This being so, and the answers throwing no new light on

to the subjects discussed, I have not thought it worth while to translate them. At the same time, it seemed advisable to sort out the specific, if not the individual, differences in diction, so that the reader may lose nothing that may prove of any value for the history either of the terms or of the concepts of Buddhism. I have also given translations of a few answers where the very difference in the terms used to obtain a virtually equivalent statement may prove helpful towards understanding the language of the Manual itself.

In respect of Pāli terms used, when there is need of referring collectively to the three modes, or worlds of all rebirth, as well as to that higher life of saintly aspiration, which is not concerned with rebirth, these four are no longer distinctively spoken of as the āvacaraṃ of this or that and the Unincluded, but are simply classed together as 'the four bhūmis.'

Again, 'Nirvana' (nibbānaṃ) invariably replaces the term 'uncompounded element.' See Appendix II.

'Form' replaces 'all form' (see § 983 *passim*), and 'fruits of the life of the recluse' the word 'fruits of the Paths.' (See § 992 *passim*.[1]) The latter variation occurs but once in the Manual itself, viz., at § 1016.[2]

Frequent allusion is now made to those 'types' of good and bad thoughts distinguished and analyzed by Book I. They are spoken of, not as cittāni, but as cittuppādā, or genesis of thought, a term occurring only once in the Manual, viz., as a title. (See above, p. 164.)

The skandhas, so frequently adduced in Book III., are never mentioned.

The term 'co-Intoxicant' (sāsavo), is no longer used except in the analysis of the Intoxicant Group.

The very frequent use of the ablative in -to (when the

---

[1] By an error presumably in the MSS., the printed text has, in § 1597, jhānabalāni for sāmaññaphalāni. *Cf.* K.

[2] Printed above by an error as [1015].

Manual would use a substantival adjective—for instance, kāmāvacara-kusalato instead of kāmāvacaraṃ kusalaṃ—betrays the later idiom. The Manual itself uses this ablative, I believe, but twice, viz., in §§ 1062, 1071: vipākato=as, or by way of, result.

The term kiriyā, so seldom used in the Manual, is now used extremely often.

* * * * * *

Taking now the three questions respecting (*a*) good, (*b*) bad, and (*c*) indeterminate states, with which Book III. (§§ 981-983, and for that matter the Manual itself) opens, we read the following concise replies, taken in order :—

> '(*a*) Good in the four planes (bhummīsu).
> (*b*) The twelve geneses of bad thought.
> (*c*) Result in the four planes; completed indeterminates[1] in the three planes;[2] form also and Nirvana.'

Now, on referring to the analysis of the twelve Types of bad states (Book I., Part I., ch. ii.), it will be seen that these cover the whole question, inasmuch as only one 'plane'—that of sensuous existence—is involved. Good and indeterminate dhammas, on the other hand, involve all four planes, and cannot be answered simply in terms of the eight types of good thoughts (ch. i.) in the one case, nor of thought genesis in the other.

* * * * * *

The next triad of questions (Book III., §§ 984-986) is answered in language which occurs at only one other passage in the whole work (§ 1268 *et seq.*), and which is of a vagueness that makes any equivalent rendering welcome.

'States associated with easeful feeling' :—

'The four geneses of thought accompanied by happiness, which belong to good (karma) in the sensuous universe. The four, which belong to bad (karma). The six, which

---

[1] Kiriyāvyākataṃ. See Introduction viii.

[2] *I.e.*, excluding that of sense (see Book I., Part III., ch. ii.).

belong to the results of good (karma) in the sensuous universe, as well as the five belonging to completed thought.[1] The threefold and fourfold[2] Jhāna relating to the heavens of Form whether it arise as good (karma), result (of good karma), or as a completed state. The threefold and fourfold Jhāna relating to the Higher Ideal, whether it arise as good (karma) or as result. The easeful feeling herewith arisen is not reckoned in.'

'States associated with distressful feeling':—

'The two geneses of thought which are accompanied by melancholy. Cognition of body, which is accompanied by distress. The distressful feeling herewith arisen is not reckoned in.'

'States associated with neutral feeling':—

'The four geneses of thought accompanied by disinterestedness, which belong to good (karma) in the sensuous universe. The six, which belong to bad (karma). The ten, which belong to the results of good (karma) in the sensuous universe.[3] The six, which belong to the results of bad (karma).[4] The six, which belong to completed thought.[5] The fourth Jhāna, relating to the heavens of Form, whether it arise as good (karma), result (of good karma), or as a completed state. The four Jhānas connected with Formless Existence,[6] whether they arise as good (karma), result (of good karma), or as completed states. The Fourth Jhāna relating to the Higher Ideal, whether it arise as good (karma), or as result (of good karma). The neutral feeling herewith arisen is not reckoned in.

'It is not proper to say that these three modes of feeling

---

[1] K. reads kāmāvacara-kusalassa vipākato ca kiriyato ca pañca. But reference to §§ 469 and 568 shows that the analysis gives six and five respectively.

[2] Excluding the highest Jhāna, as incompatible with 'easeful feeling.'

[3] Read kāmāvacara-kusalassa.

[4] Four in § 556, one in § 562, one in § 564.

[5] Five in § 566, one in § 574.

[6] For arūpāvacarā read āruppā. P. 71 *et seq.*

are associated either with themselves, or with form, or with Nirvana.'

* * * * * *

The answers to questions §§ 1007-1012 are (with the exception of that to 1009) more precise than those there given :—

'States which may be put away by insight':—

'The four geneses of thought which are associated with views and opinions, the genesis of thought which is accompanied by perplexity.'

'States which may be put away by culture [1007]':—

'The genesis of thought which is accompanied by excitement.

'The four geneses of thought which are accompanied by lust, but disconnected with views and opinions, also the two geneses of thought which are accompanied by melancholy :—these states may be put away either by insight or by culture.'

'States which may be put away neither by insight nor by culture':—

'Good in the four planes; result in the four planes; completed indeterminates in three planes; form also, and Nirvana.'

States the causes of which may be put away by insight, by culture, or by neither are described in the same terms. M o h o (dulness), however, is inexplicitly named as something the cause of which can be put away by neither.

* * * * * *

Questions 1022-1024 are answered in quite other terms than those there used :—

(*a*) 'States having limited objects of thought':—

'All result of sensuous existence; ideation that is completed action; representative cognition that is completed action but not free of causes,[1] and is accompanied by happiness.'

(*b*) 'States having objects of thought of wider scope':—

'The sphere of infinite intellect; the sphere where there

[1] Kiriyā-hetukā manoviññāṇadhātu.

is neither perception nor non-perception.' (*Cf.* §§ 267, 268.)

(*c*) 'States having infinite objects of thought:'—

'The four Paths that are the Unincluded, and the four Fruits of the life of the recluse.'

'The four geneses of thought which are disconnected with knowledge and belong to good (karma) in the universe of sense, also the four geneses of thought disconnected with knowledge which are completed acts, and all bad (karma):—these states may be (*a*) or (*b*), but not (*c*), and may not be termed both (*a*) and (*b*).

'[Again,] the four geneses of thought which are associated with knowledge and belong to good (karma) in the universe of sense, the four geneses of completed thoughts which are associated with knowledge, the Fourth Jhāna relating to the universe of form, whether it arise as good (karma), or as completed thought, and the representative cognition which is completed and free from the causes and is accompanied by disinterestedness:—these states may be (*a*), or (*b*), or (*c*), but it is not proper to call them (*a*) and (*b*) and (*c*).

'[Lastly] the threefold and fourfold Jhāna relating to the heavens of Form, whether it arise as good (karma), or as result, or as completed thought, the results of Fourth Jhāna, and the two first Jhānas connected with Formless existence, viz., the spheres of Infinite Space and of Infinite Nothingness:—these states it is not proper to call (*a*) and (*b*) and (*c*).

Form and Nirvana are without objects of thought.'

* * * * * *

One more group deserves quoting as giving answers not in terms of the subject inquired into. This is the two triads corresponding to §§ 1044-1049. The Aṭṭhakathā has the following:

'States which are

(*a*) personal (or subjective),

(*b*) external,

(*c*) personal-external.'

'With the exception of form which is not bound up with

faculties,[1] all states may be subjective or external or subjective-external. Form which is not bound up with faculties, and Nirvana are both external.'

'States which have

(*a*) a subjective object of thought,

(*b*) an external object of thought,

(*c*) a subjective-external object of thought':—

'(*a*) The sphere of infinite intellection and the sphere where there is neither perception nor non-perception.

'(*b*) The threefold and fourfold Jhāna relating to the heavens of Form, whether it arise as good (karma), as result (of good karma), or as completed thought, also results of Fourth Jhāna, the sphere of infinite space, the four Paths that are the Unincluded and the four Fruits of the life of the recluse:— —these states have an external object of thought.

'Excepting form, states, good, bad, and indeterminate relating to the sensuous universe, and the Fourth Jhāna relating to the heavens of Form, whether it arise as good (karma), or as completed thought:— all these may be either (*a*), (*b*), or (*c*).

'But it is not proper to say that the sphere of nothingness is all three.

'Form and Nirvana are without objects of thought.'

There is here a point of additional interest.

The second and fourth Āruppajjhānas are shown to have been conceived as exercises of pure introspection, and to be devoid of any implications of a World-Reason, or a macrocosmic Perception, let alone any of the 'rapt soul' being caught up to other spheres.

---

[1] Read, for Manindriyaṃ, Anindriya-baddharūpañ ca. By an oversight this sentence and the next are printed in the text as if belonging to the previous triad.

APPENDIX II.

On that which is predicted about Uncompounded Element (asankhatā dhātu) in the Dhamma Sangaṇi.

Uncompounded Element is classed as the fourth and last species of the morally Indeterminate (avyākataṃ)—in other words, of that conduct or state of mind which is not productive of good or bad karma. But it alone, of those four, does not receive separate and systematic discussion, as is the case with the other three—Result, Kiriyā, and Form. The following predicates are elicited incidentally in the course of Book III., which discusses what may be called Applied Ethics. Again, whereas the word Nirvana (nibbānaṃ) is always substituted for asankhatā dhātu in that Aṭṭhakathā which is appended as a supplement to the original text, the term 'uncompounded element' is not identified, in the Dhamma Sangaṇi, with the 'topmost fruit' of the Paths, the arahatta-phalaṃ, which is one aspect of the state called Nirvāna (*cf.* S. iv. 251, 252). The subject therefore seems to demand further inquiry. It is to facilitate this that the following results are appended, parallel more or less to the table on Form, pp. 168-171. *Cf.* note, p. 166.

Uncompounded element is

- indeterminate [983]
- neither result nor productive of result [989]
- neither the issue of grasping[1] nor favourable to it[2] [992]
- neither corrupt nor baneful [995]

---

[1] Given also in [1212]. [2] Given also in [1220].

'void of the working of conception and of thought discursive' [998][1]
to be put away neither by insight nor by culture [1008]
something the causes of which are to be put away neither by insight nor by culture [1012][2]
that which makes neither for the piling up nor for the undoing of re-birth [1015]
neither appertaining nor not appertaining to studentship [1017][3]
infinite [1021]
perfected [1027]
that which does not entail fixed consequences [1030][4]
invisible and non-impingeing [1052][5]
not a cause [1072]
without causes as concomitants [1074][6]
not associated with a cause [1076]
without material form [1092]
supra-mundane [1094]
not an Intoxicant [1102]
not co-Intoxicant [1104]
disconnected with the Intoxicants [1106][7]
not a Fetter [1124]
unfavourable to the Fetters [1126]
disconnected with the Fetters [1128][8]
not a Tie [1141]
not that which tends to become tied [1142]
disconnected with the Ties [1144][9]

---

1 Given also in [1269], [1271].
2 Given also in [1258] *et seq.*
3 In the printed text [1018].
4 Repeated in [1291].
5 Repeated in [1088] and [1090].
6 [1082] combines [1072] and [1074].
7 [1112] repeats [1104] and [1106].
8 [1134] repeats [1126] and [1128].
9 [1150] repeats [1142] and [1144].

not a Hindrance [1163]
disconnected with and unfavourable to the Hindrances [1173]
not a Contagion [1176]
disconnected with the Contagion and uninfected [1184]
without concomitant object of thought [1186]
not of the intellect [1188]
not involved in the life of sense [1190]
disconnected with thought [1192]
detached from thought [1194]
not sprung from thought [1196]
not something coming into being together with thought [1198]
not consecutive to thought [1200]
not derived [1210]
without the attribute of Grasping [1218]
disconnected with Grasping, and not favouring it [1228]
without the attribute of corruption [1240]
harmless [1242]
not corrupt [1243*a*]
disconnected with the Corruptions, and harmless [1253]
not joyous [1273]
unaccompanied by joy [1275]
unaccompanied by ease [1277]
unaccompanied by disinterestedness [1279]
Unincluded [1287]
that by which there is no going away [1289]
something having no Beyond [1293]
not concomitant with war [1295]

In the Cy. on the Dhātu Kathā nibbānaṃ (Nirvana) is always substituted for asankhato khandho.

THE END.

INDEX OF PALI WORDS.

[n is throughout printed for ṅ.]

GENERAL INDEX.

25

ERRATA.

P. 5, for ὕρεξις, read ὄρεξις.
P. 13, for citt' ekaggatā, read cittass' ekaggatā (*bis*).
P. 23, for kāya-passaddhi, read kāyappassaddhi.
P. 44, for parip-pharati, read parippharati.
P. 57, for Aruppajhāna, read Āruppajjhāna (*bis*).
P. 58, for -vilasa, read -vilāsa.
P. 63, for vimokkhaṃ read vimokkho.
P. 132, for santīrana, read santīraṇa (*bis*).
Pp. 149, 150, for aññātavindriyaṃ, read aññātāvindriyaṃ
P. 158, for thāṇaṃ, read ṭhānaṃ.
P. 165, for arupino, read arūpino.
P. 166, for Atthakathā, read Aṭṭhakathā.
P. 174, for samudīranaṃ, read samudīraṇaṃ.
P. 175, for attabhāvō, read attabhāvo.
,, divide indriyesu from guttadvāro.
P. 183, for sumukkhapakamā, read sumukhapakkamā.
,, for 'long,' short, read 'long,' 'short.'
P. 185, for sakkhusamphassajo, read sukhasamphassajo.
P. 199, for kāya-pasādo, read kāyappasādo.
P. 201, for sneho, read sineho.
P. 241, for paṭiṭṭhānaṃ, read patiṭṭhānaṃ.
P. 242 note[1], for *Mil* 317 read *Mil* 313.
P. 250, for Atthakathā, read Aṭṭhakathā.
P. 252, for thānaṃ, read ṭhānaṃ.
Pp. 264, 265, from §§ [1015] to [1019] the questions are wrongly numbered.
P. 280, for -tanhā, read -taṇhā.
P. 294, for ṭathāgato, read tathāgato.
,, for ārammanaṃ, read ārammaṇaṃ.